Reading Mahler

Studies in German Literature, Linguistics, and Culture

Reading Mahler

German Culture and Jewish Identity in Fin-de-Siècle Vienna

Carl Niekerk

CAMDEN HOUSE
Rochester, New York

Copyright © 2010 Carl Niekerk

All Rights Reserved. Except as permitted under current legislation, no part of this work may be photocopied, stored in a retrieval system, published, performed in public, adapted, broadcast, transmitted, recorded, or reproduced in any form or by any means, without the prior permission of the copyright owner.

First published 2010 by Camden House
Transferred to digital printing 2012
Reprinted in paperback 2013

Camden House is an imprint of Boydell & Brewer Inc.
668 Mt. Hope Avenue, Rochester, NY 14620, USA
www.camden-house.com
and of Boydell & Brewer Limited
PO Box 9, Woodbridge, Suffolk IP12 3DF, UK
www.boydellandbrewer.com

Paperback ISBN-13: 978-1-57113-564-3
Paperback ISBN-10: 978-1-57113-564-2
Hardcover ISBN-13: 978-1-57113-467-7
Hardcover ISBN-10: 1-57113-467-0

Library of Congress Cataloging-in-Publication Data

Niekerk, Carl.
    Reading Mahler: German culture and Jewish identity in fin-de-siècle Vienna / Carl Niekerk.
    p. cm. — (Studies in German literature, linguistics, and culture)
Includes bibliographical references and index.
ISBN-13: 978-1-57113-467-7 (hardcover: alk. paper)
ISBN-10: 1-57113-467-0 (hardcover: alk. paper)
    1. Mahler, Gustav, 1860–1911 — Criticism and interpretation.
2. German literature — History and criticism. 3. Music and literature.
I. Title. II. Series.

ML410.M23N57 2010
780.92—dc22

2010008589

This publication is printed on acid-free paper.
Printed in the United States of America.

Contents

Acknowledgments   vii

List of Abbreviations   ix

Introduction: Literature, Philosophy, and Images in Mahler's Music   1

I. The Crisis of German Culture

1: *Titan*: Symphony of an Anti-Hero   29

2: *Des Knaben Wunderhorn*: Rediscovering the "Volk"   56

3: Nietzsche and the Crisis of German Culture   83

II. German Culture and Its Others

4: Rembrandt and the Margins of German Culture   135

5: Goethe against German Culture   154

6: The Two Faces of German Orientalism   178

Conclusion: Beyond Mahler   212

Notes   223

Works Consulted   275

Index   299

Acknowledgments

EARLY VERSIONS OF PARTS OF chapter 3 were published in *German Quarterly* 77.2 (2004): 189–210, and in *Sound Matters: Essays on the Acoustics of German Culture*, ed. Nora M. Alter and Lutz Koepnick (New York: Berghahn, 2004), 49–64. Earlier versions of chapter 4 appeared in *Legacies of Modernism: Art and Politics in Northern Europe, 1890–1950*, ed. Patrizia C. McBride, Richard W. McCormick, and Monika Žagar (New York: Palgrave, 2007), 29–40, and in Dutch in *De Gids* 170.2 (Feb. 2006): 166–74. All of these texts have since been substantially rethought and rewritten. Chapter 5 is a slightly reworked version of an article published in *Musical Quarterly* 89.2–3 (2006): 237–72. I am very grateful for the excellent suggestions this journal's anonymous readers made, which not only contributed to a better text but also gave me a sense of the problems of doing truly interdisciplinary work and of the potential readership for my book. Some of the material discussed in chapter 6 was taken from my essay "The Romantics and Other Cultures," published in the *Cambridge Companion to German Romanticism*, ed. Nicholas Saul (Cambridge: Cambridge UP, 2009), 147–62. Many thanks to the editor of that collection for proposing the topic of the essay in the first place and for his many valuable suggestions.

Work on this book began in the fall of 2003 and was facilitated by a sabbatical leave from the University of Illinois at Urbana-Champaign and by a grant from the Andrew W. Mellon Foundation, which made an additional one-semester leave possible and came with a generous research account. Two conferences were especially influential in shaping this project. The Sixth Biennial Minnesota Forum "Northern Light/Northern Darkness? Rethinking Modernism after the Demise of the 'Master Narrative': Art and Politics in Northern Europe, 1890–1950," 25–27 April 2002, at the University of Minnesota in Minneapolis gave me some important stimuli to further pursue this project. My talk as a last-minute stand-in at the Thirteenth Bard Music Festival, "Mahler and His World," at Bard College, Annandale-on-Hudson, on 17 August 2002 introduced me to the work of many interesting scholars in the field of German musical and cultural studies who have shaped the intellectual contours of this project.

Conversations with Matti Bunzl, Cori Crane, Stefani Engelstein, Michael Finke, Barbara Fischer, Jeff Grossman, Martina Hamidouche, Waïl Hassan, Stephanie Hilger, Stephen Jaeger, Laurie Johnson, Brett Kaplan, Bill Kinderman, Lutz Koepnick, Francien Markx, Patrizia McBride, Jim

McGlathery, Peter McIsaac, Elizabeth Oyler, Paul Reitter, Michael Rothberg, Helmut Walser Smith, Mara Wade, Marc Weiner, Meike Werner, and Yasemin Yildiz helped form this project and contributed to a better understanding of the issues discussed in this book. Some of them also read parts of the manuscript. I am very grateful for their many suggestions and I hope that nobody will be disappointed by what I did with them. My interest in *fin-de-siècle* Viennese literature and culture goes back to my undergraduate and early graduate school days, when I took classes with Walter Schönau, Egon Schwarz, and Ulrich Weinzierl (at the time visiting critic-in-residence at Washington University) on Austrian literature, culture, and intellectual history. The latter scholar, together with my colleague Bruce Murray, has proved to be a reliable source of knowledge about Viennese culture past and present. My interest in German-Jewish culture was greatly encouraged by the DAAD-NEH seminar on the culture of masochism, led by Sander Gilman (Cornell, Summer 1995). Emma Betz, Adam Chambers, Mary DeGuire, Jim Edenstrom, and Kathleen Smith at various stages worked as perpetually reliable research assistants with me on this project and their observations at times also influenced its final profile. I would also like to thank Margaret (Peg) Flynn and Sue Innes for their careful editorial work on my text.

I am grateful to my father not just for letting me grow up in a house full of music but also for sharing some of his immense knowledge of music and musical history with me, and for giving me some insight into the functioning of a professional symphony orchestra through anecdotes about his eight-year term as vice-president of the board of the Northern Netherlands Symphony and his membership of the programming committee of that same institution. While I was working on this project, two of the people closest to me were diagnosed with cancer. On 8 July 2006, my mother, Willemien Niekerk-Timmer, one of the healthiest people I know, died after a courageous eleven-month struggle with lung cancer. A little more than half a year later, my wife Laurie was diagnosed with what turned out to be a complex case of breast cancer that necessitated a yearlong intensive treatment. Their experiences will always be with me. I would like to dedicate this book to our children, Naomi and Maaike (now 8 and 6 years old), for their (Montessori-trained) inquisitive personalities, their many jokes and seemingly perpetual good moods, and their willingness to let their father listen not just to K3 or Dirk en de Liedjesband, but also to the music of Mozart and Stravinsky, and the occasional Mahler symphony.

Abbreviations

AC	Nietzsche, Friedrich. *The Anti-Christ, Ecce Homo, Twilight of the Idols, And Other Writings.* Translated by Josefine Nauckhoff and Adrian Del Caro. Cambridge: Cambridge UP, 2005.
AF	Wagner, Richard. "The Art-Work of the Future." In *The Art-Work of the Future and Other Works*, translated by William Aston Ellis, 69–213. Lincoln: U of Nebraska P, 1993.
Br	Mahler, Gustav. *Briefe.* Edited by Herta Blaukopf. 2nd rev. ed. Vienna: Paul Zsolnay Verlag, 1996.
BT	Nietzsche, Friedrich. *The Birth of Tragedy and Other Writings.* Translated by Ronald Speirs. Cambridge: Cambridge UP, 2004.
DKdZ	Wagner, Richard. "Das Kunstwerk der Zukunft." In *Sämtliche Schriften und Dichtungen*, 3:42–178. Leipzig: Breitkopf & Härtel, 1911.
GME	Bauer-Lechner, Natalie. *Gustav Mahler in den Erinnerungen von Natalie Bauer-Lechner.* Edited by Herbert Killian. Rev. ed. Hamburg: Verlag der Musikalienhandlung Karl Dieter Wagner, 1984.
GR	Mahler, Gustav. *Ein Glück ohne Ruh': Die Briefe Gustav Mahlers an Alma.* Edited by Henry-Louis de La Grange and Günther Weiß. Berlin: Siedler, 1995.
GS	Nietzsche, Friedrich. *The Gay Science: With a Prelude in German Rhymes and an Appendix of Songs.* Translated by Josefine Nauckhoff and Adrian Del Caro. Cambridge: Cambridge UP, 2001.
GSL	Schein, Ida. *Die Gedanken- und Ideenwelt Siegfried Lipiners.* PhD diss., University of Vienna, 1936.
MP	Adorno, Theodor W. *Mahler: Eine musikalische Physiognomik.* In *Gesammelte Schriften* 13:149–319. Frankfurt am Main: Suhrkamp, 1997.

MPE	Adorno, Theodor W. *Mahler: A Musical Physiognomy*. Translated by Edmund Jephcott. Chicago and London: U of Chicago P, 1996.
RA	Wagner, Richard. "Religion and Art." In *Prose Works*, vol. 6, translated by William Ashton Ellis, 211–52. New York: Broude Brothers, 1966.
RGM	Bauer-Lechner, Natalie. *Recollections of Gustav Mahler*. Translated by Dika Newlin. Edited by Peter Franklin. Cambridge: Cambridge UP, 1980.
RK	Wagner, Richard. "Religion und Kunst." In *Sämtliche Schriften und Dichtungen*, 10:211–85. Leipzig: Breitkopf & Härtel, 1911.
SM	Goetschel, Willi. *Spinoza's Modernity: Mendelssohn, Lessing, and Heine*. Madison: U of Wisconsin P, 2004.
SSLD	Mitchell, Donald. *Gustav Mahler: Songs and Symphonies of Life and Death*. Woodbridge, UK: Boydell, 2002.
SW	Nietzsche, Friedrich. *Sämtliche Werke: Kritische Studienausgabe in 15 Bänden*. Edited by Giorgio Colli and Mazzino Montinari. Munich, and New York: DTV; Berlin: de Gruyter, 1999.
TSZ	Nietzsche, Friedrich. *Thus Spoke Zarathustra: A Book for All and None*. Translated by Adrian Del Caro. Cambridge: Cambridge UP, 2006.

Introduction: Literature, Philosophy, and Images in Mahler's Music

THIS IS NOT A BOOK LIKE OTHER BOOKS about Gustav Mahler. It is different in that it does not approach Mahler's oeuvre from a musicologist's perspective, but rather focuses on his interest in and use of literature, philosophy, and the visual arts. *Reading Mahler* is meant as a companion to Mahler's music that helps its audiences understand its literary and cultural roots. Mahler's view of German cultural history is of great importance for understanding his music in the context of its time. Only if we reconstruct this history and Mahler's perspective on it will the true polemical points underlying Mahler's compositions become clear. The goal of this study is therefore not a comprehensive view of Mahler's entire oeuvre. Not all of Mahler's symphonies, for instance, contain literary, philosophical, or cultural references that can be reconstructed. While the ambitions of this book are modest, my claim is that the perspective offered in this book will challenge and perhaps even change our view of Mahler's music.

Much has been said from a musicological viewpoint about Mahler's use of musical forms and content in relation to musical history. The assumption, implicit or explicit, is often that Mahler's interest in literature and culture merely mirrors his musical preferences. Someone with traditionalist musical preferences will probably like a figurative painting more than an abstract one. But does music history simply mirror other parts of cultural history, or is it rather that one can make us see the other in a different light? Literature and the visual arts in Vienna around 1900 underwent an intriguing period of self-reflection and renewal that manifested itself, for instance, in a critical and highly eclectic attitude toward their own past. What if Mahler's strong interest in German cultural history does not simply affirm traditions but rather seeks to take traditions apart and to reassemble them according to different priorities? If that is the case, interpreting Mahler's work in its cultural contexts may shed some new light not only on its underlying intentions but also on our current ways of looking at his work and life. Or a cultural reading of Mahler can point to innovative or critical aspects of his music that have hitherto gone unnoticed.

My book does not claim to show a complete picture of the intellectual and cultural landscape in which Mahler's work originated, but rather fragments of that picture. Others will be needed to complete it. Texts and images can help us understand Mahler's work and grasp some of the issues underlying it without giving us necessarily definitive answers. In the following, I will not pretend to be a musicologist; rather, I intend to raise questions from the perspective of a literary and cultural historian. In addition to offering a companion to the literature, philosophy, and paintings in Mahler's music, this study aims to contribute to an increasingly lively dialogue between musicologists, intellectual historians, political scientists, scholars in Jewish studies, and others who are interested in Mahler's life and works.

Cultural Contexts

Such a dialogue is highly desirable. While Mahler's music is omnipresent and the man himself has become something of a cultural icon, and in spite of the fact that Vienna around 1900 has become the object of rather prolific scholarly fascination, I still believe that too little is known about the precise cultural contexts in which Mahler's works originated. The popularity of Mahler's work today is immense. His symphonies are frequently performed on concert stages; famous conductors like to celebrate milestones in their own careers or of their orchestras by performing a Mahler symphony, and there is a seemingly endless stream of new (or reissued) Mahler performances on CDs. But what exactly intrigues us about this music? Nobody who is acquainted with or knows his music is neutral about it. Dislike for Mahler's music is as old as the music itself, as recent scholarship has documented.[1] On the other hand, Mahler enthusiasts are exceptionally devoted to his work. But is it the musical material alone that intrigues us?

Leon Botstein has argued recently that one of the most dominant stereotypes about Mahler today is that his music expresses our deepest, most personal emotions; his works are seen as a highly complex and ambivalent representation of "the inner experience of life" that includes not just the positive but also the negative.[2] That Mahler's music is perceived to be so highly personal may, to some extent, explain the radically divergent responses that Mahler's music evokes. For some, Mahler's music may be too personal, while others may enjoy exploring their emotions through his music. Elaborating on Botstein's analysis, I would argue that it is part of our contemporary perception of Mahler's music that emotions are given a sense of importance that points beyond the subjective, even though their basic subjectivity is never questioned. Because of its highly abstract nature and the fundamental, irrevocable ambiguity of any attempt to assign nonmusical meaning to it, music seems particularly well suited to accommodate a residual longing for meaning beyond the purely subjective that still exists in postmetaphysical times such as the early twenty-first century. Given that much about music relates to feelings, it is perhaps one of the last places where our metaphysical yearning can find shelter despite our "rational" knowledge that we live in a time without common values.

In addition to its appeal to our emotions and desire for values, Mahler's Jewishness can be seen as a third reason underlying the contemporary attention to his music. To explain Mahler's contemporary popularity, Botstein speaks of the "post WWII romanticization of the acculturated European Jewish cosmopolitan intellectual and artist" from before 1945.[3] Mahler stands for a tradition, in other words, that was at once largely lost in the Holocaust and long ignored by mainstream European culture. By speaking of it in terms of a "romanticization," Botstein indicates that there is something questionable about this newfound interest in Mahler; it is not necessarily based on an accurate picture of the man or his work.

As we ask ourselves why we find meaning in Mahler's music, a more important question to ask is who exactly "we" are in this context. Mahler's reception has followed quite divergent trajectories within different national contexts and sometimes even within one national context. The two men who have been most important for making Mahler's music known in the United States, Bruno Walter and Leonard Bernstein, represent widely disparate ways of looking at Mahler's music. Bruno Walter had worked as an assistant conductor under Mahler and was his friend. After Hitler's invasion of Austria in 1938 he was forced to go into exile. Walter saw Mahler's work as the culmination of Western music and of German music in particular.[4] His interpretations of Mahler's works were cautious; they emphasized the unity of Mahler's scores, their intrinsic balance, and their aim for harmony that was consistent, as he saw it, with the tradition in which they had originated. Bernstein, by contrast, who like Mahler was a prominent conductor and a prolific composer, emphasized in his performances Mahler's contradictions, moments of dissonance, ambiguities and ironies, and the music's emotional extremes. Both men stand for very different views on Mahler's music and, to some extent, on the issue of who Mahler was as a person.

This should suffice to show that our perception of Mahler's music is at least in part the product of historically and culturally specific expectations that we associate with his work. Although the enormous attention paid to Mahler's work is of course a positive thing, we should perhaps be somewhat suspicious of this attention. That Mahler's music is — among other things, I would argue — about emotions is clear, but do its audiences really understand the emotional narrative that it is telling? If we want to adopt the hypothesis that Mahler's music hints at values in a time in which most values are being debunked or seriously discredited, then we will also need to study the conditions under which the values promoted by Mahler are still possible. It is rather surprising to me that one of the most knowledgeable Mahler scholars believes that Mahler's works are the product of a deep belief in Christian dogma.[5] Such a reading completely ignores the critical attitude toward tradition that I believe manifests itself in all of Mahler's music. In the following, I will argue that Mahler in his work is deeply influenced by modernity and its acknowledgement that any form of normativity can only be subjective, and that falling back on old, dogmatic metaphysical frameworks is not an option. Finally, if Mahler's Jewishness is part of the attractiveness of his works — the fact that his music represents a legacy of German-Jewish culture of which so much is irreparably lost since the Shoah — then we are obliged to ask under which historical conditions Jews in Germany and Austria could participate in German-Austrian culture, and to what extent their works mirror the problems and dilemmas of Jews who were cultural participants. The cultural approach that I propose in this study will seek not only to answer the question of how Mahler's Jewishness influenced his music, but also to determine what the consequences of this insight are for us and for our attitudes toward cultural history, no matter what traditions we may belong to ourselves.

I am, of course, only the latest in a line of scholars to have asked these questions. But I want to ask them in a way that is different from the approach adopted in other studies on Mahler. It has, in the words of Leon Botstein, become "increasingly difficult to untangle the historical Mahler from the massive overlay of posthumous reception."[6] What I propose as a strategy for getting a clearer picture of the historical Mahler is to look at his literary and cultural interests, in particular his image of German literary and cultural history and his own place in it. Tradition is never static but is rather in a constant state of flux. Traditions often have a legitimizing function; they serve specific interests in the here and now, and the parties representing those interests do not necessarily aim at a historically accurate account of events or at a perspective that reflects the diversity inherent to all cultural history. There are periods in which the desire to locate, or rewrite, one's own national cultural history is more pronounced than in others. From 1870 to 1914 Western Europe in general underwent a particularly lively period of inventing national traditions.[7] Germany and Austria were no exception. Germany's unification in 1871 forced Germans to reflect upon and commemorate what they had in common — to invent traditions — but in Austria it also sparked a debate about the extent to which it wanted to be part of Germany or to go its own way. The invention of tradition can rely on specific historical events but can also revert to elements of "mythology and folklore"; intertwined with this, the creation of enemies inside or outside the nation can serve to establish national unity, as it did in the case of Germany.[8] Because tradition consists not of historical facts but of cultural constructions, it is easy to see how literature, music, and the other arts can not only play an important role in the construction of tradition but also be useful as a means for studying the dynamics underlying the creation and institutionalization of traditions as frames of reference.

And yet little attention has been paid to the patterns behind the literary, philosophical, and other cultural references in Mahler's music apart from a superficial identification of some sources. There is no doubt that Mahler himself is at least partially to blame for this. Mahler sometimes made quite substantial programmatic statements about his orchestral work, which he invariably retracted thereafter, sometimes almost immediately after making them. Such anti-programmatic/programmatic statements are often seen as a nuisance; many would argue that they unnecessarily complicate access to his works. Scholars are therefore often inclined to ignore Mahler's warnings against reading his music as a representation of a clear and fixed set of ideas. It is important to take this anti-programmatic impetus of Mahler's aesthetics very seriously. I will argue in the following chapters that Mahler's unwillingness to pin himself down on a specific set of principles, be they musicological or philosophical, is a constitutive element of his aesthetics. At the core of his creative work is a profound feeling of ambiguity toward representation. While Mahler himself has often addressed the issue of musical programs,[9] the most elaborate attempt to explain the anti-programmatic agenda underlying Mahler's music is a letter that Bruno Walter, presumably at Mahler's request, wrote to the musicologist Ludwig Schiedermair in December 1901. Mahler "rejects in the most energetic way every program" (perhorresziert aufs energischste jedes Programm), Walter states.[10] That seems to be a very clear and unambiguous statement. Music itself needs to be at the center; what music tells us cannot be stated in words; at best they offer a "bad translation" (schlechte Übersetzung) of what music wants to communicate (49).

In spite of this, according to the same letter by Walter, words or images can nevertheless help us to understand music: "The possibility exists to point to the region from which such sharply contoured musical expressions come by means of a fitting image" (Es besteht die Möglichkeit, die Region, aus der so scharf umrissene musikalische Äußerungen kommen, durch ein passendes Bild anzudeuten; 50). The word "image" in this context is not to be understood in a visual sense, I would argue, but rather as any type of material that comments on music from a nonmusical perspective. Such material (words, images) can help us understand what music is about, even though it is just an approximation at best. The fact that Mahler did not see his music as an unmediated expression of a text — as an illustration of something situated beyond the realm of music — does not mean that texts or images are irrelevant when it comes to understanding the meaning of Mahler's music. A composer may, again according to Walter, be able to produce "a great number of images, of which the essence is related to his work" (eine ganze Anzahl von Bildern, deren Wesen mit dem seines Werkes verwandt ist) without thereby being programmatic (51). Mahler's anti-programmatic stance is not meant to discourage listeners from formulating the free associations they have when listening to his music; his listeners should not reduce it to *one* message. While throughout its development Mahler's music propagates diverging ways to deal with the problem of "art without a program," this interest in a multitude of associations remains something constant. It shows Mahler's affinity with the early-twentieth-century avant-garde and its interest in appropriating materials from all kinds of different sources.

From Walter's letter one can draw the conclusion that Mahler's anti-programmatic impulse should not keep us from discussing texts (or images) in relation to his music. Mahler's interest in literature was quite sophisticated. Mahler's friends and intellectual companions (*Gesprächspartner*) consistently stated that Mahler was well acquainted with German literature and well versed in German intellectual history. The texts Mahler uses in his music are chosen quite deliberately. I am interested in the ways in which Mahler uses references to literature, philosophy, and the visual arts both within his music and in statements about his compositions. I propose to reconstruct what these references tell us about Mahler's thinking about his own art, and about the way in which Mahler saw German culture as a whole, including its past, present, and future. Mahler's literary interests in particular were oriented toward literary history rather than toward contemporary literature.[11] But it would, in my opinion, be incorrect to describe these interests as conventional for that reason. Mahler's interests in these areas are unorthodox and driven by a critical impulse, a spirit of rebellion. This is mirrored in Mahler's conceptualization of German culture. "Culture" does not function in Mahler's view as a monolithic whole, in the sense of a clearly defined canon — "tradition" understood in a very narrow sense — but rather as heterogeneous, pervaded by conflicts and tensions. The "cultural" approach I propose here is not new to Mahler studies; one does find frequent references to Mahler's literary and cultural interests in scholarship on Mahler. Rarely, however, are these interests at the core of an analysis; they are primarily used to illustrate musicological points or as part of a musicological analysis.

Mahler and German Cultural History

For our contemporary view of Mahler in general and his relation to German culture in particular, Adorno's monograph *Mahler: Eine musikalische Physiognomik* (Mahler: A Musical Physiognomy), first published in German in 1960, has been a landmark resource. Theodor W. Adorno (1903–69) was trained in philosophy, musicology, and sociology, and studied composition in the 1920s with Alban Berg in Vienna. Because of his Jewish background and his left-leaning political sympathies, he went into exile in 1934, returning to Germany in 1949. As a member of the Frankfurt School (*Frankfurter Schule*), he became one of the most influential cultural critics who fought for a reinterpretation of German culture in the light of Germany's fascist and anti-Semitic past. There are two aspects of Mahler's music that Adorno sees as problematic and that nevertheless structure his interpretations. One of the central ideas encountered in all of Adorno's essays on Mahler is that Mahler works with musical materials and forms that are archaic: "Because his material was obsolete, the new not yet set free, in Mahler the antiquated, what had fallen by the wayside, has become a cryptogram of the sounds as yet unheard that followed it" (*MPE*, 126; Weil sein Material veraltet, das Neue noch nicht befreit war, ist bei Mahler das Veraltete, am Wege liegen Gebliebene zum Kryptogramm der noch nicht gehörten Klänge danach geworden: *MP*, 270). Outdated form and vocabulary stand in the way of innovation: "A taboo is placed on novelty" (*MPE*, 6; Ein Tabu liegt über dem Neuen: *MP*, 155). This is of course a problematic diagnosis; it is only valid within the historical development of Western music as Adorno sees it. While Adorno sees the lack of formal innovation as an aspect of Mahler's style that is his conscious choice, such an assessment comes dangerously close to the stereotype promoted by anti-Semites that Jewish composers were *not able* to produce anything new, but instead copied what was already there — a reproach that can be found in the literature about Mahler well into the postwar period.[12] Adorno, however, does not deny a critical dimension to this use of the outdated. This explains the importance Adorno attributes to moments of fracture or breakdown in Mahler's music. But because Mahler's music makes it clear that the "obsolete" is no longer functional and is therefore to be understood ironically, it points to the necessity of a new musical language. Especially in the last chapter of his monograph on Mahler, Adorno tries to interpret Mahler's innovations in *Das Lied von der Erde* and the Ninth as prefigurations of those by composers who came later, in particular Berg, Schoenberg, and Stravinsky (*MP*, 293, 300, 304, and 307; *MPE*, 151, 157–58, 162, and 164).

A second problem that Adorno identifies in Mahler's music is the role of popular music, the fact that Mahler breaks down the barriers between high and low art. Adorno speaks of a "reactionary element" (*MPE*, 61; reaktionäres Moment: *MP*, 209) in Mahler's music. By this he means the naive aspects of Mahler's music: the presence of "folk music" (*MPE*, 31; Volksmusik: *MP*, 180, trans. modified) or what Adorno calls "vulgar music" (*MPE*, 50; Vulgärmusik: *MP*, 200): the posthorn, the ubiquitous military music, and so on. For Adorno, such elements are further proof of Mahler's formal asynchronicity, the obsolescence of his materials. They are also problematic because they are prime examples of the commodification of music; they suggest that music can easily create collectivity. The presence of such naive elements in Mahler's music runs the risk, for Adorno, of continually compromising what his music intends to express, which is a critique of such a naive understanding of music, of reading more into music than what is produced in the here and now (*MP,* 153; *MPE,* 5). Adorno maintains a strict separation between "low" and "high" art and finds any mixture of the two problematic. The reactionary element is for Adorno always present in Mahler's music, and at times it triumphs over its critical, progressive dimension, for instance in the Eighth Symphony (*MP,* 283; *MPE,* 138).

Leon Botstein has made the provocative observation that Adorno's concept of culture may have more in common with that of Mahler's enemies (well into the Nazi era) than one would expect.[13] Mahler himself once said, as Alfred Roller has reported, that the "anti-Semitic papers" of his time were "the only ones who still have any respect for me" (die antisemitischen Zeitungen sind . . . die einzigen, die vor mir noch etwas Respekt haben).[14] Of course what Mahler's critics saw as negative — the disruptive potential of Mahler's art in relation to their vision of the German national cultural tradition — was given a positive interpretation by Mahler (and later by Adorno). Mahler wanted to be subversive, and Adorno is very much interested in working out this rebellious element in Mahler. And yet the fact that Adorno refers to Mahler's achievements mostly in negative terms — only rarely or not at all does Mahler develop an advanced musical language; he instead deconstructs an older musical language — may also be read as an indication that Adorno is never really able to transcend the specific concept of culture he has in mind. While it would not be correct to say that Adorno's concept of culture is in any way naive, in his musicological writings he does emphasize historical patterns of development of musical material or its "historical 'movement.'"[15] The decisive difference between earlier, idealistic models of musical history and Adorno's version is that Adorno emphasizes the "emancipation of the Subject as a process of 'demythologization' of the material."[16] Adorno describes this development as a process of increased rationalization of the musical material, which leads to more value being placed on dissonance and atonality. Musical history will eventually debunk the ideological functions music has played in the service of creating collectivity. At the same time, however, there is also a longing for earlier (diatonal and more "subjective") modes of music making. In spite of this dialectical tendency in musical history, Adorno postulated the existence of an end point where the ideological function of music, more precisely of tonality and its mimetic suggestion, is recognized and abandoned. In the works of Schoenberg and Stravinsky this end point realizes itself in exemplary forms, as is clear from Adorno's *Philosophie der neuen Musik* (Philosophy of New Music), which juxtaposes analyses of both of these composers. In the end, their works express the inability of music to create a metaphysical substitute for a lost collectivity (even though Stravinsky is less clear on this point than Schoenberg). With that, on the one hand Adorno offers a radical counterreading of cultural history that denies any of the idealistic functions culture once performed. On the other hand, in some respects it remains quite uncritical. In the end, it is still culture that articulates this message. Culture, in other words, still plays a primary role in man's understanding of his relation to the world.

In some respects Mahler is for Adorno, and despite the latter's respect for the composer, a questionable case. One could say that Adorno's ideology, to some extent, stands in the way of his appreciation of actual works of art, even though he also seems, at times at least, to be willing to question at least part of his interpretative model in favor of Mahler's actual music production. My reservations about Adorno have to do with the premises of Adorno's work, the structure behind his thinking. Leon Botstein has stated that after Adorno the elements of "criticism and resistance" present in Mahler's work and Adorno's interpretation of it vanished from public perception.[17] This may be true, but I would argue that Adorno himself is also to blame, at least partially. Criticism and resistance remain very abstract categories in Adorno's analysis of Mahler. In spite of the range of Adorno's knowledge and interests, the image of Mahler that emerges from Adorno's essays remains remarkably anemic and colorless. Mahler, in Adorno's view, leaves us with the impression of a person with a masterly but very technical interest in musical structures and ways to manipulate them, but certainly not as a full-fledged intellectual with broad literary and cultural interests who may also have been, at least to some extent, aware of the ways in which society was changing around him. This image cries out for correction. In spite of my great respect for the not only highly original but also very detailed and complex writings by Adorno on Mahler, I wish to make three main objections to his analyses.

Adorno, in spite of a sophisticated model of historicity that combines insight into historical development with a respect for the individuality of musical works that may contradict general patterns, sees cultural development as linear and closely tied to formal innovation. Formally, the use of dissonance and atonality are the most important markers for Adorno of a musical piece's place in musical history. It is questionable whether Mahler indeed relies on "outdated" forms and materials to the extent Adorno suggests. It is also important to stress that Adorno offers *one* specific way of looking at musical history. If one were to use not tonality but, for instance, heterogeneity of forms and materials as a defining criterion, Mahler's music would have to be considered among the most advanced of his time. Paradoxically, Adorno believes that Wagner is, in terms of his place in musical history, more progressive than Mahler in some respects, because Wagner's innovative development of musical form does play with dissonance, at least from time to time (in other respects Wagner is highly reactionary).[18] Mahler's music, in Adorno's view, does not participate in the linear development of formal means at the disposal of the composer (*MP,* 167; *MPE,* 19); in fact, like Stravinsky after him, he intentionally works "archaic" elements into his musical vocabulary. In Mahler's music, the individual dreams of the "irresistible collective" (unaufhaltsamen Kollektiv); at the same time, his music expresses the impossibility of the individual's identifying with the collective (*MP,* 182; *MPE,* 33).

Adorno radically downplays the importance of text for Mahler. This is surprising, because Adorno's own cultural interests were very broad, and he was quite active as a literary critic as well. It is an interesting phenomenon that literary and cultural approaches dominate in scholarship on Wagner,[19] while for Mahler, as I have already stated, attention is paid to literary and cultural aspects but is generally subsumed into a musicological approach. This is quite clear in Adorno's work, as he admits: "For musicians, words happen to be vehicles for their compositions" (Für Musiker sind nun einmal Worte Vehikel ihrer Kompositionen).[20] To phrase it another way: words are tools to communicate what is at stake in the music; their value is thus purely instrumental. By this, in my view, Adorno does not mean that in a specific work words serve to illustrate merely what the music communicates (words mirror the music), but rather that in the text the same developments and conflicts are articulated as in music. This in turn implies that an analysis of the text merely confirms what the music has already told us. But is this really the case? One of the reasons why Wagner is and always has been so much a part of the public sphere, I would argue, is because of his textual production — the texts of his operas, but also his essays and journalism. Because of Wagner's texts, we are forced to look at his works in their relationship to the German cultural tradition and his place therein, on the one hand, and the ways in which art and politics, more specifically Wagner's art and its political legacy, are interconnected on the other. Paying attention to the text in Mahler's works may also mean reclaiming Mahler for the public sphere; it forces us to ask difficult questions that go beyond our purely subjective, non-discursive enjoyment of his music. The text forces us to acknowledge the historicity of our experiences and of our ways of experiencing the world. The text has the potential to function as a form of cultural memory.

Surprisingly, Adorno is mostly silent about the "Jewish Question" in Mahler's work and life. This is astonishing because Adorno was, of course, well aware of the anti-Semitic undercurrent in German-speaking cultural history. His book on Wagner is quite explicit not only about Wagner's anti-Semitism but also about Wagner's tendency to use and abuse the Jews surrounding him whenever it suited him.[21] In Adorno's book and essays on Mahler, one can find references to the anti-Semitic reception of Mahler (*MP,* 151; *MPE,* 3). Adorno, however, has little to say about what Mahler's Jewishness meant for his activities as a composer in Vienna around 1900. In a passage on *Das Lied von der Erde* Adorno summarizes his views on Jewish aspects of Mahler's music. The oriental setting in *Das Lied* functions, according to Adorno, as a "cover for Mahler's Jewish element" (*MPE*, 149; Deckbild von Mahlers jüdischem Element: *MP*, 291). Such a statement suggests that Mahler attempted to think through his Jewishness intentionally in his music, albeit indirectly. But Adorno does not pursue this line of thinking. He argues that there is very little evidence for the inclusion of Jewish folk melodies in Mahler's work, but the music does nevertheless contain a more abstract Jewish aspect that Adorno acknowledges is hard to grasp on a conceptual level. In particular, Mahler's late style is characterized by an unfamiliar element that irritates Western audiences: "the shrill, sometimes nasal, gesticulating, uproarious aspect" (das Grelle, zuweilen Näselnde, Gestikulierende und durcheinander Redende) appropriates "that quality of Jewishness that provokes sadism" (*MPE*, 149; jenes Jüdische, das den Sadismus reizt: *MP*, 291, trans. modified). Such statements raise more questions than they answer. One may wonder whether Adorno's characterization of Mahler's late style (as shrill, nasal, gesticulating, uproarious) is accurate. Adorno's characterization also evokes strong associations with anti-Semitic stereotypes of Jewish speech (mauscheln). The separation between the familiar and the unfamiliar in Mahler's music also seems highly arbitrary. Since musicology does not seem to be able to help us further on this issue, could a cultural approach shed light on it?

Mahler's "Jewish Question"; Mahler and Wagner

Adorno is not alone in his hesitancy in discussing Mahler's Jewishness; it may be seen as part of a trend in postwar literary and cultural studies, in particular in the first two decades after the Second World War. Carl E. Schorske, in his seminal work *Fin-de-Siècle Vienna: Politics and Culture* (1981), acknowledges the enormous importance of Jews in Vienna's cultural life but interprets their artistic activities as independent from their ethnic background.[22] In Schorske's opinion, Freud, Klimt, Mahler, and Schnitzler first and foremost responded to the failed political liberalism of their fathers by embracing an ideal of culture that was detached from political power. To understand such an approach, which sidesteps ethnic and racial issues, it is important to realize that the discourse of race in German-Austrian culture was not introduced, but was certainly popularized enormously, by the Nazis. Through their instrumentalization of anti-Semitism, particularly in the realm of culture, they broke with a long German tradition that emphasized "aesthetic immanence": the idea that art was to function independently of other areas of society such as politics. To insist on discussing art in terms of race and ethnicity after the demise of the Third Reich might appear, in particular to scholars who had lived through the Third Reich themselves, possibly in exile, as an act that assigned importance to a reprehensible mode of thinking. Besides, if Mahler himself did not conceive of his own music as "Jewish," at least not in public, then why should we do so?

While Schorske's importance for scholarship on fin-de-siècle Vienna has been generally acknowledged, other scholars have started to reevaluate the methodological presuppositions underlying his research.[23] The problem is not so much that Schorske does not pay attention to anti-Semitism in fin-de-siècle Vienna (he does),[24] but rather that he appears to assume that culture at the time remained unaffected by it. It is important to see that when ethnicity and race are introduced as categories for cultural analysis, our image of fin-de-siècle Vienna changes as a result. Around 1900, the ideal of "aesthetic immanence" increasingly came under fire. It is harder to maintain the view that turn-of-the-century art and culture were in essence apolitical if one takes into consideration the Jewish background of men like Freud, Mahler, and Schnitzler, on the one hand, and the increasingly anti-Semitic environment surrounding them on the other. In *Reading Mahler*, I will show that for Mahler his Jewishness was of importance, even though he said little about it in public. My argument is that there is a critical potential in his music that one misses if one overlooks Mahler's Jewishness, or, to phrase it another way, the way Mahler was perceived as a Jew in the public sphere of Vienna around 1900.

Political anti-Semitism was on the rise in fin-de-siècle Vienna. This development in the political domain was paralleled by the great importance attributed to Wagner's legacy in the Viennese cultural scene. In the literature on Mahler, whether cultural or musicological, remarkably little is said about the issue of Mahler's relationship to Wagner as a person and to the cultural agenda he stood for, and yet it raises difficult questions. Wagner's attractiveness to young composers can be partially explained by the fact that Wagner provided, musically speaking, in the words of the composer Ernst Křenek "the most progressive idiom available" for its time.[25] The fact that Wagner was seen as an outlaw by the musical establishment may have furthered such an identification with him by a new generation. Furthermore, Wagner's essays offered a complex agenda, incorporating literature, philosophy, and a cultural program with a clear political vision. His operas were a genuinely new form of synthetic art combining music, literature, drama, and the visual. And yet, there was also Wagner's anti-Semitism. There is no question about the anti-Semitic tendencies in Wagner's theoretical writings and personal communications, even though there are scholars in German culture who have long attempted to ignore or downplay them.[26] This component of Wagner's thinking, of course, also problematizes Mahler's undeniable admiration for Wagner's work. One might even reproach Mahler — of course very much in hindsight! — for ignoring Wagner's anti-Semitism.[27] I do not believe that he did, however. Mahler was not only aware of the problematic sides of Wagner's political and cultural agenda but sought to counter them with an alternative agenda of his own.

Mahler's stagings of Wagner's operas, for instance, were not uncritical. In their legendary and pathbreaking cooperation, Alfred Roller, one of the founding members of the *Secession*, and Mahler developed a concept that moved away from Bayreuth's "fussy realism" and instead aimed, through an "innovative use of color and light," for an experience that allowed for a more abstract vision of what was happening on stage, a synthesis of "the real and the ideal."[28] One could interpret Mahler and Roller's staging of *Tristan* at the Vienna Court Opera in 1903 as the first break with the traditional naturalism that had dominated the productions of Wagner's operas.[29] This critical attitude is also clearly seen in other areas. From his recently published correspondence with Anna von Mildenburg, we know that Mahler was not exactly excited to go to Bayreuth.[30] With this in mind, what do we make of the fact that Mahler, before accepting his job in New York, explicitly stipulated that he did not want to be forced to perform *Parsifal*?[31] Against the wishes of Wagner's heirs, *Parsifal* had been performed in New York in 1903 (and before that under Mengelberg in Amsterdam). Mahler was clearly hoping to be able to perform Wagner in Bayreuth and did not want to do anything to harm that chance. But does this necessarily imply that Mahler is in full agreement with Wagner's cultural agenda? As a musical director, Mahler did not follow all of Wagner's ideas. But there is also a fundamental difference between Mahler's work as a conductor and his identity as a composer — a question that is not often addressed in current research. It is interesting, for instance, to read Mahler's decision to concentrate on symphonic forms, often with a strong vocal element, in the context of Wagner's statement that, after Beethoven's Ninth, choral symphonies had no future.[32] This suggests that the differences between Wagner and Mahler are clearer when one focuses on the latter as a creative artist and not solely as a conductor.

Despite the silence in the literature on Mahler's relationship to Wagner, the scholarly consensus appears to be that Mahler was an admirer of Wagner and his works and that their relationship was largely untroubled. But are there any (biographical) indications that this relationship was problematic? In 1872 Guido Adler, Felix Mottl (who was sixteen at the time), and Karl Wolf had founded the *Wiener Akademischer Wagner Verein* (Vienna Academic Wagner Society) to promote Wagner's work in Vienna in general and at the Vienna Conservatory in particular.[33] Mahler had joined the society in 1877 but gave up his membership in 1879 together with his friends Anton Krisper, Rudolf Krzyzanowski, and Hans Rott.[34] Hugo Wolf stayed on as a member. The exact reasons why Mahler and some of his friends decided to leave but Hugo Wolf did not are not known. The political agenda of fierce

German nationalism and the anti-Semitism associated with Wagner as a cultural icon in Vienna around 1880 may very well have had something to do with it.[35] Around the same time that Mahler renounced his membership in the Wagner Society, his relationship with Wolf started to cool as well, until the two were barely on speaking terms.[36] Wolf had started to translate his admiration for Wagner into a philosophy of life. In his letters starting in 1881, Wolf articulates an unprecedented hatred for Jews and for composers such as Brahms who, for him, personified an anti-Wagnerian program, and Wolf's visit to see *Parsifal* in Bayreuth in 1883 reinforced his anti-Semitism.[37] There is some anecdotal evidence that Mahler was aware that Wolf thought about art in racial terms. Once when Wolf complimented Mahler on his songs, Mahler responded by saying: "We now have surpassed Mendelssohn" (Ja, ich glaube, dass wir jetzt Mendelssohn eingeholt haben);[38] "we" clearly refers here to Mahler's Jewish background, and Mendelssohn's name stands for an outdated artistic model.

Mahler's break with Vienna's Wagner Society is *one* clear indication that Mahler experienced at least part of Wagner's legacy as problematic, especially where its political agenda was concerned. However, one could argue that such political forms of appropriation of Wagner did not concern Wagner's art itself but only the use that was being made of it. Following this line of argumentation, one would have to distinguish between Wagner's operas as complex and many-layered creations that are in essence not political, and the politically and racially motivated use that is being made of these works of art. Such a strict separation between "pure" art and its time-bound reception is of course highly artificial and thus problematic, and, moreover, is not supported by Wagner's own essays, which emphasize the political implications and racial agenda of his operas. There is also evidence that Mahler viewed anti-Semitism not as something that was constructed by Wagner's disciples but that was inherent to his operas.[39] In the book she authored on her friendship with Mahler, Natalie Bauer-Lechner refers to her conversations with Mahler in the context of the September 1898 rehearsals of Wagner's *Ring des Nibelungen*. Mahler was upset with one of his singers, who was scheduled to perform the role of Mime in *Siegfried*. Mahler reproached him for playing the role too much as a parody instead of a straightforward characterization; he also chided the singer for his "Mauscheln" — a stereotypical Jewish and therefore deficient way of speaking that had long been part of the anti-Semitic vocabulary.[40] In that context Mahler says a few things about what exactly Wagner intended with Mime:

> Although I am convinced that this figure [Mime] is the embodied persiflage of a Jew, as intended by Wagner (with all the traits which he gave him: his petty cleverness, greed, and all the complete musically and textually excellent jargon), that should not be

exaggerated and dished up so thickly here, for heaven's sake, as it was by Spielmann — especially in Vienna, at the "k.k. Court Opera," it is clearly laughable and a welcome scandal for the Viennese! I know only *one* Mime (we all looked at him anxiously) and that is *me*! You will be surprised to see what lies in the part and what I could make of it!"

[Obwohl ich überzeugt bin, daß diese Gestalt [Mime] die leibhaftige, von Wagner gewollte Persiflage eines Juden ist (in allen Zügen, mit denen er sie ausstattete: der kleinlichen Gescheitheit, Habsucht und dem ganzen musikalisch wie textlich vortrefflichen Jargon), so darf das hier um Gottes willen nicht übertrieben und so dick aufgetragen werden, wie Spielmann es tat — noch dazu in Wien, an der "k.k. Hofoper," ist es ja die helle Lächerlichkeit und den Wienern ein willkommener Skandal! Ich weiß nur *einen* Mime (wir sahen gespannt auf ihn): und der bin *ich*! Da solltet ihr staunen, was alles in der Rolle liegt und wie ich es zutage fördern wollte!" (*GME*, 122; not in *RGM*)][41]

Is Mahler here repressing the anti-Semitic subtext in Wagner's opera? I would argue that he is not; it is very clear to Mahler that Mime is intended by Wagner to personify an anti-Semitic stereotype. I would read Mahler's emphasis on the fact that he himself is meant ("that is *me*"/"der bin *ich*") as a statement that such stereotypes are not part of an archaic mythological imagery but concern the "here and now." Yet, as a conductor, newly appointed at the Court Opera House, Mahler chose not to emphasize this aspect of Wagner's opera in order to avoid a scandal. It is important to see that this is a conscious choice Mahler makes that bespeaks the pressures under which he had to work at the Court Opera and in Vienna in general, where his Jewishness was, from the outset, a topic of controversy. It would be wrong, in my opinion, to believe that Mahler did not care about Wagner's anti-Semitism or that he unconsciously decided to repress this aspect of Wagner's work; the above quote clearly shows that he was aware of it and that he did care. I hope to show in this book that in his own creative work Mahler takes issue with the cultural/political agenda underlying Wagner's works, including its anti-Semitic aspects. In comparison to Wagner's agenda, Mahler's work can be understood as a counterreading of the German cultural tradition, a reading that, among many other things, is also a critique of Wagner's idea of a German national culture.

Even while acknowledging the importance of Mahler as a conductor for the dissemination of Wagner's operas, it is hard to refute the claim that Mahler as a composer made choices that were quite different from the models Wagner promoted in theory and practice. Among Mahler's student friends, Siegfried Lipiner (1856–1911) stood out as a great admirer of Wagner (whom he had also visited in Bayreuth). And yet Lipiner was aware that Wagner's trajectory through German musical and cultural history was only one option among many. He was in particular critical of the connection between text, image, and music in Wagner's concept of the "total work of art" (Gesamtkunstwerk), and he explicitly questioned the tendency to see Wagner as the only possible artistic model or trajectory for cultural history, while simultaneously paying tribute to Wagner's unique role in German music:

> The interaction of music and poetry in dramatic form may be legitimate in an extraordinary artistic phenomenon like Richard Wagner, who masters both forms of art equally well and for whom music cannot lose its transcendental sense. Whether, however, a symphony by Beethoven is not a more perfect, greater creation than the most splendid works of Wagner — who can decide? Unquestionably, however, his opinion that only through a unification of all arts could the one true work of art come into being was a fundamental mistake.
>
> [Das Zusammenwirken von Musik und Dichtkunst im Drama mag in einer phänomenalen Kunst-Erscheinung wie Richard Wagner gerechtfertigt sein, der beide Künste ebenbürtig beherrscht und bei dem die Musik ihren übersinnlichen Sinn nicht verlieren kann. Ob aber eine Beethovensche Symphonie nicht immer noch eine vollendetere, größere Schöpfung bleibt als die herrlichsten Werke Wagners — wer kann's entscheiden? Doch fraglos ein Grundirrtum war seine Meinung, daß nur aus einer Vereinigung aller Künste das wahre einzige Kunstwerk hervorgehen könne!][42]

Lipiner's statement shows that one could respect Wagner and yet at the same time favor an alternative trajectory for musical history. His opinion is also relevant here because it reflects a choice that Mahler himself made (in spite of his high regard for Wagner): in his own creative work, leaving aside some early projects that never materialized,[43] Mahler decided to focus not on opera but on the symphony.

There are other differences between the musical trajectory Mahler chose and that of Wagner, in particular if we focus on the issue of "text." Wagner's music is highly programmatic. Not only does the text in his operas explain what the music is about (and vice versa), but he also built up an elaborate essayistic framework that comments in detail on the meaning of his compositions. Speaking from the perspective of a literary scholar, one may describe Wagner's operas as offering its audiences a closed narrative: a plot with a clear beginning and a clear end, connected by a chain of events that the audience is supposed to reconstruct. With very few exceptions (*Das klagende Lied*), Mahler's musical works offer open narratives. Textually speaking, there is no clear plot in his compositions; there is no clear beginning or end marked by text or within a text. This even applies to the First Symphony, even though, as I will show in the first chapter, it plays with the model of the *Bildungsroman*. Because of Mahler's use of narrative ambiguity and irony, it is often not even possible to distill a single unambiguous message out of his symphonies or song cycles.

All of this shows that Mahler's relationship with Wagner as a historical person, as the composer of some very influential operas, and as a theorist of German culture was a complex one and by no means without ambivalence. We can only understand Mahler's relationship to Wagner and to the agenda of German national renewal through art that Wagner advocated (especially in his theoretical writings), if we take into account Mahler's Jewishness. At the core of Wagner's cultural agenda is the idea that German culture needs to be cleansed from foreign influences: this means not just the French and Italians, but especially the Jews, the foreigners dwelling within German culture. Anti-Semitism is not at the margins of Wagner's essayistic work: it is at its center. It is not limited to essays such as "Das Judentum in der Musik" (Jewishness in Music, 1850/69), which long played a marginal role in the literature about Wagner, but it is part, in one form or another, of many other writings as well, among them "Religion und Kunst" (Religion and Art, 1880), an essay that is one of the more central texts in Wagner's theoretical work. In Vienna around 1900, anti-Semitism was not an abstract cultural issue. In 1897, the year in which Mahler returned to Vienna to work at the Court Opera, Karl Lueger — who was the leader of the Christian Social party and who had run for mayor of Vienna on an openly anti-Semitic platform — was finally appointed to the position of Mayor by Emperor Franz Joseph, who had refused to do so earlier, after he had been elected for the fifth time.[44] Lueger's appointment shows unambiguously that anti-Semitism had become a powerful political force in turn-of-the-century Vienna.

Within Vienna fin-de-siècle culture, Mahler's Jewishness was therefore an important factor. As a Jew working in the German(-Austrian) culture industry around 1900, he had only a limited number of options available to him. Many Jews identified with the Enlightenment ideal of assimilation.[45] Jews were to be tolerated and given civil rights, provided they would renounce or at the very least downplay their Jewish background. Mahler's conversion to Catholicism, shortly before starting his tenure at the Court Opera, should be understood in this context. To realize the attraction inherent to this idea of Jewish assimilation at the time, it is important to see that it was linked to the promise that every human being would only be judged as an individual, and not as the member of a specific ethnic group — clear signs of progress. Culture was an important platform for the assimilation of Jews into Western European society. Austrian Jews tended to identify primarily with German culture; in their eyes German culture stood for progress; it was associated with tolerance, civilization, and order; Germany was seen as a nation of "poets and thinkers."[46] In this respect, Mahler's path is remarkably similar to that of other prominent Jewish intellectuals of his time, such as Freud, Schnitzler, and Kafka. All these men saw themselves as representatives of German culture, and yet, in different ways and with varying degrees of success, they sought to establish a Jewish presence within German culture as well. At times this Jewish identification with German culture took the form of overt German nationalism.[47]

In his student days, Mahler was a member of a group of intellectuals, the so-called *Pernerstorfer Kreis* (Pernerstorfer circle), that was heavily influenced by Nietzsche and Wagner, and that combined an interest in art and philosophy with a political tendency toward German nationalism.[48] Some of the members were more interested in the circle's cultural ambitions, others in its political dimension, which was particularly pronounced in 1878, when Mahler joined the group.[49] The circle's affinity for the politically conservative cause of German nationalism can be partially explained as the rebellion of (Jewish) sons against the liberalism of their fathers, which to them seemed naive and remarkably ineffectual.[50] The *Pernerstorfer Kreis* therefore had strong critical motives; it saw itself as an anti-establishment group. This may to some extent explain the diverse political impulses to which it gave rise. Members of the group ended up representing very different political movements in later years; some of them became involved in conservative politics, but Victor Adler, a prominent member, became leader of Austria's Social Democratic party.[51] In hindsight, identifying with the conservative agenda of German nationalism may seem naive for Jews like Mahler, but one has to remain mindful that for some this identification may have been primarily cultural, and only secondarily a political matter, and may therefore have appeared quite harmless at the time.[52] It is important to keep this episode of Mahler's intellectual development in mind, even though there are good reasons to believe that Mahler later felt an affinity for a progressive political agenda.[53] In addition to the political aspect, there is another reason why the legacy of the *Pernerstorfer Kreis* is important for understanding Mahler. It is one of the decisive characteristics of Mahler's intellectual development that he viewed German culture holistically — that is, as a unified whole — and was never interested in any regional or ethnic particularism. His literary and philosophical interests (Goethe, Jean Paul, and Nietzsche) are an indication of this; the same goes for the texts he worked with in his compositions (*Des Knaben Wunderhorn*, Klopstock, Rückert, and of course, again, Jean Paul and Nietzsche).

It is in the context of this holistic view of German culture that one must interpret the importance of the tradition of Jewish-German culture for Mahler. In his everyday interactions, but also in explaining his artistic goals, he tended to avoid references to his Jewish background. His hesitancy to take a position against, or even to refer to, Wagner's anti-Semitic ideas is to be understood in this context. Yet, as I will argue in the following chapters, Mahler's work is not an example of assimilation. While the idea of a German national culture is very important for him, his aim is not to immerse himself in it, even though this is one of the predominant stereotypes about him. It would be wrong to see Mahler as someone who passively subjugated himself to the ideas of German *Bildung* and culture. Mahler's literary and philosophical preferences alone are indicative of his intellectual independence. Jean Paul and Friedrich Nietzsche, to name two prominent examples, not only represent a cosmopolitan thread in the fabric of German culture, but they also quite explicitly see themselves as critics of the prevailing trends in German culture and society. Even Mahler's reading of Goethe focuses on that author's cosmopolitan agenda.

Simultaneously, it must also be said that Mahler is not interested in establishing an independent Jewish cultural canon that is diametrically opposed to the assimilationist approach. Specifically, the decade between 1893 and 1904 was a period characterized by a "revitalization of a distinct Jewish culture" in German-speaking countries.[54] The interest in different subcultures coincides with an increase in nationalist tendencies in German culture. Michael Brenner has made the interesting observation that this revival of Jewish culture did not focus on a revival of "traditional Judaism" but rather attempted to "integrate selected aspects of this tradition into the framework of a modern secular culture" (21). One cannot speak of Mahler's music as an example of a Jewish cultural revival. Nevertheless, the motives underlying Mahler's creative works may have something in common with those seeking a revival of Jewish culture. Not only is Mahler interested in a specifically modern cultural agenda, but he is also highly aware of the nationalist connotations of German culture and he consciously positions his works vis-à-vis the nationalist agenda accompanying the idea of a German national culture as it manifests itself in his time. When he refers to his Eighth Symphony as "a gift to the nation," as I will discuss in chapter 5, he is clearly invoking the national discourse surrounding music.

While Mahler rarely addressed his Jewish background, I do not believe that he repressed his Jewishness. His attitude toward his Jewishness is maybe best described by Alfred Roller's statement that "Mahler never hid his Jewish origins. But he had no joy from them" (Mahler hat seine jüdische Abstammung nie versteckt. Aber sie hat ihm keine Freude gemacht).[55] To some extent Mahler's "Jewish identity" was something that the outside world constructed for him, and not something that Mahler himself felt he needed. Given the very public nature of Mahler's job in Vienna, repressing such identity politics was impossible.[56] It may also be significant in this context that a statement on Wagner's anti-Semitism such as the one reported by Natalie-Bauer-Lechner regarding the actor playing Mime in *Siegfried* most likely was part of a private or semi-private conversation.

But if Mahler did not want to repress his own Jewishness, how are we to interpret this public silence on anti-Jewish trends in the cultural discourse surrounding him? One could argue that he had no other option than to remain silent on the issue, at least in public. Had he chosen to address the issue openly, this would have had immediate consequences for his position of music director of the Court Opera. But what does this mean for Mahler's creative works; does he reflect his Jewishness in them or not? The question of the Jewish aspect of Mahler's music has been examined primarily on the basis of musicological deliberations; against such an appropriation, however, one could echo the argument of Talia Pecker Berio, who stated that music is "too complex a phenomenon to be reduced to a channel for the expression of ethnic and national sentiments and affiliations."[57] What I propose in the following is to follow a cultural, text-centered approach that attempts to do at least some justice to these complexities.

Modernism, the Avant-garde, and the Importance of Text

By focusing on the relevance of literature, philosophy, and the visual arts for Mahler's creative work, I hope to lay bare the critical dimension inherent in these works. Mahler's use of text in his symphonies is unusual in the symphonic tradition, in relation to which he positions himself as a creative artist (Beethoven's Ninth Symphony is the only major exception). Text is one of the defining features of Mahler's work. To make it part of music — either through the integration of song, or through extramusical deliberations — is also a polemical and emancipatory move. Because music without words or images is primarily a nonrepresentative form of expression, it could serve as an easy way for Jews to assimilate into German culture.[58] Mahler's use of text in his symphonies indicates that he wishes to take issue explicitly with the German cultural tradition. This explicit engagement with German cultural history assumes different shapes in his music.

In the first section of this book, which discusses his first four symphonies and the *Wunderhorn* songs, I show how Mahler seeks a critical reading of German cultural history. He identifies a crisis at the core of German culture, in particular where its normative ambitions are concerned, but nevertheless remains within the boundaries of that cultural tradition. In the second section, which deals with the Seventh and Eighth symphonies, the *Kindertotenlieder* and other Rückert songs, and the *Lied von der Erde*, I show how Mahler gradually develops an interest in alternatives to German culture, in what this culture perceives as its "others." Mahler's notion of alterity, however, is still deeply embedded in, and yet not identical with, what the German intellectual tradition understood the concept to be. In his interest in the "other side" of German culture, Mahler articulates an investment in cultural diversity beyond the German tradition that prefigures but is nevertheless very different from current notions of cultural diversity. I go on to argue that Mahler's relationship with German culture is largely a rational one. Mahler actively seeks to reflect its normative dimensions; it is not that his thinking and music are articulations of discourses beyond his grasp. It is impossible to understand the dynamics underlying Mahler's relationship with German culture without taking into account Mahler's Jewishness and the role of anti-Semitism in fin-de-siècle culture. It is at the core of the aforementioned "critical potential" in Mahler's creative works.

The crisis informing Mahler's earlier works is, to some extent, the crisis of modernism in general. In modernism, in Patrizia McBride's words, an "awareness" articulated itself "about the insufficiencies of established ways of thinking the human, of conceptualizing individual and collective experience, as well as an anxiety about the disastrous effects that could ensue if the admittedly inadequate categories currently being deployed were to be dismissed."[59] It is precisely in this sense of crisis that the relevance of modernism lies for understanding the later twentieth century. But how did Mahler relate to the crisis of modernism? It has become commonplace to view Mahler as a nostalgic modernist, as someone who mourned the loss of tradition, of the old certainties, and whose view of the past was mostly melancholic. This is essentially the vision that informs Adorno's essays. In his monograph on Mahler, Ernst Křenek, in contrast, mentions surrealism and the avant-garde as being more appropriate frames of reference for his creative efforts.[60] Drawing parallels between Mahler's music and surrealism may strike one, from our current perspective, as out of place; nevertheless, Křenek makes some very interesting points. Mahler's relation to tradition is eclectic; he chooses symbols that seem to be "outworn, obsolete" and appear to be quotations, and yet in their context in Mahler's music they achieve an aura of "grandeur and monumentality." His music very much lives off the (emotional) effects of these obsolete symbols in the listener. Yet while his symphonies contain plenty of "extra-musical associations," many of which can be traced back to popular culture, they nevertheless refuse a precise program. With such observations Křenek points to the liberties Mahler takes with tradition; one could call it a certain "playfulness." When I use the word "playfulness" in this context, I do not mean to suggest that Mahler's music is not intended seriously, but rather as a mode of expression that wishes to change the ways we see tradition and the way it has constituted what we view as reality.

This artistic freedom in relation to tradition is typical not only for surrealism but for the historical avant-garde in general. Peter Bürger's definition, in his classic study on the avant-garde, emphasizes that the avant-garde artist views the "totality of artistic means" that cultural history has produced as available in creating a new work of art.[61] It is interesting to note in this context that critics at the time had already noticed that Viennese fin-de-siècle artists were far less afraid of using past traditions than was the case for their Berlin contemporaries, for example.[62] Bürger also notes that the historical avant-garde is capable of self-reflection and self-critique and has a desire to break down the boundaries between art and life.[63] All these tendencies can also be found in Mahler's work. (Mahler's interest in the *Wunderhorn* folk songs is certainly an example of the desire to bring art and life together.) Vienna around 1900 was of course a place where exciting artistic innovations were happening. Mahler's proximity to the aesthetic philosophy of the avant-garde is not, or is not primarily, based on a conscious identification with the most innovative artists (the "avant-gardists") of his day — Klimt and Kokoschka for instance, although there are some interesting connections (see chapters 3 and 5) — but rather through a shared view of tradition (see chapter 5). Mahler's use of the melody of *Bruder Martin* for the third movement of his First Symphony is not much less daring than the exhibition of a urinal in a museum by Marcel Duchamp in 1917, I would argue. Of course, looking at Mahler in connection with the historical avant-garde is only possible in hindsight; in connection with twentieth-century German and Austrian art history, the term "avant-garde" is in general adopted for a group of artists who started to become active in the years around the First World War. However, it is a plausible perspective. For one thing, it makes us aware that Mahler certainly intended to provoke his audiences.

I am not going to claim that Mahler's works in every aspect prefigure the characteristics of the historical avant-garde as discussed by Bürger. What I am suggesting, however, is that we keep some of the characteristics of that avant-garde in mind when thinking of Mahler's place in Western culture. Leonard Bernstein, by the way, did not reintroduce Mahler solely to American audiences. Mahler's breakthrough in Vienna during the 1960s and 1970s must, to a large extent, be attributed to him as well. Mahler was reintroduced to Austrian audiences by someone from the "outside," a Jewish-American who also happened to be a composer with avant-gardist traits (for example, an interest in tearing down the boundaries between "high" and "low" culture). This reintroduction of Mahler in Vienna began with the performance of *Das Lied von der Erde* in April 1966 by the *Wiener Philharmoniker* under the direction of Bernstein, and included a complete recording of Mahler's symphonies on video in the 1970s and a highly symbolic tour to Israel in 1988, during which Mahler's Sixth Symphony ("The Tragic") was performed.

Bernstein's arduous rehearsals of Mahler's works with the *Wiener Philharmoniker* are well documented.[64] At least in part, this can be explained through the performance styles of Bernstein's predecessors in Vienna. The kind of Mahler to whom the musicians and audiences of the Vienna Philharmonic were accustomed stood in stark contrast to Bernstein's agenda. Bruno Walter, the most prominent among Bernstein's predecessors, could because of his personal relationship with Mahler be assumed to be in possession of an authentic view of the composer's works; in his approach, he emphasized the stylistic unity of Mahler's scores and thereby their "classical" lineage. Walter's performances, one could argue, sought to make Mahler's music acceptable by performing it in a very balanced, measured way and thus taking the provocative angle out of this music for an audience accustomed to the classics. Leonard Bernstein, in contrast, not only paid far more attention to the music's emotional content, but above all stressed the music's inherent contradictions. Bernstein clearly offered an avant-gardist's view of Mahler, but not that of an avant-garde mostly occupied with formal procedure and innovation, but rather as a representative of an avant-garde that made the point that music does not just have to be beautiful but can also be violent, exuberant, provocative, uncanny, ironic, or banal. Furthermore, Bernstein's insight into the heterogeneous nature of Mahler's musical textures was at least in part due to a certain ethnomusicological sensitivity that not only recognized but also sought to articulate in performance the diverse range of stylistic sources in Mahler's music. One can argue that Bernstein also reacquainted Austrians with their own cultural roots. These roots included Jewish music making as well, even though Bernstein simultaneously was also very hesitant — generalizations make him uncomfortable, he states — to mark certain aspects or elements of Mahler's music as "Jewish." For Bernstein, the Jewishness of Mahler's music is associated with its stylistic heterogeneity and translates into a fundamental ambiguity of the music's content.[65]

Bernstein conducting Mahler in front of the Vienna Philharmonic little more than twenty years after the end of the Holocaust and the Second World War was a highly symbolic event in many respects, and all the parties involved were well aware of this. What was less clear or at least, I would argue, what remained largely unreflected upon was that Bernstein's engagement with Mahler was also very much a statement about what culture is and what it does. Bernstein's struggle with the Vienna Philharmonic over Mahler was also (among many other things) on a fundamental level a clash between very different concepts of culture. While German cultural history always had been heterogeneous, both regarding the artifacts it produced and the different motivations with which individual artists created art, attempts had been made throughout German intellectual history to define "culture" in ways that would clearly set it apart from other European (or non-European) traditions. "Culture," according to this line of thinking, had unified German-speaking countries long before its political unification in 1871. It provided national cohesion in the realm of literature and the arts at a moment when, in reality, political unification was not possible. After the French revolution of 1789, "culture" was also increasingly seen as a superior German alternative to the political bloodshed in neighboring France. This ideal of "culture" was homogenous or homogenizing in that it emphasized a common base for all Germans within the realm of their ethnic tradition. "Culture" was also seen as something apolitical or, in the words of Wolf Lepenies, "a noble substitute for politics"[66] (in particular for the social experiments of eighteenth- and nineteenth-century France), although this argument turned out to be highly ambiguous, since culture was, on the one hand, supposed to be giving guidance to politics, while, on the other hand, the argument could also be made that politics should be enforced in order to protect culture.[67] This view of culture is still very much alive in modernism, which is one of the main targets of Lepenies's analysis.

But the potential for reading German culture differently — for, in other words, a more heterogeneous and political reading of the German cultural tradition — was always there. In an exemplary way, this is made visible by Bernstein's performances of Beethoven's Ninth Symphony on 23 and 25 December 1989 at the West-Berlin *Philharmonie* and the East-Berlin *Schauspielhaus* with a multinational cast of performers in celebration of the fall of the Berlin Wall on 9 November that year.[68] In his performances Bernstein diverged from the score regarding one crucial aspect: in the symphony's final movement with Schiller's "Ode an die Freude" (Ode to Joy) at its center, he replaced the key term "joy" (Freude) with "freedom" (Freiheit), giving the piece a decisively political (rather than aesthetic) message. Bernstein's action is a prime example of a critical appropriation of the German cultural tradition, a form of appropriation that raised fundamental questions about the functioning of art in German history. "Freedom" in this context could stand for many things: at that moment it certainly referred to a political goal, but Bernstein's change of vocabulary could also be interpreted as a call to look at one's own history differently. By substituting "Freiheit" for "Freude," Bernstein took up a mid-nineteenth-century debate on the question of whether Schiller had originally intended to write a more political version of the poem, one that thematized "freedom" and not "joy."[69] Bernstein's substitution was a critical act; it was meant to have his audience rethink what their tradition and Beethoven's music, as part of it, were about — very much *unlike* Simon Rattle's performance of the same symphony with the Vienna Philharmonic, but with its original text, the "Ode to Joy," at the site of the former concentration camp Mauthausen on 7 May 2000, celebrating the fifty-fifth anniversary of the concentration camp's liberation.[70]

It is possible to reconstruct German cultural history — or any national cultural tradition for that matter — critically or uncritically. It is also possible to think that one is doing something critical while one in reality is doing something very uncritical. For Bernstein, working with Mahler was clearly one possible path of working through German musical and cultural history critically. In Bernstein's view, that meant more than just identifying a "Jewish" element in Mahler's music: it meant developing a sense of awareness of the many different traditions and narratives present in Mahler's music and of its critical potential vis-à-vis German culture. *Reading Mahler* tries to do something similar, but with a focus on the texts that are important for Mahler's music. Mahler's texts are highly ambiguous and diverse, and it is precisely in this ambiguity and diversity that a critical impulse resides, something that is especially clear when we look at Mahler's music as a reflection on the historical and cultural conditions that shaped it. If we want to do justice to Mahler's place in German-Jewish culture beyond the kind of naive romanticization that has been problematized by Leon Botstein, we need to do justice to Mahler's text. Interpreting Mahler in the context of German literary and cultural history means reconstructing what was, but also what could have been, and what is perhaps still relevant today.

I. The Crisis of German Culture

1: *Titan:* Symphony of an Anti-Hero

Mahler's First Symphony has come to be associated with a little-known novel by the German author Johann Paul Friedrich Richter — commonly known as Jean Paul — entitled *Titan*, which was first published in four volumes between 1800 and 1803. This association between symphony and literary text is intriguing but quite problematic. The assumption that the two works are somehow connected is based on a handful of rather contradictory references. In spite of the fact that the works are mentioned in relation to each other frequently, and that "Titan" has become the First's unofficial title, the exact connections between novel and symphony are only rarely explored. Today Jean Paul's novel is largely forgotten, and even among specialists very few have read its more than 1,000 pages.

Mahler himself did not exactly help things with his conflicting statements about the symphony's (nonexistent) program. In a letter of 20 March 1896 to the critic Max Marschalk Mahler comments that he had added the references to Jean Paul to the notes accompanying performances of the First in an attempt to satisfy audiences' request for programmatic explanations of his symphony (*Br*, 169). He did not address the issue of whether Jean Paul's novel had in fact been important for its genesis. Indeed, the program notes accompanying the symphony's first performance in Budapest in 1889 do not contain any references to Jean Paul's novel or to any other literary or philosophical framework.[1] This may, however, be explained by the fact that this performance was for an audience whose primary linguistic and cultural environment was not German. Mahler may, in other words, have avoided references to the novel because he could not assume that his audience had any knowledge of Jean Paul's works, which were not part of the German literary canon.

Natalie Bauer-Lechner writes in her memoirs on Mahler that he did not intend his symphony to be associated with Jean Paul's *Titan*, but that others were responsible for this association:

> [Audiences] connected his "Titan" with Jean Paul's. But all he had in mind was a powerfully heroic individual, his life and suffering, struggles and defeat at the hands of fate, "while the true, higher resolution comes only in the Second Symphony."

> [So brachte man ihm seinen "Titan", mit dem Jean Paul'schen in Verbindung. Er hatte aber einfach einen kraftvoll-heldenhaften Menschen im Sinne, sein Leben und Leiden, Ringen und Unterliegen gegen das Geschick, "wozu die wahre, höhere Auflösung erst die Zweite bringt." (*RGM*, 157; *GME*, 173)]

But why would audiences associate a symphony by Mahler with a novel that was little known around 1890? No doubt Bauer-Lechner in her statement reiterates a version of what Mahler had told her, even though she appears to contradict Mahler's own statements. Her account of Mahler's ideas has strongly influenced contemporary thinking on the First (and Second) symphonies. And rightfully so: the above statement alone contains a number of important insights into the First. However, if Mahler did not intend his symphony to be associated with Jean Paul's *Titan*, he should have avoided the many references to Jean Paul in early scores of the symphony and in the program notes accompanying its early performances.

Bruno Walter, in sharp contrast to the statements by Mahler and Bauer-Lechner discussed here, claims in his biographical essay on Mahler that a connection between the First Symphony and Jean Paul's *Titan* was intended. Walter and Mahler discussed Jean Paul and his novel *Titan* frequently, we are told, and using the title *Titan* to designate the First is meant as a homage to Jean Paul. The third movement of the First, the Funeral Procession (Trauermarsch) that was originally meant to be the fourth movement when the symphony still consisted of five movements, is according to Walter based on the figure Roquairol, one of the principal characters in Jean Paul's *Titan*.[2] The same association between Roquairol and the "Trauermarsch" is made in Bruno Walter's letter of 6 December 1901 on Mahler's anti-programmatic programs (see "Introduction"). In this letter, however, Walter is more careful about the connection: the content of the movement "could appear to be related to the image of Roquairol from Jean Paul's novel" (könnte ... als dem Bilde des Roquairol aus dem Jean Paul'schen Roman verwandt erscheinen).[3] However, Walter makes it clear that other associations are possible as well, for instance with the images of Callot, in particular his popular depiction of the dead hunter accompanied to his grave by animal musicians. Walter, in other words, attempts to retain the (programmatic) *Titan* connection while simultaneously maintaining Mahler's anti-programmatic stance.

Mahler's hesitancy in formulating an explicit literary or philosophical program for his symphonies is clearly grounded in the era's aesthetic debates about the extent to which music should be autonomous or rather define itself in relation to other forms of art (see my introduction to this volume). In the case of the First Symphony, however, evidence exists that Mahler had psychological reasons for suppressing its "program." He reportedly referred to this work as a very personal piece that could only be understood by those who were familiar with what was going on in his life at the time.[4] Certain statements by Bruno Walter after Mahler's death regarding the genesis of the symphony support this, as I will discuss further hereinafter. Such contradictory explanations are typical for Mahler's antiprogrammatic programmatic art, and we will encounter them frequently in subsequent chapters. In spite of these contradictions, I believe that it is productive to follow Mahler's idea (at one point in the symphony's genesis) that studying Jean Paul's text can yield helpful insights into his First Symphony or can at least help us gain an impression of some of the literary and intellectual traditions that informed it (or that Mahler associated with it). Even though we should be cautious and not, for instance, equate Mahler's intentions with those of Jean Paul in his *Titan*, there is a characteristic ambiguity in the hero of Jean Paul's novel that we also find, for instance, in Bauer-Lechner's statement about Mahler's First (even though she claims that there is no connection between the works).

In his symphony, Mahler narrates a story that in some ways resembles a *Bildungsroman* — a genre built around a male hero preoccupied with finding love and a position of social responsibility, who goes through a learning process that eventually develops into a philosophy of life.[5] Upon closer examination, however, this seemingly straightforward narrative evoked by the symphony's "title" falls apart. The story that Mahler wants to tell his audiences in his symphony is not about a conventional hero but rather about a sort of anti-hero who is very much like the main character in Jean Paul's novel *Titan*, which was very critical of the idea of *Bildung* (often translated as "self-cultivation"[6]). It is very significant that, in Bauer-Lechner's version of Mahler's program for the First Symphony, the hero does not win but loses — a fact often overlooked by scholars. Jean Paul's *Anti-Bildungsroman* resists formulating a normative ideal for its hero. In fact the novel is skeptical toward any attempt to find unambiguous norms (in, for instance, religion, nature, or love), a skepticism that is mirrored in Mahler's symphony and is expressive of a notion of crisis that both have identified at the roots of German culture. Both Jean Paul's novel and Mahler's First Symphony seek to make this notion of crisis productive by experimenting with open forms of narration. Rather than offering a linear narrative, the story that is told is characterized by digressions, contradictions, intentional obscurities, and fundamental ambiguities. It is this openness that calls for the participation of the recipient in making sense of text and music. Finally, we find in the music (as in Jean Paul's novel) a mode of temporality that insists on the continued relevance of aspects of our past for our present, even if history, or the dominating construction thereof, decided to discard those aspects. Mahler reads German cultural history critically. This critical reading is only possible if we in turn read Mahler's symphony in the context of German literary and cultural history.

Mahler and Jean Paul

It is sheer historical coincidence that both Jean Paul and Richard Wagner spent the last years of their lives in Bayreuth. Around 1900 Bayreuth, with its Festival Hall and *Wahnfried*, Wagner's residence, had become a popular destination among nationalistic Germans. Wagner was *the* icon of middle-class German culture. The fact that Jean Paul's grave was also located in Bayreuth was mostly forgotten; not many knew where it was.[7] A few authors and critics, among them Alfred Kerr,[8] commented on this marginalization of Jean Paul in comparison to Wagner and its possible interpretation as the victory of nationalism over cosmopolitanism. It is unlikely that Mahler knew of these writings, but he was certainly aware of the fact that Jean Paul's status in German culture was very different from that of Wagner.

Jean Paul is a pseudonym for Johann Paul Friedrich Richter (1763–1825). As a homage to Jean-Jacques Rousseau, he chose the pen name Jean Paul.[9] When Richter adopted this pseudonym in 1792, Rousseau had come to be perceived, in spite of his death in 1778, as one of the intellectual forefathers of the French Revolution and therefore as a radical and controversial author. Most other German authors, for that reason, sought to dissociate themselves from the French Revolution (and Rousseau). But there are other reasons why Jean Paul is an anomaly in German literary history. He was a satirical and humoristic author with an interest in popular literature — a rarity in German literary history. Even though Jean Paul achieved fame overnight with his novel *Hesperus* (1795), which also put an end to his financial worries, he remained an outsider in German literature until the end of his life. This was at least partially due to his political radicalism. Jean Paul was a relentless critic of contemporary society, and his works were exceptionally harsh in their condemnation of institutions such as the church and the government.

One can see how Jean Paul became an identificatory figure for Mahler. Mahler's childhood was certainly not as harsh as that of Richter, who had grown up in great poverty with only modest prospects for success in society, but it is well documented that Mahler, especially in his student days, also had to live off very little at times.[10] Both were outsiders in German culture, albeit for very different reasons. Jean Paul's literary narratives resemble Mahler's musical narratives: Jean Paul's interest in humor and satire, in combination with philosophical musings and a deep interest in nature, can also be found in Mahler's music. There is no doubt that Jean Paul anticipated Mahler's philosophical interests. One characteristic of Jean Paul's psychology as an artist was a seemingly unquestioning belief in his own artistic talents; the same can be said of Mahler. It is remarkable that, as we can read in surviving autobiographical documents, Jean Paul does not simply deny the harsh realities of his youth but manages to turn them into their opposite: the idea of a happy and privileged childhood.[11] According to Alma, Mahler likewise never acknowledged the poverty of his childhood home.[12]

Titan is representative of Jean Paul's oeuvre in many respects. With its four volumes, two "humoristic" supplements, and a sort of philosophical treatise called a "supplement to the first humoristic supplement," it is a very long novel. Jean Paul attacks the double standards of the upper classes — *Titan* is a critique of both the aristocracy and the bourgeoisie or middle class. It can also be read as a *Bildungsroman* in search of philosophical answers about the relationships between men, women, their fellow human beings, and the world around them. It documents a fundamental crisis in this relationship. The novel depicts a world without values; metaphysics has come to an end and nothing speaks for the existence of a better world anymore.[13] Yet most characters are not satisfied by an exclusive focus on the here-and-now. Because of this crisis — the notion that nothing matters any more, an insight that would later be called "nihilism" — Jean Paul can accurately be called a precursor to Nietzsche. In the late eighteenth and early nineteenth centuries, within Romanticism a radical current developed whose advocates believed in the purely subjective nature of all knowledge and therefore, in many respects, anticipated Nietzsche's diagnosis of German culture eighty years later (see chapter 3). While Nietzsche ultimately seeks to embrace this new lack of values, Jean Paul's characters suffer from this crisis. Their identities, as we will see, are deeply affected by the crisis of values articulated in *Titan*. Virtually all of the main characters in the novel are profoundly insecure about who they are and what they want to be, while "death," as a symbol of the futility of all that is on earth, seems to be the only certainty left.

By 1888, when Mahler composed the First Symphony, the general public had largely forgotten Jean Paul.[14] Working with Jean Paul's *Titan* at the end of the nineteenth century meant rehabilitating a neglected author. More importantly, one could argue that Mahler's focus on Jean Paul allows for an against-the-grain rereading of German literary history. Jean Paul's novel was often seen as being in opposition to the "classical" tradition of Goethe and Schiller. The roots of this perceived opposition can in fact be found in Goethe's work. In 1797 Goethe published a satirical poem about Jean Paul in which he compared him to a Chinese man looking at ancient ruins in Rome. The Chinese man is fundamentally unable to understand or appreciate antiquity's greatness; Goethe draws a parallel between him and someone who is ill and who views something he sees as pathological, not realizing that his own illness prevents him from recognizing what is healthy.[15] Later in life, Goethe was more appreciative of Jean Paul's work, even though he still considered him an outsider. While working with oriental texts in the context of his *West-östlicher-Divan* project, he once characterized Jean Paul's style as "oriental" because the heterogeneous nature of his narratives made the strangest of connections and combined elements that did not belong together, even though Jean Paul was ultimately able to synthesize his materials into a unified whole.[16] In some of his later works — the *West-östlicher Divan*, but also the second part of *Faust* — Goethe embraces an eclectic style of writing that moves far away from the classical norms of unity and simplicity to which he and Schiller had earlier aspired.[17] Some literary critics saw similarities between *Titan* and Goethe's *Faust*; the principal characters of the two texts are seen as kindred spirits,[18] but readers must have also noticed the similarly heterogeneous and eclectic nature of both texts.

In addition to its stylistic characteristics, there may have been another, less obvious reason why Goethe described Jean Paul's work as "oriental." What makes a novel like *Titan* stand out in comparison to the work of contemporaries like Goethe and Schiller is that it pays attention to Jewish life. Jean Paul's portrayal of Jews in *Titan* is generally respectful. The statement in *Titan*, for instance, that 12,000 Jews did not design the coliseum that they built[19] may have a specific rhetorical function within an argument, but it also shows an awareness and appreciation of Jewish contributions to Western culture that is atypical for the period in which Jean Paul wrote his novel. Another example is the portrayal of the "Jewish peddler" (Schnurrjude)[20] early on in the novel (81) — a wandering merchant, collecting and buying hair in the villages (for a wigmaker in the city?) whose collection has been set on fire by local children. Jean Paul belongs to a small group of non-Jewish authors in German literary history who actively engage with Jewish life.[21] At a young age Jean Paul avidly learned Hebrew.[22] A motivating factor for Jean Paul's interest in Jewish culture and Orientalism may have been his close friendship with the Jewish merchant Emanuel Samuel in Bayreuth; not much is known about this relationship, but one of Jean Paul's early biographers emphasizes its importance for Jean Paul's knowledge of Jewish and Oriental culture.[23]

Titan, the Anti-Hero

Because Jean Paul's *Titan* is little known (even among Mahler scholars) and its complex aesthetic and philosophical aims were unquestionably a major influence on Mahler, I will discuss the novel here in some detail. The most obvious continuity between Mahler's First Symphony and Jean Paul's novel is the main heroic figure, the Titan character. I have already quoted Bauer-Lechner's statement that Mahler "had a powerfully heroic individual in mind" (Mahler hatte einen kraftvoll-heldenhaften Menschen im Sinne) when composing his First Symphony. The section of Bauer-Lechner's memoirs in which she reports this is based on a letter she wrote much earlier to the Vienna music critic and friend of Mahler Ludwig Karpath, on 16 November 1900. There is no doubt that the letter was written at the request of Mahler himself. Bauer-Lechner's letter to Karpath tells us something more, something left out of the memoir, that makes Mahler's Titan figure much more complex. In clarifying the heroic character of the symphony's main figure, Bauer-Lechner writes:

> The First is still altogether written from the standpoint of a *young* man, unarmed and defenseless against all attacks, who experiences and suffers in the most direct way.
>
> [Die Ite ist noch ganz vom Standpunkte des unbewehrten (— wehrlos allem Ansturm preisgegeben —) unmittelbarst erlebenden und erleidenden *jungen* Menschen aus geschrieben.] (*RGM*, 237 and 239, trans. modified; not in original German edition)

While the memoir emphasizes Titan's active attributes, the letter in contrast points to his passivity and suffering. Reading Bauer-Lechner's clarification, one could say that Mahler's hero is more of an anti-hero, and that it is at the very least questionable whether he determines his own fate through his own actions.

This ambiguity is also typical of Albano, the main character in Jean Paul's *Titan*. Jean Paul himself speaks occasionally of his "Anti-Titan" when referring to the novel.[24] Albano is, one could say, very impulsive, a character trait that is described in the text as "warm-bloodedness" (warme Seele; 183); in other words, he is a typical Romantic hero in that he believes that emotion and intuition should guide his actions, not rational deliberations. Equally characteristic of Albano is his strong focus on the here and now. This is particularly clear in his relation to his first love interest, Liane, to whom he says that he is "happier" than she because he "believes in a *long* life here" on this earth (ich bin glücklicher als du, denn ich allein glaube an unser *langes* Leben hier; 390). Albano is a modern hero: he believes in creating his own values in the here and now instead of relying on models passed down by previous generations. He is no classical hero representing a set of given ideals, and he is certainly not a hero who can be expected to represent Jean Paul's own philosophy of life. The attitude of the narrator toward his "hero" is one of deep irony. *Titan* is not a *Bildungsroman* but rather an *Anti-Bildungsroman*, even though many "classical" *Bildungsromane* are also critical of their protagonists.[25]

This fundamentally ironic attitude toward Albano is also seen in the many contradictions in the way Albano is characterized. In spite of his down-to-earth philosophy of life, he is attracted to the deeply religious Liane, who tends toward mysticism and lives for what lies beyond; Albano's realism feels drawn to Liane's idealism. Albano's fascination for and eventual friendship with Roquairol, the novel's main antagonist, represents another inconsistency: Albano is a deeply moral person who believes in sincere emotions; Roquairol — who is introduced to the reader as he attempts to gain Linda de Romeiro's heart by (ineptly) reenacting the suicide scene in Goethe's *Die Leiden des jungen Werther*) (The Sorrows of Young Werther) — is the exact opposite: he is dishonest and manipulative. The strongest argument for claiming that the narrator is treating Albano ironically is the fact that, up until the end of the novel, Albano is almost completely ignorant of his own family background and the future tasks connected to it. Many of his statements and insights are therefore to be taken with a grain of salt.

The passive nature of *Titan*'s main character means that secondary figures in the novel play relatively important roles. Their narrative function is to clarify the main character's development to the reader by offering contrasts with it. Roquairol is the son of a government official and the brother of Liane, Albano's first love interest. Roquairol is as focused on the here and now as Albano claims to be, but while Albano is driven by high moral standards in his actions, Roquairol is not. He is indifferent toward the moral implications of his actions. There is a decidedly aesthetic dimension to his way of life; he plays with emotions, his own and those of others.[26] He is always looking for new opportunities to live out his fantasies.[27] This is seen not only in his seduction of Rabette, Albano's adoptive sister, and his subsequent abandonment of her, after which she is psychologically a broken woman with no future in society, but also in his rape of one of Albano's later love interests, Linda de Romeiro, while pretending to be Albano (494). Roquairol, in his own words, does "not believe in anything anymore" (ich glaube nichts mehr; 486).[28]

Albano and Roquairol's interactions with the world represent divergent responses to a worldview that could be characterized as post-metaphysical or modern. There is no doubt that *Titan* portrays a world in which people have lost their sense of orientation. Philosophically, the crisis at the core of Jean Paul's *Titan* manifests itself as a lack of values, or, to be more precise, as the modern world's inability to provide a substitute for the old metaphysical systems. However, the metaphysical crisis in *Titan* also has a psychological dimension. *Titan* is rich in psychology, in particular where it concerns knowledge of psychosomatic phenomena, that to a degree anticipates Freud's theory of psychoanalysis. Like Roquairol, Albano sometimes suffers from overexuberant emotions, an excess of feelings and fantasy.[29] Albano remedies this situation by cutting himself and thus causing "pain and even small bleedings" (Schmerzen und sogar kleine Verblutungen; 4). Albano's masochism, to use Freud's terminology,[30] is the logical consequence of a new philosophy of life that emphasizes one's inner development and the cultivation of one's emotions, but that does not provide any kind of social sphere where this inner development could find a productive outlet. One could speak in this context of a psychopathology of modernity: these symptoms are the direct result of uncertainties typical of a post-metaphysical age. But does *Titan* offer a form of therapy for remedying these time-bound ailments?

The novel makes it clear that *religion* is not an effective form of therapy. Despite the novel's rather severe criticism of the church as an institution, not all forms of religious experience are entirely without merit. On the one hand, Liane demonstrates that some forms of religious experience are still possible in a post-metaphysical world. In her case, religion takes the shape of a nearly total withdrawal into herself, an extreme mysticism. On the other hand, however, the novel demonstrates that such religious mysticism is not viable; Liane's mystical experiences almost exclusively center on death and dying as the central aspects of her inner life. Her obsession with mysticism is connected to her own death, which appears to result from a sheer inability to live, from a physical breakdown caused by overwhelming negative emotions. Bruno Walter, strangely enough, claimed that Jean Paul's work, in particular *Titan*, brought him back to Christianity.[31] This is a highly intriguing remark, especially since it makes one wonder about Mahler's influence on Walter here. If Liane can be seen as a model of religious experience at all, then only as a very masochistic one.

Nature seems to offer a more plausible form of therapy, albeit an imperfect one. Rousseau is mentioned repeatedly (136, 694) with at least some respect, but it is made clear that his criticism of civilization and advocacy of nature have been reduced to a fashionable construction of the rich. This is particularly clear in the description of Lilar, one of the settings of the novel, which is described as a "play with nature and bucolic poem of the romantic and at times deceptive fantasy of the old ruler" (Lilar ist das Naturspiel und bukolische Gedicht der romantischen und zuweilen gaukelhaften Phantasie des alten Fürsten; 202). Attempts to construct such a utopian realm are as flawed as any other metaphysical fabrication. And yet nature is not entirely without value. It is false to say that nature represents a fixed normative order or provides man with some sort of moral code. However, nature — or more accurately the experience of nature — can have intrinsic value, as the following description by *Titan*'s narrator makes clear:

> Grand nature! When we see and love you, then we love human beings more warmly, and when we must mourn or forget them, you remain with us and pose before our teary eye like a greenish mountain range in the red evening sun.
>
> [Hohe Natur! wenn wir dich sehen und lieben, so lieben wir unsere Menschen wärmer, und wenn wir sie betrauern oder vergessen müssen, so bleibst du bei uns und ruhest vor dem nassen Auge wie ein grünendes abendrotes Gebirge. (23)]

This passage describing Albano's arrival at Isola bella and his experience of nature's awakening is located at the end of the first book of *Titan*; Mahler depicts this scene musically at the beginning of his First Symphony, as I will show below. After the passage quoted above, the narrator describes a soul that has lost its initial idealism, unquestionably anticipating Albano's later development. However disillusioned one may be, nature will always be there and can have a consoling function (23). The function ascribed to nature here is primarily aesthetic and psychological. Nature does not offer us an objective "order of things" in the sense of a hierarchy that tells us how to organize our lives. The importance of nature is rather located in the psyche of the individual[32] and is to some extent indicative of the individual's ability to deal with the world. The interaction of humankind with nature is highly relevant for Jean Paul in that it is symptomatic of one's relation to the world. Roquairol's remark in his farewell speech, just before his suicide, that he does "not even appreciate beautiful nature anymore" (nicht einmal die schöne Natur mag ich mehr; 747) clearly refers back to the quote above; it is indicative of his problematic relationship with the world in general.

Titan suggests that *love,* as well as nature, can have a therapeutic function, even though the novel strongly resists an idealization of love. Albano's first lover, Liane, dies; Linda de Romeiro, his second lover, is raped by his former friend Roquairol and disappears into a convent. Only his relationship with Idoine shows some promise. One could say that these three women are instrumentalized in the interest of the "hero's" development, a situation that is not atypical for a *Bildungsroman*; Goethe's novel *Wilhelm Meisters Lehrjahre* (Wilhelm Meister's Apprenticeship), the archetype of the genre, is structured along similar lines. Here too, however, Jean Paul does not reproduce the rules of the genre uncritically. In the end, "love" is for Jean Paul not about the realization of the self, the finding of personal fulfillment in being with a specific partner, but about a way of relating to the world around us. After losing Liane and Linda, Albano has learned that "compassion" (Mitleiden; 761) is perhaps more important than love. Such a criticism of "romantic love" at least partially explains why Albano's image of Idoine remains strangely detached throughout the novel. She is not his real love in the sense that she is the person for whom he has the most intense feelings (the latter is obviously Liane). As Albano's last love interest, however, Idoine offers a sort of synthesis of utopian moments in the novel. Marriage to Idoine would end existing rivalries between his family and hers. At a moment when Albano is in deep despair over Liane's death, Idoine, who can pretend to be Liane's spirit since there is a strong resemblance between them, appears to him to wish him peace. After that a healing process begins (549–50). Albano's relationship with Idoine has, in other words, a clear religious dimension. Idoine's Arcadia project, a model village where people live in harmony with nature, is an attempt to realize Rousseau's philosophy of nature in a more realistic and societally productive setting than Lilar's world of fake nature (461–62). Finally, through their physical similarity, Idoine reminds Albano of his first, "real" love, Liane. Idoine, therefore, synthesizes the different utopian elements in the novel.

I mention the semi-utopian elements in *Titan* in such detail because they all play a significant role in Mahler's intellectual landscape. The texts used in Mahler's music are full of references to religion, nature, and love. It is important, however, to emphasize that in Jean Paul's world there are no real utopian realms but only memories of past utopias: there is an element of ambiguity inherent to these projects that has been there from the beginning and simply cannot be ignored. Jean Paul's writing is characterized by a basic questioning of normative claims; his version of Romanticism emphasizes notions of crisis not unlike Mahler's. In his groundbreaking study on Mahler, Adorno states that "Mahler's Romanticism negates itself through disenchantment, mourning, long remembrance" (*MPE,* 47; Mahlers Romantik negiert sich selbst durch Entzauberung, Trauer, langes Eingedenken: *MP,* 196). One could counter this observation by arguing that an element of negation is already inherent in the version of Romanticism on which Mahler bases his work: there is no naive Romanticism in Mahler that remains unaware of it own fallacies. From the outset, the intellectual agenda informing Mahler's music displays a fundamental skepticism toward the metaphysical. Mahler's literary source for his First Symphony, its "program," does not try to reconstruct a utopian past no longer available in the present; there is no such nostalgic longing for a past presence in Jean Paul's *Titan*. To phrase it in philosophical terms, Jean Paul's *Titan* confronts its readers with the paradoxical insight that despite the basic unreliability of metaphysical projects, humankind cannot live without some form of substitute for metaphysics. The question it asks is: how can humanity find anything of value in a post-metaphysical world?

In contrast to the prototypical *Bildungsroman,* understood in a traditional sense, Jean Paul's *Titan* does not suggest that an emancipatory program toward a future of human autonomy is possible. The orientation shared by Jean Paul's novel and Mahler's music is that they turn not to the future but to the past. In the words of one contemporary Jean Paul scholar: "The secret telos of the novel [*Titan*] is a present that *simultaneously* is also memory" (Das geheime Telos des Romans ist eine Gegenwart, die *zugleich* Erinnerung ist).[33] Albano is the personification of this type of memory; in contrast to Roquairol, who only lives in the present,[34] Albano is able to live in the present and the past. The novel offers only memories of utopia, or to be more precise "a quotation-like memory of projections that were once thought, but that are nothing but fictions" (zitathafte Erinnerung an Projektionen, die schon einmal gedacht wurden, aber allein Fiktionen sind).[35] The kind of memory Jean Paul aims for in *Titan* is not a historical memory — a reconstruction of the facts that constitute history — but a form of memory that incorporates lived experience, emotions, and the lessons and hopes derived from them; one that also incorporates literature and other arts as testimonies of one's experience. This makes Jean Paul's novel into a *Bildungsroman* that is very different from its classical model. The novel documents a profound crisis and offers no easy solutions to it. Moreover, history is not something that has to be overcome in order to make a better future possible; history is precisely where hope is still possible.

The First Symphony and Its Programs

To arrive at a more precise understanding of the connection between Jean Paul's novel and Mahler's First Symphony, it is helpful to look at some of the notes accompanying early versions of Mahler's score and the program notes for some of the early performances, in particular two concerts in Hamburg in 1893. Initially the symphony had five movements; in the following I will consistently refer to this original version, even though it is only rarely performed today. The reason for my choice is that Mahler's programmatic statements that connect the symphony to Jean Paul's work almost exclusively refer to the symphony in its original, five-movement form.

Bruno Walter, in his explanations of the (anti-)programmatic aspects of this work, states that Mahler is not interested in representing actual events of his life but rather in evoking a specific mood or frame of mind — Walter literally speaks of a certain "disposition of his soul" (Stimmung seiner Seele) — combining memory and a feeling that is present in the here and now, resulting in thematic clusters that are an organic part of Mahler's compositions.[36] Walter speaks of a vision emphasizing organic unity and closure in Mahler's music that perhaps tells us more about Walter than about Mahler; it is a well-known fact that Walter's musical preferences focused on the classical, with its emphasis on harmony and linearity, and not the modernist tradition, with its preference for contrasts, fragments, and open-endedness. Nevertheless, Walter's deliberations tell us something essential that could easily be overlooked. They offer a key for understanding the relation between music and the images associated with it. Only if we pay attention to the "mood" that Mahler's music attempts to evoke are we able to understand the references within it.

At times, Jean Paul's novel also seeks to suggest very specific "moods" or "emotions." One reason why I believe that Mahler's First Symphony is indeed based on Jean Paul's *Titan* is that the idea underlying the first movement, the articulation of nature's awakening, has a clear parallel in the novel's opening scenes, specifically the passage depicting Albano's arrival at night at Isola bella, the island on which he had spent the earliest years of his childhood. In order to experience the awakening of the coming day more purely — as a listening experience! — Albano has himself carried up the mountain blindfolded (20–22). In the novel, this event is also described as the advent of spring (20). The fact that the first movement portrays, according to Mahler's programmatic notes of 1893 (see appendix), the awakening of nature from its winter slumber in itself explains a certain mood that the listener will recognize. When Mahler revised the programmatic notes he had written in Hamburg (1893) for the Weimar performance of this symphony, one year later (1894), he explicitly referred to "the awakening of nature in the very early morning" (das Erwachen der Natur am frühesten Morgen) in connection with the first movement;[37] this ties Mahler's program into Jean Paul's text even more closely.

A clear correlation between symphony and literary text also exists for the second movement. To Bauer-Lechner, Mahler has characterized the second movement, the "Blumine" movement, which was later dropped from the symphony, as "sentimentally indulgent" (sentimental schwärmerisch), as a "love episode" (Liebesepisode), but also as "youthful folly" (Jugend-Eselei) of his hero (*RGM*, 158; *GME*, 173). Following the arrival scene described above, we find the novel's hero behind the palace on Isola bella, intoxicated by the smell of blooming orange trees. He is opening his veins to find relief from his overwhelming emotions — a habit, we are told, he took up as a child (34–36). Suddenly Don Gaspard, the man whom Albano assumes is his father, appears. The scene that follows can certainly be characterized as a love episode in that Albano's meeting with his presumed father is followed by a profound declaration of the love of the son for his father: "Let me bleed, I want to die with you, if you die" (Laß mich bluten, ich will mit dir sterben, wenn du stirbst; 38). Considering the fact that Albano's wounds are entirely self-inflicted, it is hard for the reader to take this seriously; neither does Don Gaspard, who appreciates the sentiment but wants to take care of practical things first: "All good and well, but put a bandage on first" (Recht gut, verbinde dich aber; 38). Later on Don Gaspard reproaches Albano for being in "too romantic" a mood that day (du bist leider heute zu romantisch; 39). Albano's love for his "father" is therefore to be taken with a grain of salt; the text does express an ambiguity quite similar to the one that Mahler, according to his programmatic notes, had intended for his original second movement. Whether the movement does in fact express the ambiguity that Mahler aimed for in his programmatic explanations in a way that was recognized by audiences is another question. Mahler himself seems to have doubted it; there are indications that he considered it too sentimental.[38]

Little information is available regarding the intended program for the third movement. In the program notes of October 1893, this scherzo is only accompanied by the somewhat enigmatic description "Under full sail" (Mit vollen Segeln). Of some help is the subtitle for the first section of the symphony, comprising the first three movements, in the same program: "Flower, Fruit, and Thorn Pieces" (Blumen-, Frucht- und Dornstücke), a reference to Jean Paul's novel *Siebenkäs*.[39] While the first two movements in the original five-movement structure clearly depict positive moods, albeit not without irony, as I have shown, and indeed evoke associations with flowers and fruit — that is, they could count as "Blumen-" and "Frucht[stücke]" — one could argue that the third movement is pessimistic in tone (and therefore a "Dornstück"). The chronology of the first book of Jean Paul's *Titan* is helpful here. After the encounter with his "father," Albano goes out into the night and encounters a figure dressed in black bearing a depiction of a skull on his chest, who introduces himself as a "father of death" (ein Vater des Todes; 48). The mysterious figure, who resembles a monk and at the end of the novel is revealed to be a brother of Don Gaspard, announces the imminent death of Albano's sister in Spain and asks Albano to follow him into a boat, a gondola, onto the lake (this may explain the nautical imagery in Mahler's program notes). On the lake a mysterious voice tells Albano to love the figure that will appear to him, after which a female figure rises halfway out of the waves (49). The monk adds that, on the upcoming Day of the Ascension, his sister will announce the name of his bride to him from heaven.

The three aforementioned events in the first book of *Titan* foreshadow the fortunes of the principal character and are therefore highly significant for the plot line of the remainder of *Titan*. Albano's search for the bride promised to him by the mysterious monk is a major structural element in the novel. A literary reading of Mahler's program underlying the first three movements of his First Symphony makes it possible to discern a developmental model. Not unlike the psychoanalytic theory of Mahler's contemporary Sigmund Freud, the development of the individual is tied to the relationships he develops with his primary caregivers. In the first movement, the protagonist is totally alone and, as it were, in complete unity with the world around him. In the second movement, a parental figure appears, the "father," who becomes the primary object of the hero's emotions and is also seen as a source of knowledge about the world. The third movement then articulates the transition from this parental relationship and its accompanying hierarchies to a relation of equals or partners; the hero is promised a future love object and the realization of his sexual identity. Albano's sister functions here as a transitional figure. On the one hand, she is part of the parental world; on the other, she points to a realm beyond that constrictive world, a realm of freedom and autonomy. It is important to recognize that the three movements discussed here also concern the emotional development of the individual at the center of the symphony; they narrate a *Bildungsroman*. The cognitive and sensual awakening of the principal character (first movement) is followed by the experiences of love (second movement) and death as irrevocably intertwined with love (third movement). The third movement is particularly important here, since it articulates the end goal of this development. Death and love are intertwined in an unexpectedly productive way here; it is as if only the recognition of death makes it possible for the hero to love.

Mahler abandoned his programmatic explanations for the First Symphony with the Berlin performance on 16 March 1896; he also shortened the symphony from five movements to four by dropping the second, "Blumine," movement.[40] At the same time — in his letter of 20 March 1896 to Max Marschalk, discussed above — he downplayed the importance of Jean Paul's *Titan* for this work. The conventional wisdom contends that he had had enough of the speculations that his programmatic statements had engendered. Indeed, his letter to Marschalk suggests this, when he states that the titles and explanations give only "incomprehensive" (nicht erschöpfend) and (therefore?) "not even correct" (nicht einmal zutreffend) accounts of the symphony's content, and seem to have led audiences in the wrong direction (*Br,* 169). It is interesting that Mahler does not deny the relevance of Jean Paul's *Titan* for the symphony here, but rather points out that extramusical elements can lead to only a partial understanding of the (far more complex) music. Keeping the (literary) *Bildungsroman* sketched above in mind, another explanation for Mahler's abandonment of the *Titan* program arises: without the original second movement, "Blumine," the story of the hero's youth and development traced by the music made little sense anymore; in fact, it is no longer possible to distinguish the developmental sequence originally underlying the first three movements.

While Mahler's programmatic statements about the first three movements of the original version of the First Symphony are sparse, there is an abundance of information for the fourth movement — so much so, in fact, that Bruno Walter, as I have already shown at the beginning of this chapter, repeatedly used this movement as an example for explaining Mahler's stance on programmatic music. Mahler himself also wrote an extensive explanation for this movement in the program notes for the Hamburg performance on 27 October 1893 (see appendix). There he refers to an engraving by the French artist Jacques Callot (1592/3?–1635), "The Hunter's Funeral Procession," to explain his intentions. Mahler calls Callot's engraving the "stimulus" or "inspiration" (Anregung) behind the movement and claims that it is simultaneously relevant for its interpretation. He is interested in the ambiguity expressed by Callot's engraving. It depicts a funeral procession for a hunter staged by his prey: the hunted woodland animals who also are responsible for the procession's music. The music that these animals produce is a medium for widely diverging emotions — sadness, perhaps, but especially joy — and this fundamental ambiguity is exactly what interests Mahler. The funeral march is nothing but a parody of ritualized grief, and in fact is more genuine in its celebration of life. It lives off a tension between what a specific social occasion demands the musicians to feel and what they really feel. Interestingly, a connection also exists between Jean Paul and Callot. In 1814, the German author, composer, conductor, and music critic E. T. A. Hoffmann published a collection of novellas entitled *Fantasiestücke in Callots Manier* (Fantasy Pieces in Callot's Manner). Jean Paul wrote the preface to this collection,[41] in which he claims that Hoffmann's novellas are not written in "Callot's manner" at all; nevertheless, he appreciates their ironic and satirical aspects and their aim to save serious art from abuse by those who think they know better than its creator. Most of the preface is in the form of a fictitious review, supposedly copied by Jean Paul from a prominent literary journal. The result is that the reader is also left with a profound feeling of ambiguity regarding Jean Paul's exact intentions.

Bruno Walter adds an important additional piece of information to Mahler's program for the fourth movement of the First Symphony in his biographical essay on Mahler, in which he states, as I have already noted, that the funeral march of the First is influenced by the figure of Roquairol in Jean Paul's *Titan*. This is a cross-reference to Jean Paul's novel *Titan* that we can be reasonably sure originates from Mahler. There is no description of Roquairol's funeral in *Titan*. There are, however, two passages in which "death" is thematized with a sense of ambiguity that is highly reminiscent of the ambiguity associated with Callot's "Hunter's Funeral Procession." First, there is Roquairol's suicide attempt in the second book of *Titan* — the event that actually introduces Roquairol to the reader. Roquairol believes himself to be very much in love with a friend of his sister's, Linda de Romeiro. Around 1800, the impossible love of Werther for Lotte in Goethe's best-selling epistolary novel *Die Leiden des jungen Werther* (1774) provided the quintessential model of the unhappy love affair. Jean Paul refers to this in *Titan*. One day Roquairol encounters Linda at his sister's, and "unfortunately" she is "coincidentally dressed like Werther's Lotte" (Zum Unglück ging sie zufällig als Werthers Lotte gekleidet; 97). Roquairol immediately demands her love, and when she refuses, goes home, dresses up like Werther, and brings back a pistol. Roquairol, "half-drunk from Lotte's charms, from Werther's sufferings, and from punch" (halb trunken von Lottens Reizen, von Werthers Leiden und von Punch), threatens to kill himself and eventually — after Linda's fifth or sixth refusal — pulls the trigger but only nicks part of his left ear (97). A similarly staged scene, but with a very different outcome, can be found later in the novel in book 32,[42] and this is the second passage of relevance here. After Roquairol concludes that Linda will never love him and only loves Albano, he decides to seduce and rape her. Exploiting Linda's night blindness, Albano's temporary absence, and the similarity between his voice and Albano's, he seduces her and rapes her, all while maintaining the illusion that he actually is Albano. Soon thereafter, he invites his friends and acquaintances to a performance of a play that he has written incorporating many of his life's important moments in a veiled manner that is nonetheless recognizable to his audience. At the end of the play, and in the audience's presence, he commits suicide (755).

Both passages are characterized by an ambiguity very similar to the one found in Callot's "Hunter's Funeral Procession." On the one hand, we are asked to take what happens very seriously; on the other hand, doing so is impossible. Both Roquairol's suicide attempt and his actual suicide are highly staged events. The Werther scene in book 2 of *Titan* is, of course, meant to manipulate Linda into at least admitting feelings for Roquairol that she does not have. In relation to Roquairol's actual suicide in book 32, Don Gaspard remarks that Roquairol was in debt to his regiment and was afraid of an official investigation with the pending change of government (755–756). His behavior toward Linda alone does not motivate his suicide. Both passages have a highly satirical undertone. The first passage discussed criticizes the kind of public madness evoked by Goethe's *Werther*, in particular the culture of irrationalism to which it led. The satirical function of the passage describing Roquairol's actual suicide becomes particularly clear when the response of the audience and other actors is taken into account. The initial response to Roquairol's death comes from an actor, Bouverot, who asks who is going to pay him now (755). One of the members of the audience uses the occasion to launch a lengthy aesthetic discourse.

In his text Jean Paul uses musical means to underscore the fundamental ambiguity underlying the scene of Roquairol's suicide. This is one of the few passages in *Titan* where Jean Paul works with concrete examples of existing music. Roquairol's play starts with the "eternal overture from Mozart's *Don Giovanni*" (die ewige Ouvertüre aus Mozarts Don Juan; 46). The sequence of events that result in Roquairol's shooting himself is introduced by the wedding music (Hochzeitsmusik) from *Don Giovanni*, suddenly interrupted by frightened screams instigated by Roquairol (752). These references to *Don Giovanni* are highly significant; they, too, underscore the fundamental ambiguity of what happens onstage. The passage in *Don Giovanni* to which Jean Paul's text refers is the end of act 1, where Don Giovanni organizes a ball at his castle, ostensibly in honor of the farmer couple Zerlina and Masetto, who will be married that day. In reality, however, he hopes to use the occasion to seduce Zerlina and other women present. Don Giovanni's plan fails when Zerlina starts to scream — this is the moment to which Jean Paul's text alludes — when he tries to drag her out of the ballroom and the other guests, among them Donna Elvira and Donna Anna (also seduced by Giovanni), come to her aid, confront Don Giovanni with his misdeeds, and threaten to expose him to the world.[43] Of course, Roquairol is afraid that his crimes will be exposed; the allusions to Mozart's opera therefore provide a better insight into his psyche. It also allows Jean Paul to emphasize the ambiguity of Roquairol's character and actions. When Jean Paul wrote this, performance practice sought to deemphasize the demonic aspects of *Don Giovanni,* and there was a tendency to interpret it as a sort of comedy.[44] Jean Paul offers a major exception to this interpretation and his view was to gain support later, in particular through the efforts of his friend E. T. A. Hoffmann. Roquairol's presentation of his ultimate demise, in itself a tragic event, as a sort of comedy — even though a failed one — is consistent with his philosophy of life (and is prefigured by that of Don Giovanni): if one lives one's life not believing in anything, death is no tragedy. Of course, Don Giovanni manages to escape the scene of his public humiliation; for Roquairol this is no longer an option.

Reading Mahler's First Symphony in conjunction with Jean Paul's *Titan* yields intriguing questions. For instance, how does the First Symphony's fourth movement (in its original design), with all its ambiguities, relate to the narrative of the earlier movements, in particular the third? The first three movements suggest a *Bildungsroman,* culminating in the third movement, where the experience of death is constitutive for the emotional development of the symphony's hero. It is only the awareness of death's reality that makes the protagonist realize the importance of love. The fourth movement makes a radical break with such an interpretation. Whether one follows the model of the Callot engraving, the figure of Roquairol in *Titan,* Jean Paul's vision of Goethe's *Werther,* or Mozart and da Ponte's *Don Giovanni,* only one conclusion is possible: death is pointless and life goes on. Death is not a learning experience but confirms life's lack of meaning, its lack of a metaphysical center. Death is the end of something and not the beginning of something new. Humor does nothing to soften the experience of death but emphasizes life's purposelessness. Mahler's First Symphony does not in the end offer a program of *Bildung* but, having dallied with one, demolishes it.

The fifth and final movement of the original version of the First Symphony fits into this interpretation. Here again, Mahler's programmatic explanations are sparse. It is possible to read the motto of its final movement, *"Dall' Inferno al Paradiso,"*[45] in connection with Jean Paul's *Titan.* Mahler's heading for the fifth movement (which later became the fourth movement) is an indirect quote from *Titan;* it refers to the "Road *from* Tartarus to Elysium" (Weg *aus* dem Tartarus ins Elysium; 203), a sign placed between the two sections of the artificial garden complex belonging to Hohenfließ, the commemorative cemetery and the idyllic nature park, to help travelers find the road from one section to the other. In relation to Jean Paul's *Titan,* Mahler's choice of motto is highly appropriate; both terms, "Inferno" and "Paradiso," properly describe the two poles delimiting the hero's growth into adulthood.

Albano's intense experiences of love are followed by equally intense experiences of loss. Liane, his first love interest, dies after she has been forced to abandon her love for Albano. Linda de Romeiro, his second great love, disappears into a convent after being seduced and raped by Roquairol. And yet the motto of the fifth movement also leaves open an important question: will Albano eternally, so to speak, be tossed back and forth between experiences of love [Paradiso] and death [Inferno] or is he on the road from "Inferno" to "Paradiso"?

Jean Paul's text does not allow for a clear answer to this question. The novel appears to end on an optimistic note. Albano's relationship with the idealistic Idoine promises to end political rivalries. However, the funeral arrangements for Albano's brother Luigi are taking place at the same time, and we know that every earlier romantic relationship in Albano's life has ended in disaster. The end of Mahler's First Symphony is similarly ambiguous. In his conversations with Natalie Bauer-Lechner, Mahler commented that he intended his hero to be victorious, but that his victory over fate is only possible in death (*GME,* 175; not in English edition). The final movement of the symphony also presents its listeners with memories of earlier stages of the hero's development: the nature scenery of the first movement and its associations with the hero's innocence and happiness.[46] These references to innocence lost are not integrated into the turmoil but remain apart from it. The melodies that dominate the symphony's last movement articulate a wide range of emotions: bright and triumphant, but also dark and threatening. To phrase it another way, the symphony insists on the conflicted nature of the traumatic events at its heart and does nothing to even them out or smooth them over.

In Jean Paul's *Titan,* Albano does not die at the end, but his fate is very much linked to that of his alter ego, Roquairol, who does die and thereby enables Albano to live. Mahler, in inventing an alternative ending for his symphony, follows the spirit of Jean Paul's novel: death and love are irrevocably interwoven; neither one is thinkable without the other. The end of Mahler's symphony, in other words, is as ambiguous and paradoxical as Jean Paul's novel. What may seem like a victory can also be a defeat. The possibility of a *Bildungsroman* is fundamentally called into question. Like Jean Paul's *Titan,* Mahler's First Symphony may end with a utopian vision, but it is a vision that cannot make the reader forget about the price to be paid for such a "happy ending."

Mahler's Werther

Thus far I have used Mahler's references to literature and the visual arts in his programmatic statements as a means for working out the thematic structure of the First Symphony. These references allow us to describe certain developmental patterns at the roots of the music more clearly (but do not exhaust its semantic or emotional content). References to texts and images helped us understand certain subtleties of the music that are, or should be, highly relevant for the performance practice of the piece. In the case of the First Symphony, however, such references also allow for something else: they make it possible to establish a link between Mahler's music and his biography.

One of the literary texts other than Jean Paul's *Titan* that I mentioned above in my analysis of the fourth movement of the First Symphony is Goethe's *Die Leiden des jungen Werther*. The reference to Goethe's *Werther* in Jean Paul's *Titan* is especially interesting when we consider that Bruno Walter, seemingly in passing, refers to the First Symphony as Mahler's *Werther*: "The First Symphony I would like to call Mahler's *Werther*; in it, a heartbreaking event is acted out by means of art" (Die *Erste Symphonie* möchte ich Mahlers *Werther* nennen; in ihr wird ein herzzerreißendes Erlebnis künstlerisch abreagiert).[47] As is often the case with the information that Walter provides about Mahler and his works, whether certain data originate from Mahler or Walter himself is not entirely clear. Walter suggests that the characterization of the First Symphony as Mahler's *Werther* is his own invention, but how does he come to this observation? Does he base it on information provided by Mahler himself?

Mahler's correspondence, along with the memoirs by Natalie Bauer-Lechner and Alma Mahler, shed some light on the "heartbreaking" event Walter writes about. Mahler composed this symphony during his tenure as second conductor in Leipzig (1886–88), reportedly in only six weeks. At the time, he was deeply in love with Marion von Weber, the wife of the grandson of Carl Maria von Weber and mother of three children.[48] There is a striking similarity between Mahler's "affair" with Marion and Werther's relationship with Lotte in *Die Leiden des jungen Werther*. Both men had a "good" relationship not only with the woman they loved herself but also with her husband and the children involved (in the case of *Werther*, Lotte's younger brothers and sisters; in the case of Marion von Weber, her children). In comparison to her husband, Marion is clearly the more artistically gifted one, as is made clear in Natalie's notes (*GME*, 175; *RGM*, 159). It is also beyond question that Marion von Weber reciprocated Mahler's feelings to some extent but in the end decided against breaking with society's norms and values and stayed with her husband. According to Alma, Gustav and Marion decided to elope, but in the end did not.[49] The veracity of this claim is unclear, but it would have been a move truly worthy of Goethe's Werther.

There are a number of pieces of information that tie the First Symphony directly to the "affair" with Marion von Weber. From Natalie Bauer-Lechner's memoirs, we know that Mahler composed the symphony during a period of six weeks in Leipzig, while he was in close contact with the Webers (in very similar fashion, Goethe had claimed that he had written his *Werther* in only four weeks[50]). According to Bauer-Lechner, when Mahler had finished the first movement at around midnight, he went to the Webers and played it for them on their piano. Afterward, they went walking in the Rosental (*GME,* 175; *RGM,* 159). The close connection of the symphony's origins to the Weber family is confirmed by another source. According to the Dutch conductor and Mahler friend Willem Mengelberg, who visited Marion von Weber in 1907, she was at the time in possession of an early version of the score, including the "Blumine" movement, the second movement in the original design, which then bore the heading "In happy times" (In glücklicher Stunde). It also contained the personal dedication "To M., on the occasion of M.'s birthday" (An M. zum Geburtstage von M.).[51] Since this information is from a letter by Mengelberg to his wife drafted immediately after the visit, I assume it is correct, even though the scores he discusses are now lost.

Such biographical tidbits are interesting, but how do they help us understand the First Symphony? There is, of course, quite a discrepancy between the characterization of the second movement as an expression of unambiguous happiness in the original score in the possession of Marion von Weber and the words "youthful foolishness" (*RGM,* 158; Jugend-Eselei: *GME,* 173), which Mahler later used in characterizing the movement to Natalie. Such contradictory classifications of the movement are interesting, because they give insight into the nature of Mahler's creativity and ultimately help us understand the symphony. Clearly, Mahler went through a very intense emotional period when creating this work. This was also a period of enormous, previously unexperienced creativity for Mahler, especially taking into consideration the fact that he composed the whole symphony in only six weeks. Mahler's contradictory subsequent characterizations, in particular with reference to the "Blumine" movement, can be read as a sign that the psychological function of the symphony had changed over time for him. In its first stage, the symphony was clearly intended to be a "declaration of love." But thereafter, Mahler's compositional work on it was guided by the need to shake off his younger, "naive" self.

The fact that Mahler spent so much time and energy on explaining the fundamental ambiguity underlying the fourth movement, and in so many different ways, indicates that it was very important to him to have this second aspect, the abandonment of youthful naiveté — the heading for the first part of the symphony, consisting of the first three movements, was originally "*Aus den Tagen der Jugend*" (From the Days of Youth; see appendix) — recognized by his audiences. Jean Paul's *Titan,* with its highly ironic attitude toward its main protagonist and its abundance of satirical and parodic elements, also helped Mahler to gain perspective on the original emotional core of his work. In this context it is interesting that Mahler, in a letter of 20 March 1896 to Max Marschalk mentioned at the beginning of this chapter, states that the titles and explanations for the symphony were something he invented "afterward" (nachträglich; *Br*, 169). Were these inventions really meant only to facilitate the audiences' understanding of the symphony, as the letter suggests, or were they part of Mahler's working through his own feelings and gaining perspective on his own emotional life at the time, a process that had already started with the bitter/humoristic fourth movement? In a third stage, Mahler takes out the "Blumine" movement, his testimony to happy hours, maybe even a declaration of his love for Marion von Weber, and he rejects all of the programmatic statements that had previously accompanied the symphony. The usual explanation for Mahler's dropping of the second movement is that he was not satisfied by it on a musical level. The above suggests that Mahler may have had emotional reasons for doing so; the movement reminded him of something in his life that he wished to forget. Jean Paul's *Titan* helped him with this because it, too, is a text about lost dreams, about utopian projects from the past that no longer function in the present.

These insights into the biographical circumstances in which the First Symphony was composed and the multi-layered process through which it achieved its final form lead us to another question: to what extent is this work, in its original five-movement form, intended to be therapeutic? To what extent, in other words, is its music meant to help the composer work through the emotions evoked by his liaison with Marion von Weber? The attempt to overcome certain emotions is clearest in the fourth movement. In the end, it is Jean Paul's satirical account of *Werther* — note the ubiquitously recognized humoristic element in the fourth movement of the symphony — that allows Mahler some perspective on his own feelings. However, "humor" is only a phase in Mahler's symphony. The final movement does not offer reconciliation but rather articulates a confrontation between strongly divergent emotions, as the motto of the movement discussed above also indicates. This is not the symphony of a man who has worked through his emotions and mastered them; it is the music of a man torn by extreme contradictory impulses who, not unlike the main character of Goethe's *Leiden des jungen Werther*, sees death as the only means to end the conflict he faces. If Bruno Walter was right in saying that the First Symphony is Mahler's *Werther*, then it must be added that it is a symphony that, in the end, does not resolve its many conflicts but rather insists on their irreconcilability.

Mahler's Anti-Bildungsroman

Mahler's references to Jean Paul's *Titan* in the context of his First Symphony make it possible to read this symphony in the tradition of the *Bildungsroman*. However, neither Jean Paul's *Titan*, Goethe's *Leiden des jungen Werther,* nor Mozart and da Ponte's *Don Giovanni* — to name the texts that can be assumed to have played a role in the First's origins — offer a traditional narrative of self-cultivation. Goethe's text ends with its protagonist's demise; in Mozart's opera and Jean Paul's *Titan* the protagonists survive but it is difficult to be optimistic about their future.[52] Mahler, in his symphony and his statements about it, emphasizes the ambiguity of his hero's victory in the symphony's last movement. Like Jean Paul's writings, Mahler's art presents a counterreading of sorts; his engagement with the German cultural and intellectual tradition is highly critical, and his works are intended as statements about the society in which he lives, even though the cultural framework he uses to make them may no longer be familiar to us. Mahler's symphony reproduces a form of temporality also constitutive for Jean Paul's novel by insisting on the present importance of those hopes and dreams that could not be integrated or were discarded. Precisely because the music insists on the relevance of what was cast aside for the present, it does not fall victim to an easy melancholy that does nothing but mourn what is lost.

Nineteenth-century scholarship has been important in shaping our current view of the *Bildungsroman* as a novel of self-education that traces its hero's development, his self-realization, through love and work. Even though the term *Bildungsroman* can refer to eighteenth-century writing — Wieland's *Geschichte des Agathon* (History of Agathon, 1766/67), Goethe's *Wilhelm Meisters Lehrjahre* — the concept originated in the nineteenth century. Nineteenth-century scholars were interested in the normative potential of this type of novel; as its goal they saw the integration of the individual into the collective.[53] The *Bildungsroman* was seen as a specifically German genre.[54] While battling reality, its hero finds love and friendship, learns from experience, and eventually finds himself and his task in life. In essence it is a very optimistic genre, to paraphrase the views of one prominent nineteenth-century scholar.[55] The problem with this view is that very few *Bildungsromane* actually meet its criteria. This is certainly the case for the Romantic generation (among them not only Jean Paul but also Novalis and Tieck); more specifically, newer research has emphasized that even a text such as Goethe's *Wilhelm Meisters Lehrjahre*, the prototypical *Bildungsroman*, is upon closer examination quite critical of the concept of self-cultivation.[56]

Mahler's First Symphony is not an attack on the *Bildungsroman* understood in the traditional (nineteenth-century) sense. Rather, Jean Paul's *Bildungsroman* functions as a catalyst for Mahler to rethink issues of memory and the relationship between past and present in individuals' lives. In line with Jean Paul's novel and its critical appropriation of the legacy of the classical generation (Goethe, Schiller), Mahler emphasizes the elements of crisis inherent in this tradition. His intention is to produce the musical equivalent not of a closed text but rather of an open narrative[57] (that happens to be at odds with traditional, nineteenth-century models of reading the *Bildungsroman*). By a "closed" text, I mean a text with a linear approach to chronology, little ambiguity about the possibility of the hero's achieving his goals, and a clear ideological message at the end. A text is "open" when it breaks through linear narratives, its protagonists (and antagonists) are portrayed ambiguously, and the text is without a clear ideology. Jean Paul and Mahler both had an essentially "open" concept of art. This explains the significant stylistic resemblance between Mahler's symphony and Jean Paul's novel. Both unite very heterogeneous materials and produce art characterized by a certain eclecticism.[58] Just as Jean Paul's text unites very different narrative styles — psychological, philosophical, anthropological, medical, essayistic, humorous, satirical, and parodic, to name a few — Mahler's symphony unites very diverse musical styles. Humor, satire, and parody are important stylistic means for both artists, but they are not these artworks' final word. They make room for what could be call an insight into the fundamental ambiguities of life. Heterogeneity is a stylistic marker of *Titan* and Jean Paul's work in general. It is also one of the defining features for all of Mahler's oeuvre (with the possible exception of his very early cantata *Das klagende Lied*).

By aiming for an open work of art, Mahler also sets parameters for the reception of his music. There is a connection between the openness of Mahler's text and the necessity, in Mahler's eyes, of the audience's collaboration in constructing the narrative underlying his symphonies and its message. It is in this context that we are to understand Mahler's anti-programmatic programs. While there are some arguments in favor of reading a temporal element into the anti-programmatic logic of Mahler's music (initially he endorsed programs for his music, later he rejected them), I have argued in this chapter that both impulses, Mahler's anti-programmatic considerations and his desire for a program, are simultaneously present. As we will see in relation to Mahler's Third Symphony, Mahler still developed programmatic statements after renouncing all programs. Mahler's and Walter's programmatic statements in relation to the First Symphony, at the very least, do make it clear that there is not *one* program or *one* precise set of images or concepts underlying Mahler's symphony, but that his music is instead meant to evoke a multitude of textual references and images, and the emotions that come with them. The clearest example of this is the fourth movement with its references to a variety of texts and images. Mahler may have intended the programmatic statements discussed above to be received in a playful way. His objections to audiences' suggesting specific literary references in his music are well documented. But did he object to their speculating about his music, or was he simply criticizing their attempts to reduce the multiple references in his music to *one specific reading*? In relation to the Seventh Symphony, one of Mahler's Dutch friends, the composer Diepenbrock, complained that Mahler "tells" him "something different every time" ([h]ij zegt . . . telkens wat anders)[59] about the intentions behind his music. In view of the widely variable programmatic explanations of his music that we know of, this appears to be an accurate assessment. No doubt the same held true for different people; Mahler seems to tailor the message behind his music in different ways in order to appeal to different intellectual partners. Could this have been the case because Mahler hoped that his educated listeners would actually look for and find different things in his music?

The fact that the First Symphony can be associated with a broad variety of images and texts is a constitutive element for the aesthetic program underlying this symphony. To borrow a term from psychoanalysis, the symphony wants to set into motion a process of "free association" in its audiences.[60] If we take seriously the openness of Mahler's art, this means that the associations we have when listening to his music can take us into the realm of literary and intellectual history, into cultural and musical history, into Mahler's biography, and in the end also into *our own time* and *our own lives*. This is the ultimate consequence of the freedom of association that Mahler strives for. If we embrace an aesthetics of reception of this type, one that is at once programmatic and anti-programmatic, we have to face the fact that Mahler's music tells a different story to each listener.

Appendix

Title page of the First Symphony, January 1893:

SYMPHONY ("Titan")
in 5 Movements (2 Parts)
by
GUSTAV MAHLER

Part I: *"From the Days of Youth"*
  1. *"Spring without End"*
  2. *"Blumine"*
  3. *"Under Full Sail"*

Part II: *"Commedia humana"*
  4. *"Funeral March in the Manner of Callot"*
  5. *"Dall' Inferno al Paradiso"*

[SYMPHONIE ("Titan")
in 5 Sätzen (2 Abteilungen)
von
GUSTAV MAHLER

I TEIL: "Aus den Tagen der Jugend"
    1. "Frühling und kein Ende"
    2. "Blumine"
    3. "Mit vollen Segeln"

II TEIL: "Commedia humana"
    4. "Todtenmarsch in Callots Manier"
    5. "Dall' Inferno al Paradiso"]

Program notes from the performance of 27 October 1893:

TITAN, a Tone Poem in Symphony Form

PART I
"From the Days of Youth," Flower, Fruit, and Thorn Pieces

1. "Spring without End" (introduction and allegro comodo).
   The introduction portrays the awakening of nature from its long winter sleep.
2. "Blumine" (andante)
3. "Under Full Sail" (scherzo)

PART II
"Commedia humana"

4. "Stranded" (a Funeral March in "the Manner of Callot").
   The following serves as an explanation of this movement: the author received the external stimulus for this piece of music from a parodic image that all children in Austria know well: "The Hunter's Funeral Procession," from an old fairy-tale book for children: the animals of the woods accompany the coffin of the deceased hunter to his grave; hares carry the little flag, in front a band of bohemian musicians, accompanied by music-making cats, toads, blackbirds, and so on, and stags, does, foxes, and other four-legged and feathered animals of the woods escort the procession in comic poses. At this point this piece is conceived as the expression of an at times ironic and humorous, at times uncanny and brooding mood, after which then immediately
5. "Dall' Inferno" (allegro furioso)
   follows, as the sudden outburst of desperation from a deeply wounded heart.

[*TITAN, eine Tondichtung in Symphonieform*

I TEIL
"Aus den Tagen der Jugend," Blumen-, Frucht- und Dornstücke

1. *"Frühling und kein Ende"(Einleitung und Allegro Comodo).*
   Die Einleitung stellt das Erwachen der Natur aus langem Winterschlaf dar.
2. *"Blumine"(Andante)*
3. *"Mit vollen Segeln"(Scherzo)*

II TEIL
"Commedia humana"

4. *"Gestrandet" (ein Todtenmarsch in "Callots Manier").*
   Zur Erklärung dieses Satzes diene Folgendes: Die äussere Anregung zu diesem Musikstück erhielt der Autor durch das in Oesterreich allen Kindern wohlbekannte parodistische Bild: "Des Jägers Leichenbegängnis," aus einem alten Kindermärchenbuch: die Thiere des Waldes geleiten den Sarg des gestorbenen Jägers zu Grabe; Hasen tragen das Fähnlein, voran eine Capelle von böhmischen Musikanten, begleitet von musicirenden Katzen, Unken, Krähen etc., und Hirsche, Rehe, Füchse und andere vierbeinige und gefiederte Thiere des Waldes geleiten in possirlichen Stellungen den Zug. An dieser Stelle ist dieses Stück als Ausdruck einer bald ironisch lustigen, bald unheimlich brütenden Stimmung gedacht, auf welche dann sogleich
5. *"Dall' Inferno" (Allegro furioso)*
   folgt, als der plötzliche Ausbruch der Verzweiflung eines im Tiefsten verwundeten Herzens.][61]

2: *Des Knaben Wunderhorn:* Rediscovering the "Volk"

JEAN PAUL WAS NOT EXACTLY FORGOTTEN around 1900, but his texts, while of interest to some, were clearly not part of the German literary canon. This was not the case, however, for the poems collected by Achim von Arnim and Clemens Brentano in *Des Knaben Wunderhorn* (The Boy's Magic Horn). Achim von Arnim and Clemens Brentano were prolific German authors, belonging to the second Romantic school affiliated with the city of Heidelberg. While the first generation of Romantic authors (Novalis, Friedrich and August Wilhelm Schlegel, Tieck, and Wackenroder) was primarily a protest generation, the second generation, partially influenced by the French occupation of large sections of the German states, was characterized by a nationalistic, conservative, and religious turn; many of these Romantics converted to Catholicism. *Des Knaben Wunderhorn* is the most comprehensive and best-known collection of German folk songs and was first published in 1806 (volume 1) and 1808 (volumes 2 and 3). The songs experienced a renaissance much earlier than Jean Paul's works, around 1870; interestingly, this coincided with Germany's national unification.[1] And yet one should not exaggerate their popularity; first-edition copies of *Des Knaben Wunderhorn*, for instance, were still available from the publisher in 1900.[2]

While the subtitle of the collection is "Alte deutsche Lieder" (Old German Songs), Achim von Arnim refers to the songs in an essay accompanying the first volume as "Volkslieder."[3] It was Johann Gottfried Herder (1744–1803) who had invented the term "Volkslied"; in fact, *Volkslieder* was the title of a collection of songs that he edited almost three decades before von Arnim and Brentano published their collection.[4] Herder's introduction of the "Volkslied" concept into cultural history is significant for two reasons. By using this term, Herder initiated the study of what today is called "world music" or ethnomusicology,[5] a discipline guided by the idea that music should be studied in its global diversity and local contexts. Simultaneously, however, the early-nineteenth-century interest in "Volkslieder" is undeniably linked to a surge of nationalism in Germany. *Des Knaben Wundernhorn* is one of the first texts documenting this turn toward the national that typified second-generation Romantics. One could say that this interest in folk songs in early-nineteenth-century Germany was, on the one hand, guided by descriptive interests (an inventorying of available materials and the knowledge contained in them), while, on the other hand, it is marked by a prescriptive dimension (this material is meant to represent the "real" Germany). The latter motivation made the *Wunderhorn* collection into fascinating material for those pursuing a German-nationalist agenda.[6] It is precisely this tension between a descriptive and prescriptive component that, in my eyes, makes Mahler's songs so compelling. Mahler shows that a close reading of traditional German folk songs — the tradition some conservative cultural critics sought to mobilize — brings to light narratives that are clearly at odds with a reactionary idealization of the past. The seemingly naive folk songs collected by von Arnim and Brentano in *Des Knaben Wunderhorn* are documents of crisis; they record what is problematic in German culture and society. Here too, Mahler is driven not by lighthearted nostalgia but by a critical agenda.

"Volk" and "Volkslieder"

To better understand the literary and cultural functions of the "Volkslieder" collected under the title *Des Knaben Wunderhorn*, it is useful to consider briefly the history of the term "Volk." As a concept, "Volk" did not gain a political dimension until Johann Gottfried Herder (1744–1803) began to give it a privileged position in his writings on literary and cultural history. Trained as a philosopher and theologian, Herder is now primarily known for his writings on cultural history and anthropology. His interest in the concept "Volk" can be explained by his desire to free German literature from classicist models and from foreign influences (in particular that of the French, who were a major force in eighteenth-century German culture).

Within Herder's work, "Volk" is a central but ambiguous concept. A *first* ambiguity: to whom or to what does Herder refer in using the term "Volk"? Herder used the concept in a much broader sense than did those who preceded him, and historians have argued that the term "Volk" in Herder's writings is equivalent to "nation" and "no longer" refers to "a social group within or beneath the nation."[7] Such a statement is not entirely incorrect, but it is somewhat misleading. The concept of "nation" was, around 1800, largely an abstract one for Herder, since what is now Germany then consisted of many small, largely autonomous states. It could be said that Herder was referring to the essence of a nation in using the "Volk" concept. When using the term, he meant at once a language community and an idealized notion of what one might call the "common man," so the term for Herder is not entirely free of the original social associations that connected it to the lower classes. His idea of culture was profoundly anti-elitist. Herder was interested in culture as a basic manifestation of human activity. He saw language and culture as means through which humans created identity. The most decisive feature uniting the members of a "Volk" was, for Herder, the fact that they share a language and, as a consequence, a literary and cultural tradition. Language builds community: "A people is not in possession of an idea if it does not have the word for it" (Ein Volk hat keine Idee, zu der es kein Wort hat).[8] Only through the ability to articulate an idea can it be part of memory, tradition, and the wisdom of humankind, Herder states in the same context.

There is a *second* ambiguity underlying Herder's use of the concept "Volk," one that is related to the first one. For Herder the term had both descriptive and prescriptive dimensions, and it is not always easy to distinguish between the two. The poetry of different nations, according to Herder, was "always and in every language the quintessence of the mistakes and perfections of a nation, a mirror of its views, the expression of its highest aspirations" (in jeder Zeit und Sprache war sie der Inbegriff der Fehler und Vollkommenheiten einer Nation, ein Spiegel ihrer Gesinnungen, der Ausdruck des höchsten, nach welchem *sie* strebte).[9] Literature offers a source for studying the belief systems of a people from an anthropological perspective. Herder acknowledges that the knowledge thus gained may be both positive and negative and believes that comparing the literatures of different nations can be instructive (575). And yet one of Herder's main interests in studying folk literature was strengthening Germany's cultural presence in Europe.[10] The above quote shows how close the descriptive and prescriptive dimensions of literature can be: literature mirrors the nation in its virtues and vices, but it also advances certain ideals for it.

Behind Herder's curiosity about popular forms of writing there is a clear interest in rethinking the function of literature. It is in this context that we must read Herder's repeatedly addressed concern that literature has lost its public function — that literature is no longer the organic part of society it once was (see, for example, 70, 71, and 305). What Herder envisions in order to counter this trend is a return to the foundations of literature in the "Volk." While Herder emphasized the national characteristics of language and culture, it is not correct to say that he was a nationalist. He accepted the legitimacy of cultural differences; one could characterize his approach as being genuinely comparative. For Herder, no single nation is privileged over another.[11] It should, however, also be clear from the above that Herder, despite his cosmopolitanism with roots in the Enlightenment, offered an interesting model for nationalistic and conservative intellectuals well into the Third Reich, although constructing such an agenda based on Herder's writings is only possible through a one-sided reading of his work. Not simply Romanticism but the nineteenth century in general made use of certain ambiguities inherent to the "Volk"concept from the very beginning of this discourse in Herder's writings.[12]

Versions of these ambiguities return in Achim von Arnim's essay "Von Volksliedern" (On Folk Songs), a text of which Mahler was most certainly aware, since it appeared as an afterword for the first volume of *Des Knaben Wunderhorn*. In this essay, too, the notion of "Volk" functions as a critique of existing cultural institutions. The author is critical of the fact that in German literary and cultural history the theater had become the location of a national revival;[13] this exclusive focus on the theater was at the expense of interest in folk songs. Moreover, according to von Arnim, governments suppressed interest in folk songs because they feared social unrest (388, 390). But to whom was von Arnim exactly referring when he used the concept "Volk"? Folk songs have survived among the lower classes and farmers (389, 391), but they cannot really count on von Arnim's sympathies. It is highly interesting that von Arnim finds travel to be a necessary prerequisite for the type of folk literature in which he is interested; he specifically mentions Gypsies, wandering craftsmen, soldiers, and (traveling) students (393–94). They carry with them a form of knowledge that is a precondition for folk literature. Paradoxically, it is knowledge of the world that can bind a person to her or his fatherland, and poetry in particular can establish such a bond (394–95). Von Arnim's essay here mirrors the great importance the Romantics in general attributed to poetry.

In view of the subsequent nationalistic appropriation of the Romantics' ideas, this is of course a very provocative notion. Von Arnim, it seems, was not interested in a narrow-minded nationalism that sought to block out the outside world but rather aimed for a cosmopolitan sense of national identity (represented by certain figures of mobility) that quite consciously lived off a knowledge about other peoples and their cultures. For von Arnim, folk songs additionally have an anthropological function in that they allow a nation to find its own cultural identity by comparing itself with other cultures. However, a version of the ambiguities underlying Herder's use of the term "Volk" can be found in von Arnim's essay as well. While von Arnim in the first half of his essay, as I have shown, gives very concrete examples of what he means by the "Volk" concept and emphasizes the term's social connotations that would potentially make a politically progressive interpretation possible, toward the end of the essay it turns into a very abstract category. According to von Arnim, only the artist who is close to the "Volk" can bring it together under his "flag" (Fahne); he can do this even though it may be separated by "language, national prejudices, religious errors, and superfluous fashion" (Sprache, Staatsvorurtheile, Religionsirrthümer und müßige Neuigkeit; 413). The question to ask here, then, is: what is the constitutive component of the "Volk" if it is not language, a sense of national identity, or religion? The only answer that von Arnim allows is, surprisingly, the activity of the poet-archaeologist. In the end, the role of the "Volk" is to legitimize the efforts of the poet, and not the other way around. Little remains of the openness to alterity evoked earlier when von Arnim, at the end of his essay, speaks of the folk-song project as a "public monument for the greatest new people, the Germans" (allgemeinen Denkmahle des größten neueren Volkes, der Deutschen; 413–14). Folk songs are meant to serve the goal of national unification. Here von Arnim is no longer interested in the anthropological, descriptive function of folk poetry; instead, he evokes its prescriptive, normative potential, its ability to create a nation superior to others. It is precisely this element that would later be picked up on by the anti-modern, nationalist, and conservative *Völkische Bewegung* that played an important, even crucial role in the rise of German and Austrian fascism.[14]

The contradictory ways in which von Arnim conceptualized the "Volk" in his essay indicate a shift from the concrete to the abstract. While at the beginning of his essay the influence of the Enlightenment's social agenda and Herder's ideas clearly manifest themselves, at the end these have moved into the background in favor of more abstract ideals. It is not just in von Arnim's works that this shift can be found; his text is symptomatic of broader changes that occurred over the course of the nineteenth century. In its new interpretation, the term "Volk" functions primarily as an imagined category with strong national connotations, no longer as a term that was meant to refer to a historically existing entity. This shift is also documented in some of Wagner's early writings.

Following Herder and von Arnim's line of thinking, Wagner, in his 1849 essay "Das Kunstwerk der Zukunft" (The Art-Work of the Future), writes that a renewal of German art is only possible through art's reorientation toward the "Volk," an idea that he would repeat in many later texts, even though it is clear that he relied on highbrow literature or philological publications for the narratives of his operas.[15] But what does Wagner mean when writing about the "Volk"? Wagner defines the "Volk" as "the epitome of all individuals who made up a collective" (der Inbegriff aller der Einzelnen, welche ein Gemeinsames ausmachten) and, echoing Herder (who remains unnamed), mentions the use of a single language as a criterion that unites the "Volk" into a nation (*DKdZ*, 3:47; *AF*, 74). Later he will clarify his definition by stating that the "Volk" consists of people who "feel a common and collective need" (*AF*, 75; eine gemeinschaftliche Noth empfinden: *DKdZ* 3:48, trans. modified). This is ambiguous language, in particular because Wagner embeds this argument in a discourse that criticizes luxury and fashion, and their effects on society and culture. This could be read as a remnant of a socioeconomic understanding of "Volk" that is possibly in line with a progressive political agenda. "Noth" would accordingly refer to the basic needs of life. But this is not what Wagner means. A little later in his essay he clarifies this "Noth" in an abstract sense as something "unconscious" and "involuntary" (*AF*, 79; unbewußt, unwillkürlich: *DKdZ* 3:52, trans. modified), as an intrinsic (but abstract!) drive propelling the people. In clear contrast to von Arnim, Wagner believes that intellectuals should learn from the "Volk" and not the other way around (*DKdZ* 3:53; *AF,* 80–81). A subtle transition from the descriptive to the prescriptive can also be found in this essay. In later texts such as "Was ist Deutsch?" (What is German?, 1878) the second, prescriptive function dominates entirely. Here Wagner draws explicit connections between the German "Volk" and a German spirit (deutscher Geist) that remains largely abstract, although we learn that it is associated with a "conservative temperament" (konservativen Sinn).[16]

While Wagner never mentioned *Des Knaben Wunderhorn* in his writings, Nietzsche discusses von Arnim and Brentano's collection in chapter 6 of *Die Geburt der Tragödie aus dem Geiste der Musik* (The Birth of Tragedy out of the Spirit of Music), first published in 1872. Read on a programmatic level — and this was certainly what Nietzsche originally intended — *Die Geburt der Tragödie* can be interpreted as a call for a revitalization of German culture, which had become too rational, too constructed, and above all, too lifeless. In the context of the work of earlier folk-song theorists (Herder, von Arnim), it is interesting to note that folk songs, for Nietzsche as well, represent a critical potential in relation to the epic tradition dating back to Homer (antagonist of Antilochus, the father of the folk song; *SW* 1:42–43; *BT,* 29) and also, if compared to the later dramatic tradition, Greek tragedy (*SW* 1:52–57 *BT,* 36–40). Nietzsche mentions the *Wunderhorn* songs as an example of Dionysian art, or at least of a form of art that harbors many traces of what he calls "Dionysian" (*SW* 1:49; *BT,* 34).[17] The superiority of folk songs over other forms of art manifests itself in the fact that music prevails over language in them. Language serves music; it tries to imitate music, and one melody can lead to many different poetic images (*SW* 1:49; *BT,* 34). Such statements are to be understood in the context of the philosophy of Schopenhauer, for whom music, in contrast to text, was an unmediated manifestation of the will underlying all life (*SW* 1:46–47; *BT,* 31–33). Nietzsche points out that folk songs are, consistent with their Dionysian foundation, neither objective nor subjective, but that the artist functions only as a medium, and that therefore this type of poetry cannot be considered the expression of an individual will (*SW* 1:47; *BT,* 32).

Nietzsche's reflections on the critical potential of folk songs are relevant because they point to a certain tension with the main message of the work: its goal of renewing German (musical) drama. Nietzsche wrote *Die Geburt der Tragödie* — a book that destroyed his scholarly career almost overnight — under the influence of Wagner (to whom it is dedicated). One could say that Nietzsche's book invents a philosophical program for Wagner's dramatic works. But the excursus on "Volkslieder" and *Des Knaben Wunderhorn* in chapters 5 and 6 investigate what could be a different trajectory for German culture, one that Wagner did not follow. Nietzsche clearly had the above-mentioned writings by Herder, von Arnim, and Wagner in mind when he wrote *Die Geburt der Tragödie*. What is significant is that he seeks to preserve the potential for cultural criticism in their texts. It is tempting to read such a hesitation as a foretaste of Nietzsche's later criticism of Wagner's nationalistic and religious turns (see chapter 3). That may overstate the case, but it was, I would argue, Nietzsche's promise of an alternative trajectory for German culture that attracted Mahler when he started work on his *Wunderhorn* compositions — a trajectory very different from that of Wagner. By the time Mahler started work on the *Lieder eines fahrenden Gesellen* (Songs of a Wayfarer) and the *Wunderhorn* songs, the intolerant side of this conservative agenda had become much clearer than had been the case during Wagner's lifetime. But what kind of knowledge do these folk songs contain that makes them suitable as a platform for a counterreading of German culture?

Masculinity in Crisis — Lieder eines fahrenden Gesellen

While there are connections between the First Symphony and the *Lieder eines fahrenden Gesellen*, there are also indications that Mahler wants to do something very different in these songs. At the roots of the *Lieder eines fahrenden Gesellen* is a program that, I will argue, is similar to the programmatic deliberations underlying the songs collected under the title *Des Knaben Wunderhorn*. The titles of both cycles could easily evoke a reductionist Romantic image of an idealized and unproblematic past, but if one looks at them more closely, it becomes clear that it is precisely such a tendency toward idealizing the past that is fundamentally questioned by text and music. By giving his first cycle the title *Lieder eines fahrenden Gesellen*, Mahler may have sought to profit from the name recognition provided by Rudolf Baumbach's popular book of poems with the same title from 1878[18] — it is not clear whether Mahler knew the book, but it is not unlikely — but the intentions underpinning Mahler's cycle are very different from Baumbach's. While Baumbach offers his readers harmless entertainment, Mahler's songs are much more serious in nature, despite their occasionally lighthearted façade.

Donald Mitchell has pointed out that there is a clear connection between the origins of the *Lieder eines fahrenden Gesellen* and Mahler's failed relationship with the singer Johanna Richter during his Kassel period (1884–85),[19] reminiscent of the way in which the composition of (parts of) the First Symphony was influenced by Mahler's failed relationship with Marion von Weber. One could say, however, that Mahler resists an autobiographical model of interpretation by naming his cycle *Lieder eines fahrenden Gesellen*. The title alone indicates that they are about much more than the adventures of one individual; the protagonist functions as a representative of a certain social group. It is commonly translated into English as *Songs of a Wayfarer* — the songs of someone who travels by foot, in other words. The German word "Geselle," however, contains a dimension that is lost in this translation. The primary translation for "Geselle" is "apprentice"; a "fahrender" or "wandernder Geselle" has finished an initial training period with a master ("Meister") and has entered a period of traveling around in order to refine his skills as a craftsman before settling down somewhere permanently.[20] The "Geselle" mentioned in the title is one of the "figures of mobility" described in von Arnim's essay accompanying the first volume of *Des Knaben Wunderhorn*. The social connotations of the term are important; they are indicators of one's status within a group in society. This may strike us as self-evident today, but in this context the observation is relevant, because such a social and historically specific interpretation clearly sets Mahler's cycle apart from the "abstract" conservative conceptualizations of the *Volk* in Mahler's day.

And yet in spite of the social function of the term "Geselle," the social status of the "fahrender Geselle" is also characterized by a certain uncertainty. The first song of the cycle, "Wenn mein Schatz Hochzeit macht" (When my love has her wedding day), the only text of the *Gesellen* cycle not written by Mahler himself,[21] points to this separation of the apprentice from society — the song consists of his imagining his lover getting married while he remains alone. This song clearly establishes a contrast between public space, where the marriage of the protagonist's former lover is celebrated, and the private space of the "dark little room" (dunkles Kämmerlein) which, we are to believe, is the protagonist's (temporary) living quarters. In one of the very few statements Mahler made about the cycle, he emphasizes the element of separation: the apprentice "moves out into the world" (zieht in die Welt hinaus; Br, 57). The song imagines the marginality of the apprentice, but the image Mahler evokes here is also one of emasculation. The protagonist's marginality implies an inability to find a partner, to establish one's sexual identity in society. Even though sex is not directly discussed in these songs, they all contain a strong sexual undertone.

One could say that the term "fahrender Geselle" refers to a transitional stage in life that also has philosophical connotations. Mahler's cycle was originally supposed to consist of six songs. Donald Mitchell has made accessible an early untitled poem by Mahler that one can assume was meant to belong to the cycle but was ultimately not included. We find the apprentice wandering around at night, having lost his "way and orientation" (Weg und Weiser), surrounded by soft imaginary voices speaking seductively.[22] Then the wanderer wonders when his travels will end and compares himself to someone who encounters a Sphinx "staring" at him and "threatening" him with "tormenting riddles" (Es starrt die Sphinx und droht mit Rätselqualen) that he cannot solve. One can debate the poetic merits of this image — a sphinx imagined in the middle of what we assume is a predominantly German landscape? — but the image makes clear what is at stake here: the poem is asking a philosophical question about the meaning of life. Not surprisingly, it ends on a rather negative note: "And when I cannot solve the riddle — — I must pay for it with my life" (Und lös' ich's nicht — — muß es mein Leben zahlen). It is not clear how we are to interpret these lines, however. It could be that this is what the protagonist really thinks, but it could also be that this is what the soft and threatening voices tell him — what they want to make him believe.

The fact that "wandering" is to be understood as a metaphor for humanity's lack of orientation should not come as a surprise to German audiences. "Wandering" as a literary image has a long tradition; it plays a prominent role in the works of Rousseau, but also within German literary and cultural history of the eighteenth and nineteenth centuries (Jean Paul, Goethe, and Heine come to mind).[23] In late-eighteenth- and early-nineteenth-century German literature the wanderer is a rebel, but he is also looking for a place in society.[24] While for Goethe and the Romantics the wanderer is a central figure searching to make sense of life, in the later nineteenth century the wanderer is a marginalized figure, a journeyman or vagabond driven by unrest, unhappiness, and a pathological urge to travel.[25] In his songs Mahler seeks to rehabilitate the figure of the wanderer by referring back to the older tradition (represented by Goethe and the Romantics) while simultaneously emphasizing the critical potential and heterogeneity of that tradition. In Mahler's time German audiences may very well have associated the image of the wanderer with Goethe's classical Bildungsroman, *Wilhelm Meisters Lehrjahre* (Wilhelm Meister's Apprenticeship), and in particular also with its sequel: the *Wanderjahre* (Wilhelm Meister's Journeyman Years). While the *Lehrjahre* promise readers a clear ideal, albeit ambiguously, the *Wanderjahre* are characterized by the lack of a philosophy of life. The lack of philosophical perspective associated with the wanderings of the *Wanderjahre*'s hero is mirrored by a dissolution of the novel's formal structure: the linear narrative is abandoned and makes way for individual novellas, essayistic fragments, letters, and aphorisms. In the following, I will argue that this same openness of form is also characteristic of Mahler's song cycle.

The first song of the cycle, "Wenn mein Schatz Hochzeit macht," hints of a counterworld to the protagonist's desolation. The flower and bird briefly mentioned in the middle stanza provide the leading images for the second song, "Ging heut morgen übers Feld" (Walked this morning through the field). Text and music express, throughout the song, the happiness and naiveté associated with nature, or at least with a certain image of nature. (Mahler used the main melody in the first movement of his First Symphony, intended to evoke a similar atmosphere of nature's innocence and simplicity.) Nature provides some relief to the tortured soul; the second song describes a walk over the fields early in the morning with the birds and flowers speaking directly to the protagonist. And yet, as in the First Symphony, the song does not allow for an unambiguous idealization of nature. As much as nature may provide the protagonist with aesthetic pleasure, it always remains a subjective experience and is therefore dependent on his perception and imagination. "Will my happiness now begin as well?!" (Nun fängt auch mein Glück wohl an?!) the song asks in the end, only to answer with a clear "no": "No! No! That, I believe, will never be able to bloom for me!" (Nein! Nein! Das ich mein, mir nimmer blühen kann!). The subjective element "for me" is very important in this context; it is not so much that nature will not bloom again; nature will continue to go through its natural cycles — but in the perspective of the subject speaking here, it will not.

Scholars have commented on the importance of contrasts for the structure of this cycle[26] (and of Mahler's music in general, one might add). The second and third songs of the cycle are built around such contrasts. The general tone of the second song is peaceful and friendly; the third song is agitated and loud. The latter song, "Ich hab' ein glühend Messer" (I have a glowing knife), counters the second song's imagery of nature with that of a knife in a chest — a knife that is always there. In psychoanalytical terms one could speak of a masochistic scenario in this song. The violence is not directed against the other but against the self, and it is tied closely to feelings of lust; "joy" (Freude) and "lust" (Lust) are mentioned in relation to violence in the first stanza of the song. But what does the knife mean; what does it stand for? In one scholar's view it is the protagonist's imagination, as he thinks about his lover, that is at the root of this violent imagery.[27] Indeed, in the last stanza of the song, hearing her laugh makes him long for death. But it is not just this (imagined) renewed acquaintance with his lover that evokes the imagery of violence. The middle stanza, which connects the third song with the preceding and following songs, gives a further clue leading to an answer. The underlying structure of "Ich hab' ein glühend Messer" is A — B — A; like the first song of the cycle (and the fourth), the middle stanza contrasts sharply with the first and last stanzas, both musically and textually.[28] While the first and third stanzas are dominated by masochistic imagery, the middle stanza of the third song seeks to revive the natural scenery (the sky, the field) from the second song, and also mentions "blue eyes" — a prominent image in the last song. However, this middle stanza reminds the song's narrator of the impossibility of returning to nature as innocent. The imagery prompts reminiscences of earlier days: the sky reminds him of his lover's eyes and the field recalls her blond hair. "Nature," in other words, is always also the product of the subject's imagination; there is no nature outside the subject. The song is deeply skeptical about the consoling powers of nature. In the end, the contrasts evoked by the poem collapse; what once offered consolation now causes pain.

The cycle's last song, "Die zwei blauen Augen" (The two blue eyes), is perhaps the most puzzling of all. The song reiterates the story of loss, separation, and isolation (first stanza). It reminds the listener that nature offers no consolation; we see the protagonist wandering alone at night through the heather fields (second stanza). In the third and final stanza, however, something changes. While the first stanza seemed to argue that it would be better for love never to have existed — "Oh blue eyes, why did you look at me" (O Augen blau! Warum habt ihr mich angeblickt?) — the final stanza does accept love, or to be more precise: the memory of love. The beginning of the final stanza features the memory of the linden tree under which the protagonist first slept after leaving his love. Peter Revers has pointed out that the linden tree is an important literary topos that functions as a symbol of love; it also plays this role in Schubert's song "Der Lindenbaum" (The Linden Tree), part of the *Winterreise* cycle.[29] The tree is associated with sleep, and sleep is seen as a recapturing of a time of childlike innocence: "There I did not know how life treats us" (Da wußt ich nicht, wie das Leben tut). And yet this evocation of childlike innocence is not the final message of the song. The song in the end does not offer a clear path to a (brighter?) future, nor does it idealize the past in any way; Mahler's instructions are clear: it should be played "without sentimentality" (ohne Sentimentalität).[30] What remains is a seemingly indiscriminate listing of human experience brought back to its essentials: "Everything! Everyting! Love and suffering! And world and dream!" (Alles! Alles! Lieb und Leid! Und Welt und Traum!). It is possible to read these final lines as a poetic program legitimizing the cycle: real art does not offer easy answers or "ideology" but rather insists on experience, negative or positive, real or imagined. One can also read these final lines as language's failure to organize experience (by means of syntactical structure) — a failure that is meant to be positive, in the end, in that it allows a more complex view of reality.

On Love and Art — Des Knaben Wunderhorn

In the orchestral songs based on von Achim von Arnim and Clemens Brentano's *Des Knaben Wunderhorn*, too, Mahler is interested in a historically specific and concrete definition of *Volk*. This is noticed by Adorno (among others), who writes of the "historical" nature of the "world of images" in Mahler's music (*MPE*, 47; Geschichtlich ist seine Bilderwelt: *MP*, 196). This is especially true for the characters populating this world. In Mahler's music we find "pressganged soldiers" (wider ihren Willen gepreßte Soldaten), "peasant scheming against the overlords" (Bauernlist gegen die Herren); its protagonists are "outsiders, the incarcerated, starving children, the persecuted, lost soldiers" (*MPE,* 46; Außenseiter, Eingekerkerte, darbende Kinder, Verfolgte, verlorene Posten: *MP,* 195, trans. modified). In his choice of texts Mahler may have been motivated by the hardships of his own youth, Adorno suggests; more recent biographical research is inclined to downplay these hardships.[31] Even if the marginality of the figures populating Mahler's songs is self-evident, it is worth investigating further. It is not just memories of his youth that made Mahler pick these specific poems; they are part of a program. In spite of the marginality of these figures, they are representatives of the "Volk." In the way they describe their protagonists, the poems that Mahler chose for his songs remain remarkably close to the original meaning of "Volk." In German, "Volk" originally meant a "group of soldiers" or a small group that has something in common, for instance a profession.[32] It had, in other words, a strong social connotation, and it is precisely this aspect that is emphasized in Mahler's songs.

How did Mahler select texts from von Arnim and Brentano's three-volume collection entitled *Des Knaben Wunderhorn?* To answer this question, it should be remembered that Mahler's criteria were by no means exclusively literary. He may have chosen certain texts because they offered good building blocks for the musical intentions he had in mind or because they allowed him a certain amount of artistic freedom. In this sense I would interpret Mahler's comment to Ida Dehmel that von Arnim and Brentano's *Wunderhorn* texts "are not perfect poems, but rather rocks, from which everyone can make what they wish" (Das seien keine vollendeten Gedichte, sondern Felsblöcke, aus denen jeder das Seine formen dürfe.).[33] The content of the *Wunderhorn* texts, however, also influenced Mahler's choices. Mahler chose texts on topics that interested him and that had some thematic similarities, as I will show in greater detail below. Another question is: which poems did Mahler not include? An undeniable undercurrent of anti-Semitism exists in *Des Knaben Wunderhorn.* In total, ten texts in *Des Knaben Wunderhorn* are characterized by openly anti-Jewish content; in most cases these texts are about Jews interfering with Christian rituals.[34] Mahler must have encountered these. Yet he may not have been aware of the fact that von Arnim and Brentano were both members of the *Christlich-deutsche Tischgesellschaft* (Christian-German Dining Club), a conservative and fiercely nationalistic group that openly propagated anti-Semitism. He also may not have known that Clemens Brentano was the author of *Der Philister vor, in und nach der Geschichte* (The Philistine before, in, and after History, 1811), one of the most notoriously anti-Semitic texts of German Romanticism and originally read at the inaugural meeting of the *Christlich-deutsche Tischgesellschaft.*[35]

One observation to be made in this context is that the characters populating Mahler's *Wunderhorn* cycle are again, with very few exceptions, figures of mobility. While mobility in the *Lieder eines fahrenden Gesellen* is seen as predominantly negative, in *Des Knaben Wunderhorn* mobility, at least initially, seems to be something positive — the protagonists of these songs tend to accept it as a part of life. This is consistent with von Arnim's programmatic statement in the essay accompanying the first volume of *Des Knaben Wunderhorn*, in which he argued that only those who travel (or wander) could represent his ideal of folk art. "Wandering," however, is also part of an iconography that can be associated with Jewishness in Western culture, most prominently in the figure of Ahasverus, the wandering Jew.[36] In the nineteenth century, for instance, the "wandering Jew" was the subject of a popular woodcut by Gustav Doré and a novel by Eugène Sue. The image was increasingly used by anti-Semitic propagandists as a countertype to more positive forms of masculinity,[37] but had originally had more positive connotations. We know that Mahler was aware of the iconography surrounding the "wandering Jew" from a letter he wrote at a very young age to his friend Josef Steiner. The letter is a highly personal document, written over three days and organized in three parts. The second part contains a rather dark dream-like sequence in which figures of Mahler's past, as well as mythological figures, play a role. It ends with Mahler's dream vision of Ahasver, who is rejected by an angel and "picks up his walking stick and moves on, dry-eyed, forever, immortal" (dann nimmt er seinen Stock, und ziehet weiter, ohne Tränen, ewig, unsterblich).[38] On some level — unconsciously, one would be inclined to say — Mahler must have identified with the figure of Ahasver. This may explain, at least in part, his fascination with "wandering figures" in the *Lieder eines fahrenden Gesellen* and *Des Knaben Wunderhorn*. They are likeable figures, and in Von Arnim's view, as representatives of the "Volk," they are at the core of the German cultural tradition.

The order in which Mahler published his orchestral settings for the first ten orchestral *Wunderhorn* songs most likely followed their order of composition (between 1892 and 1896).[39] These songs were published in two volumes of five songs each in 1899; two additional songs ("Revelge" and "Der Tamboursg'sell") were published separately in 1905. In the following, I will discuss these songs more or less in the order in which they were published. While I do not believe that they present a linear narrative — a *Bildungsroman* in the traditional sense — they do respond to and communicate with each other. Mahler himself did not have them performed in their original order,[40] and many performances or recordings today do not do so either. Nevertheless, one runs the risk of overlooking some of the associations that exist among them if they are only considered individually and out of their original sequence.

One striking thematic difference between the *Lieder eines fahrenden Gesellen* and the orchestral *Wunderhorn* cycle is that "love" is dealt with in an entirely different manner in the *Wunderhorn* cycle. The *Gesellen* songs were about love as passion — a conceptualization of love that emphasizes feelings independent of social or moral responsibility, associates the feeling of love with self-realization,[41] and includes both a spiritual and a physical element. These songs also depicted the suffering experienced when this kind of love cannot be fulfilled. At the end of the cycle, the protagonist has understood that this love can only be a memory and that life moves on. The protagonist of "Der Schildwache Nachtlied" (Sentinel's Night Song),[42] the first song of the *Wunderhorn* cycle, resolutely rejects the idea of love as passion. In an imaginary conversation between the sentinel and his (imaginary) lover,[43] this lover represents love as passion for him: she tries to seduce him into leaving his post by promising to wait for him in the "rose garden," among the "green clover" (im Rosengarten, / im grünen Klee) — symbols that may very well be understood to signify a sexual promise. But the sentinel does not want to be seduced and counters her proposal with images of weaponry and a garden used to store weapons ("Waffengarten"). When his lover invokes God to protect him in the field, the sentinel refers to king and emperor. He goes so far as to order his lover to stay away from him — the text emphasizes physicality: "Bleib' mir from Leib" (Stay away from me [literally: from my body]) — and even calls for the patrol to join him in order to prevent her from coming closer. Only the knowledge articulated in the final stanza by an anonymous narrator, who is not the soldier, that the song is sung at midnight by a "Verlorne Feldwacht" (lost watchman in the field), opens a new perspective on the message of this song. What does it mean that the sentinel is "lost"? Does it have something to do with the anti-idealist tendency of the song, the rejection of love and religion in a traditional sense?

The second and third songs in the first book of Mahler's *Wunderhorn* cycle are closely related. In von Arnim and Brentano's collection, too, they can be found next to each other.[44] "Verlor'ne Müh" (Wasted effort) consists of a dialogue between, we assume, a young man and woman, in which the woman again tries to seduce the man. To do so, she evokes various images. First, she associates love with innocence; she invites her male counterpart to watch some lambs with her. When that does not work, she tries to trick him with food: "Would you like to nibble on some sweets, / Get some from my pocket!" (Willst vielleicht a Bissel nasche? / Hol' dir was aus meiner Tasch'!). One does not need to be psychoanalytically inclined to see that both "naschen" — the word "nibble" is a good translation, even though "naschen" generally implies something sweet — and "Tasche" (pocket) have a strong sexual connotation in this context. The male figure's response, "ich nasch' dir halt nit" (I don't want to nibble on anything from you), is equally unambiguous. Finally, the woman offers him her heart and appeals to his feelings so that he will forever think of her ("Immer! Immer! Immer!") and is nevertheless rejected again. The text here returns to love as "passion," and not just as physical pleasure, even though the listener will take this turn with a grain of salt, since love as "passion" comes only in third place after descriptions of love as child-like innocence and physical pleasure. Read this way, the song is about the impossibility of turning something physical into something spiritual (a topic that recurs in the fourth song).

The third song "Trost im Unglück" (Consolation in Hardship) is another dialogue, this time between a soldier (hussar) and a girl. Here both partners agree that they are not destined for each other, as is clear from the verse "I love you only out of folly" (Ich lieb dich nur aus Narretei), first announced by the hussar and repeated by the girl. The term "Narretei" reminds the listener of the "foolish girl" (Närrisches Dinterle) with which the male figure in "Verlor'ne Müh" addressed his female companion. It is not love as passion (with its associations of permanence and self-fulfillment), but rather love as a harmless game that both figures agree upon; both can live very well without each other, they believe. And yet there are also references to another kind of love in the song; there is, for instance, a reference by the girl to the "flower" growing in her "father's garden" (In meines Vaters Garten / wächst eine Blume drin); she wants to wait until it has become bigger before she starts taking love more seriously. This can be read as a reference to society's expectations, in particular the expectations that families (fathers) have of their daughters. The end of the song, which contains a rather unexpected turn, confirms such a reading. Both figures agree that they would be ashamed of each other if they were to be seen together in the company of others. This tells us something about society's pressures that keep these two from finding each other. While the girl may refer to middle-class morality or her parents' expectations that forbid her from being seen with a (wandering) soldier, the hussar must have his army buddies in mind who, no doubt, would frown upon anyone pursuing such a conventional relationship. This could be a lighthearted ending, if it were not for the title of the song that speaks of "Unglück" (Hardship or Misfortune).

The pressures of society return more prominently in the fourth and fifth songs of the cycle. "Wer hat dies Liedchen erdacht?" (Who thought up this little song?)[45] is, like the second song, about the impossibility of translating physical into spiritual love. This song is considered to be one of Mahler's more enigmatic.[46] I would argue, in contrast to one commentator,[47] but in line with all other *Wunderhorn* songs discussed thus far, that to understand it, it is important to see that it presents a dialogue between two partners, one male and one female. The first stanza is narrated from the perspective of a man who is standing at the foot of a mountain with a big house from atop which a girl is peering; she is the daughter of the innkeeper, but, we are told, does not live at the house. Here the song addresses a social issue, I would argue. Women of lower standing are easy prey for those higher on the ladder of society. The second stanza is from the perspective of the girl, who is bemoaning her life — "My heart is wounded" (Mein Herzle ist wund) — and hoping that the man, whom we can now assume is a former love interest (she addresses him as "Schätzle," Sweetheart), can help her. This middle stanza ends with images of death and illness, yet it also envisions love as a healing power. It is not part of the original poem in von Arnim and Brentano's *Wunderhorn* collection but was added by Mahler. In other words, it is Mahler who transformed the poem into one about the conflict between physical and spiritual love.[48] The first verse of the third stanza, "Who thought up this nice nice little song?" (Wer hat denn das schön schöne Liedlein erdacht?), refers to the previous second stanza. The meaning of this line is ambiguous. Mahler plays a little joke on his listeners by asking them to guess who wrote the previous lines, not part of the original *Wunderhorn* poem. But the line also allows for a second reading. It can be read as a rejection of the type of romantic love to which the innkeeper's daughter had alluded, as if the protagonist is asking: "Who believes in such a silly story? This kind of love does not exist in the real world; it is sheer fiction." The reference to three geese — two of them are grey; one is white — at the end of the song remains enigmatic. There is little justification for reading them as folkloric parallels of the "stork announcing pregnancy," as Paul Hamburger has suggested (77). But the idea that the song has something to do with unwanted pregnancy is not entirely out of the question;[49] this would explain the references to illness and the call for youth to be wiser at the end of the second stanza. Does the white goose symbolize an illegitimate child? At the very least, the symbolism reinforces the impression of someone who is "out of place" within a community.

If it is true that Mahler conceived of the two books of *Wunderhorn* songs as separate cycles, how is the final song of the first book, "Das irdische Leben" (Life on Earth[50]), connected to the previous songs? Its tone and general atmosphere are very different: not humorous, but tragic — a tragedy to which the middle stanza of the previous song, with its images of illness and death, already alluded. It is also meaningful that this last song does not have a man and woman but a woman and child as its main protagonists. It is tempting to assume that this may be the child to which "Wer hat dies Liedchen erdacht?" implicitly referred. Several commentators have remarked on the similarity of this poem to Goethe's "Erlkönig" (King of Elves),[51] one of Goethe's most famous poems, also because of Schubert's adaptation of it for voice and piano. However, little has been made of this implied intertextual reference. How does an insight in the connection between both texts help us to better understand Mahler's song? "Erlkönig" argues that parents must acknowledge children's spiritual needs; because the father ignores the fears of his son, the child dies. The message of "Das irdische Leben" is the exact opposite: because the mother ignores her child's need for food (bread), the child dies. Parents, in other words, need to acknowledge their children's material, bodily needs; if they don't, their children will die.

There is, in my opinion, a clear connection between this emphasis on the physical rather than spiritual side of human nature and the theme of "love" that so clearly dominates this first series of *Wunderhorn* songs. In the first four songs the material world, including humans' physical needs, was powerfully rejected by the male protagonists. In the final song a woman is at the center, and the text offers a powerful defense of the physical side of human nature. One could also say about "Das irdische Leben" that it reintroduces society's realities (already referred to a few times previously) into the cycle. This puts the female figures' concerns, particularly in the third and fourth songs, into a very different perspective. Simultaneously, this forces us to reevaluate the male perspective in these songs. All these songs have a dialogic component. It is, however, inaccurate to identify the message of the songs with the (dominant) male perspective present in the first four songs. These songs do not give us a straightforward message or ideology but rather present a clash of viewpoints or a dilemma. Masculinity asserts itself in these songs but is also questioned. Who believes the man who claims to be able to live without love, without physical needs, or without a home?

Initially Mahler considered the term "Humoresken" as a genre designation for these songs, at least for the first four songs and "Das himmlische Leben," which he composed at the same time, but which was used for the Fourth Symphony instead of the collection of 1899 (*Br*, 206).[52] I will discuss the term "Humoreske" in relation to Mahler in greater detail in the context of the final movement of the Fourth Symphony (chapter 3), but for the moment I would like to note that, as in the Fourth Symphony, the songs' undeniable lightheartedness is to be taken with a grain of salt.

The second book of *Wunderhorn* songs from 1899 is quite different in character from the first book. "Love" is still present as a topic, but not in all of the songs and not as prominently as in the first series. The center of attention shifts to issues of art and representation, and many of these songs are critical of art's functions in society and of its potential. What is interesting about these songs is how art and nature are intertwined in them; in this second series, "nature" does not function as mere scenery for the songs' texts, but the question is rather: what is nature and how can it help us understand, not only "art," but perhaps even human culture, understood here broadly as "human activity"?

The first song of the second *Wunderhorn* series, "Des Antonius von Padua Fischpredigt" (Anthony of Padua's Sermon to the Fishes), the melody of which Mahler also used for the third movement of his Second Symphony, is without a doubt one of the most humorous pieces of music that Mahler composed. Its narrative line is simple: Anthony of Padua — an actual historical figure, a Portuguese saint who lived from 1195 to 1231 — finds the church empty and so decides to preach to the fishes. The fishes are described in detail and with great wit; each specimen represents a specific human vice and character type. The fishes are attentive and enjoy the sermon, but none of them, in the end, change anything about their behavior. This is summarized in the last two lines of the final two stanzas: "All were pleased by the sermon, / but they remained like everybody else!" (Die Predigt hat g'fallen, / sie blieben wie allen!). How are we to interpret this? The "sermon" functions here as a metaphor for the work of art and its ambition to teach something, as musicologist Hans Eggebrecht has noted.[53] Nature is chaotic and always in movement. Wanting to change that is an illusory undertaking. There is a broader issue behind the song that concerns human knowledge in general: as convinced as we may be of the "truth" of our convictions, nature is essentially indifferent to such moral pronouncements or to any normative pronouncement. Such a conceptualization of nature is very much in line with the philosophy of Nietzsche (see chapter 3). The song, in the end, is highly critical of any form of ideology.

The song that in terms of its message and language most closely resembles the "Fischpredigt" is the last song of the second series, "Lob des hohen Verstandes" (Praise of a Great Mind). This song is often taken to be Mahler's response to his critics; an earlier version was in fact called "Lob der Kritik" (Praise of Criticism).[54] It is certainly possible to read the song that way, but such a reading, based primarily on Mahler's biography, is perhaps more a statement about the song's origins than indicative of the song's interpretative potential. "Lob des hohen Verstandes" presents a fable: a cuckoo and a nightingale organize a competition to determine who can "sing a masterpiece" (zu singen um das Meisterstück). A donkey will be the referee. Of course the donkey thinks that the nightingale's melodies are far too complex, and he lets the cuckoo win (whose sounds are as repetitive as his own). Thus, one could say that the song illustrates the narrow-mindedness of critics and their failure to recognize true art. The song, however, also makes a more subtle point. The donkey does not just decide intuitively, but presents an argument to back up his decision: the cuckoo sings a much better "chorale" and is rhythmically stronger than the nightingale ("Aber Kuckuck, singst gut Choral / und hältst den Takt fein innen!"). In other words, the donkey bases his decision on specific aesthetic norms, set according to his own priorities. These norms, however, are arbitrary and like all other normative statements they are manmade and not reflective of any objectively existing order in nature (as the "Fischpredigt" had already shown).

This insight into the relative nature of aesthetic norms is particularly relevant if one keeps in mind that most audiences at the time when Mahler composed his song would have recognized an intertextual reference to Wagner's *Meistersinger* in it. Wagner's opera also relates to a competition between singers and can likewise be read as Wagner's response to one of his critics, Eduard Hanslick.[55] There are two crucial differences between Mahler's and Wagner's pieces. In the *Meistersinger*, "true" art wins through a unanimous decision of the "Volk"; in "Lob des hohen Verstandes" "true" art loses out through an arbitrary decision of the referee. The relative nature of artistic norms is addressed in *Die Meistersinger* as well,[56] but in the end the opera is about distinguishing "pure" from "impure" art — a distinction that we are to believe is objective and based on consensus, and not subjective or relative. Mahler's song, in contrast, insists on the arbitrary nature of all norms. Beckmesser, the contestant representing impure art in *Die Meistersinger*, has been interpreted, quite convincingly in my opinion, as a Jewish caricature.[57] We are not sure whether Mahler saw it that way, even though he did recognize, for instance, Mime in Wagner's *Siegfried* as a Jewish caricature (see introduction). At the very least, Mahler in his song opposes the effort to juxtapose "pure" with "impure" art for ideological reasons, as Wagner did in *Die Meistersinger* with its nationalistic agenda, the presence of which even Wagner's most ardent defenders do not contest. Mahler revisits *Die Meistersinger* in the last movement of the Seventh Symphony (see chapter 4).

While the first and last songs of the second orchestral *Wunderhorn* cycle are critical of art's potential and function, the general atmosphere and textual content of the three middle songs are quite different. These songs are critical as well, but they also illustrate ways in which art can be meaningful. The second song of the cycle, "Rheinlegendchen" (Little Rhine Legend)[58] presents itself as a naive and sentimental love song: the protagonist, who we learn is cutting grass or possibly herbs along the Neckar and Rhine rivers,[59] ponders the fate of his girlfriend, who has left him to serve at a distant court. Art in this song is symbolized by a small golden ring that the man keeps as a memento of his absent lover; art, in other words, serves memory. He throws the ring into the Rhine, and he imagines that it is swallowed by a fish and ends up on the plate of the king, his lover's employer. When the king asks to whom the ring belongs, the girl recognizes it and, in the imagination of the protagonist, brings it back to him. Art, in other words, in the service of memory eventually will find the audience for which it was intended. However, the crux of the song is that this only happens in the imagination of the shepherd. When Mahler characterizes the song's atmosphere as "childlike and naughty" (*RGM*, 33, trans. modified; kindlich-schalkhaft: *GME*, 29), he certainly also has the naiveté of the main character's thoughts in mind.

The next two songs also portray cases of successful communication, albeit ambiguously (as was the case in "Rheinlegendchen"). The title "Lied des Verfolgten im Turm" is often translated as "Song of the Prisoner in the Tower." This translation is not incorrect, but it eliminates a dimension that is at least implicitly present in the German text. A "Verfolgter" is someone who is being persecuted, and the question is, of course, for what reason and by whom? It is not possible to answer this question precisely. It is safe to assume that the protagonist has been in trouble with the authorities, possibly by exercising his freedom in ways not sanctioned by them. One cannot help but be reminded of Florestan in Beethoven's *Fidelio* in this context. In spite of the love story implied in the words of the girl responding to the prisoner, the song has a clear political dimension. A second question that needs to be asked of this song regards the status of the girl responding to the prisoner's litany. Is she real or imagined? Is the song a true dialogue or an interior monologue within the prisoner's mind? I am inclined to assume the latter. The girl's responses to the prisoner's words do not so much articulate an independent point of view but rather seem to function as figments of the prisoner's imagination: she is a projection, the ideal love object, who would rather die with him than live a life without him. Two verses in the third stanza spoken by the prisoner suggest this projective function of the girl's words: "My wish and desire, / no one can take away from me!" (Mein Wunsch und Begehren, / niemand kann's wehren!). Here the song thematizes the creative act as compensation for grim reality. In doing so, these verses hold the key for understanding the song's first line, "Thoughts are free" (Die Gedanken sind frei), which also functions as a refrain. The prisoner's freedom is relative to his circumstances: He can think what he wants, but this changes nothing about the fact that he remains locked up where he is and that he may die soon (as the sixth stanza suggests). In showing the ambiguity of this "freedom," the song debunks one of the most pervasive ideas on the role of art in German cultural history: the idea that art should resist interfering with society and instead focus on what is possible in the aesthetic realm — the notion that art is, in other words, a "noble substitute for politics"[60] — can be found in Kant, Goethe, Schiller, and many Romantics. Sociologically this idea has been explained as an attempt by intellectuals, who in Germany during the eighteenth and nineteenth centuries had little political power, to safeguard their intellectual freedom at the price of actual political power. Allowing this idea to be articulated by a prisoner (who may be awaiting execution) is a powerful commentary on the status of intellectuals in German culture; it makes the song into a political statement.

"Wo die schönen Trompeten blasen" (Where the beautiful trumpets blow),[61] the fourth song of the second book, is another imaginary dialogue and can be understood as a response to the previous song in that, this time, it is the female figure who imagines a dialogue with her lost companion, her "ghost lover,"[62] who we assume is a soldier. The (distant) sound of trumpets sparks the girl's imagination. She imagines her lover knocking at her door. Here too, I would say, we are dealing with a projection: her lover consoles her but also explains his absence; he has to go to war; his "home" is the "green field" (mein Haus, von grünem Rasen). Here too, art functions as a form of consolation, but also, I would argue, as a form of memory. The associations or images evoked by the distant trumpet sounds allow the protagonist to "remember" what otherwise would have been an anonymous death on the battlefield. When we hear the "beautiful trumpets" again at the very end of the song, we know what they mean (and what we perhaps should have understood at the outset): they are commemorating the fallen soldiers. However, whatever the protagonists of this and the previous songs imagine remains a fantasy; they offer an escape from reality as much as they offer access to reality.

All the songs in Mahler's second orchestral *Wunderhorn* collection problematize art in ways that we associate with Vienna around 1900 and with modernism in general, but certainly not with the Romantic and seemingly naive texts that von Arnim and Brentano collected under the title *Des Knaben Wunderhorn*. What is at stake is the capacity of art to create community and whether art is successful at facilitating a process of communication from one subject to another. The answer to the latter question is highly ambiguous; in particular, the middle three songs suggest that art can be an important medium of communication, but they also leave open the option that the communicative power of art exists solely in the artist's imagination. While the *Wunderhorn* songs tend to be perceived as being full of naive folk wisdom, in this set of songs there are actually several references to major issues in German cultural history, specifically the issue of how art relates to society. I also believe that the associations that these songs evoke with major works of German musical and cultural history — I have mentioned *Die Meistersinger* and *Fidelio* — are far from coincidental. Not only must Mahler have been aware of these associations, but the audiences for whom he composed these songs would have recognized them as well. Increasingly, Mahler conceives of himself as an active participant in German cultural history who positions himself vis-à-vis other major figures who are part of this tradition.

Mahler's last two orchestral *Wunderhorn* songs were composed considerably later than the others and with a considerable time interval between them. "Revelge" (Reveille) was composed in July 1899 and "Der Tamboursg'sell" (The Drummer Boy) in August 1901.[63] Both are marches, and one could characterize them as "tragic, ironic, sometimes desperate songs."[64] There are significant thematic continuities between these songs and the earlier series, while both songs are also closely connected to each other. The protagonists in both songs are (again) soldiers, drummer boys, and Mahler thus again reverts to the older meanings of the concept "Volk."[65] Furthermore, both songs thematize death, albeit in very different ways. "Revelge" describes the fate of a soldier shot on the battlefield and left to die by his fellow soldiers. The plot of "Der Tamboursg'sell" is less clear. The protagonist is awaiting the gallows and nobody wants to have anything to do with him anymore — we assume, because he has deserted: "Had I remained a drummer boy, / I would not be lying around here as prisoner!" (Wär' ich ein Tambour blieben, / dürft ich nicht gefangen liegen!). These songs remind us of the miseries of war and are decidedly anti-militaristic.[66] In them, violence is omnipresent and sometimes described rather graphically: "My brothers are all over the ground, / as if they were mown down!" (Die Brüder, dick gesä't, / sie liegen wie gemäht; Revelge). Moreover, it is worth noting that the narratives of these two songs supplement each other. Taken together, they point to the limited options available to the simple soldier, the exemplary representative of the "Volk," and the hopelessness of his situation: he can either choose to be part of the collective and die on the battlefield ("Revelge"), or decide to break with the collective and be hanged as a deserter ("Der Tamboursg'sell"). One could characterize these songs for that reason as being deeply anti-ideological: they do not offer any point of orientation, any form of ethical directive.

And yet there is some hope, maybe not for the songs' poor soldier boys, but for posterity. "Revelge" ends with the image of a ghost army, led by the protagonist on his drum, first defeating the enemy army and then walking up to the house of his sweetheart ("Schätzlein"), so that she can see him (and his fellow soldiers) one last time. What is the meaning of this image of an army of skeletons showing up at someone's doorstep? The situation is similar to "Wo die schönen Trompeten blasen," where the protagonist (also a dead soldier) visits his lover after his death, at least in her imagination, to remind her of his fate. This song, too, is about memory. The same is the case with "Revelge." The deaths of the protagonist and his fellow soldiers are no longer anonymous if they are remembered, and if not merely the individual's suffering but also the miseries of war are part of individual *and collective* memory, because the song transforms death from something private or individual into something of collective relevance. This act of remembering the dead is also explicitly dealt with in "Der Tamboursg'sell." When soldiers come by — we assume by the gallows? — and ask the main figure who he has been ("wer i g'wesen bin") — note the use of the perfect tense — he replies that he used to be "the drummer of the sovereign's company" (Tambour von der Leibkompanie). Again, an individual's death is no longer anonymous but is made part of public memory. This passage has a parallel in "Revelge" when the soldier on the battlefield addresses his fellow soldiers ("brothers"; Brüder), reminding them of his fate. The last two stanzas of "Der Tamboursg'sell," which we assume are the drummer's final words, address posterity: he bids goodnight to the officers, corporals, musketeers, and grenadiers — all those who outrank him, in other words. This is a powerful reminder of the inequality inherent to military life (and perhaps to society in general?). The poor die; the privileged survive.

Do these last two songs offer a conclusion to what was said in the first and second *Wunderhorn* series? I would argue that they do to some extent.

Both "Revelge" and "Der Tamboursg'sell" thematize art's function as a form of remembering; as such, they assign to art a specific function — as problematic, momentary, random, and unreliable as this function may be. The protagonists of both songs are what I have previously called "figures of mobility" and outsiders; not, however, by their own choice. "Revelge" thematizes love and loss (the soldiers march by the house of the protagonist's sweetheart). This can be read as a comment on the first cycle, but a significant difference is that the main figure does not proudly reject love and is not an outsider by his own choice, but suffers from the loss of his love object. "Der Tamboursg'sell" is also about loss, again as the result of circumstances beyond the main figure's control. Both songs question the ideal of masculinity put forward in the first four songs of the first *Wunderhorn* cycle: they show men as being weak rather than strong. Both songs reintroduce society's harsh reality (not unlike "Das irdische Leben"), and they leave little space for an idealization of the simple man, of the "Volk." Both songs are at odds with the rhetoric of nationalism that was increasingly surrounding "Volkslieder."

Because they synthesize and comment on so much earlier material, the last two *Wunderhorn* songs affect our perspective on the earlier songs; one needs to keep the later songs in mind when listening to the earlier ones in order to understand them fully. When studying the orchestral *Wunderhorn* songs, it is important to be aware of the kinds of connections among them that I have just identified. While there would be some merit, in my opinion, in performing the songs in the order in which they were composed and published, I would not argue that the songs should only be performed in the original order (nor did Mahler do so, as I mentioned above). The fundamental openness of these texts allows for seeing new continuities and contrasts when they are performed in a different order. Mahler maybe also had his audiences in mind when he characterized the *Wunderhorn* texts to Ida Dehmel as "rocks from which everyone can make what they wish" (see note 33). In the end, none of these songs offers an ideology in the form of a clear "final" message; instead they present divergent perspectives on problems that can be found throughout Mahler's works.

Against Tradition

The social historian Eric Hobsbawm speaks of the era from 1870 to the First World War — the period during which Mahler composed all his works — as one of "mass-producing traditions," as I mentioned in my introduction.[67] In Germany this trend was particularly pronounced; as a result of the Franco-Prussian War (1870–71) Germany became a political unity, and there was a sudden need to back up this newfound unity by establishing a German national culture, even though Germans had long viewed themselves as culturally unified. Mahler was certainly aware of these trends. At the very least, his interest in Wagner and his membership of the German-nationalist *Pernerstorfer Kreis* would have made him familiar with the phenomenon. He was certainly also aware that he, as a Jew and an Austrian, was marginalized by these developments. Instead of establishing alternative traditions, however, he sought to debunk the normative aspects implied in the idea of a German national culture from within, by composing songs that deepened and complicated this concept.

When one speaks of the "production" or "invention" of traditions, the assumption is that traditions are not something stable, something that has always been in place, but that they are continually being redesigned or even developed from scratch ("invented"). This seems to contradict a basic notion about traditions: that they are characterized by stability and go back far into the past. Historical research, in particular scholarship in cultural history, however, has emphasized the fact that traditions can be remarkably versatile and that they are often multifunctional. The cultural interest in the "Volk" among German intellectuals throughout the nineteenth century can be traced back to the French Revolution of 1789 and is predominantly a legacy of German Romanticism.[68] The importance that Wagner and in his wake the *Völkische Bewegung* attributed to the concept "Volk" must be understood in the context of burgeoning nationalist movements and art's complicity in them. Mahler does not engage Wagner's philosophy of the "Volk" *directly* in his *Wunderhorn* songs (with the possible exception of his "Lob des hohen Verstandes"). In fact, he makes very different choices from Wagner. The way in which "Volk" is used in the late nineteenth century in order to reinvent tradition is, in other words, truly multifunctional. Of Wagner's operas, one could say that they invent tradition by what Hobsbawm calls "creating an ancient past beyond effective historical continuity."[69] Wagner's semifictional mythological operas shaped a historical genealogy for the German nation that was almost completely independent of historical reality, and in doing so they defined the characteristics of the nation, quoting Eric Hobsbawm again, "in terms of its enemies."[70] Mahler's *Wunderhorn* songs, on the other hand, insist on their rootedness in historical reality, and one may also say that they identify with outsiders in society.

Before something like a tradition can be invented — or to use a somewhat more careful phrase: "redesigned" — something else has to happen that concerns the collective memory of the past. The insight that traditions are constructions of one kind or another raises the question as to what "ancient materials" are being used in their production.[71] Cultural history can be seen as a reservoir of such materials, but not all its contents are equally useful. By necessity there exists a tension between these available materials and traditions that are continually redesigned; one could therefore define tradition as "nothing but deformed memory."[72] When traditions are established, a decision is made regarding which cultural materials are to be used and which are to be discarded: some things are considered worth remembering and others can be forgotten. But what kind of memory are we referring to when we talk about tradition and cultural history? Even though individuals participate in the process of remembering, the type of memory discussed here is not primarily individual but rather collective.[73] It can involve historical reality, but historical accuracy is not its primary concern. It is rather about the interpretation of historical reality — in other words, the attitudes, values, and even emotions that we associate with objects from the past. To express the collective character and the normative aspects inherent to this form of memory, the field of cultural studies has developed the term "cultural memory." "Cultural memory" has been defined as the "intentional remembering through actual records and experiences or symbolic interpretations thereof by any community that shares a common 'culture.'"[74] "Culture" in this context is understood anthropologically as the basic symbolic activity through which humans interpret the world around them and express feelings and values.[75] To be sure, such an anthropological definition does not solely refer to "high" culture, but can include "low" culture as well. In fact, one of the provocations underlying Mahler's *Wunderhorn* songs is his use of "low" culture for these highly artificial songs.

Mahler's songs actively take issue with what Hobsbawm calls the mass-producing of traditions in Europe from 1870 to 1914; they do so by pointing to a crisis, whereas others sought to use the "Volk" concept for ideological gain. Many of Mahler's songs, as we have seen, reflect and problematize the function of art, in particular its ambition to create community or to establish intersubjective communication. They also problematize memory as a process. A number of the songs discussed above — for instance, the last *Gesellen* song "Die zwei blauen Augen," and the later *Wunderhorn* songs: "Rheinlegendchen," "Wo die schönen Trompeten blasen," "Revelge," and "Der Tamboursg'sell" — are concerned with the processes through which memories are transmitted and the randomness with which memories may or may not survive. The deliberations on memory within these songs function as a form of work-immanent poetics. When these songs thematize memory, they also contemplate their own status: the role of art in society and history. The same phenomenon can be found in another early work by Mahler: art and memory are also closely linked in the cantata *Das klagende Lied* (Song of Lament), Mahler's first major work, which he completed in 1880. He wrote the text of this cantata himself but based it on the fairytale *Der singende Knochen* (The Singing Bone), which exists in versions by the Brothers Grimm and Ludwig Bechstein.[76] At the center of the fairytale is the possession of a red flower; he who finds it will be allowed to marry the queen. Two brothers go on a quest to find the flower; the younger one finds it but his older brother kills him and hastily buries his body under a willow tree. A passing minstrel ("Spielmann"), however, finds a bone belonging to the murdered man's skeleton, makes it into a flute, and goes to the castle to sing at the royal wedding. The flute tells the story of the fratricide, the guests flee, and the castle vanishes. Art serves the recovery of what is repressed; it serves as a counternarrative to the "official" version of history. Art speaks for the abused.

The memories contained in the *Gesellen* and *Wunderhorn* songs are guided by equally critical intentions. In relation to dominant cultural memory, Mahler searches for images and texts that do not fit the prevailing model. His songs are descriptive in that they search for material that is repressed and problematic at this time, when German nationalism is seeking to mobilize the concept of the "Volk," and do not seek an ideal image of the "Volk" in a prescriptive sense. In doing so, Mahler's songs go back to older semantic contours of the term "Volk." In the *Wunderhorn* songs the prototypical representative of the "Volk" is the military man, the soldier of lower rank — and not the mythological hero, the farmer or the merchant, to name a few figures who also functioned as ideal representatives of the German "Volk" in nineteenth-century discourse.[77] In particular in the *Lieder eines fahrenden Gesellen*, but also in some of the *Wunderhorn*-songs ("Wer hat dies Liedchen erdacht?"; "Der Tamboursg'sell") the social aspect of an older understanding of the term is very clear. The descriptive dimension of the songs is also clear in that all of the characters are individuals and anti-heroes with their own narratives, set in their own specific situations, with their own desires and their own fears. One could say that there is no "Volk" in Mahler's songs, at least not as a monolithic unity. "Volk" is always something very concrete for Mahler and tied to material conditions of life. His songs emphasize mobility. In his cosmos, wandering figures are the ideal representatives of the "Volk," as they were for von Arnim in the essay accompanying the first volume of the *Wunderhorn* songs. All of these elements call into question politically conservative appropriations of the "Volk" around 1900 that emphasized unity, stability, and attributed racial or ethnic characteristics to the term.

The use of the "Volk" for nationalist purposes had a gendered dimension as well. Culturally speaking, 1870–71 marked the beginning of a "'militarisation' of public life" that meant simultaneously a "'masculinization' of culture."[78] The cultural historian George L. Mosse interprets the establishment of an ideal of masculinity as being motivated by a desire to stabilize Western societies, a desire that began in the eighteenth century and lasted well into the twentieth.[79] Mahler's songs are against this idealization of masculinity, which was very much part of the conservative idolization of the "Volk" (even though tendencies to idealize manhood can be found in the socialist movement as well).[80] Not only do his songs focus on outsiders and underdogs in society, but these figures also represent countertypes[81] when compared to dominating images of manhood. The *Gesellen* songs still assert a type of masculinity that emphasizes control, in particular over physical impulses or women's demands on the male subject. Yet they also ironically undercut this ideal and show its unfeasibility. The *Wunderhorn* songs challenge the masculine ideal even more by focusing on men who are cowards, lack self-control, or transgress social norms. Mahler's men are vagrants, without roots in society, and yet at least the military men among them are also supposed to represent society's core.

Mahler's songs are severely at odds with an idealization of the past that is often associated with Romanticism but in fact runs through the entire nineteenth century. Behind the criticism of a naive Romanticism that thinks it can return to an unproblematic past without the troubles of modern society, there is a skepticism regarding all ideology — a skepticism that, as Mahler's songs show, is also part of the Romantic legacy. It is remarkable how many of these songs contain violent imagery and how closely intertwined violence and culture are in these songs. Violence in these songs is not incidental or individual, but deeply embedded in society. In view of such violence, art's legitimacy itself is at stake. In spite of art's ability to serve as a medium of cultural memory, it is questionable whether art can teach its audiences anything ("Fischpredigt") or that there are any objective criteria for distinguishing "pure" from "impure" art ("Lob des hohen Verstandes"). "All singing is over" (Alles Singen is nun aus) is a line in the *very first song* of the *Lieder eines fahrenden Gesellen*. That is no coincidence; Mahler is deeply skeptical of the conventional understanding of the normative powers of art — his songs are art after the end of art. If these songs are meaningful, it is perhaps not because of their message or ideology but only because the images and sensations contained in them lead us to associations that are meaningful for us. For Mahler, cultures are in movement and they are not monolithic but heterogeneous.

Paradoxically, within German cultural history Romanticism has been associated with nationalism, conservatism, and anti-Semitism on the one hand, but simultaneously with more positive developments, for instance with an increased interest in Germany's cultural roots, with an interest in the figure of the outsider and artist in German cultural history, and, last but not least, with an increased respect for the alterity of other cultures (going back to the work of Herder).[82] Romanticism can be normative and monolithic, but it also embraces humor, irony, and fragmentary ways of thinking and writing. It is possible to understand Mahler's interest in the *Wunderhorn* texts as an attempt to rescue this critical and humoristic side of Romanticism (commonly associated with early Romanticism) at a time when the public was mostly interested in the conservative and nationalistic side of Romanticism (usually associated with late Romanticism) which, for instance, dominates Richard Wagner's work. Mahler is not alone in his desire to revisit Romanticism and rewrite German cultural history; both impulses can also be found in the writings of Friedrich Nietzsche, whose influence is difficult to overestimate in fin-de-siècle Vienna.

3: Nietzsche and the Crisis of German Culture

To understand the importance of Nietzsche for Mahler and many of his contemporaries, it is crucial to realize that Nietzsche was seen not as just another figure in the history of Western philosophy but rather as someone who personified an endpoint and also the chance for a new beginning. Around 1900 Nietzsche's name was synonymous with a fundamental crisis that indicated the end of Western metaphysics. One did not read Nietzsche; one "experienced" his thought.[1] Nietzsche had come to be associated with "the death of God," a maxim he first put forward in his 1882 book *Die fröhliche Wissenschaft* (The Gay Science), the title of which Mahler would borrow for an early version of the program for his Third Symphony. While Nietzsche's thinking was certainly directed against the church as an institution, his atheism was more comprehensive, in that it questioned the validity of any kind of normative claim, be it ethical, aesthetic, or cognitive. Nietzsche was a nihilist who dared to question not only the "truths" of Christianity but also the materialist and positivist foundations of mid-nineteenth-century science and philosophy, along with their ideals of scientific "objectivity." Many also saw Nietzsche as a rebel against the middle class's morals and lack of ingenuity[2] who countered conventional bourgeois moralizing with a new vitalism.

Such radical ideas made Nietzsche into a cult figure for a new generation of artists and intellectuals, among them Siegfried Lipiner and his close friend Gustav Mahler. To understand Nietzsche's significance for Mahler, it is necessary to reconstruct the critical impulses underlying the former's works. But it is also important to realize that criticism represents a starting point for Nietzsche. While a critique of Western metaphysics underlies his philosophy, the fin-de-siècle generation of artists to which Mahler belonged was more interested in those aspects of Nietzsche's philosophy that articulated a new beginning, in his "sweeping visions of cultural and political redemption."[3] It is part of the paradoxical nature of Nietzsche's thinking that despite all of the criticism they contain, Nietzsche's works are "ideological" in the sense that they intend to prescribe a post-metaphysics way of life. It is important to take these critical and reconstructive impulses in Nietzsche seriously when looking at the texts in Mahler's Second, Third, and Fourth symphonies. Underlying the following deliberations is the assumption that Mahler did not simply borrow a few ideas or images from Nietzsche, but rather that the worldview underlying the Second, Third, and Fourth Symphonies is fundamentally Nietzschean.[4]

Nietzsche and the Meaning of Art

William McGrath has correctly pointed out that Nietzsche's early texts and in particular his first book, *Die Geburt der Tragödie aus dem Geiste der Musik* (The Birth of Tragedy out of the Spirit of Music, 1872), had a great impact on Mahler, Lipiner, and their generation who were still in high school or were beginning their university studies in the 1870s.[5] We encountered *Die Geburt* in the last chapter when I discussed the opposition between the Apollonian and the Dionysian in order to understand Nietzsche's interest in folk songs. Nietzsche developed this terminology as part of a critical agenda whose roots can be traced back to German Romanticism. He not only revitalized Romanticism's critique of a world that had become too rational and scientific but also agreed with the foundational function it assigned to the work of art in order to counter such a worldview. It is in this context that the early Romantics developed the idea of a "new mythology." Its central idea is that although it is no longer possible to legitimize political structures by referring to a divine order of nature, art might be able to take on some of the legitimizing functions formerly assigned to religion.[6] In order to do so, the early Romantics believed, a new "general symbolism" was needed to create new forms of community.[7]

One of the key insights in *Die Geburt der Tragödie* that summarizes the function Nietzsche assigns to art is the statement that "only as *aesthetic phenomenon* is existence and the world eternally *justified*" (*BT*, 33; nur als *aesthetisches Phänomen* ist das Dasein und die Welt ewig *gerechtfertigt*: SW 1:47).[8] This insight is a clear variation on the Romantics' concept of a "new mythology."[9] It is also of fundamental importance for understanding turn-of-the-century aesthetic theory and practice, precisely because of the preeminent and yet highly ambiguous function it assigns to art. On the one hand, Nietzsche acknowledges that there is no traditional metaphysics in place that can make sense of life and the world. On the other hand, however, he clearly states that it is the task of art to find substitutes for the old metaphysical frameworks. Such substitutes, however, can never completely replace those frameworks, but rather function as surrogates. Art is a privileged medium through which the relativity of any metaphysical framework can be articulated. In his aesthetic theory too, Nietzsche shows himself to be a profoundly modern thinker.

For Nietzsche, the concept of ideal art — art that is not superficial, that does not make the mistakes of the past — is necessarily tragic, yet nevertheless becomes the source of what might be described as a new optimism or form of joy. This constellation — joy derived from the deepest pessimism — is highly interesting in the context of Mahler's reception of Nietzsche. One of the more baffling features of Mahler's music, and one that has long been viewed as one of its most controversial aspects, is his seemingly contradictory use of diverging emotions: the sometimes very sudden shifts from deep desolation to (ostensibly) uninhibited and unambiguous joy, in particular in the symphonies discussed in this chapter (for instance, the transition from the fourth to fifth movement in the Third Symphony or from the third to the fourth movement in the Fourth). These contradictory emotions are part of the Nietzschean agenda informing this music. Pessimism is one of the key concepts in *Die Geburt der Tragödie*. Tragedy is characterized by pessimism. Its epistemological function consists in a glum and yet truly "profound" (tiefsinnig) view of reality that acknowledges that individuality is not a useful concept and in fact is the "primal source of all evil" (*BT*, 52; Urgrund des Uebels: *SW* 1:73). Tragedy teaches humans to overcome their individuality — an important topic not just in *Die Geburt der Tragödie* but also, for instance, in a later text such as *Also sprach Zarathustra* (Thus Spoke Zarathustra). Pessimism is not tragedy's final word. At the end of tragedy there is the "joyous hope" (freudige Hoffnung) that accompanies the insight that humans are part of a larger whole (*SW* 1: 73; *BT*, 52). For Nietzsche, tragedy ideally has a cleansing, healing function (*SW* 1: 132; *BT*, 98) that manifests itself in the ability to find optimism or joy in spite of this tragic worldview — it is Nietzsche's interpretation of the Aristotlean theory of catharsis in tragedy.[10] While Nietzsche associates pessimism with individualism and therefore with the Apollonian heritage (*SW* 1:103; *BT*, 76), through "joyfulness" a Dionysian view of the world is reintroduced into tragedy. One could say that with Nietzsche Greek tragedy returns to its Dionysian roots. Such a return is associated with a specific insight, a vision of life, that Nietzsche describes in multiple ways in *Die Geburt der Tragödie*, often using nature imagery. At the core of tragedy, Dionysian joy functions as a form of consolation that is to be understood as an affirmation of life, since it articulates the idea "that eternal life flows on indestructibly beneath the turmoil of appearances" (*BT*, 85; dass unter dem Wirbel der Erscheinungen das ewige Leben unzerstörbar weiterfliesst: *SW* 1:115), even though, Nietzsche adds immediately thereafter, such an image can in turn only be an illusion.[11]

Music plays a key role in *Die Geburt der Tragödie* and in Nietzsche's work in general because it alone can somewhat adequately represent the Dionysian element at the root of Greek tragedy. Nietzsche quotes Schopenhauer's statement that music is like nature in that both express the same thing; music provides a general language that has not lost touch with the inner essence of things (*SW* 1:105; *BT*, 77–78). Music is, in the words of Schopenhauer, "directly a copy of the will itself" (*BT*, 78; unmittelbar Abbild des Willens selbst: *SW* 1:106), referring to the most elemental force underlying all of life in Schopenhauer's philosophy, not unlike the Dionysian in Nietzsche's philosophy. According to Nietzsche, German music in particular has succeeded in preserving the Dionysian element in Western culture, as Bach, Beethoven, and Wagner show (*SW* 1:127; *BT,* 94). The expressive power of (instrumental) music succeeds where word and image alone are bound to fail (*SW* 1:134; *BT,* 100). To illustrate these ideas Nietzsche adds a lengthy analysis of Wagner's *Tristan und Isolde,* in particular its third act (*SW* 1:135–37; *BT,* 10–102). After his split with Wagner, Nietzsche would distance himself from endorsements like these, and he no longer believed that his musical ideals would be realized during his lifetime.[12] In the new introduction for the 1886 edition of *Die Geburt der Tragödie,* Nietzsche alludes to a new form of "Dionysian" music that has no roots in German Romanticism and is still waiting to be invented (*SW* 1:20; *BT,* 11).

Many of Nietzsche's ideas discussed here are constitutive elements for Mahler's music making. And yet Mahler is not a dogmatic "Nietzschean" thinker. When discussing the impact of Nietzsche and Wagner on fin-de-siècle Viennese culture, it is important to realize that Nietzsche and Wagner were still alive when Mahler and Lipiner became interested in their works as members of the *Pernerstorfer Kreis* in the late 1870s. A serious literary reception of Nietzsche's thinking, however, did not start until the early 1890s, when Nietzsche became the object of a cult-like following.[13] Mahler, incidentally, did not publicly identify with Nietzsche's thinking until he was composing his Third Symphony (1895–96), with its multiple Nietzschean references. The interest of the *Pernerstorfer Kreis* in Nietzsche therefore developed significantly earlier than that of other, "mainstream," intellectuals.

Among the members of the *Pernerstorfer Kreis,* Mahler's friend Siegfried Lipiner played a key role in sparking the circle's interest in Nietzsche, and after Lipiner sent Nietzsche his epic poem *Prometheus entfesselt* (Prometheus Unbound), a brief correspondence between the two ensued.[14] Nietzsche's ideas and those of his followers and associates were still greatly in flux; they were very much part of an ongoing "conversation," literally and figuratively speaking. In a letter that Lipiner, Pernerstorfer, and fellow members of the *Circle* wrote to Nietzsche marking his thirty-third birthday (18 October 1877), Nietzsche's *Schopenhauer als Erzieher* (Schopenhauer as Educator) is mentioned specifically and the letter draws a parallel between Nietzsche's admiration for Schopenhauer and that of the *Circle* for Nietzsche.[15] This vision of a new form of cultural community that Mahler and his friends imagined would be gravely disturbed soon after they had sent their letter to Nietzsche. Nietzsche broke with Wagner — a fact that, for the larger public, first became clear upon the publication of the first volume of *Menschliches, Allzumenschliches* (Human, All Too Human) in 1878.[16] Nietzsche criticized the religious turn displayed in Wagner's later works, and his capitulation to German nationalism. This souring of his relationship with Richard Wagner had profound consequences for Nietzsche's thinking; it led, in fact, to a fundamental reconceptualizing of his intellectual priorities. From a critic of Western culture who had generally held a favorable view of German culture's potential and Wagner's operas, Nietzsche increasingly turned into a critic of German culture and of Richard Wagner.

Where did Mahler stand ideologically in the conflict between Nietzsche and Wagner? Scholars have frequently voiced doubts on Mahler's intellectual commitment to Nietzsche's philosophy, in particular in relation to the Third Symphony.[17] An interest in Nietzsche's thinking is particularly at odds with the religious agenda that many have wished to read into Mahler's music, specifically with regard to the Second and Third Symphonies. On the other hand, if Nietzsche did have a significant impact on Mahler, such a link would connect Mahler's music firmly to the agenda of fin-de-siècle Vienna modernism. To answer the question of Mahler's philosophical and ideological alliances, we will need to look to his music, since there are no other records clarifying them. The fact that Nietzsche plays an important role in Mahler's music is very clear, but how does this affect his attitudes toward the ideas Wagner stood for?

Religion — Symphony No. 2

To what extent is the Second Symphony a Nietzschean symphony? The religious imagery used here and elsewhere in Mahler's work seems to clash with Nietzsche's anti-metaphysical — and more precisely, anti-Christian — agenda. To understand the function of religion in the Second Symphony (and other later compositions), it is useful to look at Siegfried Lipiner's essay *Über die Elemente einer Erneuerung religiöser Ideen in der Gegenwart* (On the Elements of a Renewal of Religious Ideas in the Present), based on a talk given on 19 January 1878 at the *Leseverein der deutschen Studenten Wiens* (Reading Society of German Students in Vienna). Lipiner starts his essay by asserting that a crisis exists in humankind's attitude toward religion. This crisis among his contemporaries, Lipiner claims, can take the shape of vulgar worship of certain images — religion as a naive and unreflective form of idolization — or as indifference toward religion.[18] By way of solution, Lipiner proposes not a renewal of dogmatic forms of religion but rather an investigation of what the roots of religion exactly are. All humans are driven by a metaphysical need, defined as a longing for what is beyond the empirical realm of the here and now, that expresses itself as religion, art, or philosophy (4, 5). While this desire is common to humankind as a whole, artists play a privileged role because they are able to articulate this need for an alternate reality (4, 9). Lipiner sees the function of art, echoing with the early Romantics and Nietzsche, as being primarily "symbolic": art is "a *symbolic* abbreviation of life" (eine *symbolische* Abbreviatur des Lebens; 9). The function of the artist is to create symbols that function as substitutes for a metaphysical framework. To be able to intuit "*the world as a work of art*" (*die Welt als Kunstwerk*; 9) is to experience not just a high point of art but also the recapturing through aesthetic means of a religious moment lost by humankind's overly empirical worldview.

In his text Lipiner gives few concrete examples of such an intuitive aesthetic experience of the world, but it may be no coincidence that the passage just quoted is followed soon thereafter by a reflection on pantheism — a philosophical doctrine that rejects the belief in a conventional God and instead argues that only through nature can humankind become aware of a divine dimension. Pantheism according to Lipiner is often misunderstood as the external manifestation of God in nature. Instead, Lipiner argues for a more complex view of pantheism:

> True and serious Pantheism we can only grasp if we see nature from inside, if in our interior the great transformation has taken place, if we have stopped to think and feel about ourselves as individuals: then we are Pan, all-and-one, and then we are Theos, the divine — and that great transformation is the tragic event, the tragedy; in it we suffer the most deeply, because only when he is bleeding does man tear himself away from his transient self, and in it we experience the joy of all joys, because in this tearing-ourselves-away-while-bleeding we experience the omnipotence and magnificence of a higher self, of our own divinity.
>
> [Den wahren und ernsten Pantheismus erfassen wir nur, wenn wir diese Natur von innen sehen, wenn in unserm Innern die grosse Wandlung vorgegangen ist, wenn wir aufgehört haben, uns als Einzelwesen zu wissen und fühlen: dann sind wir Pan, das All-Eine, und dann sind wir Theos, das Göttliche, — und jene grosse Wandlung ist der tragische Vorgang, die Tragödie; in ihr leiden wir am tiefsten, denn nur blutend reisst der Mensch von seinem vergänglichen Selbst sich los, und in ihr durchströmt uns die Freude aller Freuden, denn in diesem blutenden Sich-Losreissen empfinden wir die Allmacht und Herrlichkeit des höhern Selbst, unserer eigenen Göttlichkeit. (11)

Lipiner is interested in pantheism because it acknowledges that nature can function as a source for our aesthetic sensitivity, provided that "nature" is not perceived merely as something entirely exterior or material but as an entity that engages our inner senses. Nature teaches us to see ourselves no longer as individuals ("Einzelwesen"), but as part of a larger whole. While Nietzsche — in contrast to Goethe, Schopenhauer, and Wagner — is nowhere mentioned by name in Lipiner's essay, his influence is omnipresent. Lipiner's call to conceive of the world as "*a work of art*" is of course reminiscent of Nietzsche's statement in *Die Geburt der Tragödie* that humans can only make sense of the world and their lives as an "*aesthetic phenomenon*" (*SW* 1:47; *BT,* 33). Moreover, Lipiner's references here and elsewhere in his essay to tragedy and the "tragic" (7, 12, and 17) are clearly influenced by Nietzsche. Like Nietzsche, Lipiner is interested in the tragic as a moment of transformation. In tragedy, suffering turns into joy; humankind overcomes individuality and realizes that it is part of a larger whole. The central importance of this insight is also clear from the fact that Lipiner returns to it at the end of the essay, when he quotes a passage from the memoirs of Malwina von Meysenbug, a friend of both Wagner and Nietzsche whose name also goes unmentioned, in which she reports a semi-mystical experience on a sea coast, and earlier in the French Alps, that led her to realize the unity of all things in contrast to the loneliness of the individual.[19] While the exact circumstances of these experiences remain vague, it is clear that nature plays a key role in articulating such experiences; at the very least it functions as a catalyst.

To understand the importance of Nietzsche and von Meysenbug for this text, in spite of the fact that both remain unnamed in it, it is important to realize that Lipiner's essay was meant primarily as a way to attract the attention of Wagner, as Jens Malte Fischer has suggested,[20] and was written when Nietzsche's interest in Lipiner had already come to an end. Interestingly, Nietzsche had recommended von Meysenbug's *Memoiren einer Idealistin* (Memoirs of an Idealist) to Lipiner and other intellectuals of his generation.[21] By integrating Nietzsche and von Meysenbug's thinking into his essay, Lipiner was attempting to mend the rift between Nietzsche and Wagner, at least intellectually speaking, but very much on Nietzsche's terms. This agenda underlying Lipiner's essay has thus far not been recognized, but is quite important for understanding not only Lipiner's position on the growing division between Nietzsche and Wagner, but also that of Mahler.

Wagner did respond to Lipiner's provocative essay in his own way. In 1880, two years after Lipiner's essay had appeared in print, Richard Wagner published his seminal essay "Religion und Kunst" (Religion and Art). Wagner's essay is certainly a response to Nietzsche, but also to Lipiner. From Cosima's diaries we know that Wagner read Lipiner's essay, which the author had sent to him, and discussed religious topics with Lipiner when he visited Wagner in Bayreuth in September 1878.[22] Wagner's starting point is very similar to that of Lipiner. Without using the term explicitly, Wagner too is interested in the Romantic idea of a "new mythology" according to which art takes on the metaphysical function lost by religion. In an exemplary way this is articulated in the essay's first sentence:

> One might say that where Religion becomes artificial, it is reserved for Art to save the spirit [core (CN)] of religion by recognizing the figurative value of the mythic symbols which the former would have us believe in their literal sense, and revealing their deep and hidden truth through an ideal presentation.
>
> [Man könnte sagen, daß da, wo die Religion künstlich wird, der Kunst es vorbehalten sei den Kern der Religion zu retten, indem sie die mythischen Symbole, welche die erstere im eigentlichen Sinne als wahr geglaubt wissen will, ihrem sinnbildlichen Werthe nach erfaßt, um durch ideale Darstellung derselben die in ihnen verborgene tiefe Wahrheit erkennen zu lassen.]²³

Like Lipiner, Wagner is interested in "symbolism" as a medium for resolving humankind's metaphysical homelessness. But what does Wagner mean by "symbols" in this context? The classical definition of the symbol within German cultural history goes back to Goethe, who defines "symbolism" as the ability to transform phenomena into ideas, but in such a way that in the image the idea remains "indefinitely operative and unattainable" (unendlich wirksam und unerreichbar); true symbolism is a "momentary lively revelation of the unexplorable" (lebendig-augenblickliche Offenbarung des Unerforschlichen).²⁴ The "mythic symbols" Wagner has in mind are the narrative manifestations of a truth that is "deep" and "hidden": his own operas. Wagner in his essay quite explicitly seeks to save religion, or at least its "core." While Lipiner is looking for alternatives to both conventional religion and atheism, Wagner is specifically interested in a renewal of Christianity. In the motto accompanying his essay he quotes Schiller who, in his correspondence with Goethe, wrote that he found in Christianity "the potential disposition for that which is highest and most noble" (virtualiter die Anlage zu dem Höchsten und Edelsten), and that any attempt to capture these later in one's own life can only be "inadequate" (*RA*, 213, trans. modified; verfehlt: *RK*, 211).²⁵

But why does religion need to be saved? Religion, according to Wagner, is in decline (*RK*, 223; *RA*, 224). This is particularly clear if one compares Christianity to Brahmanism — the term that Wagner, like many of his contemporaries, uses for Hinduism — and Buddhism. Wagner is interested in Brahmanism because of its belief that it is a sin to kill and eat animals. Like many of his contemporaries Wagner accepts Friedrich Schlegel's thesis that there is a straight developmental link between ancient India, Europe in general, and Germany in particular (see chapter 6 for a detailed discussion of this idea). The history of this link is a history of decline. The decline of religion (and culture in general) Wagner attributes to the fact that Brahmanism's original vegetarianism was replaced by the practice of eating meat. In this context he uses the term "degeneration" (in German: "Degeneration" and "Entartung"; for example, *RK*, 230;

RA, 231). Eating meat means that humankind is abandoning its natural nourishment, resulting in disease and degeneration (*RK*, 230; *RA*, 231). Wagner interprets Christ's sacrifice of his own flesh and blood as an attempt to remedy the unnecessary slaughter of animals (*RK*, 231; *RA*, 231). Later in his essay, he speaks repeatedly of "regeneration" in this context ("Regeneration"; *RK*, 241; *RA*, 239). While Christ, and therefore also Christianity, point toward such a "regeneration," Wagner associates Judaism with animal sacrifices; to illustrate this point he refers to Abel's sacrifice of the lamb (*RK*, 241; *RA*, 241).

One observation we can make is that Wagner's use of symbolism in his essay is very different from Lipiner's. While Lipiner emphasizes the creative potential of symbols and their openness, Wagner's primary goal is to establish a direct and unambiguous link between symbol and what is symbolized, between signifier and signified. This is clear, for instance, toward the end of the first section of Wagner's essay, in which symbolism is discussed most extensively, when Wagner discusses music vis-à-vis other forms of art. The difference between painting and music is that painting ultimately relies on concepts to assign meaning to its figures, while music gives presence to meaning and thus abolishes the difference between the sign and its meaning (*RK*, 222; *RA*, 224). It is music's task to abolish the interpretative uncertainty that comes with the symbolic mode. Wagner returns to the issue of symbolism toward the end of his essay. He is looking for one central symbol to create a new form of community (*RK*, 249; *RA*, 248). What this symbol exactly is he has already told his readers; only a daily glance at the "Redeemer on the cross as last sublime refuge" (*RA*, 247, trans. modified; Erlöser am Kreuze als letzte erhabene Zuflucht: *RK*, 247) can convince us of the inherent "tragedy" (*RA*, 247; Tragik: *RK*, 247) of being in the world and thus bring humans together in a new community. In Lipiner's essay, Christ is mentioned as the prototypical martyr in the section immediately following his discussion of pantheism. For Lipiner he exemplifies the moment of "*tragic metamorphosis*" (*tragische Wandlung;* 12), understood in accordance with Nietzsche's *Geburt der Tragödie* as the moment when a new attitude toward life originates (pantheism's insight that man is part of nature). This is perhaps the clearest indication that Lipiner and Wagner have a fundamentally different understanding of symbolism. Wagner, by making Christ into the central symbol of (all) religion, and by making meat consumption into the central issue at stake within religious tradition, ignores the principal openness associated with symbols since Goethe. Lipiner, by contrast, in his search for a pantheistic aestheticization of nature defends precisely this open model of the "symbol."

These different ways of understanding symbolism translate into fundamentally different views on the role of religion in society. Wagner advocates a return to Christianity or, to be more precise, to what he conceives of as a more authentic form of Christianity. Doubt about Christianity's truth is merely a passing phase; it is a characteristic stage to be overcome. For Lipiner, doubt is a constitutive element for any religion, which is clear from a sentence such as "He who means well toward religion should protect and support the efforts of those critics who want to kill its dogmas" (Wer der Religion wohl will, schütze und stütze die Bestrebungen der dogmenmörderischen Kritik; 8). Any attempt to give a very specific content, material or ideological, to humankind's metaphysical longing is futile. Humankind, in Lipiner's view, is driven by a "dark intuition" (dunkle Ahnung) rather than by a longing for something more specific (6). Lipiner is not concerned about seeking an aesthetic foundation for a new community. It would be more accurate to say that his ideas mirror what has been called Nietzsche's "aristocratic" skepticism toward creating forms of communality in this way.[26] One can add to this that, from the perspective of intellectual history, both essays construct the heritage of Jewish thinking for German culture very differently. Wagner sees Judaism in "Religion und Kunst" as negative, because he associates it with the sacrifice of animals. Lipiner, by contrast, defends pantheism, a philosophical movement often associated with Jewishness because Baruch de Spinoza was seen as one of its intellectual founders; in German culture Lessing, Mendelssohn, Goethe, and Heine either subscribed to pantheist thinking themselves or were associated with pantheism by others.[27]

There is no doubt in my mind that when Mahler composed his Second Symphony he was not simply aware of the essays I just discussed and the debate they engendered, but also viewed his symphony as a contribution to this debate. Some of the key issues in this debate (nature's symbolism; tragic denial versus affirmation of life; how to understand pantheism) reappear in different ways in materials related to this work. The religious setting of the Second Symphony can, at least in part, be explained by Mahler's initial intention to use a funeral scene as its point of departure: At the outset of the symphony "we stand at the coffin of a beloved person" (wir stehen am Sarge eines geliebten Menschen), Mahler states in his programmatic deliberations of 1901 for a performance of this symphony in Dresden (*GR*, 87). In a letter of 6 March 1896 to Max Marschalk — another important source for Mahler's thinking about this composition — Mahler interprets his Second Symphony as a commentary on his First: at the moment of his death, the life of the hero of the First Symphony is examined, and the central question is "*Why did you live?*" (*Warum hast du gelebt?*; *Br*, 172). The Second Symphony, in other words, seeks to think through the philosophical issues raised by the First. The question is very explicitly for Mahler whether life makes sense or whether it is nothing more than a "big abominable joke" (ein großer, furchtbarer Spaß; *Br*, 172). In such statements, regardless of their programmatic value, there is a fair amount of skepticism regarding any conventional understanding of religion, and it is important to keep this in mind when studying the Second Symphony.

In his letter to Marschalk (and elsewhere), Mahler refers to the first movement as "Todtenfeier" (Celebration of the Dead). This could be taken as a literary reference: in 1887 Siegfried Lipiner had published a German translation of the epic poem *Dziady* (*Todtenfeier*; a more accurate translation would be The Forefathers[28]) written by the Polish-Lithuanian author Adam Mickiewicz (1798–1855). Mahler had read Mickiewicz's text,[29] and there are some interesting parallels between the text and topics that were preoccupying Mahler when he composed the *Todtenfeier* movement in 1888. This text too, like Jean Paul's *Titan* and Mahler's First Symphony, can be read as a response to Goethe's *Werther*.[30] Nevertheless, the Second Symphony's first movement responds to Mickiewicz's text in a fundamentally different way when compared, for instance, with the connection between Mahler's First Symphony and Jean Paul's *Titan*. The difference is that the references to Jean Paul were very much part of the program Mahler invented for the symphony's audiences: they encouraged his listeners to explore what he saw as an important piece of German cultural history. Interestingly, Jean Paul's *Titan* ends with a "Totenfeier" (for Albano's predecessor on the throne, Luigi, also named Ludwig).[31] As important as Mickiewicz's text and Lipiner's notes may have been for Mahler, he did not intend his audiences to follow in his footsteps here; the name "Mickiewicz" is, for instance, nowhere mentioned in relation to the Second Symphony (or to the original independent movement). The importance of Mahler's reference to the first movement as a *Todtenfeier*, for an interpretation of the Second Symphony, lies in the suggestion that this symphony will be about a protagonist's working through the past (as the programmatic notes discussed above also show). Mahler, in other words, is more interested in the ideas behind Mickiewicz's text as they are explained in Lipiner's foreword. Mickiewicz's *Todtenfeier* is about the memory process: in three hours Gustav, one of the book's protagonists, must "relive his life and come to a conclusion about it" (sein Leben nochmals erleben und das Facit desselben ziehen).[32] Mickiewicz, as Lipiner puts it, is not so much interested in establishing a continuous narrative but rather presents "a series of snapshots" (eine Reihe von Momentbildern), or individual scenes, that allow the hero to reexperience meaningful but painful moments of his life.[33] The religious theme of the Second Symphony is framed as a search, a highly personal quest that is simultaneously a working-through of one's past.

The second movement does precisely this. It is designed, in Mahler's words, to be a "*memory*" (*Erinnerung*) and evokes what seems to be an entirely unproblematic glance into the past, "A sunny view, pure and untarnished, from the life of this hero" (Ein Sonnenblick, rein und ungetrübt, aus dem Leben dieses Helden; *Br*, 173). It is followed by a movement that problematizes such a nostalgic view of the past and thereby shows that it is not possible to live solely through one's memories. In his letter to Marschalk Mahler writes of the chaotic impression that the Second Symphony's scherzo, the third movement, may have on its audiences: an impression that may lead us to experience it as incoherent and meaningless (*Br*, 173).[34] It is as if one sees people dancing, but without being able to hear the music accompanying them. In this movement we hear again some of the humorous element of the scherzo (third movement) of the First Symphony (the same humor found in the *Wunderhorn* song "Des Antonius von Padua Fischpredigt," on which it is based). Here too, however, the humor is highly ambiguous. The movement's atmosphere is slightly threatening, as is expressed by the drum solo's "call to attention" at the very beginning of the movement, which Mahler added at a relatively late stage[35] and what Mahler, in Bauer-Lechner's recollections, calls the "appalling shriek of this tortured soul" (*RGM*, 44; furchtbarer Aufschrei einer so gemarterten Seele: *GME*, 40) at the end. According to the Dresden program the movement is about a hero plagued by a "spirit of disbelief, of denial" (Geist des Unglaubens, der Verneinung; *GR*, 87). As such, it mirrors our interpretation of the "Fischpredigt" song: nature is chaotic and in movement; any attempt to read a moral message into it is futile (see chapter 2). Hans Heinrich Eggebrecht's primarily musicological reading of the movement confirms its emphasis on art's futility and the world's banality.[36]

The symphony's fourth movement stands in sharp contrast to the third. "Urlicht" (Primal Light), the text that Mahler uses for the fourth movement, is another *Wunderhorn* poem.[37] The song is about the symphony's protagonist's confrontation with a naive form of religion: in his notes for the Dresden performance Mahler writes that "the moving voice of naive faith sounds in his [the protagonist's] ear" (Die rührende Stimme des naiven Glaubens tönt an sein Ohr).[38] This is important, because Mahler makes it clear with his remark that the text and music are not meant to preach a return to a naive form of belief but are to be understood as a reminder of innocence lost, of times in which the protagonist of Mahler's symphony could still believe naively. Adolf Nowak has pointed out that "Urlicht" in an exemplary way illustrates Nietzsche's anthropological explanation of the origins of religion: heaven is a figment of the imagination, a product of rather mundane, earthly desires meant to counter human suffering.[39]

Read in the context of the essays by Lipiner and Wagner discussed above, "Urlicht" illustrates and questions art's symbolic function. The possibility of a return to a naive form of belief depends upon the symbolic function of nature. Only if we can read the rose — representing nature in general — as a symbol for a different order, another dimension, is it possible to believe in that order. The symphony's hero's reaching for the rose, for nature, describes humankind's longing for this other dimension: it is the rose that leads the protagonist to the wish to be somewhere else, "to be in heaven" (im Himmel sein) beyond humankind's "misery" (Not) and "torment" (Pein). Mahler, interestingly, breaks up the *Wunderhorn* poem into two parts: the first stanza articulates this longing for another dimension; the second stanza its fulfillment: the protagonist is confident that God will receive and redeem him. The two stanzas relate to each other as a symbol relates to what is symbolized, as signifier to signified. By breaking up the poem into two parts, Mahler constructs a rupture between them. With the second stanza he also introduces a new melody. It is unclear what the role of the second stanza is: does it articulate a premonition or vision, something the protagonist desires, or does it contain the realization of the desire articulated in the first stanza? In the second stanza, light — the other important symbol in the poem along with the rose — is associated with an act of revelation: through light the divine instance shows the way, reveals the road to blessed life. It is precisely this revelatory understanding of religion that Mahler questions in a comment on this work. In a letter to Alma, Mahler writes, in the context of discussing the Second Symphony, about his skepticism toward "all revelatory religions" (alle Offenbarungs-Religionen; *GR*, 102).[40]

How is it possible that the rose in "Urlicht" is symbolically associated with redemption? Within Western cultural history, the rose can be a symbol of love (Aphrodite), but, more specifically within Christianity, it can also be associated with Christ, his suffering, and the image of paradise.[41] The fact that the poem, however, problematizes such symbolism as much as it evokes it is particularly clear if we follow some of the intertextual connections associated with the "Urlicht" movement. "Urlicht" is one of the *Wunderhorn* poems that inspired one of Clemens Brentano's best-known novellas, the *Geschichte vom braven Kasperl und dem schönen Annerl* (The Story of Brave Kasperl and Lovely Annerl), first published in 1817.[42] In the story, it is through a red rose that one of the characters, the grandmother who also narrates most of the story, is recognized in church by her lover; she hopes the same will happen in the hereafter.[43] The story explains how a rose can turn into a symbol of life after death (although it remains an open question whether the grandmother indeed encounters her former husband in the hereafter). However, the story in many ways illustrates the arbitrariness and unreliability of such symbolic readings. The rose, for instance, that the grandmother attaches to Annerl's chest after she has been executed is not from her lover but rather from the man who seduced and impregnated her, using medications to make her forget her love for Kasperl (804, 806). The veil that was supposed to bring her pardon, instead ends up, the reader is told, symbolizing her honor — in a rather ambiguous way, one might add (804). Both Kasperl and Annerl strive to be honorable, but precisely in their striving both end up acting dishonorably (betraying father and stepbrother; suffocating a newborn child). This seems emblematic of the world of symbols in Brentano's text in general: nothing is what it seems; nothing symbolizes what it is supposed to symbolize.

There is another intertextual link in "Urlicht" that points to the arbitrary nature of symbols. In the piano version of the fourth movement of the Second Symphony, in between the well-known lines "O Röschen roth!" (Oh little red rose!) and "Der Mensch liegt in grösster Noth" (Man lies in deepest need), Mahler had another text printed in parentheses under the piano part:

(Star and flower! Spirit and gown!)
(Love and suffering! Time! Eternity!)

[(Stern und Blume! Geist und Kleid!)
(Lieb und Leid! Zeit! Ewigkeit!)][44]

Renate Stark-Voigt, who discovered this literary reference, which cannot be found in any other editions, has traced it to Clemens Brentano's *Märchen von Gockel, Hinkel und Gackeleia* (Fairy Tale of Gockel, Hinkel, and Gackeleia, first published in 1838).[45] The formula "O Stern und Blume, Geist und Kleid/ Lieb, Leid und Zeit und Ewigkeit!" is repeated many times in the fairy tale. Its origin is a maxim handed down to Hinkel, one of the fairy tale's protagonists, by her ancestors, ostensibly as a source of inspiration and wisdom, while in reality only offering a nonsensical listing of objects and concepts arbitrarily associated with each other.[46] The verses are meant to express a certain desire, and with it a philosophy of life. What the verses convey stands in diametrical opposition to the philosophy of the oriental seal makers — the antagonists in the story — whose deepest desires are also expressed in a maxim: "Youth and riches, all the goods of the world! — Money! — Money! — Money! — Money!" (Jugend und Reichtum, alle Güter der Welt! — Geld! — Geld! — Geld! — Geld!; 666). While Hinkel searches for spiritual values, the oriental seal makers, who embody an anti-Semitic stereotype, are looking for happiness in material things. Mahler's knowledge of this text — we know that he read it to his daughter Anna[47] — makes it perfectly clear that he was aware of the anti-Semitic dimension in Brentano's writings.

Such intertextual references confirm a reading of the fourth movement as an expression of humankind's longing for metaphysical orientation, but they also question the possibility of a return to a naive form of religious experience. After the third movement's emphasis on nature's chaos, the fourth movement articulates the impossibility of going back to a way of looking at nature as a symbolic representation of God's order, offering a variety of entirely nonsensical symbols in its stead. It is, however, not just through questioning the symbolic function that Mahler's movement debunks the functioning of religion. The text, as Martha Nussbaum has shown in her highly original reading of this movement, also points to the exclusive, restrictive nature of religious communities — personified by the angel who tries to reject the child attempting to enter heaven: "An angel came who wanted to reject me" (Da kam ein Engelein und wollte mich abweisen).[48] Mahler's ideal of community is, instead, inclusive in the sense that it is aware of and open to human diversity (see chapters 5 and 6).

Based on our interpretation of the Second Symphony thus far, the concept of religion underlying this symphony is closer to Lipiner's questioning attitude toward all manifestations of religion than to Wagner's attempt to reinstate an unambiguous form of religion (one that makes us forget about the arbitrary nature of all symbols) centered on the figure of Christ. And yet the fourth movement is not Mahler's final word on how or whether nature can be the foundation for a religious experience. A number of scholars have read the symphony's fifth and final movement as having something to do with Judaism. Martha Nussbaum, for instance, writes of the "distinctively Jewish picture of the afterlife" that the movement paints; it is a vision that mirrors what she describes as Judaism's "insistence on finding the worth and meaning of a life within history, in its choices and striving in this life" (641). Nussbaum's insight explains Leonard Bernstein's musicological observation that in the symphony's final movement Mahler mimics the sound of the shofar (ram's horn) used in synagogue services, by using off-stage horns.[49] Vladimir Karbusicky supports Bernstein, pointing out that the Jewish Museum in Prague houses about 500 shofars originally belonging to synagogues in Bohemia and Moravia.[50] For him, the apocalyptic imagery of the Second Symphony's final movement has roots in the Jewish world of the Old Testament, especially the Book of Daniel (198).

Such observations make it likely that Mahler had the Jewish cultural tradition in mind when he composed this music. In order to illustrate the idea that "worth and meaning" can only be found in the here and now, to use Nussbaum's formulation, Mahler did not delve further into Jewish tradition but went back to German literary history to arrive at the same insight. Mahler chose the poem "Die Auferstehung" (The Resurrection) by Friedrich Gottlieb Klopstock (1724–1803) as the literary point of departure for this last movement. Although Klopstock belonged to the generation of the Enlightenment, his own sympathies were clearly with Pietism — a radical Protestant movement dating back to the seventeenth century, which sought a renewal of religion and defined religion primarily as an inward experience, independent of revelation, religious tradition (with the exception of reading the Bible), or the church as an institution. Even though there is a tension between the Enlightenment and Pietism, it is fair to say that Pietism aimed for a clearly modern form of religion and was therefore often at odds not only with institutionalized religion but also, to some extent, with society's institutions in general. Klopstock's importance for German literary history consists of his abandoning any system of poetological rules along with developing a subjective vocabulary that enabled an innovative way of interpreting the world, considered revolutionary by his contemporaries.[51]

Through its thematic focus on resurrection, Klopstock's poem "Die Auferstehung" is associated with his most famous work, the epic poem *Der Messias* (The Messiah, first published between 1748 and 1773). What is unusual about *Der Messias* is that all creatures are forgiven and redeemed, also those suffering in hell, something that was a decisively anti-orthodox, progressive position within eighteenth-century theology.[52] While Mahler, in his adaptation of Klopstock's poem, refrains from explicit references to biblical accounts of the last judgment, his Dresden program for the symphony, and in particular the discussion of the fifth movement, quite explicitly adopts apocalyptical imagery: the last judgment is announced, the dead rise from their graves and are summoned before God. In sharp contrast to New Testament accounts, however (see Matthew 13: 40–43; 25: 31–34, 41, 46), there is no separation of the virtuous and the wicked, the pious and the sinners:

> And look: there is no judgment — There is no sinner, no righteous man — no great and no small man — There is no punishment and no reward! An almighty feeling of love illumines us with blessed knowing and being!

> [Und siehe da: Es ist kein Gericht — Es ist kein Sünder, kein Gerechter — kein Großer und kein Kleiner — Es ist nicht Strafe und nicht Lohn! Ein allmächtiges Liebesgefühl durchleuchtet uns mit seligem Wissen und Sein. (*GR, 89*)][53]

In spite of Mahler's use of religious imagery, one can say that in this programmatic statement he deconstructs as much as he constructs a religious framework. What Mahler presents in his program here alludes to the Nietzschean transformation of tragedy into joy (also articulated in the text of the poem itself, as we will see) that left its traces in Lipiner's essay. But beyond that, the ideal world that Mahler portrays, in the end, is a world beyond good and evil — another leitmotif in Nietzsche's thinking — and one in which human differences no longer matter. But how is it possible to arrive at such a philosophy of life?

While the first two stanzas of Klopstock's "Die Auferstehung" and Mahler's adaptation of this poem are more or less identical,[54] the remainder of the text Mahler used for the last movement of the Second Symphony is written entirely by Mahler. In the first two stanzas, Klopstock compares the "dust" (Staub) that is left over from the human body after death (first stanza) to grain that is collected to be sown and to produce a new harvest (second stanza). In doing so, Klopstock's poem offers a relatively conventional example of the symbolic use of nature imagery:

one thing symbolizes another. It is at this point that Mahler breaks with Klopstock's text. While Klopstock goes on, in the third stanza, to praise God — "Day of God!" (Du meines Gottes Tag!) — and mentions Jesus, Mahler avoids mentioning either one. This omission of the Jesus figure is one indication that Mahler's priorities are quite different from those of Wagner, for whom Jesus was the pivotal symbol in "Religion und Kunst," as discussed above. Mahler in fact does not mention God until the very last line of the last stanza of his adaptation. Instead he describes the effect of the second stanza's image on his protagonist as a self-admonishment to believe in the continued existence of things: "Oh believe, my heart, oh believe: / Nothing will be lost for you" (O glaube, mein Herz! O glaube: / Es geht dir nichts verloren!). In other words, Mahler describes the process of symbolization: how something, in this case an image from nature, can mean something else. It describes this process as a dynamic act: the text is about the *desire* to read something into nature; but at the same moment it makes clear that any attempt to read something into nature is a subjective act and that nature does not provide any stable symbolic order. What Mahler alludes to here is a dynamic, cyclical understanding of nature: "What has come into existence must perish! / What has perished [must] rise again!" (Was entstanden ist, das muss vergehen! / Was vergangen, auferstehen!). As unlikely as it may seem, for those who read these lines in the context of fin-de-siècle Vienna, there is also an echo of a Nietzschean idea here. The *"thought of eternal recurrence"* (der *Ewige-Wiederkunfts-Gedanke*) is one of Nietzsche's most foundational ideas, which also underlies his criticism of religion.[55] Because nature is cyclical and chaotic instead of linear, it is not possible to use nature as evidence of a benevolent creator-God.

To attempt, after Nietzsche, to find in nature a basis for some form of existential orientation, one must acknowledge this insight in the cyclical, unstable essence of nature. It is precisely nature's inability to signify anything, its lack of stability, that becomes the basis for a new relationship to nature. And, as Lipiner's ideas on pantheism in his essay on the renewal of religious ideas show, the insight that we are all part of nature can be the foundation for a new, post-metaphysical ethics — one that acknowledges Nietzsche's critique of metaphysics while also picking up on the reconstructive component in his thinking. For Mahler, the image of nature's cyclical quintessence, nature's eternal back-and-forth movement between destruction and creation, turns into an image that can help us understand and explain human emotions: after death comes love; death is "defeated" (bezwungen) by love ("in love's ardent pursuit / I will drift away"; in heißem Liebesstreben / werd' ich entschweben). One misunderstands these lines, I believe, if one reads an opposition between the material and spiritual world into them. The message is rather that both pain (Schmerz) and love are emotional states, and that in their emotions humans find an anticipation of what is valuable in life. It is not a statement about life after death but rather a philosophy of how to lead one's life that the symphony espouses: "Stop trembling! / Be prepared to live!" (Hör auf zu beben! / Bereite dich zu leben!). The fact that we find something positive in our negative emotions — the message behind the symphony's most famous line, "I will die to live!" (Sterben werd' ich, um zu leben!) — is reminiscent of Nietzsche's interpretation of Aristotle's theory of catharsis. Tragedy can have a cleansing function; through awareness of life's tragic essence, humankind can find a new optimism associated with the insight that humans are part of a larger whole. "Love," here as in the second movement of Mahler's Eighth (associated with striving), is the central emotion in the stanzas that Mahler added to Klopstock's materials.

It is the awareness of nature's perpetual back-and-forth between destruction (death) and creation (love) that makes it possible to overcome humankind's solipsistic individualism. Emotions play a crucial role in the Second Symphony. It is through feelings that human beings can not only make sense of nature but also intuit a sense of communality and value. Mahler has very much the pantheistic vision of Lipiner's essay in mind here that Lipiner saw illustrated in the Memoirs of Malwina von Meysenbug. Mahler's text does not create new symbols — certainly not in the form of a hierarchical order of things that is normative and beyond history — but is rather interested in symbolic thinking as a modality, as a means of approaching nature and the world. Rather than establishing one central symbol to which all our perceptions of the world are to be subordinated, Lipiner's text and Mahler's Second Symphony point to an ongoing and infinite process of symbolization. In the context of her discussion of Mahler's music, Martha Nussbaum speaks of musical works' ability, on basis of their emotional core, "to embody the idea of our urgent need for and attachment to things outside ourselves that we do not control" (272). Interpreted in this way, the Second Symphony's last movement offers not only a philosophy of life that finds in an aesthetic sensibility a substitute ethics for a postmetaphysical age, but implicitly also an aesthetic agenda that legitimizes the kind of work of art that lives off its emotional impact. In many respects, the finale of the Second Symphony with its religious imagery prefigures the second movement of the Eighth Symphony (see chapter 5). But it is in the Third Symphony that Mahler works out his ideas on nature in greater detail.

Nature — Symphony No. 3

Nowhere in Mahler's oeuvre is the importance of Nietzsche as clear as in his Third Symphony. The symphony was originally to have the title "Die fröhliche Wissenschaft" (The Gay Science), after Nietzsche's 1882 book of the same title. For the symphony's fourth movement Mahler set to music a poem from Nietzsche's *Also sprach Zarathustra* (for the fifth movement he again used a *Wunderhorn* song). Mahler also left us an abundance of (anti-)programmatic statements for this work in which Nietzschean ideas figure prominently. These statements are important, even though Mahler eventually decided, as he did with the First Symphony, not to have performances accompanied by a "program." Furthermore, William McGrath has pointed out that Mahler in the first movement of his Third Symphony used the melody of a student song, "Wir hatten gebauet ein stattliches Haus" (We had built a stately house) for the opening theme — a song that was sung on the occasion of the government's suppression in 1878 of the *Leseverein der deutschen Studenten*, the conservative, pro-German nationalist organization in which members of the Pernerstorfer Circle played a leading role (and where Lipiner gave his talk on the necessity of a renewal of religion).[56] Such an autobiographical reference is intriguing but somewhat speculative and its contribution to a better understanding of the symphony can only remain fragmentary, since it is not possible to read the entire symphony as an autobiographical narrative. What is significant, however, is that it links the symphony to the literary and philosophical interests of Mahler and his student friends in the late 1870s.

While working on the Third Symphony in the summer of 1895, when he composed all its movements except the first, Mahler repeatedly wrote to his friends about the program he intended to accompany his new symphony. The most comprehensive version of this program was outlined on a separate sheet accompanying a letter to Friedrich Löhr, one of the friends with whom he had stayed in touch since his student days:

Symphony No. III.
»THE GAY SCIENCE«
A SUMMER MORNING'S DREAM

I. Summer marches in.
II. What the flowers in the meadow tell me.
III. What the animals in the woods tell me.
IV. What the night tells me. (Contralto solo).
V. What the morning bells tell me.
(Women's choir with contralto solo).
VI. What love tells me.
Motto: »Father, look at my wounds!
Let no creature be lost«!
(From The Youth's Magic Horn)
VII. Heavenly life.
(Soprano solo, with humor).

[Symphonie Nro. III.
»DIE FRÖHLICHE WISSENSCHAFT«
EIN SOMMERMORGENTRAUM

I. Der Sommer marschiert ein.
II. Was mir die Blumen auf der Wiese erzählen.
III. Was mir die Tiere im Walde erzählen.
IV. Was mir die Nacht erzählt. (Altsolo).
V. Was mir die Morgenglocken erzählen.
(Frauenchor mit Altsolo).
VI. Was mir die Liebe erzählt.
Motto: »Vater sieh an die Wunden mein!
Kein Wesen laß verloren sein«!
(Aus des Knaben Wunderhorn)
VII. Das himmlische Leben.
(Sopransolo, humoristisch).][57]

At this stage Mahler was planning a seven-movement symphony. When he wrote this letter, he intended to include a seventh movement, "Das himmlische Leben," which he later used for the Fourth Symphony. Mahler's plans acknowledge Nietzsche's importance for the symphony in a number of ways. Most importantly, there is the symphony's title, "Die fröhliche Wissenschaft." Furthermore, there is the fact that he used a text from *Also sprach Zarathustra* in the fourth movement. And finally, in a letter written a few months later to Natalie Bauer-Lechner, Mahler says he is still unsure about the first movement's title; he is considering "Procession of Dionysos" (Zug des Dionysos) — a clear reference to *Die Geburt der Tragödie* — or "Summer marches in" (*RGM*, 41; Sommer marschiert ein: *GME*, 37–38).[58] Without a doubt, this Nietzschean subtext is important to Mahler, but it seems strangely at odds with other elements of the symphony's program, in particular its view of nature. Surprisingly, Nietzsche does not figure very prominently in scholarship on this work. One reason may be that it is hard to reconcile the Nietzschean references with other programmatic statements on it by Mahler, in particular those emphasizing the importance of nature for the symphony. But what concept of nature does Mahler advance here?

Here too, Mahler himself contributed to the confusion about his symphony. Twice in his letters, he talks about the Third Symphony as a comprehensive tableau of nature, understood in a hierarchical sense. In the above-mentioned letter to Friedrich Löhr, Mahler characterizes the second, third, fourth, and fifth movements as expressing a "chain of being" (Stufenreihe der Wesen; *Br*, 150). In a letter to Anna von Mildenburg that he wrote a year later, in the summer of 1896 while he was working on the first movement, Mahler speaks of "all stages of development in gradual progression" (alle Stufen der Entwicklung in schrittweiser Steigerung) — a thought he clarifies by pointing out that the symphony "starts with lifeless nature and builds up to the love of God" (Es beginnt bei der leblosen Natur und steigert sich bis zur Liebe Gottes! *Br,* 189–90; see also *GME,* 56; *RGM,* 58–59). In contrast to the earlier version of the program, now the first and last movements are included in the developmental hierarchy. Mahler's concept of nature here is hierarchical, developmental, and linear. This idea of a hierarchical order of nature, a "chain of being," has a long tradition in Western thinking and has always had a strong religious dimension: in the order of nature, God's wisdom showed itself.[59] Such thinking was by no means obsolete in the nineteenth century; the evolutionary patterns in nature that Darwin had described in *On the Origin of Species* (1859) and *The Descent of Man* (1871) are still to some extent indebted to the model of a "chain of being," even though, from the eighteenth century onward, the idea is given a scientific and chronological interpretation.[60] And yet it is clearly not a rigorous exercise in natural history that Mahler presents here — "angels" or "God" as a category in nature's hierarchy? — but rather a free-floating poetic improvisation on the question of what nature may mean to humankind.

If the Third Symphony's message, a depiction of the hierarchical order of nature, was relatively straightforward, why is Mahler concerned about it being misunderstood? Mahler repeatedly expresses doubt that critics and the public will truly understand his intentions with the symphony, in particular its humor (*Br,* 190). From the outset, "humor" was an important element in its design.[61] But what does Mahler mean when he refers to the symphony's humorous side? Interestingly, when explaining the symphony's humor to Bruno Walter, Mahler seems to have a very different concept of nature in mind: "Friends of a good joke will find the wanderings I am preparing for them very amusing" (Freunde eines gesunden Spaßes [werden] die Spaziergänge, die ich ihnen da bereite, sehr amüsant finden; *Br,* 190). To characterize the symphony as a series of "wanderings" (Spaziergänge) seems to preclude the kind of developmental and hierarchical reading proposed in the symphony's programmatic notes. Here and elsewhere, Mahler alludes to a much less rational view of nature in relation to the symphony.

Mahler also deals with the question of the extent to which audiences and critics will understand this symphony correctly in a letter to musicologist Richard Batka. In it, he writes of his fear that the semi-evolutionary depiction of nature in the symphony might stand in the way of an appreciation of the symphony's multi-layered message:

> That this nature [in the Third Symphony] harbors everything, whether eerie, great or charming (exactly what I wanted to articulate in the entire work through a kind of evolutionary development) — nobody experiences that of course. It always strikes me as strange that most

people, when they talk about "nature," only think of flowers, birds, and the smell of the woods, etc. Nobody knows the god Dionysos or the great Pan. So there you have already a kind of program — that is, an example of how I make music. It is always and everywhere only the sound of nature!

[Daß diese Natur alles in sich birgt, was an Schauerlichem, Großem und auch Lieblichem ist (eben das wollte ich in dem ganzen Werk in einer Art evolutionistischer Entwicklung zum Aussprechen bringen), davon erfährt natürlich niemand etwas. Mich berührt es ja immer seltsam, daß die meisten, wenn sie von »Natur« sprechen, nur immer an Blumen, Vöglein, Waldesduft etc. denken. Den Gott Dionysos, den großen Pan kennt niemand. So: da haben Sie schon eine Art Programm — d.h. eine Probe, wie ich Musik mache. Sie ist immer und überall nur Naturlaut!][62]

The fact that Mahler writes of "a kind of evolutionary development" is interesting, because it shows the impact that developments in natural history and biology (Darwin) had on Mahler's thinking. His criticism in this fragment concerns not just the reception of his own music but, more broadly, how nature is seen by his contemporaries. Humankind has a tendency to objectify nature (flowers, birds, and so on), but that is not what should interest us about nature. Mahler wants to experience "nature as a whole" (Natur als Ganzes; *Br*, 203), and not just in fragments, as he states later in the same letter. Instead of an objective or a quasi-scientific view of nature, he is interested in nature as a source of subjective experiences that may assign both positive and negative characteristics to it. Such a subjective way of experiencing nature for Mahler does not necessarily contradict a developmental view of nature (hence the semi-evolutionary organization of the symphony), but it does contrast with a tendency to perceive nature only in the form of distinct entities. Dionysos is mentioned as an example for an alternative way of looking at nature; this is in line with Nietzsche's *Geburt der Tragödie*, in which Apollo stands for rational and scientific knowledge, but Dionysos is associated with intuitive, subjective modes of experiencing the world.

The other mythological figure mentioned in Mahler's letter to Batka is Pan. Pan is brought up frequently in Mahler's deliberations on this symphony from the summer of 1896 onward (and appears to assume the place Dionysos had held before that). For instance, Mahler considers the title "Pan awakening" (Pan erwacht) in combination with "der Sommer marschiert ein" as titles for a first movement of the symphony, consisting of two parts (*Br*, 191; see also 196). At one point he also thinks about naming the entire symphony "Pan," whom he identifies as the "ancient Greek god who later would be identified with the universe" (die altgriechische Gottheit, die später zum Inbegriff des "Alls" geworden; *Br*,

192–93). Like Dionysos, to whom Mahler compares him in his letter to Batka, Pan stands for the subjective experience of nature in ancient Greek mythology. As a mythological figure he represents nature's demonic and uncanny aspects; he is one of the "satyrs and other such rough children of nature" (Satyrn und derlei derbe Naturgesellen) mentioned by Mahler in a conversation about this work with Natalie Bauer-Lechner (*GME*, 56; *RGM*, 59). Mahler's references to Pan are interesting for other reasons. Pan is associated with music through the "pan flute." When Pan was thwarted in his attempt to seduce the nymph Syrinx, because the gods changed her into river reeds to protect her from him, Pan decided to make a flute out of these reeds after hearing the wind blow through them and produce a melody.[63] Pan, in other words, stands for nature's ability to produce music without human interference. This aspect may have interested Mahler, since in his description of the genesis of the Third Symphony he also tended to emphasize how small a role he himself played in it. In a letter to Anna von Mildenburg in which he writes about the composition of this work, for instance, he states, "one is oneself, as it were, only an instrument, on which the universe makes music" (man ist, sozusagen, selbst nur ein Instrument, auf dem das Universum spielt"; *Br*, 187; see also *GME*, 56; *RGM*, 59). It is also noteworthy in this context that "Pan" is etymologically associated with "pantheism," as Lipiner notes in his essay on religion.[64]

Interestingly, the human perception of nature, and in particular the values we attribute to nature, are also a major topic in Nietzsche's *Die fröhliche Wissenschaft* (The Gay Science), the text that was originally to have provided the Third Symphony with a title. This programmatic reference has also been questioned.[65] What does Nietzsche's *Fröhliche Wissenschaft* tell us about nature? The core of *Die fröhliche Wissenschaft* consists of 383 numbered aphoristic fragments, loosely organized around certain topics. The book is best known for the phrase "God is dead" (*GS*, 109; Gott ist todt: *SW* 3:467). While, as in all texts by Nietzsche, in *Die fröhliche Wissenschaft* there is a fair amount of criticism of the church as an institution and its impact on the lives of citizens, the text's main aim lies elsewhere: it wants to show how metaphysical principles have infiltrated Western thinking in unexpected areas, such as the sciences. In particular, nature has been used to provide humankind with a purpose; the first fragment is accordingly titled "*The teachers of the purpose of existence*" (*GS*, 27–29; Die Lehrer vom Zwecke der Menschheit: *SW* 3:369–72). In Nietzsche's analysis, humankind's attitude toward nature is driven by a desire to read something into nature that is fundamentally not there. This thought is developed in fragment no. 109, immediately following the famous fragment no. 108 announcing the death of God. In fragment no. 109, Nietzsche writes of the error in thinking that the world is like an organism: "The total character of the world . . . is for all eternity chaos" (Der Gesammt-Charakter der Welt ist . . . in alle Ewigkeit Chaos); any attempt to find order is aesthetic and anthropomorphic (*SW* 3:468; *GS,* 109).[66] Nietzsche is very skeptical regarding attempts to read a teleology into nature. Humankind is not in any way associated with the purpose or endpoint of nature, even though it is very much part of the natural world.

And yet this insight into nature's chaotic essence and lack of purpose, other than an elementary will to survive (*SW* 3:369; *GS,* 27), is not Nietzsche's final answer. The title of Nietzsche's text is indicative of its agenda. In *Die fröhliche Wissenschaft* Nietzsche is interested in recapturing a sense of humor: humankind needs to learn to "laugh at itself" (*GS,* 27; ueber sich selber lachen: *SW* 3:370). On the one hand, this laughter is to be understood as a criticism of the "serious" scientific search for truth; on the other hand, it is also the expression of a "sense of truth" (*GS,* 27; Wahrheitssinn: *SW* 3:370). In other words, while being aware of the futile and therefore tragic nature of our search for "truth," since nature is chaotic, our own truthfulness paradoxically forces us to acknowledge the relativity of a search for meaning in nature. As in *Die Geburt der Tragödie*, comedy is born out of tragedy. In a number of fragments Nietzsche points to art as an antidote to science's seriousness. By asserting its "*freedom over things*" (*Freiheit über den Dingen*), art can counteract the "delusion and error" (Unwahrheit und Verlogenheit) of science (fragment 107, *SW* 3:464–65; *GS,* 104). What is needed is a higher synthesis that unites art and the "practical wisdom of life" (praktische Weisheit des Lebens) with science (fragment 113, *SW* 3:474; *GS,* 114). Humans capable of contemplation — that is, artists and intellectuals, among whom Nietzsche also counts himself — distinguish themselves through their ability to see and hear more than others. More specifically, they are able to create order where it does not really exist. One of the examples Nietzsche mentions in this context is, interestingly, "scales" (*GS,* 171 Stufenleitern: *SW* 3:540). Contemplative humans conceive of value where nature intrinsically has no value, and thus they are able to create a world "*that concerns human beings*" (*GS,* 171; *die den Menschen etwas angeht*: fragment 301, *SW* 3:540). Unfortunately, such a world can only exist momentarily before it eludes the contemplative person, who is forced to realize the futility of making the effort.

Nietzsche's attitude toward any attempt to interpret nature can therefore be described as highly skeptical, albeit not without ambiguity. Mahler's use of "Die fröhliche Wissenschaft" as a title for the Third Symphony in its early version, the references to Dionysos in the early version of its program, and the reference to Pan in its later versions all seem to indicate that Mahler shared some of Nietzsche's skepticism, and in this work was more interested in a chaotic, intuitive understanding of nature than in a rational, quasi-evolutionary view. But how does the symphony express this, if not through the program originally intended to accompany it? In this context, it is useful to look at the texts Mahler chose for the fourth and fifth movements, and also at some of the programmatic deliberations accompanying the final, sixth movement of the symphony.

For the fourth movement Mahler set to music a text from *Also sprach Zarathustra* (1883–85). Here, as in the Jean-Paul-inspired programs accompanying the First Symphony, Mahler promises to resolve one programmatic reference (the symphony's projected title "Die fröhliche Wissenschaft") by referring to another Nietzsche text (a poem from *Also sprach Zarathustra*). However, in this case there is a clear connection between the two texts. Nietzsche worked on both texts simultaneously and the figure of Zarathustra is even mentioned in Fragment 342 of *Die fröhliche Wissenschaft* (*SW* 3:571; *GS*, 195), which was originally the last fragment of the book. This fragment is more or less identical to the first section of the "Prologue" in *Also sprach Zarathustra* (*SW* 4:11–12; *TSZ*, 3). Stylistically there are great differences between *Also sprach Zarathustra* and Nietzsche's other works. It is Nietzsche's most poetic text, characterized by an exuberant but largely hermetic imagery.[67] The text is organized around the prophetic/messianic figure named Zarathustra, who is loosely based on the ancient Persian priest and prophet Zarathustra or Zoroaster, founder of Zoroastrianism, one of the oldest documented religions. More than in any other text, in *Zarathustra* Nietzsche is interested in translating his epistemology into a vision of how one should live one's life without succumbing to outdated metaphysical certainties. I will argue that it was precisely this "ethical" vision in Nietzsche's text that attracted Mahler and led him to use it for his Third Symphony.

In early versions of the program of the Third Symphony, for instance in the letter to Löhr discussed above, the fourth movement was entitled "What the night tells me" (Was mir die Nacht erzählt), although in his letter Mahler made it clear that this movement was meant to be about "*man*" (der *Mensch*; *Br*, 150). In later versions the movement is simply called "What man tells me" (Was mir der Mensch erzählt; see *Br*, 188 and 196). Thus the fourth movement introduces humankind into the symphony, but the text Mahler uses does not portray man as an integral, organic part of nature, as the earlier program accompanying the letter to Löhr would suggest, but rather as a creature at nature's margins.[68] The text that Mahler chose for the fourth movement is one of the key texts in *Also sprach Zarathustra*. It can be found in the penultimate chapter of book 3, where it is called "The Other Dance Song" (*TSZ*, 183–84; Das andere Tanzlied: *SW* 4:285–86) and again in the penultimate chapter of book 4, where it is called "The Sleepwalker Song" (*TSZ*, 264; Das Nachtwandler-Lied: *SW* 4:404). We find Zarathustra alone — illustrative of the fact that he is not the living example of the new way of life but only its prophet (*SW* 4:277; *TSZ*, 178) — at midnight. The fact that Mahler chose what is informally known as Zarathustra's "midnight song" (Mitternachtslied) for this symphony is interesting in the context of other programmatic deliberation on it. It creates a marked contrast to the original subtitle for the symphony: "A Summer Morning's Dream" (Ein Sommermorgentraum), later changed to "A Summer Noon's dream" (Ein Sommermittagstraum; *Br*, 188 and 196). With the introduction of humankind, a fundamentally different way of looking at reality enters the symphony: day is replaced by night, consciousness by the irrational or intuitive. The fourth movement, it seems, is diametrically opposed to what the symphony as a whole wants.

In Nietzsche's text too, Zarathustra's song articulates a moment of transition; it indicates a shift in Zarathustra's attitudes. It unites radically diverging impulses, characteristic of Zarathustra being torn between different worlds. Zarathustra in his dream-like state anticipates another, deeper way of experiencing reality, of which he himself cannot really be a part, but the (momentary) experience of which he can communicate to his followers. In "Das Nachtwandler-Lied," we find Zarathustra soliloquizing. The first two lines of the poem address humankind in an imaginary conversation, while in the rest of the text Zarathustra engages into a conversation with the night-side of his personality. The song captures Zarathustra at a stage between sleep and wakefulness. Precisely because Zarathustra is between two states of consciousness, he is able to grasp a deeper truth and bring to the surface an insight that goes beyond what we think possible in broad daylight: "The world is deep! / And deeper than day thought possible!" (Die Welt ist tief! / Und tiefer als der Tag gedacht!). The wisdom that Zarathustra has found has something to do with the complexity of emotions: the deepest despair can turn into something positive; out of pessimism can come an affirmative attitude toward life. To be more precise, Nietzsche's "Nachtwandler-Lied" articulates a moment of healing: a deeply negative experience of "pain" and "heartache" (Weh, Herzeleid), turns into something positive: "pleasure" and "eternity" (Lust, Ewigkeit) — very much like Nietzsche's interpretation of Aristotle's theory of catharsis in *Die Geburt der Tragödie*. Pleasure and pain are deeply intertwined; it is impossible to strive for pleasure without experiencing pain.[69]

Critics have been astonished by Mahler's juxtaposition of Nietzsche's rather dark and introverted text in the fourth movement with a seemingly innocuous and superficial *Wunderhorn* song, the "Armer Kinder Bettlerlied" (Poor Children's Begging Song).[70] The affirmative attitude, to which the Nietzsche text alluded, now seems fully articulated. A textual reading, however, should be skeptical of the song's seemingly innocuous or optimistic message. For one thing, the song's title, "Armer Kinder Bettlerlied," should make us question the song's religious message: is this what these children really believe, or does the song articulate what they think their audiences, those who are supposed to give them money, would like to hear? At moments, the song anticipates the joyful irreverence toward the Christian tradition that articulates itself fully in the final movement of the Fourth Symphony. And yet the song is perhaps less naive than one would believe at first glance. It is very much about isolation and the longing for community. Mahler created continuity between the Nietzsche text and the *Wunderhorn* setting by allowing the contralto who sang the "Nachtwandler-Lied" in the fourth movement to sing the part of Saint Peter in the "Armer Kinder Bettlerlied" in the fifth movement. It is, in other words, Nietzsche's protagonist longing for community — he who has "broken the Ten Commandments"(übertreten die zehn Gebot) — whom we are facing here again. But how are we to understand the religious message at the end of the song, the promise of "heavenly joy" (himmlische Freud) and "beatitude" (Seligkeit)?

The promise of heaven is not necessarily the poem's ideology or final answer, but rather part of an exchange. Through his setting of the *Wunderhorn* text, by assigning individual lines to either contralto or choir, Mahler makes explicit the dialogue that remained implicit in von Arnim and Brentano's *Wunderhorn* text. The dialogue allows Mahler to stage a clash of emotions. St. Peter's words articulate guilt and sadness, while the choir speaks of religious confidence and happiness. But does the song resolve this clash of convictions? I would argue that it does not. The contralto, for instance, does not join the choir in its last stanza; it is therefore not clear whether she has become part of the collective and shares its view of life. But the question of the function the boys' choir's "Bimm, bamm, bimm, bam . . ." has in relation to the dialogue should also be addressed.

Commenting on a friend's criticism of the abrupt transition between the fourth and fifth movements, Mahler speaks about the fifth movement's humor, which he was afraid would not be understood: "Humor must be put in here for what is highest, which can no longer be expressed in any other way" (*RGM*, 60; Der Humor hier [muß] nur für das Höchste einsetzen, das anders nicht mehr auszudrücken ist": *GME*, 57, trans. modified). What intrigues me about this quote is Mahler's statement that his ideal "can no longer" be articulated. This suggests to me that it should be read in the context of Nietzsche's critique of metaphysics. Understood in a negative way, humor points to the insight that the old metaphysical truths no longer hold. However, for Nietzsche humor can also be something positive; it can be indicative of a basic joy of life. Humor and laughter are important topics not just in *Die fröhliche Wissenschaft* but also in the fourth and last part of Nietzsche's *Zarathustra*. In a chapter entitled "The Welcome" (Die Begrüssung), Zarathustra is searching for "*the higher human*" (*der höhere Mensch*), whom Nietzsche defines in a number of ways, among them as "someone to make you laugh again" (*TSZ*, 226; Einer, der euch wieder lachen macht: *SW* 4:47, trans. modified). At the end of the chapter it becomes clear that for Zarathustra children best represent this ideal of higher human beings (*SW* 4:351; *TSZ*, 229–30). Zarathustra is driven by a longing not for his fellow human beings but for news about his children. Children find reasons to laugh where others don't; the lack of laughter is equated with a lack of love (*SW* 4:365; *TSZ*, 238). In the same context, Zarathustra stresses that humans need to learn to laugh about themselves (*SW* 4:364, 367, and 387; *TSZ*, 238, 240, and 253).

The importance of the image of the child for Zarathustra's intellectual cosmos is clear at the beginning of *Also sprach Zarathustra*. In the first chapter following the prologues, entitled "On the Three Metamorphoses" (Von den drei Verwandlungen), Zarathustra speaks of the "three metamorphoses of the spirit . . .: how the spirit becomes a camel, and the camel a lion, and finally the lion a child" (*TSZ*, 16; drei Verwandlungen . . .: wie der Geist zum Kameele wird, und zum Löwen das Kameel, und zum Kinde zuletzt der Löwe: *SW* 4:29). The camel stands as a symbol for human beings who have no trouble kneeling down and carrying the weight of others (*SW* 4:243; *TSZ*, 154). The lion represents the exact opposite of this attitude; he represents protest and is associated with assertiveness and the revival of humankind's vital instincts (see *SW* 4:385, and 406–7; *TSZ*, 251, 265–66). By far the most complex symbol is that of the child. At the end of "On the Three Metamorphoses" Zarathustra seeks to clarify the complex associations one can have with children: "The child is innocence and forgetting, a new beginning, a game, a wheel rolling out of itself, a first movement, a sacred yes-saying" (*TSZ*, 17; Unschuld ist das Kind und Vergessen, ein Neubeginnen, ein Spiel, ein aus sich rollendes Rad, eine erste Bewegung, ein heiliges Ja-sagen: *SW* 4:31). The important thing, for Nietzsche, is that children represent an affirmative attitude toward life, an innocent beginning of something new that is simultaneously an act of forgetting, that is instinctive and not rationally planned; children are also associated with play.[71]

Scholars have been baffled by Mahler's use of religious imagery in the fifth movement of the Third Symphony, because it seems to constitute a clear break with the *Zarathustra* text in the fourth movement and with Nietzsche's anti-Christian philosophical agenda in general; in fact, this has been one reason to doubt Mahler's Nietzschean agenda in this work.[72] When returning to the symbol of the child at the end of book 4 of *Also sprach Zarathustra*, in the section just before the "Nachtwandler-Lied," Nietzsche himself somewhat surprisingly uses religious imagery to express his thoughts. He wishes the people assembled around him to be "pious" (fromm) again, so "that at last you did again as children do, namely prayed, folded your hands and said 'dear God!'" (*TSZ*, 257; dass ihr endlich wieder thatet wie Kinder thun, nämlich betetet, händefaltetet und 'lieber Gott' sagtet!; *SW* 4:393). In reference to the Gospel of Matthew (18:3) Zarathustra preaches: "Unless you become as little children, you shall not enter *that* kingdom of Heaven" (*TSZ*, 257; So ihr nicht werdet wie die Kinderlein, so kommt ihr nicht in *das* Himmelreich; *SW* 4:393). How are we to understand this? Is this a possible example of irony in Nietzsche's text? Does Zarathustra intentionally send his followers in the wrong direction?

What argues against an ironic interpretation is that prayer constitutes an example of what at the beginning of *Also sprach Zarathustra* was called children's "sacred yes-saying" (*TSZ*, 17; heiliges Ja-sagen: *SW* 4:31), their affirmative attitude toward life — something Nietzsche clearly saw as positive. What makes an ironic interpretation even more unlikely is that, at the end of the fragment, Zarathustra adds something: he is not interested in heaven but in *"the kingdom of the earth"* (*TSZ*, 257; *das Erdenreich*: *SW* 4:393), indicating nothing less than a complete reversal of Christianity's focus on the hereafter. Here, as in the Second Symphony, religious imagery is not meant to convert to a religious worldview but rather as cultural material expressive of worldly wisdom, for which language possesses very few alternative modes of communication (a problem that will return in the second movement of the Eighth Symphony). Through the image of the child, humankind can find its way back to a revitalized way of living. Tragic denial of life is turned into its opposite: the affirmation of life, as Nietzsche envisioned it. Children's humor and their ability to laugh stand for the ability to see the relativity of things, to have a playful outlook on life combined with an affirmative attitude and a new sense of community. This is the meaning of the children's choir's "Bimm bamm" accompanying the text of the Third Symphony's fifth movement.

The juxtaposition of Zarathustra's "Nachtwandler-Lied" and the children's song from *Des Knaben Wunderhorn* is not a random combination but the result of a deliberate decision by Mahler that follows the ideas underlying the last book of Nietzsche's *Zarathustra*. The importance of the child as a symbol of something is also clear from the fact that Mahler originally intended to end his Third Symphony with a seventh movement, which in some of the symphony's intended programs carries the title "What the child tells me" (Was mir das Kind erzählt; *Br*, 150), after the *Wunderhorn* song on which it is based, "Heavenly Life" (Das himmlische Leben). This movement would eventually become the last movement of the Fourth Symphony.

Mahler decided to let the Third Symphony end with a movement about love. As in Nietzsche's *Die fröhliche Wissenschaft*, humor is not the final answer in this work. Mahler wanted to offer a philosophy of life here, albeit one that is decisively post-metaphysical. Its final Adagio is a hymn to love, not to compassion, as Wagner had it in *Parsifal;* there "Mitleid" (compassion) plays a major role.[73] In his *Zarathustra*, Nietzsche was highly critical of such an ethics. In fact, at the very end of the book, "Mitleid" is what threatens to endanger Zarathustra's philosophy (see *SW*

3:323; *GS*, 210). Love functions as an alternative to compassion, which at one point is called Zarathustra's final sin (*SW* 4:301; *TSZ*, 194). This polemic against compassion is characteristic of many of Nietzsche's writings after his break with Wagner. In the last book of *Zarathustra*, love replaces compassion, or to be more precise, compassion has evolved into love. That is how I would understand Zarathustra's statement: "All creators are hard, all great love is above pitying" (*TSZ*, 215; alle Schaffenden sind hart, alle grosse Liebe ist über ihrem Mitleiden: *SW* 4:330–31; see also *TSZ*, 69; *SW* 4:115).

Nietzsche's *Also sprach Zarathustra* gives us some indication as to how Mahler may have understood "love" in his Third Symphony. But what kind of love does Mahler have in mind? In the manuscript score of 1896, the last movement has a somewhat enigmatic motto: "Father look upon my wounds! / Let no creature be lost!" (Vater sieh an die Wunden mein! Kein Wesen laß verloren sein!)[74] — a motto that Mahler claims, in his letter to Löhr, was taken from *Des Knaben Wunderhorn* (*Br*, 151). There is no exact match for these words in *Des Knaben Wunderhorn*; Mahler most likely adapted (or misremembered) a few lines from the poem "Redemption" (Erlösung).[75] The same verses are mentioned in a different letter, wherein Mahler elaborates on them further:

> It should be nothing less then the "Macrocosm"; the motto of the last movement: "What love tells me" is:
> "Father, look upon my wounds
> Let no creature be lost."
> It is the last stage of differentiation: *God!* Or, if you like, Overman.
>
> [Es soll nichts weniger als der "Macrocosmos" sein; das Motto zum letzten Satz: "Was mir die Liebe erzählt" ist:
> "Vater, sieh an die Wunden mein
> Kein Wesen laß verloren sein."
> Es ist die letzte Stufe der Differenzierung: *Gott*! Oder wenn Sie wollen, der Übermensch.][76]

What should surprise us is that Mahler speaks about God and "Overman" (der Übermensch) as if both stood for more or less the same thing. Such a comparison is very much against Nietzsche's intentions. In fact, in texts that Nietzsche wrote after *Also sprach Zarathustra* he repeatedly warned against a Christian interpretation of the Zarathustra figure.[77] As paradoxical as it may seem, attempts to reconcile Christianity with Nietzsche's Zarathustra were not uncommon around 1900. The prevailing argument was that Nietzsche's philosophy would allow humankind to return to a rejuvenated, more authentic, and more vital form of Christianity.[78] To understand Mahler's equation of God and "Übermensch," however, it may be more productive to look into the latter term's meaning in

Nietzsche's work. Nietzsche introduces the idea of the "Übermensch" in the prologue of *Also sprach Zarathustra* (*SW* 4:14; *TSZ*, 5). In explaining what he means by the concept, he uses imagery derived from Darwin's theory of evolution: "Human being is something that must be overcome" (*TSZ*, 5; Der Mensch ist Etwas, das überwunden werden soll: *SW* 4:14). "Overman" relates to "man," he adds in the same context, as "man" does to "ape." Our contemporary understanding of the "Übermensch" is tainted by National Socialism, which understood the concept biologically and racially.[79] This is not in line with Nietzsche's own conceptualization of the "Übermensch"; in this context, biological imagery is clearly meant metaphorically for Nietzsche. But how are we to understand this idea that humankind must "be overcome"?

To some extent Nietzsche leaves this question unanswered. It is clear that the "Übermensch," like Dionysos in *Die Geburt der Tragödie*, is associated for Nietzsche with an affirmative attitude toward life on earth, a rediscovery of nature, optimism rather than pessimism, and joy rather than suffering. But how this transformation, the "overcoming of humankind" can exactly be achieved remains an open issue in Nietzsche's text; he is not "describing a determinate goal we ought to achieve."[80] The very openness of the concept leaves the recipient ample space to (re)design the term, to fill in its semantic contours according to her/his own ideas. The fact that Mahler remembers the *Wunderhorn* line "let no *sinner* be lost" (Kein Sünder laß verloren sein) as "let no *creature* be lost" (Kein Wesen laß verloren sein) is somewhat indicative of the direction in which his thinking is taking him. While the first line, "Father, look upon my wounds," stands for humankind's alienation and isolation from nature — echoing the longing for community articulated in movements 4 and 5 — it is precisely this estrangement from nature that leads to a longing to be part of nature, to accept nature as she is. An emphasis on humankind's relation to other living beings in the context of the last movement of the Third Symphony can also be seen in Mahler's letter to Friedrich Löhr. Here Mahler speaks about this movement as "a summing up of all my feelings regarding all living beings" (ein Zusammenfassen meiner Empfindungen allen Wesen gegenüber; *Br*, 150). What needs to be overcome is humans' individualism and their alienation from nature. "Nature" functions in this work, in other words, not as an objective or "divine" order of things but as the object of a subjective experience. It is highly interesting that Mahler, in a letter he wrote during the summer of 1902 — with a little more than half a decade between him and the creation of the Third Symphony — speaks of the symphony as an example of a "steadily more complex articulation of one's feelings" (stetig sich steigernde Artikulation der Empfindung; *Br*, 297). Initially, in the fourth movement, it is about humankind's alienation from nature. But the symphony is also, in its final Adagio, about humankind's finding its way back to nature. The most perfect form of experiencing nature is through our emotions.

"Love" is the metaphor Mahler uses to describe a specific attitude toward creation. It is through our emotions that we find value. This involves the shedding of one's individuality, but also the insight that all creatures matter and that humans are not privileged within nature and yet are part of it. The Third Symphony is about the perspective from which humankind watches nature, and how it is impossible for humankind not to see itself as part of nature. This is in line with Nietzsche's thinking. In the words of John McCarthy, Nietzsche argues for a "repositioning of humanity within the total economy of nature as a constituent part, not as its teleological end."[81] At the end of the Third Symphony humankind finds its way back to nature. It is not a naive belief in nature, but an awareness of nature that knows of its chaotic essence. One could speak in this context of a "renaturalization" of humankind — a term sometimes used in Nietzsche scholarship.[82] The fact that Mahler sometimes speaks about the symphony in cosmological terms — the symphony is to articulate the feeling that one leaves "earth and human destiny" (Erde und Menschenschicksal) far behind until they are but a "tiny dot" (*RGM*, 62; ein Pünktchen: *GME*, 59, trans. modified) — fits this image. Seen negatively, all existence on earth is relative. However, a positive interpretation of mankind's dependence on nature is possible as well. The insight that all creatures matter makes it possible to enjoy nature's diversity.

Scholarship has called the final movement a "celebration of transcendent reconciliation."[83] For William McGrath, the ending points to the "possibility of redemption" away from "Nietzsche's tragic view" of reality.[84] Both interpretations miss the point. Mahler's music, even in the Adagio of the Third, belongs very much to the here and now. It is about the materiality and chaos of the natural world, not about a world beyond the here and now. Mahler's view of the world is tragic, but Mahler — and in this he follows Nietzsche — is interested in finding joy in spite of his fundamental pessimism about life. If Nietzsche's philosophy has something in common with Christianity, it is the insight that humans are more than just individuals, that they are part of a larger whole. One could say that Mahler, not unlike Nietzsche in *Also sprach Zarathustra*, seeks to return to the roots of religion, of all religions. And the origins of religion are humankind's relationship with nature.

Humor — Symphony No. 4

From the symphony's earliest sketches onward, humor played a major role in Mahler's ideas for the Fourth Symphony. One could see this work as a further development of the ideas first articulated in the fifth movement of the Third Symphony (which also shares some musical material with the Fourth). The Fourth further elaborates on the role of humor in this movement, in line with Nietzsche, who associated humor, as we have seen, not only with the ability to downplay humankind's metaphysical homelessness through laughing at one's own destiny, but also with the "joy of life" best expressed in the behavior of children. The kind of humor Nietzsche has in mind is the expression of very contradictory emotions; it can be constructive and destructive. This is how we should understand Nietzsche's remark that Zarathustra "laughed with love and malice" (*TSZ,* 227; lachte vor Liebe und Bosheit: *SW* 4:348). Humor in Nietzsche can be the expression of an uncritical joining of the crowd or, in contrast, of an ability to laugh at one's own predicament, to embrace the eternal return of things, and to create one's own self and set one's own values, an ability Nietzsche sees represented especially well in children.[85] It is precisely this ambiguous character of humor that is at the core of Mahler's Fourth Symphony.

Among Mahler's first designs for the Fourth Symphony is a sheet of paper with a plan featuring the subtitle "Symphonie humoresque."[86] While this suggests a humorous piece of music, the term "Humoreske" also includes the meaning "a free, rather than a more formalized, expression" of "emotion."[87] Mahler used the same term for his first cycle of *Wunderhorn* settings (see chapter 2). A number of early programs for the symphony exist, but in the end Mahler decided against programmatic notes. Text is nevertheless important for an understanding of this work. It has been argued that the text of the final movement functions as a substitute program for the entire symphony.[88] This last movement is a musical adaptation of "Das himmlische Leben" (Heavenly Life), a text originally published in von Arnim and Brentano's *Wunderhorn* collection as "Der Himmel hängt voll Geigen" (Heaven is full of violins).[89] Mahler initially composed this song in 1892 as part of the first orchestral *Wunderhorn* cycle, then for a time considered making it into the seventh movement of his Third Symphony, until he eventually settled on making it the final movement of the Fourth, when he was composing that symphony in 1900/1901. Musicologists have shown that the symphony's first three movements all contain thematic material from the last movement.[90] This confirms that the song functioned as a matrix for the other movements, but it also raises the question as to what the relationship between the four movements may be.

When Mahler, in his conversations with Natalie Bauer-Lechner, characterized the Fourth Symphony as a "symphonic Humoresque" (symphonische Humoreske) that (unexpectedly) turned into a symphony (*GME,* 162; *RGM,* 151), he was suggesting not only that humor plays an important role in the symphony but also that his original intention was to create a shorter piece more or less in one movement (perhaps not unlike Strauss's symphonic poem *Ein Heldenleben*). The first piece of information that Mahler gives after mentioning this original design is that the symphony has one "basic tone" (Grundstimmung) which he compares to "the even-toned blue sky" (dasununterschiedene Himmelsblau); this basic tone sometimes darkens and may appear as "spookily eerie" (*RGM*, 152; spukhaft schauerlich: *GME*, 162, trans. modified) and yet becomes blue again once these momentary obstructions of our view have gone. The symphony has one basic tenor, but this basic mood can take very different shapes. One can interpret this to mean that Mahler's intention was to experiment with different kinds of humor. It does appear as though the symphony's last movement returns to the seemingly unclouded innocent atmosphere of the first movement. But is that really the case? And what kind of metamorphoses does the humoristic theme of the symphony undergo exactly? To answer these questions, it is useful to look at the imagery Mahler uses in explaining humor in the symphony's four movements.

The idea of humor is already present at the very beginning of the symphony's first movement. Mahler refers to the opening bells as belonging to a "jester's cap" (*RGM*, 182; Schellenkappe: *GME*, 202); the importance of the motif of the jester's cap is emphasized by its return in many different guises throughout the first movement and in the final movement. What does it mean that the movement's humorous agenda is visualized by this cap? Again, Mahler chooses a very complex image to express the music's intentions. What is interesting about Mahler mentioning the jester's cap is that it links his symphony to a tradition of humor as a form of social critique (a tradition also present in "Das himmlische Leben" and, for instance, in most works by Jean Paul). The cap is part of the costume that the jester ("Narr") wore either at court or in society in medieval and early modern times.[91] The cap guaranteed the jester the freedom to say things otherwise not accepted from a subordinate or censored by society in general. It granted a special status to the person who wore it and thus functioned as a signifier of the temporary suspension of societal norms. One could say that the jester lives in the "eternal here and now" (ewige Jetztzeit);[92] he does not have to worry about past or future. The price he pays, however, is that he stands outside society. The jester is thus a very ambiguous figure.

Some of this ambiguity can be found back in other statements about the first movement of this symphony. Bruno Walter, in an important letter outlining Mahler's intentions to the musicologist Ludwig Schiedermaier, writes that the movement was meant to articulate "an unheard-of joy, an unearthly delight that attracts but also appears strange" (eine unerhörte Heiterkeit, eine unirdische Freude, die ebenso oft anzieht wie befremdet).[93] In other words, the movement's intended ideal audience should hesitate to embrace its humor wholeheartedly. It is interesting to link such a programmatic deliberation with an examination of the movement's structure. One of the most striking formal features of the first movement is that the melodic organization seems very simple and yet upon closer examination turns out to be highly complex.[94] These contradictory gestures inherent in the music also concern the symphony's humor: is this humor really the result of a naive, unprejudiced way of looking at the world, or is it a highly artistic construct? Mahler used a classical sonata structure for the first movement.[95] Throughout the symphony he employs what has been described by musicologists as a "classical idiom," and the score asks for an archaic orchestra by 1900 standards (without trombones and with a conservative use of brass in general).[96] This raises the question of the extent to which, for Mahler, humor and ambiguity were ways of relating to the musical past. The answer that the Fourth Symphony gives is clear: an unambiguous return to the past is impossible; a composer of Mahler's generation can relate to compositions by Haydn and Mozart — Mahler's Fourth is often linked to their music — only in a humorous and ambiguous way.[97]

In the second movement of the Fourth Symphony the listener is confronted with humor's uncanny side. Mahler described the scherzo as being so "mystical, confused and uncanny that it will make your hair stand on end" (*RGM*, 152; mystisch, verworren und unheimlich, daß euch dabei die Haare zu Berge stehen werden: *GME*, 163). The movement is associated with death. According to Natalie Bauer-Lechner, the violin — tuned one note higher than the rest of the orchestra and thereby creating an effect of dissonance — should sound "as if Death were fiddling away" (*RGM*, 162; wie wenn der Tod aufspielt: *MGE*, 179). Bruno Walter writes in his letter to Schiedermaier that the movement is to sound as if "the Grim Reaper is striking up a dance" (Freund Hein spielt zum Tanz auf).[98] Willem Mengelberg's score of the symphony characterizes it as a "dance of the dead" (Totentanz) in the style of the woodcuts of Hans Holbein (1497–1543); it is also possible that a painting by Arnold Böckling (1827–1901) inspired Mahler.[99] We have encountered the link between humor and death before in our analysis of the third movement, the funeral march based on *Frère Jacques*, in the First Symphony (originally its fourth movement). Nevertheless, there are considerable differences between that movement and the scherzo of this later work. In the First Symphony humor secured the affirmation of life in the face of death (see chapter 1); humor and death were antagonists. In the second movement of this work, however, humor allies itself with death and serves as a reminder of the transitory nature of all things. Death is the dissonant in life. And yet part of the uncanny nature of this movement — Mahler himself used the word "unheimlich," as we have seen — is that the fiddle's melody offers something fascinating and seductive as well. Keeping in mind that the movement was designed as a "Totentanz," one could say that it wants us "to dance out of life into death."[100]

Surprisingly, humor plays a role in the Fourth Symphony's third movement as well, in spite of the fundamentally Brucknerian, tragic basic tenor of this Adagio. In a conversation with Natalie Bauer-Lechner, Mahler compared the movement's mood to that expressed in "St. Ursula's smile" (das Lächeln der heiligen Ursula); this smile reminded him in turn of his mother's "face laughing through her tears" (*RGM*, 152–53; durch Tränen lachende Antlitz: *GME*, 163, trans. modified). This is, of course, a rare glance into the autobiographical meaning this music held for Mahler; the unhealthy relationship between his father and mother is well documented.[101] Bruno Walter's letter on this symphony, too, contains the reference to the smiling St. Ursula in relation to the third movement, describing her as "the most serious of all Saints" (die ernsteste der Heiligen); her smile is expressive of "solemn blessed rest; serious, gentle joy" (feierliche selige Ruhe, ernste, milde Heiterkeit); the movement is full of painful (schmerzliche) contrasts — "reminiscences of life on earth" (Reminiszenzen des Erdenlebens).[102] If one follows these heuristic hints, the idea of humor in the third movement is diametrically opposed to that in the second movement (and also very different from the *Trauermarsch* of the First Symphony). St. Ursula's smile here functions as a metaphor of acceptance and also of inner distance. It points to humor's ability to transform sadness into something that is not sadness, although it is not exactly joy either (certainly not the joyfulness articulated in "Das himmlische Leben"). Such a conversion of tragedy into something that may be neither comedy nor joy, but at least presents an affirmative attitude toward life, connects this symphony not only to Mahler's Second and Third Symphonies, but also to Nietzsche's *Geburt der Tragödie*. It is another reincarnation of Nietzsche's interpretation of Aristotle's theory of catharsis. While the second movement illustrated Nietzsche's laughter out of "malice" (Bosheit), in the third movement laughter is associated with love.

To what extent does the humor in the first three movements help us understand the fourth movement? "Das himmlische Leben," I would argue, at once presupposes, synthesizes, and transgresses upon the different types of humor presented in the symphony's first three movements. This is expressed by Mahler himself when he states that the child "in a chrysalis state" (im Puppenstand), whose perspective is presented in the last movement, explains what was meant by the "joy" (Heiterkeit) of the other, higher world in the earlier movements (*GME*, 198; *RGM*, 178, trans. modified[103]). The image of the child in the last movement replaces that of the jester in the first and somehow incorporates the attitudes articulated in the second and third movements. One could take this to mean that this symphony offers a chronologically organized narrative, something like a reverse *Bildungsroman*, culminating in the desire to return to one's childhood, or to a state of mind associated with it, in the last movement. One of the questions this raises is how the symphony's end, if understood in this way, relates to its (seemingly) innocent beginnings in the first movement. Summarizing his views on this last movement, Donald Mitchell speaks of "music that awaits us when Experience has been purged. Not paradise perhaps, but Innocence Regained."[104] This would suggest some form of cyclical model underlying the symphony. But how is it possible to regain innocence? And if something along those lines is possible, how is the humor of the fourth movement different from that of the first movement?

In particular, it is hard to reconcile the presence of death in "Das himmlische Leben" with an interpretation that emphasizes the last movement's promotion of a childlike innocence. It is a rather bizarre sort of innocence that would embrace the sometimes very violent imagery in the poem. Rather than some sort of musical *Bildungsroman*, the Fourth Symphony is, I would argue, the equivalent of a philosophical essay on humor and represents within Mahler's oeuvre a clear break with the temporally oriented narrative model informing Mahler's first three symphonies. The experience to which Mitchell refers certainly includes the evocation of death in the symphony's second movement ("Freund Hein spielt zum Tanz auf") but may already have been thematized in the first movement as well.[105] Death, however, is not absent from the final movement, either. While the first stanza of "Das himmlische Leben" seems unambiguous in its praise of heavenly life, this is not at all the case for the second stanza, which narrates how heaven's inhabitants "lead a meek, / innocent, meek / a sweet little lamb to its death" (führen ein geduldig's, / unschuldig's, geduldig's / ein liebliches Lämmlein zu Tod) and how, subsequently, St. Luke slaughters an ox. These contradictions are inherent to the text, and even though Mahler suppresses one of the references to dying — the few verses he suppresses in the fourth stanza include a reference to St. Lawrence's death[106] — one cannot say that Mahler downplays the text's violent undertone. While in the second stanza, after the slaughter of the lamb and ox, the narrative goes on to describe how in heaven "wine does not cost a penny" (der Wein kost' kein Heller) and angels are baking bread, the horns in the background (in one of Mahler's more bizarre musical jokes) mimic the ox's final moments at length. The music reminds the listener of the text's conflicted message. According to the oldest programmatic sketch, Mahler originally intended "Das irdische Leben" — the tragic song about a child's death from starvation, which broke with the lighthearted atmosphere of the first set of *Wunderhorn* songs (see chapter 2) — to be the symphony's second movement.[107] This is another indication that the symphony's contradictions are not incidental but part of its design.

The message behind the humorous subtext vis-à-vis the reality of death is that only with the help of humor can we face life's harsh realities. It is in essence a version of Nietzsche's embracing of laughter in order to lighten the burden of human existence. To some extent, what happens to the animals in the second stanza is the key to understanding the polemical impetus contained in "Das himmlische Leben" and in the Fourth Symphony in general. The allusion to the ox in "Das himmlische Leben" can be taken to refer to St. Paul's question "Doth God care for oxen?" (1 Cor. 9:9–10) — a rhetorical question that even today is quoted to argue that the Bible does not acknowledge animals' suffering.[108] Animals have to die to make the Fourth Symphony's version of heaven possible. In this context it is hard not to be reminded of Wagner's attempt to provide a Christian defense of vegetarianism in "Religion und Kunst," the essay that inspired Mahler and some of his friends to become vegetarians, at least temporarily. In a highly implausible reading, Wagner had argued in his essay, as I showed above, that Christ's sacrificing himself was meant as a reconciliation for all unnecessary slaughter of animals.

The image of Christianity that emerges from "Das himmlische Leben" is a very different one. It is not simply that this paradise is not one for animals, that animals there suffer the same fate as on earth. The image that the song sketches of human life in heaven is in many respects like that on earth. While the first two verses of the first stanza state that life in heaven is nothing like that on earth — "We enjoy the heavenly pleasures, / that is why we avoid earthly things" (Wir genießen die himmlischen Freuden, / drum tun wir das Irdische meiden) — life in heaven is far from perfect. This is expressed, for instance, two lines later in the first stanza: "We lead an angelic life! / And nevertheless we are quite merry in addition to that!" (Wir führen ein englisches Leben! / Sind dennoch ganz lustig daneben!). The expression "englisches Leben" is more ambiguous in German than my translation suggests: it could be translated both as "life of angels" or as "life of the English." For citizens of still very provincial eighteenth-century Germany, when the song was first recorded,[109] England was the prime example of an urban, luxurious life style with its advantages (prosperity) and disadvantages (those associated with an overabundant lifestyle). The ambiguity of this term is one indication that life in heaven is very much judged by earth's standards, that it is about leading a materially good life and the joy that (perhaps) comes with it. But there is another subtle hint in these verses that points to ambiguity. The word "dennoch" (nevertheless) expresses unequivocally that life in heaven is usually not that much fun: it is in spite of the angelic (English) life that the inhabitants of heaven can enjoy themselves. The second and third stanzas in Mahler's version — stanzas 2, 3, and 4 in the song's original version in *Des Knaben Wunderhorn* — illustrate how this is done: they are above all about food and drink, the simple joys of life. Heaven is not about avoiding, but rather about embracing, "earthly things" (das Irdische).

Through such contradictions "Das himmlische Leben" simultaneously utilizes and deconstructs traditional Christian iconography. This is also clear from the portrayal of some of the saint figures in "Das himmlische Leben."

Regarding St. Ursula, who, as we saw, was also mentioned in Mahler's comments on the symphony's third movement, Mahler admitted in his conversation with Natalie regarding the Fourth Symphony that he knew nothing about her or the legend associated with her name (*GME*, 163; *RGM*, 152). He was therefore most likely not aware of the fact that the "eleven thousand" dancing "virgins" (Elftausend Jungfrauen / zu tanzen sich trauen!) of the song's last stanza were the ones who were slaughtered by the Huns when they accompanied the fourth-century St. Ursula on a pilgrimage.[110] The fact that St. Peter is in charge of catching fish, St. Martha is the cook, and St. Cecilia is in charge of music in heaven is in line with biblical accounts. But what does it mean that St. John, in tandem with King Herod, is at least complicit in slaughtering the lamb that is his attribute and symbolically represents his relationship with Jesus? And that St. Luke slaughters the attribute he is commonly associated with, the ox? These could be interpreted as acts of religious self-destruction, as forms of cultural masochism that radically call into question the values we associate with these figures. At stake here is the symbolic function that is *sine qua non* for the construction of a religious narrative. This symbolic function, here as in the Second Symphony, is questioned. It is as if the figures themselves protest against being made to function as symbols in the service of religion, against losing their freedom.

Some scholars have proposed the term "irony" to understand the contradictions underlying the text and music of "Das himmlische Leben."[111] Jean Paul, rightly in my view, observes that irony on the surface is always serious, even though that seriousness may only be a veil and not be supported by a text's actual message.[112] In this sense the *Trauermarsch* of Mahler's First Symphony, which the critic Max Kalbeck called Mahler's "Sinfonia Ironica," basing his argument in particular on the funeral march,[113] is an ironic piece: on the surface, it is serious and focused on death and suffering, below the surface, however, it is humorous and life-affirming, and thus articulates a very different message. "Das himmlische Leben" does not have such a serious surface. What speaks further against an ironic interpretation of the symphony's final movement is the fact that irony, as a rhetorical device, is always highly constructed. Mahler, however, asserts a childlike attitude as the narrative attitude for this text. The perspective is that of a child spontaneously imagining a different world. This is also emphasized by a note that Mahler had printed in a relatively late stage with the score of the fourth movement: "Voice with childlike, joyful expression; throughout without parody" (Singstimme mit kindlich heiterem Ausdruck; durchaus ohne Parodie!).[114] A final objection against irony is that it privileges one level of articulation over another: it seeks to identify the real message under the text's surface. "Das himmlische Leben" instead explores the tension between two levels of articulation, the inconsistency of a Christian concept of heaven.

The key to understanding the Fourth's final movement, and with it the entire symphony, is not irony but humor. But why does this movement come across as humorous? In the words of Jean Paul, humor "humiliates what is great, . . . in order to place what is small at its side, and it puts what is small on a pedestal . . . to place it alongside what is great, in order to destroy both" (erniedrigt das Große, . . . um ihm das Kleine, und erhöhet das Kleine, . . . um ihm das Große an die Seite zu setzen und so beide zu vernichten).[115] At least in part, the humor in "Das himmlische Leben" has to do with the utter inappropriateness of the images it presents, in particular the insistence on the material world: we expect heaven to be a pious, spiritual, and restful place and not loud, playful, and focused on the kind of earthly pleasures that the song portrays. Humor is the result of an incongruity between what we expect and what we are offered.[116] Such a discrepancy can very well function as a critique of society: "Jokes are *anti-rites*. They mock, parody or deride the ritual practices of a given society."[117] "Das himmlische Leben" is indeed critical of social rites — a form of criticism to which the first movement, with its use of the jester's cap (which returns in the final movement), already alluded. As a medium of revolt the song uses the body. Humor's affinity for the body is something many of its theorists have noted, among them Jean Paul.[118] "Das himmlische Leben" insists on the materiality of life: heaven is primarily about eating and drinking. And yet such an embracing of earthly pleasures is only possible after recognizing that life is finite. This is what happens in the symphony's second and third movements, in which humor is associated with death (second movement)[119] and the ability to turn destruction into something life-affirming (third movement). In an exemplary way, "Das himmlische Leben" illustrates an understanding of humor as a back-and-forth between ideal and material reality, as the ability to be relativistic and yet also to embrace reality.

"Das himmlische Leben" shares with Nietzsche's philosophical agenda a profound skepticism, not only toward Christianity's normative claims, but also regarding the motives underlying religion in general. But in contrast to (moments in) the Second and Third Symphonies, it refuses to see humankind's metaphysical homelessness as a tragic predicament. The Fourth Symphony's final movement offers a rather playful version of Nietzsche's criticism of Christianity and a complete irreverence toward its professed norms and values. It draws the ultimate conclusion from Nietzsche's insight that "only as an *aesthetic phenomenon*" can we make sense of the world and of our existence. If our values are nothing but imaginary constructions or wishful fantasies, then we may as well try to indulge in these fantasies while also embracing the materiality of life, instead of mourning certainties that we, in hindsight, never possessed. I would interpret the fact that Mahler attributes this attitude to a child as a statement that we are dealing not necessarily with "innocence" but rather with a more authentic attitude toward life: an attitude that intuitively understands the big questions of life better than after it has been indoctrinated by religious or philosophical doctrines, and that combines such an understanding with an ability to enjoy life in freedom in spite of its many vicissitudes.

At the end of his interpretation of the Fourth Symphony, Adolf Nowak signals similarities between the thoughts underlying "Das himmlische Leben" and Freud's theories. In his view, the song articulates the kind of childish wishful thinking that is normally repressed.[120] Interestingly, Mahler himself referred to Freud, albeit implicitly, in the immediate context of his work on this symphony. In a statement directly preceding Natalie Bauer-Lechner's summary of her conversations with Mahler about this work, Mahler speaks about his creative powers as a dream-like force:

> "We know," said Mahler "that our second self is active while we sleep, that it grows and becomes and produces what the real self sought and wanted in vain. The creative artist, in particular, has countless proofs of this. But that this second self should have worked on my Fourth Symphony throughout *ten months* of winter sleep (with all the frightful nightmares of the theatre business) is unbelievable!"
>
> ["Man weiß," sagte Mahler, "daß unser zweites Ich im Schlafe tätig ist, das wächst und wird und hervorbringt, was das wahre Ich vergeblich suchte und wollte. Dafür hat besonders der Schaffende unzählige Beweise. Daß dieses zweite Ich aber über *zehn Monate* Winterschlafs (mit all den furchtbaren Träumen des Theatergetriebes) an meiner Vierten Symphonie gearbeitet hat, ist unglaublich!"] (*GME*, 161; *RGM*, 150)

The approximate date of the conversation (July or early August 1900) from which Natalie derived this information in her (chronologically organized) memoirs is interesting, because here Mahler is building on ideas that Freud introduced in his *Traumdeutung* (The Interpretation of Dreams), which had been published in November 1899. Mahler clearly became familiar with some of the basic tenets of Freud's book relatively shortly after its publication: he acknowledges that the unconscious functions differently from our conscious mental activity, that it is active during sleep, and that it produces or articulates what we consciously look for in vain (Freud's notion of wish fulfillment[121]).

At least as important as recognizing Freud's influence here is the turn that Mahler gives to his ideas: he uses Freud's model of the conscious and unconscious levels of our psychic life in order to understand the creative process, a process not unlike that analyzed by Freud himself in 1908 in his essay "Der Dichter und das Phantasieren" (The Creative Writer and Day-Dreaming).[122] Freud's dream theory leads Mahler to ponder the existence of a creative drive diametrically opposed to everyday reality, not unlike the type of fantasy at work in "Das himmlische Leben." Mahler's comment to Natalie does make it clear how he is starting to conceive of his music's ideas in a vocabulary that has roots among his contemporaries in Vienna around 1900. With this Freudian connection in mind, it is good to remember that "Das himmlische Leben," in the end, is also about art: "no music exists on earth, / that can be compared to ours" (Kein Musik ist ja nicht auf Erden, / die uns'rer verglichen kann werden). The song pays homage to the imagination, to a form of free, aesthetic playing with tradition that imagines an ideal world while acknowledging that such a world can only be fantasy.

Using dream imagery to explain an aesthetic program was not uncommon in fin-de-siècle Vienna. In 1908 the 22-year-old Oskar Kokoschka published a book of poems entitled *Die träumenden Knaben* (The Dreaming Boys), which was accompanied by eight color and two black-and-white lithographs. It is not clear how well Kokoschka knew Mahler's works, although one may wonder whether the words "rattler of bells" (Schellenrassler) and "cymbalist" (Beckenschläger) in a stanza dedicated to music, refer to Mahler.[123] In addition to introducing the "Narrenschelle" as a musical instrument, Mahler's symphonies were also known for their innovative use of percussion. The poems of *Die träumenden Knaben* have been compared to those of *Des Knaben Wunderhorn*.[124] The very first lines "red little fish / little fish red" (rot fischlein/fischlein rot)[125] could be interpreted as referring to the first lines of the *Wunderhorn* poem "Urlicht," which Mahler used for his Second Symphony. The imagery employed by Kokoschka in his collection shows a remarkable similarity to that of Mahler's songs and symphonies: the poems are about nature (fish, birds), about dreaming and art, about love as a vague promise, about death, about the inability of language to express what matters, but also about the promise of other cultures, one of them being China. The world portrayed in these poems and lithographs is very much the product of a child's fantasies — the original commission was to create an illustrated children's book[126] — but it is nevertheless also the product of a childhood that is endangered and marked by the knowledge that such a world cannot last. The individual episodes of the poem are organized as dream sequences: they consist of associations without a clear protagonist (or protagonists), without a clear location, and without a clear plot or narrative, very much like the world of "Das himmlische Leben." At the root of their world is violence. The dream sequences are set in motion by a violent act: the killing of fish.[127] Kokoschka dedicated his poems and lithographs to Gustav Klimt; this was no doubt because the penniless Kokoschka[128] hoped to attract the attention of the more established artist, who at that point was far more famous than himself. But one could also read this as an effort to seek support for an aesthetic program of unlimited artistic freedom (not unlike the final movement of Mahler's Fourth).

Mahler contra Wagner?

Mahler's Second, Third, and Fourth Symphonies all take issue, implicitly or explicitly, with the philosophy of Friedrich Nietzsche. The Second Symphony tries to cast its Nietzschean message in a relatively conventional religious language — so conventional, in fact, that its underlying critical message was often not recognized. It seeks to answer the question of the conditions under which religion still has a function in a post-metaphysical age. The Third Symphony, by contrast, is much more explicit about its Nietzschean framework. Nietzsche's name stands here for the transition to new ways of looking at the world, in particular through a rethinking of nature. One could say that the Third Symphony shows Nietzsche as the founding father of a new philosophy of life. Finally, the Fourth Symphony emphasizes the critical impulse in Nietzsche's philosophy. In the end, Mahler prefers Nietzsche the skeptic to Nietzsche the ideology-builder. Mahler himself has called his Fourth Symphony a kind of "conclusion" (Abschluß) to his first three (*GME*, 164; *RGM*, 154). If one sees the Fourth as Mahler's final word regarding his views of Nietzsche, then it is not just Nietzsche the critic of Western culture but also Nietzsche the humorist who triumphs. One could say that this symphony is conceived as an essay on humor, with the individual movements offering different insights into the functioning of humor. Nietzsche's insight that existence and the world can be justified only aesthetically turns into an argument for art as a free form of aesthetic play that conceives of itself as highly critical of tradition.

Bruno Walter has written that Mahler was "outraged" (empört) by Nietzsche's anti-Wagnerism and later in life rejected Nietzsche entirely.[129] Alma Mahler in her memoirs supports Walter's view, when she reports the (often-repeated) anecdote that Mahler, upon discovering her copy of Nietzsche's works, recommended that she throw the books into the fire burning in the open fireplace.[130] As unambiguous as such statements may seem, they do not necessarily mean that Mahler broke with Nietzsche (or with the Nietzschean agenda of his early symphonies). Regarding Alma's comment, one may wonder whether, in Mahler's idealized image of Alma, there was perhaps simply no place for the nihilist Nietzsche, whom he associated with his friend Lipiner and his fellow students from the Pernerstorfer circle.[131] In a sometimes quite patronizing way, Mahler idealized Alma's naiveté and spontaneity;[132] an interest in Nietzsche on her part did not exactly fit into that picture. Concerning Bruno Walter's comment, it would be interesting to know *what* exactly bothered Mahler about Nietzsche's anti-Wagnerism: was it the fact that Nietzsche's thinking had taken a different turn from Wagner's while Mahler's sympathies were with Wagner, or did Mahler reproach Nietzsche that the latter, in his anti-Wagnerian zeal, had produced an image of Wagner that was too simplistic and in particular ignored the innovative and critical dimensions of Wagner's (earlier?) works, which Nietzsche himself had so idealized in the past? It is also worth noting that Walter makes his comment on Mahler's break with Nietzsche over Wagner just after noting how Mahler in general thought through problems "independently" (selbständig)[133] — that is, without worrying too much about possible ideological affiliations.

There is certainly a turn away from Nietzsche in Mahler's later symphonies. These later works no longer evoke Nietzsche by name (although they do show parallels with Nietzsche's thinking, as I will show in the following chapters). They also move away from diagnosing the kind of cultural crisis that is at the core of the early symphonies and the *Wunderhorn* songs. But does this mean that Mahler rejected the principles underlying Nietzsche's philosophy? Not necessarily. When the Pernerstorfer circle was interested in Nietzsche in the late 1870s, Nietzsche was a little-known philosopher whose thinking was still in flux. Lipiner's essay *Über die Elemente einer Erneuerung religiöser Ideen in der Gegenwart* is very much an attempt, as I have shown, to instigate and participate in a debate between his contemporaries Wagner and Nietzsche. Nietzsche's breakthrough among the general public came in the 1890s[134] (when Mahler, in 1895 and 1896, composed his Third Symphony and Richard Strauss almost simultaneously his symphonic poem *Also sprach Zarathustra* [1896]). By the beginning of the twentieth century, however, Nietzsche had become an icon of popular culture and an emerging "kitsch industry."[135] Nietzsche had become the object of an at times rather uncritical form of idolization — the same kind of hero-worshipping that was at least one of the motives for Nietzsche to become rather skeptical of Wagner's Bayreuth enterprise.[136] This timeline is important for two reasons. Mahler's mindset may very well have remained the same as before the breakup between Nietzsche and Wagner (or at least before the split became public knowledge), when both were thinking through similar problems in a close exchange of thoughts. Mahler's dissociation from Nietzsche later in life (in the early 1900s) may have had more to do with the philosopher's new iconic status in German culture than with an inner disagreement with his ideas.

But how, then, are we to reconcile Mahler's clear endorsement of the thinking of Wagner's antipode Friedrich Nietzsche in his symphonies with his unquestionable interest in Wagner, especially as a conductor? Nietzsche himself summarized the differences that led him to break with Wagner most succinctly in *Nietzsche contra Wagner* in a chapter with the title "Wie ich von Wagner loskam" (How I Broke Away from Wagner):

> As early as the summer of 1876, right in the middle of the first *Festspiele*, I took leave of Wagner. I cannot stand ambiguities: since coming to Germany, Wagner had gradually given in to everything that

I hate — even to anti-Semitism . . . At that time it was indeed high time to take my leave: and I immediately received a confirmation of the fact. Richard Wagner, seemingly the all-conquering, actually a decaying, despairing decadent, suddenly sank down helpless and shattered before the Christian cross . . .

[Schon im Sommer 1876, mitten in der Zeit der ersten Festspiele, nahm ich bei mir von Wagnern Abschied. Ich vertrage nichts Zweideutiges; seitdem Wagner in Deutschland war, condescendirte er Schritt für Schritt zu Allem, was ich verachte — selbst zum Antisemitismus . . . Es war in der That damals die höchste Zeit, Abschied zu nehmen: alsbald schon bekam ich den Beweis dafür. Richard Wagner, scheinbar der Siegreichste, in Wahrheit ein morsch gewordner verzweifelnder décadent, sank plötzlich, hülflos und zerbrochen, vor dem christlichen Kreuze nieder . . .] (*SW* 6:431–32; *AC*, 276, trans. modified)[137]

What is highly interesting about this statement is that Nietzsche mentions anti-Semitism here first when clarifying the reasons for his break with Wagner. It is important that Nietzsche puts the responsibility for succumbing to anti-Semitism squarely upon Wagner himself and not upon the Wagnerians surrounding him. The quote illustrates, in an exemplary way, Sander Gilman's statement that Nietzsche was an "anti-anti-Semite".[138] Nietzsche's critical statements about anti-Semitism are primarily motivated, not by a concern for the fate of Jews or by a love for Jewish culture, but rather by a disdain for those intellectuals and other public figures who tried to capitalize on anti-Semitic sentiments for political gain. Wagner's anti-Semitism was by no means a secret in the late nineteenth century. The often reprinted "people's edition" (Volksausgabe) of Wagner's collected works included his "Das Judentum in der Musik" (Judaism in Music).[139] Anti-Semitism is also openly discussed as a reason for Nietzsche's distancing himself from Wagner in Elisabeth Förster-Nietzsche's biography of her brother.[140] I mentioned in my introduction that Mahler, according to an anecdote reported by Natalie Bauer-Lechner, was well aware of the anti-Semitic subtext in the *Ring des Nibelungen*.

Nietzsche's statement is about more than Wagner's anti-Semitism alone. For Nietzsche, Wagner's anti-Semitism ties into two other phenomena of which he is deeply skeptical: a turn to dogmatic religion, illustrated by the image of Wagner sinking down before the cross, and German nationalism. The preface of *Nietzsche contra Wagner* makes it clear that his diatribe against Wagner is to be understood with Germany's 1871 unification in mind, of which Nietzsche did not approve.[141] Here we may be at the core of what connects Mahler with Nietzsche and differentiates Mahler from Wagner. Mahler does not answer Wagner's anti-Semitism by openly/publicly denouncing Wagner's attitudes toward

Jews — for the director of the Vienna Court Opera, that would have been highly problematic given the many documented anti-Semitic incidents surrounding his tenure — but rather by developing and promoting a view of German culture in his own works that was very different from Wagner's. Jean Paul, Klopstock, Nietzsche, Mahler's idiosyncratic choice of poems from *Des Knaben Wunderhorn*, and his adaptation of the end of the second part of Goethe's *Faust* for the Eighth Symphony all stand for a trajectory of German literary and cultural history that was very different from Wagner's conservative, nationalistic, and anti-Semitic appropriation of that same cultural heritage. Mahler embraced a highly eclectic style of appropriation toward German culture (both its music and literature), not unlike that of Jean Paul's novels or the second part of Goethe's *Faust*, but very different from that of Wagner, who saw such eclecticism as typical for Jewish music making.[142]

The texts of Mahler's first four symphonies, the *Lieder eines fahrenden Gesellen*, and the *Wunderhorn* songs furthermore share a notion of "crisis" that resists any easy resolution. While these texts, on the surface, seem to tell us one thing, their actual message turns out to be far more complex. The narrative underlying the First Symphony resembles Jean Paul's *anti-Bildungsroman Titan* more than it does the *Bildungsroman* that nineteenth-century scholars had sought to read into "classical" German literature. The texts he used in his *Lieder eines fahrenden Gesellen* and *Wunderhorn* songs, in their insistence on both the material realities of everyday life and the inability of art to compensate for material deficiencies, greatly resisted an ideological appropriation in favor of a nationalist and conservative ideology of the "Volk." In his Second and Third Symphonies, Mahler ponders Nietzsche's question of what it means to live in a post-metaphysical age. These symphonies are to be understood as critiques of a discourse that sought to evade modernity's fundamental ambiguities in order to return to naive notions of religion, nature, and mankind; they insisted on rethinking these notions in line with Nietzsche's diagnosis of the end of metaphysics. Mahler's Fourth Symphony, with the often misunderstood *Wunderhorn*-text in its final movement, I would argue, represents an endpoint that is simultaneously the beginning of something new. It quite deliberately pokes fun at the questions asked in the Second and Third Symphonies. In the end, the symphony argues for a certain irreverence, indeed, an absolute freedom, vis-à-vis tradition.

The notion of crisis discussed in previous chapters is generally associated with fin-de-siècle Vienna modernism but in fact was rooted in German culture well before 1900. Mahler's strategy of appropriating texts for a specific purpose and with a specific agenda in mind is not unlike that of Nietzsche, who at times mobilizes the big names of German literary history in his fight with Wagner. In *Der Fall Wagner* (The Case of Wagner), for instance, Nietzsche seeks to answer the following question:

— What would Goethe have thought of Wagner? — Goethe once asked himself what danger was suspended over all Romantics: the fate awaiting Romanticism. His answer: "to suffocate on rehashed moral and religious absurdities." In short: *Parsifal* —

[— Was Goethe über Wagner gedacht haben würde? — Goethe hat sich einmal die Frage vorgelegt, was die Gefahr sei, die über allen Romantikern schwebe: das Romantiker-Verhängnis. Seine Antwort ist: "am Wiederkäuen sittlicher und religiöser Absurditäten zu ersticken." Kürzer: *Parsifal* —] (*SW* 6:19; *AC*, 239)

Nietzsche points here to the loss of a critical modern impulse in German intellectual history. The early Romantics, who could be characterized as a protest generation (see chapter 2), promoted a philosophical agenda that emphasized critical, ironic, humorous, eclectic, and fragmentary forms of thinking. While Jean Paul does not easily fit any standard periodizations of German literary history, he frames his theory of humor as a theory of Romanticism — very much in line with the agenda of the early Romantics.[143] The central issue at stake in Nietzsche's *Geburt der Tragödie* — the legitimizing of life and the world by aesthetic means; the replacement of religion by art — has its roots in early Romantic thinking. The link is very clear, even though Nietzsche himself never commented on this archaeology of his own thinking and wrote very little about the early Romantics in general.[144] Wagner represented, for Nietzsche, the prototypical late Romantic who cannot handle the challenges of modernity and feels the need to return to old moral certainties and a naive concept of religion. Anti-Semitism is a phenomenon that manifested itself with particular emphasis among the middle and late Romantics.[145] Nietzsche provides Mahler with the philosophical basis for a counterreading of German cultural history that emphasizes its moments of openness and modern impulses. For Nietzsche and Mahler, Romanticism with all its contradictions — Romanticism's association with both the creation of a new openness toward other cultures and the birth of German nationalism — is a key moment in this process of rereading German culture (see also chapter 2).

To some extent, Mahler's relation to Wagner is also one of rewriting through appropriation. Of course Nietzsche overstated his case against Wagner, and it is also clear that after his break with Wagner Nietzsche did still feel ambivalent about his music.[146] Wagner's works, too, take as their point of departure the idea of a crisis of German culture that had already been diagnosed by the early Romantics, as his essay "Religion und Kunst" makes clear. But can Wagner's operas, in spite of the anti-modern agenda of his later days, be read in a Nietzschean vein as a critique of Western culture? One thing that must be pointed out here is that Nietzsche's criticism specifically concerned the older Wagner: the

Wagner of the *Bayreuther Festspiele* of 1876 and of the "Stage-Consecrating Festival-Play" (Bühnenweihfestspiel) *Parsifal,* which had its premiere in 1882, could only be performed in Bayreuth, and was without a doubt the most public manifestation of Wagner's turn to what Nietzsche had called "moral and religious absurdities." In a conversation with the music critic Ernst Decsey, Mahler once described *Parsifal* as a work by a "Wagnerian" (eines Wagnerianers), not by Wagner.[147] Such a comment is very much in line with Nietzsche's criticism of the later Wagner, who had forsaken his (Nietzsche's!) critical agenda and catered to the uncritical masses instead. But Nietzsche himself never lost his respect for *Tristan and Isolde,*[148] the opera that was Wagner's most daring experiment with dissonance and, coincidentally, the opera that Roller and Mahler staged in 1903 in their ground-breaking collaborative re-envisioning of Wagner's work. Mahler and Roller's staging of this work can be seen as modernist re-imagination that emphasized the symbolic nature of the events on the stage. Interestingly, while Mahler and Roller unquestionably created new images that clearly broke with Wagner's directives and Bayreuth practice, they simultaneously sought to support their approach by referring to Wagner's score in order to legitimize their new visual scenario.[149] Precisely by resisting a naturalistic representation of events, Mahler and Roller produced a decidedly modernist version of Wagner's opera: a version that pointed to the artificial, constructed nature of the events on the stage and in doing so asked its audiences to question the opera's view of reality rather than accept it unconditionally.

Mahler profited a great deal from the fame that his reputation as the preeminent interpreter of Wagner's works gave him. As he brought Wagner's artistic and intellectual legacy into a debate about the nature of German culture, and in particular about the meaning of modernity and tradition within it, Mahler simultaneously tried to outsmart Wagner. Nietzsche offered him the tools to do so. Especially in his later phase, Nietzsche saw himself first and foremost as a cultural critic and a cosmopolitan, anti-nationalistic thinker. One could say that Nietzsche stood for the critical, modern, and emancipatory potential in German culture and for its internationalism; Wagner, by contrast, affiliated himself with its regressive, conservative, and nationalistic side. But there was something of Wagner in Nietzsche, and something of Nietzsche in Wagner. Wagner's idea of a new cultural community is not entirely incongruent with Nietzsche's reevaluation of all values, also in his late works. Starting in the 1890s, Nietzsche was at least as famous a cultural icon as Wagner had ever been. This is one reason why some intellectuals, in spite of their sympathy for Nietzsche's ideas, started to distance themselves from his legacy in the early twentieth century.[150] On the other hand, Nietzsche had correctly pointed not only to inconsistencies inherent in Wagner's aesthetic framework but perhaps also to a dimension that was potentially still viable, or that could be redeveloped, in Wagner's work. When Mahler in his Eighth Symphony set part of Goethe's *Faust* to music, he picked up on a project that Wagner had considered in his early years but then abandoned.[151] Here Mahler followed a trajectory that Wagner had considered but ultimately rejected.

I noted earlier that Mahler's Fourth Symphony is an endpoint that is also a turning point in Mahler's creative development. This work no longer lingers on the disappearance of old certainties but instead embraces this loss as an opportunity and as the realization of a newfound freedom. After this, Mahler initially composed a series of instrumental symphonies: symphonies that quite deliberately did not have programs but engaged the formal legacy of the symphony more explicitly and more radically than before. Eventually, however, he would return to text as a medium with which he could tackle some of the issues that occupied him and could position his own works within German cultural history. From deconstructing German culture and its normative assumptions in his early songs and symphonies, Mahler in his final works starts to embrace a rewriting of German culture that is actively interested in the margins of that tradition. In these later compositions Mahler aims for a concept of art that shows an increased awareness of the heterogeneity at the roots of German cultural history and also an interest in other cultures. In this, Mahler is very much a product of cosmopolitan Vienna and not of provincial Bayreuth: "compared with more recent political phenomena," Ernst Křenek writes in 1941 in exile in the United States, "old Austria must appear as a paradise of peace and freedom, since Czechs and Poles, for instance, had permanent representatives in the cabinet and at times even prevailed in the government. How, if Austria had been what her foes pretended [a stronghold of sinister reaction and suppression], could a Bohemian Jew have ruled with absolute power for ten years over the foremost artistic institution of the Empire?"[152]

II. German Culture and Its Others

4: Rembrandt and the Margins of German Culture

MAHLER'S SEVENTH SYMPHONY, like his Fifth and Sixth, is considered to be a symphony without a program. While denying that this work is programmatic, Alma Mahler gives us several important clues to the contrary; for instance, the fact that Mahler had Eichendorff's poetry and German Romanticism in mind while composing this symphony.[1] Interestingly, Bruno Walter also mentions Romanticism in relation to it. In his monograph on Mahler he characterizes the symphony's three middle movements as a return to the kind of Romanticism that he had assumed Mahler had overcome.[2] It is not clear whether he means Romanticism in German cultural history or in Mahler's creative development, but his statement does make the point that Mahler is interested in a particular view of Romanticism in his Seventh Symphony. In speaking about the piece, Mahler employed a very specific nocturnal idiom, not only, for instance, by using the term "Nachtmusik" for the second and fourth movements, but also by comparing the last movement to night-ending daybreak during rehearsals for the symphony's premiere in Prague in 1908.[3]

The starting point for my deliberations on the Seventh Symphony, which argue that it does indeed have an (anti-programmatic) program, is these nocturnal references and the importance of the imagery of light and darkness. Night is a leitmotif in German cultural history of the late eighteenth and nineteenth centuries. There exists an entire musical tradition that takes night as its theme. This tradition includes works by Mozart, Beethoven, Schumann, Schubert, and Wagner — to name only a few of the more prominent examples. Mahler explicitly referred to this tradition through his use of the title "Nachtmusik" for two of the symphony's slow movements. There is also a literary tradition represented, for instance, by the poetry cycle *Hymnen an die Nacht* (Hymns to the Night, 1800) by Novalis (the pen name of Friedrich von Hardenberg) or E. T. A. Hoffmann's *Nachtstücke* (Night Pieces, 1817). Both authors were important figures in the German Romantic movement, and Mahler was certainly familiar with them. Attempts have been made to match, in particular, the second movement with a specific text by the German Romantic author Eichendorff.[4] In the following, I will not further pursue the assumed Eichendorff reference but will rather pick up on the second part of Alma's assertion, that Mahler's symphony has something to do with a rereading of German Romanticism. In the *Wunderhorn* songs Mahler was primarily interested in identifying the contradictions underlying these texts. His aim was to show that Romanticism was a far more complex and contradictory phenomenon than some of the attempts of his contemporaries to read a normative framework into its texts in the service of a nationalist and conservative political agenda would suggest. Mahler was interested in these songs as documents of crisis — psychological, political, and aesthetic. In the Seventh Symphony, Mahler rereads Romanticism in the light of the post-Nietzschean, modernist discourses of his contemporaries as a vehicle to find alterity within German culture. But here he embraces a very specific version of Romanticism, very different from the mainstream view; he embraces Romanticism as a means of identifying what has been discarded, marginalized, and left in the dark. It is this revisiting of Romanticism in the Seventh Symphony, I will argue, that led to a critical rethinking of German cultural history and ultimately to constructing that history in a fundamentally different way from predominant discourses.

A Turn-of-the-Century Cultural History of Light and Darkness

In 1904, when Mahler started work on his Seventh Symphony, Theodor Gomperz (1832–1912) wrote an essay entitled "Über die Grenzen der jüdischen intellectuellen Begabung" (On the Limits of Jewish Intellectual Aptitude).[5] Gomperz belonged to a prominent Jewish family in Vienna. From 1873 to 1903 he worked as a professor of philosophy at the University of Vienna. He was a prolific writer of books, essays, and critical contributions who also frequently published on the "Jewish question." Gomperz's 1904 essay is relevant in this context because it picks up on the light/dark imagery in German cultural history and explicitly links it to the Jewish contribution to this history. The question that interested Gomperz is why, in spite of the Jews' great gifts for intellectual and scholarly accomplishment, very few of them, in his opinion, reached the absolute pinnacle of achievement in their respective fields. Gomperz does much to nuance his insights. He argues that many Jews do demonstrate great talents; he points to the difficult socioeconomic situation affecting Jews throughout much of modern Western history and clearly states that generalizations, especially those based on national or racial stereotypes, are always questionable. Nevertheless, Gomperz does wonder about the dearth of what he calls Jewish "poet-philosophers." Jews, according to Gomperz, are highly capable of critical reasoning, have a sharp judgment, and they are full of wit and esprit. They are, in other words, disciples of the Enlightenment. A name that would come to mind here is Moses Mendelssohn. Gomperz, however, is primarily thinking of Heine in this context, whom he mentions once in his essay. However, the opposite of these gifts seems to be lacking among Jews; they lack, in Gomperz's analysis, an affinity with the dark side of German culture: "what is unconscious, dusky, dreamlike, full of premonition. One would almost be inclined to say that for certain types of products it is too bright in Jewish heads" (das Unbewußte, Dämmerige, Traumhafte, Ahnungsvolle. Fast möchte man sagen: für gewisse Arten von Hervorbringungen ist es in jüdischen Köpfen zu hell; 387). Jews, in other words, have no gift for darkness. Gomperz offers a number of explanations: Jews were city-dwellers, not rooted in their local environment; they never developed their own mythology.

It is remarkable how many ideas that we would now label as blatant prejudices and would associate with a conservative or nationalistic political agenda were accepted by the general public in the late nineteenth and early twentieth centuries. Gomperz was not the only one who viewed Jews as being overly oriented toward rationality: "To most Germans [around 1900], Jews now represented the antithesis of the neo-Romanticist ideals of the time: they were mainly urbanized, not tied to the soil, and they lacked genuine folk traditions. Judaism once attacked for its superstition, was now criticized for being a *Verstandesreligion* (religion of reason)."[6] It is part of the popular image of Jews around 1900 that they are overly rational. To a degree, this is the legacy of the efforts made by nineteenth-century Jewish intellectuals against the stereotype that Judaism was a primitive, superstitious, and irrational religion.[7] But the examples just quoted from Gomperz's text can also yield a different conclusion. They show that even progressive Jews like Gomperz were still highly influenced by a way of thinking that emphasized environmental factors and biological determinism.[8] To be fair, Gomperz also attempts to question generalizations about Jewish intellectual life and he mentions one notable exception — Spinoza, of course — not only because he is a leading Jewish philosopher but also because of a tendency toward pantheism and mysticism in his work (389).

While it is unlikely that Mahler knew of Gomperz's text, the logic behind it may very well have been familiar to Mahler, since Gomperz clearly addresses cultural stereotypes that were circulating widely at the time. One prominent musical critic praised Mahler's technical achievements in the Sixth Symphony while simultaneously suggesting that it lacked emotional content, thereby drawing on the stereotype of the "assimilated Jew as intellectual and unemotional."[9] These reproaches were quite common in reviews of Mahler's music. One could conceive of the Seventh Symphony as a response to such criticism. But where did Mahler get the idea of writing a symphony about the night? In the following, I will argue that Mahler's visits to the Netherlands in 1903, 1904, 1906, and 1909 led his artistic interests into new directions and in particular got him interested in what could be called the "cultural history of the night."

Mahler Visits Amsterdam

Much has been said about Mahler's visits to the Netherlands. The consensus seems to be that Mahler was enchanted with the Concertgebouw Orchestra, founded in 1888, and its young conductor Willem Mengelberg (1871–1951). Indeed, Mengelberg and his orchestra offered Mahler the chance to present his works to players and audiences who were by no means unequivocal in their praise but were generally supportive. Jens Malte Fischer goes so far as to suggest that Mahler considered living permanently in the Netherlands.[10] But was Mahler's motivation purely logistical; was he only interested in the performance opportunities that the Netherlands offered him? It is remarkable how quickly, after his first visit in 1903, Mahler developed close friendships with Willem Mengelberg and with the composer Alphons Diepenbrock (1862–1921), both of whom were Dutch citizens of German descent and had an intense interest in German cultural history.

Unquestionably, Mahler respected Willem Mengelberg as a congenial conductor. They worked closely together to develop a performance practice not just for Mahler's symphonic works but also for works of the symphonic canon in general. It is clearly under the influence of Mahler that Mengelberg, who in his student days had written some minor compositions, began composing again. For the 300th anniversary of Rembrandt's birthday, Mengelberg composed a series of Rembrandt variations. He was one of a group of four Dutch composers asked to compose something for that occasion.[11] Mahler's friend Alphons Diepenbrock was also among them. All indications are that during his visits to the Netherlands Mahler quickly developed a remarkably close intellectual relationship with the composer Alphons Diepenbrock.[12] It is not clear how much Mahler knew about Diepenbrock's music. There is some evidence that he attempted to organize a Vienna performance of Diepenbrock's *Te deum*, but nothing came of it. What is clear, however, is that Diepenbrock appealed to Mahler as an intellectual companion. They shared an interest in Wagner and the German Romantics. Both were Catholic and yet were also staunch humanists who felt indebted to the legacy of modernity.

What was Diepenbrock working on when he and Mahler first met? Diepenbrock's compositions can be organized into three periods.[13] Initially, Diepenbrock predominantly wrote music for choir (often religious but sometimes secular) and works for voice and piano. A second period in Diepenbrock's creative development started in 1898 and is characterized by an interest in the symphonic poem — the genre with which Diepenbrock's name is now associated. The most famous of these compositions are the adaptations from 1899 of two poems from the collection that the German early Romantic poet Novalis had published as *Hymnen an die Nacht*. In 1905–6 Diepenbrock composed a symphonic aphorism based on the fragment "Im großen Schweigen" (In Great Silence) from Nietzsche's *Morgenröthe* (Daybreak), and in 1911 he completed a symphonic poem based on another German Romantic's text, Hölderlin's poem "Die Nacht" (The Night). I mention these specific compositions because they work with German texts and therefore with a cultural tradition shared by Diepenbrock and Mahler. Diepenbrock simultaneously worked with Latin, French, and Dutch materials, and in fact after 1910 he concentrated mainly on French materials; the music of Debussy clearly had a major impact on him, and the First World War, during which the Netherlands remained neutral, led to his break with Wagner and the German cultural tradition as a whole, with one notable exception: in 1918 he wrote incidental music for Goethe's *Faust* (with a few songs).

One can say that for Diepenbrock, as for Mengelberg, Mahler's visits to Amsterdam had a catalytic function. Interestingly, in 1906 Diepenbrock composed music to "Veni Creator Spiritus," the same Latin hymn that Mahler used for the first movement of his Eighth Symphony, on which he was working during the summer of that same year. A committee of members of the Dutch Roman Catholic church in charge of approving religious music for use in the church, to which Diepenbrock had submitted his piece, rejected it because the committee believed it heard a resemblance with Wagner's *Tannhäuser*.[14] There is, however, another piece of music by Diepenbrock that offers itself for comparison with Mahler's work. One of Diepenbrock's most interesting compositions is the above-mentioned symphonic aphorism "Im großen Schweigen," composed in 1905–6, after Mahler's initial visits. This is a symphonic poem about the night — one of Diepenbrock's favorite topics, as is clear from the works mentioned above, but also from many of his other compositions (often also for voice and piano). It is no exaggeration to say that night was an obsession for him. To understand his interest in "night" as a musical and cultural topic, it is productive to look at his essay "Schemeringen" (Twilights), first published in the Dutch literary-cultural journal *De Nieuwe Gids* in 1893. Diepenbrock was heavily influenced by the theoretical writings of Wagner and in particular of Nietzsche. Echoing the cultural pessimism of these two thinkers, Diepenbrock sees Western civilization approaching its end: "The old occidental, the old Latin world, the wreckage of the old Holy Roman Empire will fade away in the immeasurable cleft of infinite times."[15] Twilight is what characterizes the transition from this old world into something new. Diepenbrock regrets this loss of old certainties. Not unlike Nietzsche, however, he sees it as something to be desired rather than something that is simply inevitable. With great ambiguity, Diepenbrock writes of the "blissful destruction of the consciousness of life" (449).

In one of his earlier works, the Third Symphony, Mahler had used nocturnal imagery to describe man's existential dilemmas in postmetaphysical times (see chapter 3). In this context it is interesting to note that

Mengelberg and Mahler had first met in June 1902 in the German city Krefeld, where Mengelberg attended the world premiere of Mahler's Third. This led to Mahler's receiving an invitation to conduct this symphony in Amsterdam in October 1903[16] — the beginning of Mahler's close relationship with Mengelberg, Diepenbrock, and the Concertgebouw orchestra. It is possible to read Nietzsche's "Mitternachtslied" from *Also sprach Zarathustra*, the text that Mahler had used for the fourth movement of the Third Symphony, as an illustration of Diepenbrock's ideas (which, as I mentioned earlier, were influenced by Nietzsche's thinking). Zarathustra is a figure straddling old and new times; the "night" in "Mitternachtslied" is associated with profoundly ambivalent feelings, as I have shown (see chapter 3).

Nietzsche's fragment "Im großen Schweigen," which Diepenbrock used for his symphonic aphorism, offers an apt illustration of his ideas presented in "Twilights." Nietzsche's "Im großen Schweigen"[17] describes twilight at the seashore, with a city nearby. Church bells ring "Ave Maria" — clearly symbolizing an old order of things that, according to Nietzsche, is no longer valid. After the bells fade away, all is silent. The aphorism focuses on this moment of transition; the silence of the night inaugurates a new way of experiencing reality, a new time and new order of things. This silence is both "beautiful and uncanny" (schön und grausenhaft) and underlies a profoundly ambivalent experience. More precisely, it is nature that is silent. This silence is expressive of its evil side ("Bosheit"). Man is the object of this evil side of nature; his heart fears a new truth ("neue Wahrheit") of which the silence is a premonition. Man's heart cannot speak; language and thought turn into the objects of hatred. Knowledge is nothing but error, imagination, and delusion ("Irrthum," "Einbildung," and "Wahngeist"). The sea and the evening teach man to stop being human. "Im großen Schweigen" ends with a fundamental dilemma: should man give in to the new order of things or, as is implied, should he return to his old view of the world? Diepenbrock links the fragment to an autobiographical experience in Genoa that Nietzsche describes in *Menschliches, Allzumenschliches* (Human, All Too Human), as the autograph score of the work makes clear.[18]

It is very tempting to read Nietzsche's fragment "Im großen Schweigen" as a model for the first movement of Mahler's Seventh Symphony. In addition to the nocturnal images that Mahler's Seventh and Nietzsche's fragment share — Diepenbrock writes of the nocturnal atmosphere of the first *four* movements[19] — both also contain references to water. The first movement is one of Mahler's many compositions that are closely associated with nature. It was inspired by the sound of the oars of a rowing boat touching the water, as he reported to Alma in a letter[20] (not unlike how Nietzsche's stay in Genoa led him to write "Im großen Schweigen"). Few will disagree with the statement that this movement offers its listeners "beautiful," but also "uncanny" music — "schön und grausenhaft," to quote Nietzsche's fragment. The same ambiguity is expressed in Mengelberg's comments about it; he understands the first movement to be an expression of "night, a tragic night" or "the reign of the power of darkness" in the form of a "violent force," but at times we also "hear the unshakeable hope of humanity," its longing "for light and love."[21] It is tempting to see the dissolution of musical structure in the first movement[22] — radical by Mahler's standards — in connection with the insight in Nietzsche's fragment that all human knowledge is error. With its recurrent polyphonies, this symphony articulates the breakdown of Western tradition that Nietzsche had diagnosed (more successfully, indeed, than Diepenbrock's composition, which is far more conventional). There is, unfortunately, no direct evidence linking Nietzsche's aphoristic fragment, Diepenbrock's adaptation, and Mahler's symphony. Nevertheless, Nietzsche's "Im großen Schweigen" (but also Hölderlin's "Die Nacht" or Novalis's *Hymnen an die Nacht*) are exemplary in their thematization of the night side of German culture and can help us understand what Mahler's thinking may have been when he composed this work.

Rembrandt and the Dark Side of German Culture

Diepenbrock's obsession with nocturnal imagery makes a connection between the Seventh Symphony and Dutch culture plausible. There is another link connecting this symphony to its composer's visits to the Netherlands. Mengelberg's score of the second movement contains an allusion to Rembrandt's "Nachtwacht" (Night Watch).[23] It is assumed that Mahler himself was the source of this allusion. Mengelberg is also known to have referred to the "Nachtwacht" during rehearsals. As is the case for all "programmatic" statements by Mahler, this one is controversial. Diepenbrock questions the reference to the "Nachtwacht": "It is not true that he [Mahler] wanted to paint the Nachtwacht here. He only mentioned the painting as an analogy" (Es ist nicht wahr, daß er hier die "Nachtwache" hat schildern wollen. Er hat das Gemälde nur vergleichsweise genannt).[24] Clearly Diepenbrock is familiar with Mahler's thoughts on programmatic music. He therefore seeks to articulate a relationship between music and painting that is not referential; both try to do a similar thing, but in different ways, each bound by the rules of its own medium. Diepenbrock's skepticism is echoed elsewhere. In his diaries, the Austrian author Robert Musil, who visited Mengelberg's rehearsals of this symphony at the 1920 Mahler festival in Amsterdam, also mentions Mengelberg's reference to the "Nachtwacht" as a model. Musil disapproves; he cannot imagine Mahler would have imagined something so banal.[25] For Musil it is a misconception to assume that Mahler's art is referential or descriptive in the way that Mengelberg had suggested (or seemed to suggest). Clearly, Musil sees Mahler as a congenial modernist artist. But if Mahler's intentions were not descriptive, then what purpose did the references to Rembrandt serve? How are we to understand the importance of Rembrandt for Mahler's Seventh Symphony?

We know that Mahler, while studying at the University of Vienna, took a class on Dutch painting from the fourteenth to the seventeenth centuries.[26] Also, Mahler's close friend Lipiner is known to have had a strong interest in Rembrandt.[27] Mahler's curiosity regarding Rembrandt is documented in connection to his visits to Amsterdam. We know that he saw the "Nachtwacht" and other paintings by Rembrandt in the Rijksmuseum during his first visit to Amsterdam.[28] During a later visit he saw the Rembrandt house, which at the time was inhabited by a number of Jewish families and not open to the public. This suggests that Mahler was aware of the fact that Rembrandt's house was situated in Amsterdam's Jewish neighborhood. Can Mahler's attraction to Rembrandt be at least partially explained by that painter's interest in the Jewish life that surrounded him?[29] "Through these windows Rembrandt must have looked" (Durch diese Fenster soll Rembrandt also geguckt haben), he is said to have observed on that occasion, and according to the same source Mahler added that he would rather die than fail to grow as an artist.[30] All of this is testimony to Mahler's respect for this painter and perhaps to feelings of artistic affinity.

Within the context of Rembrandt's work and seventeenth-century portrait painting in general, the "Nachtwacht" enjoys a unique status. Rembrandt breaks in the most radical way possible with the rather strict and unimaginative cultural codes that existed for such group portraits[31] in order to produce something chaotic highlighting the individuality of all of the figures involved. As Simon Schama points out, "Nachtwacht" is "a picture threatening to disintegrate into incoherence" (495). A similar break with convention is an important aspect of the Seventh Symphony. One could describe the second movement, about which the "Nachtwacht" reference was made, as a march in which everyone walks out of order but that nevertheless moves forward. Rembrandt's citizens' militia moves from darkness into the light (not, however, into the light of day; 497). Diepenbrock has characterized the second movement as an example of a "march with a fantastic chiaroscuro" (ein Marsch . . . mit einem phantastischen clair obscur),[32] using a term often used to characterize Rembrandt's style. To understand Mahler's interest in the "Nachtwacht," it may also be significant to know that Rembrandt's contemporaries associated citizens' militias with a drive toward independence. They not only fought against the Spanish and would help the Dutch Republic gain its formal independence from Spain (1648), but they were also known as opponents of the House of Orange, the de facto rulers of the Republic.[33] While nightwatchmen in the sixteenth and seventeenth century generally were treated with contempt, Rembrandt in contrast depicts them as respectable citizens.[34] All of these diverse strands may help to explain Mahler's interest in Rembrandt from an art history perspective, at least partially.

There is however another reason why Rembrandt engaged intellectuals like Mahler, Lipiner, and Diepenbrock. In 1890 the previously unknown scholar Julius Langbehn (1851–1907) published a book on Rembrandt with the Nietzsche-inspired title *Rembrandt als Erzieher* (Rembrandt as Educator). This work would soon become the intellectual bestseller of the early 1890s; within its first two years it went through more than forty editions.[35] Its impact has been compared by some to that of Oswald Spengler's *Der Untergang des Abendlandes* (The Decline of the West) immediately after the First World War.[36] Before publishing *Rembrandt als Erzieher*, Langbehn's only claim to fame had been that he had served briefly as a caretaker for Friedrich Nietzsche, who shortly before had become insane.[37] This piece of information about Langbehn may have intrigued Nietzsche admirers such as Lipiner and Mahler; in a sense, *Rembrandt als Erzieher* could be read as the latest report on Nietzsche's thinking — through a not-exactly-reliable mediator, that is. Its reception history is complicated by the fact that Langbehn kept updating and expanding the text. No comprehensive study on these revisions and the critical response to the text has been published to date. After his inimitable success with *Rembrandt als Erzieher*, Langbehn soon disappeared from the public spotlight. And after 1892 interest in *Rembrandt als Erzieher* faded, although the book was reprinted occasionally until well into the Third Reich. To some extent, Langbehn managed to live off the reputation of *Rembrandt als Erzieher*, although he did much to destroy his newfound reputation by publishing a series of poems, some of which were perceived to be pornographic.[38]

To understand the attraction of *Rembrandt als Erzieher*, it is important to know that the book claims to document a societal crisis that is simultaneously a cultural crisis. While Germany is doing very well economically, it has, according to Langbehn, lost touch with its spiritual roots. His criticism, like that of many conservative cultural critics of his time, seeks to revive some of the ideas underlying German Romanticism. Langbehn attacks a world dominated by the sciences, mechanistic thinking, and over-specialization (103). In particular, he criticizes the lack of individualism among his German contemporaries, even though this is part of the essence of Germanness (3–5). It is this crisis of modern society that interests Langbehn and that leads him to invoke a new role for culture as a medium through which Germany can redeem itself. Only art will be able to save Germany (99). Art has the power to reassemble a fragmented society. It will enable a new synthesis, and the personification of this synthesis is Rembrandt. Rembrandt is, for Langbehn, in spite of his Dutch background, the most individual of all German artists: "a high degree of irregularity, displacement, peculiarity" (ein hoher Grad von Unregelmäßigkeit Verschobenheit Eigenartigkeit) characterizes his work (9 and 12). Yet Langbehn also expects what he calls "the creation of new spiritual values" (die Schaffung neuer geistiger Werte) by reorienting German culture toward Rembrandt and the tradition he stands for (268). More specifically, he is hoping for a deepening of German national consciousness beyond everyday politics: the old cosmopolitan attitudes should be replaced by an aesthetic politics that would counter "the often trivial interests of everyday politics" (die oft so trivialen Interessen der jeweiligen Tagespolitik; 269). In addition to Rembrandt, Langbehn also frequently mentions Shakespeare, Dürer, Goethe, and Beethoven. His preferences are extremely eclectic.

The model of cultural renewal that Langbehn promotes is, in many respects, reminiscent of that of the early Nietzsche, in particular as proposed in *Die Geburt der Tragödie*, the text that was so influential for Mahler's circle of friends during his student days (see chapter 3). Metaphors of light and darkness also play an important role in this work; Apollo is associated with light, Dionysos with darkness. *Rembrandt als Erzieher*, however, also clearly moves beyond Nietzsche's text. In the book, Langbehn proposes something very radical: he wants to rethink German cultural history by looking at its margins and what was discarded. Rembrandt symbolizes an alternative path that German culture could have taken (and potentially could still take). The choice of Rembrandt seems rather arbitrary. It has been suggested that Langbehn considered making Shakespeare the core of his argument;[39] like Rembrandt, Shakespeare's Hamlet clearly fascinates Langbehn as an intriguing, ambiguous, and important figure situated at the margins of Germanic culture. Surprisingly, *Rembrandt als Erzieher* did not contain a single concrete or detailed analysis of a painting by Rembrandt (the editions from the 1890s did not contain any reproductions of Rembrandt's paintings either). What "Rembrandt" exactly stands for remains equally unclear; the terms that Langbehn uses to characterize this alternative route are rather vague. His penchant for the dark side of German culture is an attempt to revive the Romantic tradition in German cultural history.

Such a revival is meant as a counter move to the Enlightenment — its name already associated with "light" — but also against the classical period in German literary history. Men like Winckelmann, Goethe, and Schiller were highly indebted to the Enlightenment, but also focused on the "light" world of ancient Greece (that had also been attacked by Friedrich Nietzsche). It is literally the dark side of German culture, represented by Rembrandt's paintings, that for Langbehn is a desirable alternative to the German fixation on the light of Greece (44). However, even though images of "light" and "darkness" are ubiquitous in *Rembrandt als Erzieher*, Langbehn's text does not explain how exactly "light" and "darkness" represent different modes of viewing life, different normative models. What is clear is that, for Langbehn, Rembrandt somehow represents a different trajectory for German culture. The fact that Rembrandt was Dutch and not German does not bother Langbehn. As a Dutchman, Rembrandt preserved an alternative route for German culture from which the Germans themselves had long since strayed. Langbehn, by the way, is intrigued by such geographical margins (as his interest in Hamlet shows). He was born in Hadersleben (Haderslev), a small town that was Danish when Langbehn was born, later became Prussian and then became part of the German Reich, and since 1920 has been part of Denmark again, but with a significant German-speaking population. It is precisely Langbehn's decentering of German culture and its subsequent recentering (in support of its margins) that makes his book relevant for Mahler's cultural cosmos.

Interestingly, in the context of his considerations about Rembrandt Langbehn not only addresses Dutch culture as a margin of German cultural history but also closely examines Rembrandt's views on Jews and their (marginalized) position in the Dutch-German tradition. Langbehn's statements about Jews in *Rembrandt als Erzieher* are complicated and problematic, if not downright confusing. Many of the anti-Semitic statements found in later editions did not appear in the initial 1890 edition. Perhaps Langbehn did not want to alienate potential Jewish audiences.[40] But even in the work's later editions, Langbehn does have positive, while highly ambiguous things to say about Jews:

> Strangely enough, Rembrandt's nobility shows itself, in the end, in — his love for the Jews; here his local and noble attitude, his view of what is close and what is high, meet. He saw this species of mankind every day, because he lived in the Jodenbreestraat in Amsterdam; the kernel of such artistic and intellectual particularities is often closer at hand than one would expect. . . . A real and religious Jew in the old sense has unmistakably something noble about him; he belongs to that centuries-old moral and spiritual aristocracy from which most modern Jews have strayed; in this respect, Lord Beaconsfield was half-right when he declared them the oldest aristocracy on earth. Rembrandt's Jews were real Jews who wanted to be nothing but Jews, and who also had character. For almost all Jews today, one has to say the opposite; they want to be Germans, Englishmen, Frenchmen etc., and because of that merely lose their character. . . . Jews as they are today he would have loathed or never understood.
>
> [Eigenthümlich genug zeigt sich endlich die Vornehmheit Rembrandt's in — seiner Vorliebe für die Juden; hier begegnen sich seine lokale und seine vornehme Gesinnung, sein Blick in die Nähe und sein Blick in die Höhe. Er hatte diese M[e]nschengattung täglich

vor Augen; denn er wohnte in der Judenbreitstraße zu Amsterdam; die Keime solcher künstlerischen und geistigen Besonderheiten liegen oft näher zur Hand, als man meint. . . . Ein echter und altgläubiger Jude hat unverkennbar etwas Vornehmes an sich; er gehört zu jener uralten sittlichen und geistigen Aristokratie, von der die meisten modernen Juden abgewichen sind; in dieser Hinsicht fühlte Lord Beaconsfield also halbwegs richtig, als er sie für den ältesten Adel der Welt erklärte. Rembrandt's Juden waren echte Juden; die nichts Anderes sein wollten als Juden; und die also Charakter hatten. Von fast allen heutigen Juden gilt das Gegentheil; sie wollen Deutsche Engländer Franzosen u.s.w. sein; und werden dadurch nur charakterlos. . . . diese, wie sie heute sind, würde er verabscheut oder nie begriffen haben.][41]

Bearing in mind Langbehn's anti-Jewish remarks in the later editions of *Rembrandt als Erzieher*, this passage articulates something quite unexpected. In contrast to Germans, the text suggests, at least some Jews have remained in touch with their tradition. While living among non-Jews and in cultures very different from their own, they have managed to protect their own cultural memory (in contrast, it is strongly implied, to Germans who have lost touch with their cultural memory). This Langbehn describes as the "aristocratic" and "noble" character of Rembrandt's Jews. What is in essence a very conservative impulse leads Langbehn to respect Rembrandt's Jews. Precisely for this reason it is therefore possible that these Jews, for Langbehn, represent the pinnacle of Rembrandt's art. For at least a moment in the course of his argument, Langbehn makes Rembrandt's Jews into the ultimate representatives of an ideal German culture.

There are more positive attributes that Langbehn associates with Jewishness. It is not Rembrandt's "archaic" Jews alone who represent some sort of ideal for Langbehn; his opinion of Rembrandt's Jewish contemporary Baruch de Spinoza is remarkably positive as well. Spinoza, too, exemplifies the "original aristocratic Judaism" (uraristokratisches Judenthum)[42] that Langbehn seeks. His personality is comparable to Rembrandt's; both men are heretics and unorthodox thinkers; both are interested primarily in individuality and the world;[43] both are characters with depth, they are goal-oriented workers and thinkers, and are ultimately free human beings. Not entirely convincingly perhaps, Langbehn also attempts to read into Spinoza's work a play of darkness and light; more specifically, Spinoza attempts to bring (some) light into the darkness that constitutes human existence. The fact that Rembrandt and Spinoza can be compared in such an affirmative way is highly significant in view of the great symbolic value given to Rembrandt in *Rembrandt als Erzieher*. Rembrandt and Spinoza are both described by Langbehn as being open to their environments in a cultural sense. Langbehn associates Spinoza's aristocracy of the mind, on the one hand, with an embeddedness in tradition, but on the other hand with an inquisitiveness about the cultures surrounding him, and a lack of orthodoxy not to be confused with a slavish copying of other cultures. Langbehn speaks of the "higher and truly spiritual world view" (höhere und wahrhaftig seelische Weltauffassung) in Spinoza's thinking that ultimately moves beyond individualism and bears some similarities to ascetic philosophies in the Christian and Indian world (43). Such an observation may be based more on Spinoza's biography than on his texts, but it does bear witness to a cosmopolitan impulse in Spinoza's philosophy that I will discuss at greater length in the next chapter.

In spite of Langbehn's positive portrayal of Jewish culture there is, however, both in the above quote and in Langbehn's text in general, a counterargument to the positive depiction of Jews. *Rembrandt als Erzieher* is, in this respect, emblematic for a line of thinking about Jews in German cultural history since the late eighteenth century. The text emphasizes the positive characteristics of the "old" Hebrews at the expense of modern, assimilated Jews. Jews who have stayed in touch with their own tradition distinguish themselves positively in comparison with Jews who have adapted to their new (European) environments without ever really becoming part of it. In Langbehn's eyes, these assimilated Jews are profiteers and parasites; they are the object of his scorn. While Langbehn primarily addresses his criticisms to the Jews of his time, he finds the same antagonism in Rembrandt's time as well. Rembrandt, in Langbehn's words, "mingled with aristocratic, not with plebeian Jews" (hielt es mit den aristokratischen, nicht mit den plebejischen Juden; 43). In a paradigmatic way, this distinction between "old" and "new" Jews can be found in the work of Herder.[44] In spite of the occasionally positive things Langbehn has to say about Jews, I by no means wish to trivialize the intolerant, racist, and anti-Semitic agenda underlying Langbehn's book, especially its later editions. He not only falls back on the anti-Semitic stereotypes of his time; he actively helps to create these stereotypes.[45]

And yet, there is, I will argue in the following, a deep affinity between the cultural reforms that Langbehn proposed and the ideas underlying Mahler's Seventh Symphony.

Symphony No. 7 — Composing the Night

The Seventh Symphony introduces a new phase in Mahler's creative thinking. It displays a number of features typical in his later symphonic compositions (the Eighth, Ninth, and Tenth symphonies and the *Lied von der Erde*). The Seventh Symphony is intended, I hope to have shown thus far, as a return to the cultural issues explicitly addressed in some of the (anti-programmatic) programmatic statements accompanying Mahler's first four symphonies and the *Wunderhorn* songs. Mahler's intention is to provide a rereading of the German cultural tradition that represents a new way of looking at German Romanticism, but also looks further back (as does the Eighth). Mahler is interested in forms of alterity that are marginalized by, but nevertheless present in, German cultural history. At the beginning of this chapter I mentioned Bruno Walter's remark that this symphony refers to a form of Romanticism that he assumed had outlived its usefulness. Here Mahler is interested in unearthing forgotten cultural and intellectual history, and Dutch culture seems to have played the role of a catalyst. Mahler, I believe, was intrigued by Dutch culture as a symbol of what was marginalized and discarded within German cultural history. This framework of a search for alterity within the German tradition is also highly relevant for the Eighth Symphony, as I will show in the following chapter.

One of the innovations of the Seventh Symphony is that slow movements play a very prominent role (as they do in the Eighth, Ninth, and Tenth and the *Lied von der Erde*). One could say that from the Seventh on, Adagios start to play a more prominent role in Mahler's symphonic landscape. They are no longer part of the organic structure of the symphony, understood in a more conventional way, as they were in some of Mahler's earlier symphonies (the First, Fourth, Fifth, and Sixth) that had *one* slow movement (usually one of the middle movements). Starting with the Seventh, the first and last movements of Mahler's symphonies in particular tend to develop as slow movements.

This structural development is paralleled by something else: the three middle movements of this work evoke an intimacy associated with chamber-music settings; in fact, the symphony orchestra functions as a chamber orchestra in these middle movements, whereas we are confronted with a full-scale symphony orchestra in its first and last movements. These contrasts are intentional, I would argue. Mahler's interest in a chamber-music atmosphere was first seen in the *Kindertotenlieder*[46] but can also be found in the Eight and Ninth symphonies and the *Lied von der Erde*. While working on these compositions, Mahler simultaneously, in his correspondence with Strauss, emphasizes that the *Wunderhorn-Lieder* should be performed in the chamber-music style.[47] In particular Schoenberg and Webern would, in their compositions, pick up on the preference for smaller orchestral settings seen in Mahler's later works. Contrasting with this interest in a chamber-music style in his later works, Mahler is also increasingly interested in writing music for mass audiences. One could say that his symphonies display an interest in the dynamic between the individual and the masses. In the last movement of the Seventh Symphony the idea of music for the masses is seen as something negative. But Mahler's interest in music for the masses is not just negative; in particular, the Eighth Symphony struggles with the question as to how mass and individual can be reconciled.

In order to understand these innovative aspects of Mahler's later works, it is productive to look at passages in *Rembrandt als Erzieher* that deal with music in general and with Wagner in particular. I hope to have shown convincingly that Mahler's interest in the night in relation to the Seventh was inspired by a desire to reread German cultural history. In the section "Musical Matters"(Musikalisches), Langbehn — referring to statements by Wagner, who had characterized the adagio as the "foundation of all musical determination of time" (Grundlage aller musikalischen Zeitbestimmung) — calls the adagio "the specifically German musical tempo" (das speziell deutsche Musiktempo).[48] Beethoven's Adagios are invoked to illustrate Langbehn's point; Beethoven serves here, as in much of the nineteenth-century's cultural imagination, as the quintessence of German culture. But, improbably enough, for Langbehn Rembrandt's paintings express this German Adagio as well. Langbehn's call for a "German" Adagio is followed immediately by a deliberation on how one form of art (painting) can be translated into another form (music). Through the experience of nature, music enters Rembrandt's paintings: "In Rembrandt's painting there seems to resound a bit of the soft murmuring of the sea surrounding his homeland" (In Rembrandt's Gemälde scheint etwas von dem leisen Rauschen des Meeres hineinzutönen, das seine Heimath umspült). It is very interesting that Langbehn, in his rather far-fetched example of the transition of one medium to another, uses "water" to illustrate his point. One of the very few statements of a somewhat programmatic nature that Mahler made about the first movement of the Seventh is, as I have already shown, that the beginning of this movement is inspired by the sound made by the oars of a rowboat.

The musical ideal that Langbehn advocates is characterized not merely by slowness but also by a specific mood (typical for adagios). In elaborating on this "Rembrandtian" musical ideal, Langbehn draws a comparison with "certain Northern-German folk songs" (gewisse Volkslieder des nördlichen Deutschlands) and then speaks of the melancholic character that is typical for this music, a character that can also be found in Rembrandt's paintings and in Beethoven's music. Langbehn describes the general ambiance underlying these works of art as "a sort of softspoken German grace that has turned away from the world" (eine Art von zartverschwiegener weltabgekehrter deutscher Anmuth) that is to serve as a northern European alternative to the superficial lightness of southern — that is, Italian — European music. Langbehn also characterizes this mood as "melancholic." The dark colors of Rembrandt's paintings are echoed in the melancholic nature of the musical ideal that Langbehn envisions. Much later in his text Langbehn further clarifies the musical ideal outlined here. He makes the interesting observation that "after [Wagner] music, if it wants to progress, will need to return to the highest form of intimacy" (nach [Wagner] wird die Musik, wenn sie überhaupt fortschreiten will, zur höchsten Intimität zurückkehren müssen; 278). "Intimacy" is the key word here — intimacy as opposed to superficial splendor. The second, third, and fourth movements of the Seventh Symphony exemplify, I would argue, such a program of intimate music. Mahler experiments with a reduced orchestra — reduced, as it were, to a chamber-music ensemble — in order to evoke melancholy and intimacy, in contrast to music that is interested in overpowering its audiences through pure effect. Bearing in mind that Mahler, like his contemporaries Hugo Wolf, Arnold Schönberg, and Alexander Zemlinsky, was obsessed by the question of developing a musical language that would move beyond Wagner, Langbehn's remark is especially interesting, because it gives a hint as to how this could be realized. Langbehn's deliberations here, incidentally, proved to be prophetic. Not only Mahler but the avant-gardists Schönberg and Webern would, after experimenting with large orchestral settings, turn to composing music for much smaller ensembles.

While Langbehn, in the section that I have just discussed, suggests that his ideas follow or at least are inspired by Wagner's program, a later section on music in *Rembrandt als Erzieher* sheds a very different light on his intentions. In this section, appropriately titled "Wagner,"[49] Langbehn's attitude toward Wagner is very different; Wagner does not serve as a model but as a countermodel for the musical ideal outlined by Langbehn. Here he is clearly influenced by Nietzsche's harsh criticism of Wagner, even though Nietzsche is surprisingly absent from *Rembrandt als Erzieher*. Langbehn questions how long Wagner's music will dominate the German musical landscape. He criticizes Wagner's lack of modesty; Wagner's music knows "no rest" (keine Ruhe). Wagner is interested only in superficial effects; his music is characterized by nervousness: "He is nervous and makes others nervous" (Er ist nervös und macht nervös). His music is not even German: "He wanted to be German; but his form of passion does not always achieve this; the loud lovelorn lunacy of Isolde may have something Celtic about it" (Er wollte deutsch sein; aber seine Art von Leidenschaft ist dies nicht immer; der laute Liebeswahnsinn seiner Isolde dürfte eher keltisch sein.) Wagner's music has more in common with Meyerbeer than he would like to admit.

Wagner's music — or at least a version of his music — also plays an important role in the final movement of Mahler's Seventh Symphony. The last movement, the Rondo-Finale, has often been criticized and is among the most controversial in Mahler's oeuvre. Far from creating an atmosphere of intimacy, it seems to want to appeal to a mass audience. There is an apparent critical consensus that the last movement expresses a return to light. Mahler did suggest this during rehearsals, as we have seen, and the idea has since been generally accepted.[50] Diepenbrock characterizes this movement with the words "the radiant sun; night is gone" (die strahlende Sonne, die Nacht ist gewichen).[51] Diepenbrock further links Mahler's symphony to Nietzsche's cultural criticism in *Die Geburt der Tragödie* by stating that here Apollo has defeated Dionysos.[52] The music seems excessively loud and fast. Adorno writes of a "positivity" that is rarely found in Mahler and that is indicative of a "disproportion between the splendid exterior and the meager content of the whole" (*MPE*, 137; Mißverhältnis zwischen der prunkvollen Erscheinung und dem mageren Gehalt des Ganzen: *MP,* 281). Others echo Adorno's criticism. Musicologists have criticized the final movement because of its "pompous attitude" and "superficial splendor";[53] it has been seen as typical "Kapellmeistermusik" because of its assumed compositional shortcomings and supposed lack of originality.[54] In particular, the juxtaposition of the leitmotiv of Wagner's *Meistersinger von Nürnberg* with a theme from Lehár's *Lustige Witwe* (The Merry Widow) has stupefied critics.[55] Adorno is undoubtedly referring to this juxtaposition when he speaks of the "meager content" of this movement. The suggestion has been made that this must be some kind of intentional play on the tradition of the "affirmatory finale"[56] but critics are at a loss to explain what Mahler may have intended.

It may be possible to find biographical explanations here. Is Mahler articulating his frustration with contemporary audiences, who loved the operas of Wagner and Lehár but despised Mahler's own far more demanding symphonies? The return to daylight is simultaneously a return from the margin (Amsterdam) to the center of German culture (Vienna) and the humdrum routine of running the Vienna Court Opera.

Langbehn's cultural criticism may also be helpful here. Above all, the Seventh Symphony, I would argue along with Langbehn, articulates a clash of cultural concepts, of ideas relating to what music is about, and even what music is. We know that Mahler did not have a very high opinion of Lehár's *Lustige Witwe*; for him, it exemplified a form of useless entertainment comparable to playing a game of cards.[57] The fact that Mahler quotes the leitmotiv from *Die Meistersinger* is also no coincidence. *Die Meistersinger von Nürnberg* is an opera about the competition between two singers in late medieval Nürnberg, one of them, Beckmesser, characterized in ways that contemporary audiences would have recognized to be "Jewish."[58] This quote at the beginning of the fifth movement of the Seventh Symphony not only points to the element of competition but also is to be read as a reference to Mahler's Jewishness; here the Jewish composer takes up Wagner's challenge to find a new road to German culture. Langbehn's criticism of Wagner as overly loud and pompous is to be read in the context of what, very early on in his book, he calls "Ueberkultur." At the beginning of the book he argues that the problem with German society is not a lack of culture ("Unkultur") but a surplus of culture. This German "Ueberkultur" is more damaging than "Unkultur" (3). Germans are obsessed with "Bildung" and "Kultur" — it is part of Germans' self-image — but their understanding of these concepts is no more than superficial. Wagner caters to these superficial needs. In the last movement of this symphony, Mahler, I would argue, seeks to accommodate his audiences' need for "Ueberkultur"; that is, their intense but superficial interest in things cultural. Interpreted in this way, through the lens of Langbehn, the Seventh Symphony ends with a comment on the decline of art. The negative associations in the response of many critics to this movement are programmed into the music and are part of Mahler's intention, not the result of Mahler's incompetence as a composer. And yet, in its earlier movements, this work also aims to give an impression of other forms of art, of what German art could have been and still might be.

How do the above references to literary, intellectual, and cultural history add up to a different view of the Seventh Symphony? What narrative, in other words, does it present to us? It articulates neither a trajectory from innocence to experience nor a course in the opposite direction, from experience to (regained) innocence. If one accepts the premise underlying the philosophical-literary argument in this chapter that it is in the "night" that the listener experiences some anticipation of "meaning" accompanied by a fundamentally new way of experiencing the world, then it is not at the beginning or end of the symphony, but in the middle — more specifically, in the three middle movements — that the process of *Bildung* takes place, if it can be called that: it is after all an experience of only a very temporary nature. Rather than understanding the symphony as a form of *Bildungsroman*, I propose that it should be understood, not unlike the Fourth Symphony, as the musical equivalent of an essay: an essay on the night.

All the literary and philosophical texts discussed above thematize the highly diverse ways in which the night can be experienced. The emotions associated with darkness are profoundly ambiguous. Initially, in the first movement, darkness is experienced as something uncanny and chaotic; the night here is associated with some form of the primal force of nature. Gradually, in particular in the two *Nachtmusik* movements (the second and fourth movements), this experience of uncanniness makes way for more specific and yet also highly ambivalent emotions. Night is never far away and never really disappears from the background in these pieces. In the third movement night is associated with death, and in the fourth movement with love. This speaks to the cyclical nature of the emotions associated with both death and love; they are associated with each other, respond to each other. The final movement makes us forget about the core of the symphony, about the learning experience of these earlier movements. The key movement within the symphony is unquestionably the second movement with its programmatic reference to Rembrandt. It is this movement that explains the transformation of the first movement's primal nature into something more meaningful — perhaps not into a sense of order, but rather into something that is more than chaos. It is possible to read Rembrandt's painting as a powerful argument for breaking with tradition, or as a statement about finding commonality in individuality, about mobility, and about the attempt to bring (some) order into chaos (or light into darkness). In the end, the painting functions as a powerful metaphor for the music, and the music as a powerful illustration of the painting.

5: Goethe against German Culture

IN EXPLAINING HIS Eighth Symphony to contemporaries, Gustav Mahler called it a "gift to the entire nation" (Geschenk an die ganze Nation).[1] He thereby helped create a genealogy for the work that would have occurred to few people on the basis of the music alone, and simultaneously provoked a number of questions. Mahler refers to a tradition of composing works for national occasions, but does he identify with that tradition or distance himself from it? Characterizing the Eighth as a "gift" to the "nation" does not necessarily mean that Mahler intended it to be a piece of national music. But he certainly wanted to write music that engaged critically with the tradition of composing for national occasions.

One legacy of Mahler's membership in the Pernerstorfer Circle (discussed in the introduction to this study) was his interest in the political dimension of German culture rather than in Austrian particularism — although, like other former members, by 1906 he had long distanced himself from the circle's nationalist and conservative political ambitions.[2] In the following I examine the debates about the national function of culture in Germany and Austria around the turn of the century, and in particular the role that Goethe and his works played in this debate. There was of course a powerful musical tradition of composing works for national occasions during the eighteenth and nineteenth centuries.[3] In addition to referencing this tradition in musical history, though, Mahler's comment on the Eighth Symphony also evokes a literary paradigm. Throughout the nineteenth century, Goethe and Schiller were the focal points in a prolific discourse on the national functions of German literature. The last three decades of that century in particular were marked by a lively debate that conceived of Goethe's *Faust* as a "national" text — a debate in which Wagner and Nietzsche happened to be key figures. While Mahler's literary and philosophical interests were firmly rooted in his student days in the 1870s, I want to show that in his critical reading of German cultural history, he ultimately takes a stance against the nationalist and conservative functionalization of art so characteristic of the cultural climate during his student days in general and the Pernerstorfer Circle in particular,[4] a mobilization of art that by 1900 had gained a clear anti-Semitic dimension.

Goethe, Schiller or Wagner?

For a literary and cultural historian, Mahler's choice of Goethe as the literary reference point for his symphony, in contrast to Beethoven, for instance, who used a text by Schiller for his Ninth Symphony, is striking. Throughout the nineteenth century, Goethe and Schiller competed for the status of favored national symbol. In 1827 Wolfgang Menzel had published *Die deutsche Literatur*, a handbook that would become one of the first popular histories of German literature and that remained influential throughout the century. Menzel's negative stance toward Goethe is surprising now. He admits Goethe's great talent but finds his work without inner core and religious stance.[5] He feels that Goethe was too influenced by the here-and-now and by the fashion of the day, and too materialistic and focused on the senses and on physical pleasure (217–19). Menzel also sees Goethe as too international, too fixated on other national cultures (228). Rejecting the modern materialist Goethe, Menzel worships the idealist Schiller, whose works he finds characterized by the "spirit of a *moral beauty*" (Geist einer *sittlichen Schönheit*; 121). *Die deutsche Literatur* quite explicitly promotes Schiller as the poet of the German people and in particular also of German youth (130). Menzel is full of praise for those among Schiller's followers who gave his work more of a political and patriotic interpretation (132). Menzel's ideas resonated throughout the nineteenth century. Scholars of German literary history agree that, in general, Schiller's work was preferred over Goethe's during the nineteenth century; this was certainly the case as far as popular opinion was concerned. Schiller was seen as the poet of the people, while Goethe was the object of interest for a small aristocratic elite.[6] Whereas the 100th anniversary of Goethe's birth in 1849 was celebrated by a small group of dedicated followers, the celebration of Schiller's anniversary in 1859 turned into a public spectacle in which all of Germany participated.[7] However, nineteenth-century discourse on Schiller and Goethe was by no means monolithic, and there certainly were intellectuals who preferred Goethe to Schiller.[8] Remarkably, Goethe, and in particular his *Faust* drama, was quite popular among composers (including Berlioz, Liszt, Mendelssohn, Schumann, and also Wagner).[9]

However, in accordance with the general dynamics underlying the reception of Schiller and Goethe, the predominant attitude toward *Faust* was negative during most of the century, even though *Faust I* was among Goethe's better-known texts. As a character, Faust was viewed as altogether too passive, too individual, too apolitical; Goethe's text was deemed too "precocious" (altklug), too idealistic, and too literary — to name a few characterizations to be found again and again.[10] With the achievement of German unity in 1871, attitudes started to change. There were still enough negative voices to be heard, but positive ones began to dominate. It could even be said that Mahler's Eighth participated in a rehabilitation of Goethe that was set into motion by the unification of Germany, even though the text remained controversial. That Goethe's *Faust* was seen as his "national" text may be hard to imagine nowadays, but in the late-nineteenth century the idea was taken seriously. Herman Grimm, art historian and cofounder of Germany's Goethe society, and Franz Dingelstedt, director of both state theaters in Vienna from 1875 on, proposed staging performances of both parts of *Faust* annually on Goethe's birthday as a form of national celebration. Interestingly, the location Dingelstedt had in mind for this was Bayreuth.[11] The plan never materialized, but it points out a perceived rivalry as to who was deemed worthy of a national occasion: Wagner or Goethe. But how could a literary character such as Goethe's Faust — not very masculine and far from heroic, an intellectual with a tendency to question his own decisions — become an identificatory figure and part of a nationalist discourse? Interpretations that emphasize the national aspect of *Faust*[12] tend to highlight the emotional depth in Faust's character, as well as his speculative mind, his openness to inner beauty, his enthusiasm for true humanism, and his patience — all of which were seen as typically German. And surprisingly, Faust was seen as a man of action. Attempts to read a national agenda into *Faust* sometimes went quite far, comparing Mephisto, for example, at times to Napoleon who, though unwillingly, eventually was responsible for Germany's unification.[13]

Another nineteenth-century debate compared Siegfried and Faust — a debate that could help us understand the literary dynamics between Mahler and Wagner. I already mentioned that Goethe and Wagner vied for the position of privileged national symbol during that time. The suitability of either as focal point of a national celebration was closely linked to the question as to which of their heroes would better represent the German nation: Siegfried, the hero of the anonymous medieval *Nibelungen* saga and of Wagner's *Ring*, or Faust. Both were seen as competing but also complementary figures. In 1853, Ferdinand Brockhoff stated that the Faust figure had the same importance for the Reformation as Siegfried had had for the Middle Ages, both essentially being equally "faithful and keen" expressions of the "spirit specific to the German people" (Der Eine wie der Andere ist ein treuer und scharfer Ausdruck des spezifisch deutschen Volksgeistes).[14] But there are also significant differences: Faust is more intellectual, Siegfried more sensual.[15]

Brockhoff published his ideas in a review of a book on the Faust myth in a scholarly journal most likely read by specialists alone, and yet he set a discussion in motion that would soon be part of the mainstream. Traces of this debate can be found in the editorial commentary accompanying a popular edition of *Faust* edited by Gustav von Loeper, a lawyer and high governmental official in Prussia, and first published in Berlin in 1870,[16] that marks the beginning of a national renaissance of Goethe's *Faust*. Von Loeper refers to Brockhoff's review in his commentary, and like him, sees similarities between the Faust and Siegfried figures.[17] Siegfried is described as a titanic figure, light-hearted, almost a northern Achilles. In contrast, Faust, a monk-like figure, is focused on his inner world, someone who overthinks and frets about things ("grübelnd"). Thus von Loeper denies a deeper affinity and instead emphasizes differences that for Brockhoff were only minor. In spite of his lack of "titanic" attributes, Faust nevertheless is a positive figure, according to von Loeper, because he represents man's autonomy and self-liberation, not only in religious matters, but spiritually and intellectually as well (xxxi).

While Goethe's *Faust*, in particular *Faust I*, became the object of a nationalistic appropriation, aspects of the Faust figure resist such an appropriation. After 1870 a trend critical of a political interpretation of the figure also emerged. Some of this criticism came from a theological perspective, from professional theologians but also from scholars or amateurs with strong religious beliefs, but some intellectuals objected to *Faust* for other reasons as well. Two argumentative lines dominated this critique: for some, Faust was too individualistic to be an example; for others, he was too focused on humanity in general.[18] A significant number of critics opposed what one could call the modern aspect of *Faust*; others defended this modern side against ideological abuse. An early example combining the view of *Faust* as *the* exemplary German national text with a critical perspective on a German national culture can be found in Heinrich Heine's book on German literary history from 1833, originally written for a French audience.[19] Heine read Goethe's *Faust* as a text critical of German society and culture. Of particular importance for Heine, a German Jew, was that in the original version of the text Faust broke with the medieval era, and in particular with its dogmatic religiosity. Thus the Faust saga represented one of the first attempts to replace a religious (Catholic) view of the world with a scientific, modern one. For Heine, Faust is a figure of emancipation; it is no coincidence that he is incorrectly credited with the invention of the printing process and closely associated with the Reformation. But most remarkably, according to Heine, *Faust*'s program has not been fulfilled yet; when that happens, then it will mark a true "revolution."

A second major figure in German nineteenth-century intellectual history propagated a similar view of Goethe's work vis-à-vis its nationalistic mobilization. Nietzsche's posthumously published notes include an intriguing remark about Goethe's relation to nineteenth-century German music. It is part of a larger fragment that he wrote in spring 1888, entitled "On a Critique of Wagner" (Zur Kritik Wagners), which begins with the following observation:

> Wagner's music is *anti-goethean*.
> Indeed Goethe is missing in German music, the same way he is missing in German politics. In contrast to this: how much Schiller, more specifically how much *Thekla* is in Beethoven.
> A lot of middle-class mediocrity, a lot of consecration.
>
> [Die Musik Wagners ist *antigoethisch*.
> In der Tat fehlt Goethe in der deutschen Musik, wie er in der deutschen Politik fehlt. Dagegen: wie viel Schiller, genauer geredet wie viel *Thekla* ist in Beethoven!
> Viel Biedermännerei, viel Salbung.][20]

Nietzsche refers here to both the common juxtaposition of Schiller and Goethe as well as to the nineteenth century's preference for Schiller. He may also be referring to Wagner's essay on Beethoven from 1870, in which the composer confessed a clear preference for Schiller, among other reasons because he considered Schiller a better dramatist and therefore as having a greater affinity to music.[21] Nietzsche himself is clearly on Goethe's side. Following Nietzsche's logic, to use Goethe's work for music would be an anti-Wagnerian move as well as a critique of a nationalist appropriation of the German literary tradition.

To understand the intellectual-historical constellations in the fragment quoted above, it is productive to look at some of Nietzsche's published texts of the same year. In *Der Fall Wagner* (The Case of Wagner), Nietzsche comments on the constellation Goethe — Schiller — Wagner, explaining that Schiller's popularity rests on his catering to his German audiences' need for a moral message in literature, an attitude Nietzsche characterizes as "oldmaidish" (altjungfernhaft).[22] In contrast, Goethe was seen as overly sexual and morally deprived: "The Germans were always scandalized by him; his only real admirers were Jewish women" (*AC*, 238; Er war den Deutschen immer anstößig, er hat ehrliche Bewunderer nur unter Jüdinnen gehabt: *SW* 6:18). Nietzsche repeats here a racial stereotype that associated Jewishness with sexual exuberance; he suggests that Goethe's female Jewish followers were interested in his obscenity. More specifically, he refers here to the fact that Goethe's texts played an important role in the Berlin salons of Henriette Herz, Rahel Levin (Varnhagen), and Dorothea Mendelssohn (Veit-Schlegel).[23] In Nietzsche's writings, especially in the fragments published after his death, there are other examples in which he points to a Jewish affinity for Goethe, for instance calling Heine and Goethe the only two poets Germany has produced, or writing that elements of Goethe's thinking can be found in Moses Mendelssohn, Rahel Varnhagen, and Heinrich Heine.[24]

Nietzsche was not alone in associating Goethe with German-Jewish culture. The observation has been made that the first generation of Goethe philologists included a remarkable number of Jews; as a result some people started to view Goethe as a "Jewish" author.[25] George L. Mosse interpreted Goethe's popularity among his Jewish readership as indicative of a desire to assimilate within German culture, while simultaneously stressing the progressive side of this culture: "Goethe's emphasis on individual freedom, his ambivalence toward all forms of nationalism, and finally, his belief in *Bildung* seemed to foster Jewish assimilation."[26] (The fact that Mosse uses the word "seemed" here may be taken as an encouragement to be skeptical about Goethe's real intentions toward Jews. Goethe was by no means unambiguous in his attitudes about Jewish culture,[27] but the public saw it differently.) Alma Mahler's remark about Mahler's friend Lipiner that he "goethelte" and "mauschelte" is to be understood in this context.[28] By characterizing Lipiner's way of speaking German as "mauscheln" — a deficient way of using the German language associated with Jews — Alma Mahler, who hated him, picks up one of the dominating anti-Semitic stereotypes of her time.[29] "Goetheln" is, I would argue, the cultural equivalent of "mauscheln," a purportedly deficient use of the German cultural tradition in an attempt to imitate Goethe. Goethe's reputation as a favorite of the Jews is in line with another aspect that Nietzsche highlights in his late writings: Goethe's internationalism. Goethe was a European figure; in Germany he was seen as a recluse ("Einsiedler"), and he could therefore not be identified with German culture. In fact, he defined himself in opposition to Germanness.[30] In Nietzsche's view, Wagner allied himself not with Goethe and his Jewish followers but with their opposite, with Schiller and the nationalistic tradition he stands for. Wagner saved Goethe from his hypersexuality and moral depravity with a "prayer" (*AC,* 239; Gebet: *SW* 6:19). Goethe represented for Nietzsche all that is not German in German cultural history.

What must have appealed to Mahler in Goethe's *Faust* is the fundamental ambiguity of the Faust figure in nineteenth-century cultural history. Faust was, on the one hand, an icon of nationalism, especially after 1870, and yet on the other hand also associated with his author's internationalism. Faust stood, above all, as an emancipatory figure for the effort to think German cultural history differently. The fundamental ambiguity of the Faust figure is particularly clear in relation to the nineteenth-century image of Siegfried. Both are national icons, but whereas Siegfried is deeply embedded in the Middle Ages, Faust is closely associated with the advent of modernity. That Faust can be seen as a more modern version of Siegfried means that Mahler's Eighth Symphony with its use of scenes from *Faust* competes with, but also moves beyond, Wagner's *Siegfried*. The context of nineteenth-century German literary and cultural history permits us to see that by composing a symphony based on Goethe's *Faust*, Mahler articulates a certain discontent with the conservative and nationalistic older Wagner, and that he picks up a project of the younger, more progressive Wagner (and also on Liszt's *Faust Symphony*). As a student, Wagner had composed seven songs in 1831 based on texts from *Faust I* and a work from 1840 now known as Wagner's "Faust Overture" was originally meant to be the first part of an entire Faust Symphony.

Goethe in Vienna

Before I focus on a detailed analysis of the Eighth Symphony, I want to consider whether the perceived rivalry between Goethe and Schiller, accompanied by a public preference for Schiller throughout the nineteenth century, still played a role in Vienna around 1900. If so, did the Austrians make fundamentally different choices from the Germans? Vienna's architectural history provides some clues. The façade of Vienna's Burgtheater, completed in 1888, features busts of Lessing, Goethe, and Schiller.[31] Goethe is clearly in the privileged position: his bust is in the center. That Lessing is part of this group is interesting as well; the author and dramatist consistently represented the progressive and cosmopolitan side of German culture. But the façade suggests that for the Viennese Goethe must have been the leading representative of German culture.[32] The history of Viennese monuments dedicated to Schiller and Goethe, however, tells us a different story. Monuments for Schiller and Goethe were planned as part of the projects that followed the construction of the Ringstraße (1858–65). Schiller received his own plaza, close to and clearly visible from the Opernring; the Schiller monument at its center was completed and officially dedicated in 1876 (coincidentally the year after Mahler's arrival in Vienna).[33] In contrast, the Goethe monument at the corner of the Opernring and Goethegasse was not completed and officially dedicated until 1900. While Schiller got "his" plaza, Goethe received a mere "alley" (Gasse; 36).[34] Schiller is standing tall on his enormous pedestal; Goethe sits, contemplatively staring in the direction of the Schiller monument. Fundraising material for the Schiller monument shows that it was envisioned as an expression of German-Austrian brotherhood (31). The monument's dedication in 1876 led to demonstrations of German-nationalist sentiments and a considerable number of police were needed to enforce public order (33). The Goethe monument, in contrast, was described by contemporaries as an expression of the author's "universal spirit" (universaler Geist) and humanitarian philosophy (36).

The place of Schiller and Goethe in German and Austrian culture — and, more importantly, the political and cultural programs they came to represent — was, in other words, still very much a topic of public discourse in Vienna in the late nineteenth century, with Goethe by no means attracting the kind of attention dedicated to Schiller. There are other indications of this. On 27 August 1899 the liberal *Neue Freie Presse* dedicated its entire front page to the upcoming 150th anniversary of Goethe's birth the next day.[35] The main article, an editorial, characterizes

Goethe as a cosmopolitan author who was tolerant in religious and moral matters and yet also represents the cultural unity of all German-speaking citizens. The article laments the fact that Vienna does not yet have a Goethe monument. Furthermore, it criticizes the fact that there were no plans to celebrate this day,[36] blaming the Christian Social party members on the city council and the prominent role of Roman Catholicism in the city's cultural life in general for this situation.

That reactionary forces preferred Schiller to Goethe is understandable but also surprising, given that Schiller was at the same time an icon in the work of Vienna's cultural avant-garde. In the spring of 1902 the avant-garde group of visual artists The Secession, which had been quite successful in the brief period since their foundation in 1897, organized an exhibition dedicated to Beethoven. The exhibition, for which Alfred Roller had final responsibility,[37] was a homage not just to Beethoven but indirectly also to Schiller. The most spectacular artwork exhibited was a frieze by Gustav Klimt consisting of three painted panels depicting a series of highly allegorical scenes commenting on Beethoven's Ninth Symphony and the "Ode an die Freude" (Ode to Joy), the poem by Schiller at the core of its final movement.[38] It is doubtful that the Secession had a German-nationalist agenda in mind,[39] but the fact remains that Schiller again was the focus of attention. It did not necessarily have to be that way; after all, Beethoven also composed incidental music for Goethe's drama *Egmont*. Research has shown that Klimt's composition of the panels closely followed Wagner's 1846 essay on Beethoven's Ninth.[40] When the final panel of the Beethoven frieze was exhibited again in 1903 at an exhibition dedicated to Klimt's work in the Secession house, it had a new title, the biblical "My Kingdom Is Not of This World" (Mein Reich ist nicht von dieser Welt), a quote also found in Wagner's essay.[41] Wagner's preference for Schiller in his later essays[42] may in fact very well have been one of the main reasons why avant-garde artists such as the Secession focused on Schiller and not Goethe.[43]

Mahler participated in the opening of the Secession's Beethoven exhibition, conducting a fragment from Beethoven's Ninth Symphony in an arrangement for woodwind and brass that unfortunately has not survived. Originally he had planned to perform the entire symphony with the Vienna Philharmonic, but for reasons that are not quite clear this plan fell through. Objections from musicians in the orchestra may have played a role.[44] The exhibition, with its emphasis on the public function of art, may very well have been a catalyst for Mahler's plans to compose a work of his own that was aimed at a mass audience a few years later. However, Mahler's choice of a Goethe text for his Eighth Symphony may have had many motives. He may have savored the challenge of staging a text that by all standards of the theater counted as unstageable.[45] However, the decision to use the final scenes from *Faust II* was also taking a stand against the nationalist appropriation that had characterized the Schiller reception in Vienna in the last decades of the nineteenth century. It was certainly also a turn against Wagner and the conservative and nationalistic agenda of his later days. The connection with the Secession's exhibition on Beethoven is more ambiguous; there are signs that the artists of the Secession sought to rehabilitate the freethinking, cosmopolitan Schiller tradition against its nationalistic appropriation: "This kiss is for the whole world" (Diesen Kuss der ganzen Welt) is one of lines from Schiller's poem quoted in the exhibition catalog to explain the intentions behind Klimt's frieze.[46]

Mahler's Goethe

Adapting the final scenes of *Faust II* for his Eighth Symphony was something rather radical at the time. It is true, Goethe's *Faust* had canonical status in German cultural history, but when it was referred to, it was usually *Faust I* that was meant. The first part of *Faust* is an accessible text, with a clear plotline and a substantial number of quotable verses that have become part of everyday vocabulary. *Faust II* is quite different. It neither offers a straightforward narrative nor deals with a character in the traditional sense, a figure bound to a specific time and place. The second part of Goethe's drama — the last text he finished before his death in 1832 (it was published posthumously in the same year) — moves freely through time and space and offers a highly uncommon synthesis of texts from literary history, mythology, philosophy, natural science, anthropology, and theology. Furthermore, *Faust II* is a highly symbolic text, which to a large extent aims to create meaning through images rather than narrative. Its aesthetic form makes it without a doubt the most advanced work Goethe wrote. Its intellectual curiosity and eclecticism resemble that of Jean Paul's writings. Not only does the text offer a profoundly "modern" form of writing,[47] but it also espouses a modern philosophy of life. Mahler's use of the text for the Eighth Symphony is indicative of continuity within his literary interests.

It was clear from the beginning that setting *Faust II* to music would present a challenge. One of Mahler's favorite texts by and about Goethe were the *Gespräche mit Goethe* (Conversations with Goethe) by Johann Peter Eckermann, who acted as a sort of private secretary to Goethe but was also his friend. The *Gespräche*, published after Goethe's death, proved to be one of the more popular works by and on Goethe in the nineteenth century, providing in relatively simple wordings a comprehensive view of Goethe's often very complex thinking. We know that late in life, the *Gespräche* were a frequent part of Mahler's summer-time reading,[48] a fact of some significance because Mahler did most of his composing during the summer. In his conversations with Eckermann Goethe mentions the possibility of having music composed for his *Faust*, but his stance is rather ambiguous. Initially, Goethe declares a *Faust* composition "totally impossible" (ganz unmöglich), because "the repugnant, offensive, and frightful elements that the music would need to include at certain places are against the spirit of the time" (Das Abstoßende, Widerwärtige, Furchtbare, was sie stellenweise enthalten müßte, ist der Zeit zuwider).[49] However, immediately following this statement he lists Mozart's *Don Giovanni* as an example of the type of music he imagines for *Faust*. He then adds that Giacomo Meyerbeer may be able to do the work justice. Goethe had mentioned Meyerbeer in an earlier conversation about a musical adaptation of *Faust* and had mentioned Mozart's *Zauberflöte* (Magic Flute) as a musical drama comparable to *Faust*.[50]

Surprisingly, this seems to indicate that Goethe may have imagined a musical adaptation of *Faust* as a comedy, even though he had conceived the drama as a tragedy. Two of the examples mentioned, *Don Giovanni* and the work of Meyerbeer, furthermore, combine elements of German and Romance traditions of music making. In *Don Giovanni* not only had Mozart used the libretto of Lorenzo Da Ponte, but the work is solidly in the tradition of Italian opera. And Meyerbeer (1791–1864), a Prussian Jew, worked very successfully as a composer of operas, first in Italy and later in France. In Wagner's theoretical writings Meyerbeer became the embodiment of all that is wrong with the development of German culture, not only because of his Jewishness, but also because of his ability to move between different cultural backgrounds.[51] Mahler no doubt composed the Eighth Symphony with Goethe's ideas about a *Faust* composition in mind. In fact, Goethe's deliberations in the *Gespräche* with Eckermann explain one feature of the second movement that has often baffled audiences and critics: the music's lightheartedness and positive energy.[52] Theodor Adorno even speaks of the symphony's affirmative character. The text, however, barely seems to offer any justification for this. By picking up on Goethe's challenge not only to compose music for the drama but to compose it the way Goethe imagined, Mahler constructs an alternative cosmopolitan and pluralistic trajectory for German cultural history deeply at odds with Wagner's program for German culture.

Eckermann's *Gespräche mit Goethe* may help us understand a second significant feature of the Eighth Symphony that is often misunderstood, namely its use of religious imagery. From the beginning, when Mahler was still thinking about the Eighth as a four-movement symphony, he intended to use religious themes. An early sketch demonstrates this: after the "Veni Creator," a second movement with the title "Caritas" was planned, followed by a scherzo entitled "Christmas Games with the Child [Jesus]" (Weihnachtsspiele mit dem Kindlein) and a hymn with the projected title "Creation through Eros" (Schöpfung durch Eros; *SSLD*, 529–32). Why did Mahler focus on Christian images and concepts? In his conversation with Eckermann on 6 June 1831 Goethe explained that it had been very difficult for him to write the concluding scene of *Faust II*. He had avoided vagueness and had given "form and stability" (Form und Festigheit) to his "poetical intentions" (poetischen Intentionen) only through the use of "clearly defined Christian ecclesiastical figures and representations" (scharf umrissenen christlich-kirchlichen Figuren und Vorstellungen).[53] Goethe was not a religious man in any traditional sense. I would argue that religious, and more specifically Catholic, imagery, has the same function for Goethe as for Mahler. In a letter to Alma that deals with the final scene of Goethe's *Faust* Mahler paraphrased the above-mentioned passage from the *Gespräche*, expressing hope that he has explained himself clearly (*GR*, 389). Neither Goethe nor Mahler intended to document or call for a religious conversion, but a religious framework must have seemed to both the most effective means to communicate to a broad audience the highly complex message they intended for their works. Both works are characterized by an eclectic approach to traditions; they are skeptical of and resistant to ideological use or abuse, despite their religious imagery and use of concepts such as "redemption." Goethe and Mahler both use religious imagery to communicate a philosophy of life that is in essence modern and postmetaphysical.

A thematic analysis of the final scene of *Faust II* uncovers other interesting continuities between Goethe's text and earlier literary references in Mahler's works. Mahler's approach to *Faust* can be described as intuitive. He was an avid reader and knew much about German literary, cultural, and intellectual history, but little about Goethe scholarship, as he admits in a letter to Alma (*GR*, 388). To facilitate my analysis, I propose to divide the segment of Goethe's text that Mahler decided to use into three sections, each of which introduces a new set of characters and a new issue. The first section consists of the introductory "Choir and Echo" and the contributions of Pater ecstaticus and Pater profundus. The second section introduces the Angels, the Choir of Blessed Boys, the Younger Angels, the More Perfect Angels, and, at the very end, Doctor Marianus. The final section begins with Mater gloriosia and ends with the concluding chorus.

Goethe chose a very specific landscape, a mountainous environment — similar to the mountains Mahler loved to climb during the summer when taking a break from composing — for the final scene of his final work. Mahler included Goethe's heading for the final scene, "Mountain Gorges, Forest, Rock. Solitude. Holy Anachorets on the Mountain Slopes, sheltered between gorges" (Bergschluchten, Wald, Fels. Einöde. Heilige Anachoreten gebirgauf verteilt, gelagert zwischen Klüften) in his score as title for the second movement. We know that Goethe based the landscape at the end of *Faust II* on several sources, among them a description by Wilhelm von Humboldt of the mountain Montserrat near Barcelona, which was indeed populated by hermit monks.[54] Because of the clouds covering parts of the mountain slopes, it seemed as if these monks lived in a world beyond this world. "Nature" provides the imagery for another, better world, and Goethe's text demonstrates how this functions. The mechanism to which I refer here is particularly clear in the first words uttered by Pater profundus, which are an elaborate description of nature: rocky gorges, streamlets, the stem of a tree in the air (vs. 11865–72). By having his lines start with "Like" (Wie), Goethe turns the natural imagery he employs into a metaphor for "the omnipotent love / that shapes and cherishes all things" (die allmächtige Liebe / Die alles bildet, alles hegt; vs. 11872–73).[55] And yet almost simultaneously Goethe also takes this imagery apart: nature is not always that benevolent. The second strophe spoken by Pater profundus includes very different images: a wild waterfall and lightning (Blitz), breaking through a poisonous and damp atmosphere; they too are "messengers of love" (Liebesboten; vs. 11882). Idyllic nature gives way to the violence of nature. Here too, nature resists idealization.

The text that opens the second movement of Mahler's Eighth Symphony after an instrumental interlude is generally known as the Hermits' Scene. The monks Pater ecstaticus and Pater profundus seek loneliness to find the essence of life. "Nature," "loneliness," and "love" are closely intertwined in this first section; in nature and in loneliness the real essence of love manifests itself. The monks' description of spiritual love has a decidedly masochistic bend; love is perpetually intertwined with suffering (as it is for Albano, the protagonist of Jean Paul's *Titan*). Love's ambiguity manifests itself, possibly even more radically than for Pater profundus, for Pater ecstaticus, who speaks of his desire for God as an "Eternal fire of joy" (Ewiger Wonnebrand) and a "Seething pain of the chest" (Siedender Schmerz der Brust; vs. 11854, 11856). Pater ecstaticus does not restrict himself to natural imagery; he calls not only for lightning but also for "arrows, lances, and cudgels" (Pfeile, Lanzen, Keulen; vs. 11858–60) — instruments of self-torture and flagellation — to enlighten him about the true essence of love. Despite this insight into the violent nature of love, both Pater ecstaticus and Pater profundus also articulate a desire for a more profound kind of love at the ends of their respective parts; in the words of Pater ecstaticus: "love's eternal core" (Ewiger Liebe Kern; vs. 11865) — a love beyond life's nothingness (das Nichtige; vs. 11862), a love that transcends the limitations of the senses (vs. 11886). It is tempting to interpret these evocations of a more perfect form of love as indicative of an opposition between material love on the one hand and spiritual love on the other, but that is clearly not accurate. The monks' love in the here and now is already a form of spiritual love while nevertheless clearly bound to the material world. The true nature of "love" remains an enigma, even for these monks who have dedicated their lives to it.

In his adaptation, Mahler made a few changes, the most significant of which can be found in the transition from the first to the second section, where he omitted the third hermit in Goethe's text. While Mahler kept the figures of Pater ecstaticus, representing the higher region, and Pater profundus, who is associated with the lower region, he left out Pater seraphicus, the figure representing the middle region. This, I would argue, is no coincidence. Mahler was interested in opposites, visible in the profound differences that exist between the higher and lower worlds, between body and soul. Furthermore, at the beginning of the second section, Mahler makes another significant change to Goethe's text. The passage in which the angels explain why Faust is saved (vs. 11934–41) is moved slightly ahead of, and set partially parallel with, the verses in which the Choir of Blessed Boys rejoices about Faust's redemption (vs. 11926–33). As a result of Mahler's change, more emphasis is given to the angels' verses. The rest of section 2 elaborates on the reasons for Faust's redemption and the obstacles standing in its way. The key words here are "He who always keeps on striving / Him we can redeem" (Wer immer strebend sich bemüht / Den können wir erlösen; vs. 11936–37). It is important to emphasize, in line with my earlier analysis, that here religious imagery functions as a tool and is not to be confused with the message of the text. What is saved here is modernity's normative project. Despite Faust's rejection of tradition as a source of norms and values, despite his skepticism and the profound materiality of his wishes and desires, he is not an amoral human being. Despite his suffering, man keeps striving for something. Goethe's verses highlight the individual nature of these norms and values. What complicates Faust's redemption, according to Goethe's text, is that his eternal striving is a primary condition for his redemption, but not the only one. Only if "love . . . / From above" (Liebe . . . / Von oben) participates in Faust's earthly sufferings will he receive a heavenly "welcome" (Willkommen; vs. 11937–41). Here the central topic of section 1 returns. The exact link between Faust's striving and "love," however, is only implied in this passage (and is not explained until the very last verses of the drama).

The segments that follow, the rest of section 2, seek to connect the theme of redemption with its anthropological foundations, the view of mankind underlying Goethe's *Faust*. The "Younger Angels" reiterate love's crucial role for Faust's redemption, referring back to an earlier episode in which they defeated Mephisto and his satanic aides by strewing roses (vs. 11942–46). The image of the rose as representative of nature is of course familiar from Mahler's Second Symphony. Again, nature imagery is used to visualize redemption (see also the image of the dissolving of the clouds, vs. 11970, and the advent of a new Lent, vs. 11976). However, the More Perfect Angels are more pessimistic about Faust's redemption; Faust's immortal remains are "not pure" (nicht reinlich; vs. 11957), they point out, and his body and mind are inseparably joined (vs. 11962). Even a superficial reader of the text will notice that this heaven is a place full of hierarchies in which a clear distinction is made among "Blessed Boys," "Younger Angels," and "More Perfect Angels."

Furthermore, Faust's journey is not over; the text does not support the idea of an endpoint. Faust comes to the Angels "in a chrysalis condition" (im Puppenstand; vs. 11982); that is, like a caterpillar that still has one more transformation to undergo before it turns into a butterfly. (This is a point of some interest: the transformation of caterpillar into butterfly is one of Jean Paul's favorite metaphors.) Moreover, the text alludes to the beginning of a process of transformation. Faust's immortal remains are nothing but an "angelic pledge" (Englisches Unterpfand; vs. 11984), and life after death is very much like life before death — also a thought that one can find frequently in Jean Paul's work. There is no realm of eternal value; our striving alone constitutes value on earth as in heaven. Rather, heaven is a realm of learning and teaching, as a statement by the "Choir of Blessed Boys" — among them, we can assume, Faust's son — makes clear: "this man has learned [something] / He will teach us" (dieser hat gelernt / Er wird uns lehren; vs. 12082–83). As part of this learning process angels fulfill different functions based on their merits. In Goethe's *Faust*, heaven is a realm where a process of purification takes place and to which no one comes unblemished. And above all, it is also a place where all are admitted. In fact, heaven looks a lot like earth. All of this points to a decidedly heretical conceptualization of eternal life.[56] Within the existing hierarchies of heaven, Doctor marianus is at the top ("doctor marianus" is a honorary title given to someone who excels in devotion to Maria).[57] The words of Doctor marianus, concluding section 2, provide a transition. On the one hand, he is the most devoted disciple of Maria and the living proof of spiritual love; on the other, he testifies to man's weakness (vs. 12024), and his enslavement to erotic lust (vs. 12026–27). He too is torn by contradictory impulses.

The third section begins with the introduction of Maria, here called Mater gloriosa (vs. 12032), and is dominated by female figures (Mater peccatrix, Mulier samaritana, Maria egyptiaca, Gretchen). This section is primarily a clarification of the role of "love" in Faust's redemption and refers back to the beginning of section 2 and the angels' explanation for Faust's salvation (vs. 11934–41). In those verses the reader or audience member had learned not only that Faust was redeemed through his own striving but also that love was part of Faust's redemption (vs. 11937). This section further refers back to the words of Pater ecstaticus about "Love's eternal core" (Ewiger Liebe Kern; vs. 11865). The exact nature of the "love" that saved Faust is now clarified. The introduction of Maria at this crucial part of Goethe's play might suggest that Faust was saved by a purely spiritual love. It then would be easy to distinguish such spiritual and "good" love from corporal, worldly or "bad" love. This is not, however, how Goethe wanted his readers to see it. This becomes particularly clear in the choice of characters who follow the appearance of Maria. The "blessed flock" (die selige Schar; vs. 11940) receiving Faust consists of some of the worst sinners of the Christian tradition, and their transgressions are sins of the flesh; they are prostitutes who, however, have chosen to live a life of repentance. Goethe included in his text references to the biblical and apocryphal passages on which their words are based: the gospel of Luke (7:36), the gospel of John (4), and the Acta Sanctorum (a Latin collection of biographies of saints and martyrs). Gretchen, the Blessed Boys, Mater gloriosa, and Doctor marianus all join these sinners in asking forgiveness for Faust.

The concluding eight verses of Goethe's drama, assigned to the Chorus mysticus, are among the most famous, and most debated, in German cultural history. It is clear that Mahler himself also saw these verses as the key to Goethe's work and his own symphony. While we know little about Mahler's ideas about the final scene in general, his thoughts about these final verses are well known from a letter he wrote to Alma in June 1909 from Toblach (*GR*, 388–89). While Goethe's text can be read on different levels, for Mahler the verses are first and foremost about a mode of being in the world. Goethe's text for Mahler caters to the metaphysical need of its readers, without giving in to the temptation to claim the existence of a world beyond this one. On a fundamental level, we are asked to accept that what we see around us is not all that is essential. Accordingly, Mahler begins his letter by downplaying the powers of the human mind: "the *rational* aspect of it . . . is almost always not the essential part" (das *Rationale* daran . . . ist fast immer das nicht das Wesentliche).[58] This certainly refers to the first two lines of the Chorus mysticus, which states: "Everything transitory / Is but a simile" (Alles Vergängliche / Ist nur ein Gleichnis; vs. 12104–5).[59] Any rational or empirical approach to knowledge necessarily has to remain superficial and incomplete. Interestingly, *Faust*, as a text, mirrors this cognitive problem. Any understanding of the text can only be relative; in Mahler's words: "Truth is different for everybody — and different for everybody at a different time" (Die Wahrheit ist für Jeden — und für Jeden zu verschiedenen Epochen — anders geartet).

In a second reading of the text Mahler attempts to sketch what we can know about what in principle defies knowledge, "what cannot be described" (Das Unbeschreibliche; vs. 12108). He emphasizes that any attempt to conceptualize it will be "imperfect," using Goethe's "unzulänglich" (vs. 12106). The meaning of "unzulänglich" in Goethe's text is ambiguous, and it may very well have been this ambiguity that interested Mahler. In addition to "imperfect," the concept can also mean "something that can not be grasped" in the literal sense, something that cannot be touched. For Goethe, an alternative description for this enigmatic entity is "the

Eternal Feminine" (Das Ewig-Weibliche; vs. 12110). Mahler characterizes this entity in his letter as *"what is resting,* the *end point"* (das *Ruhende,* das *Ziel*), the goal of man's striving. These final verses are extraordinarily important for an understanding of Goethe's *Faust.* Here the two elements essential for Faust's eventual redemption are finally brought together: his eternal striving, and love (vs. 11936–41). Because man's striving is directed toward the "Eternal-Feminine," man's will and love are joined together. Within our most material drives, and specifically at the core of our sexual desire, there is a need for something else, something abstract. There is a gendered agenda here that is deeply embedded in the thinking of Goethe's (as well as Mahler's) time. It is possible to argue that Goethe (and Mahler with him) makes a heterosexual model of love the core of his program. By doing so, Goethe naturalizes difference, and assumes that culture is determined by biology. Man is the active instance, woman the passive and receiving instance. Man is the subject, woman the object. Mahler seems to be aware of the gendered nature of this dynamic when he says that it only makes sense to speak of the "Eternal Feminine" "in opposition to eternal desire, striving, moving toward this goal — in other words: to what is eternally masculine!" (im Gegensatze zu dem ewigen Sehnen, Streben, sich Hinbewegen zu diesem Ziele — also dem Ewig Männlichen!). This should not, however, detract from Goethe's radical move, and the emancipatory potential behind it: at the end of the drama, man is in essence reduced to a passive role, very unlike the male heroes of other exemplary "national" artworks. Read within the tradition of the search for a text with the potential to become the symbol of German nationhood, *Faust* is about accepting alterity, about accepting the limits of our own will. Our actions as human beings should be geared toward one another, and maybe women do a better job at this than men.

In addition to the two readings of Mahler's letter proposed thus far, my claim is that his letter allows for a *third,* less obvious, reading of Goethe's text. It is possible to read Mahler's deliberations on the final verses of *Faust II* as the core of an aesthetic program. When he compares Goethe's *Faust* to Beethoven's symphonies as examples of the phenomenon that great works of art are always understood only partially, he establishes a philosophical-aesthetic context for his Eighth Symphony. In alluding to Beethoven, Mahler also refers back to a letter written to Alma a few days earlier, in which he explains his understanding of "entelechy," an idea that has played an important role in interpretations of the final scene of *Faust II.* In an earlier version of the text, Goethe had introduced the crucial verses about Faust's redemption (11934–41) with the remark that the angels bring in "Faust's entelechy" (Faustens Entelechie).[60] Mahler refers to the principle of "entelechy" in both letters to Alma (*GR,* 385 and 389). In the earlier letter he clarifies it as a self-conscious productive force that is a challenge to man's ethical essence. The works of a genius — Mahler mentions the *Meistersinger*, Beethoven's Ninth, and *Faust* — are of only secondary importance in comparison to what is at their roots: "this incessant and truly painful striving" (dieses unaufhörliche und wahrhaft schmerzvolle Streben; *GR*, 385–86). This may at least partially explain why Mahler, in the second letter to Alma, states that any understanding of these works is necessarily limited. By associating art with self-reflection and with a challenge to man's ethical essence, art is given, on the one hand, a task that in previous times had been reserved for religion, or possibly philosophy. Yet, on the other hand, we can never fully understand what a work of art wants to communicate. In spite of his high ambitions for art, it would be missing the point to assume that Mahler intended to propagate a program that makes art into a form of religion, as some critics have suggested.[61] In the end, art is not the center of Mahler's philosophical program. Rather, art can serve to help our understanding of the realities surrounding us. Goethe's *Faust* propagates a view of reality that is aesthetic in nature. If we view reality as a simulation of something else, then this view has an aesthetic dimension inherent in it. Art may be a privileged medium that makes this principle clear, but it should not become the object of a (semi-)religious adoration itself. What Mahler advocates is a dialogue between all manifestations of this aesthetic consciousness. This would explain the remarkable freedom with which he uses philosophy, literature, and the visual arts as resources to illustrate the meaning of his music.

Lipiner Reading Goethe

It is generally assumed that Mahler's understanding of the final scene of *Faust II* was influenced by Siegfried Lipiner's 1894 dissertation on Goethe's *Faust* and by conversations between the two friends.[62] Unfortunately, Lipiner's thesis, entitled *Homunkulus: Eine Studie über Faust und die Philosophie Goethes* (Homunculus: A Study on Faust and Goethe's Philosophy), has been lost.[63] However, it is possible to gain some insight into Lipiner's ideas about Goethe's text based on another dissertation, *Die Gedanken- und Ideenwelt Siegfried Lipiners* (Siegfried Lipiner's World of Thoughts and Ideas), defended in 1936 in Vienna by a student named Ida Schein, who had access to Lipiner's unpublished writings, including *Homunkulus*. Schein does not give a comprehensive overview of the central argument of Lipiner's thesis, but she refers to and quotes from it a number of times. For our interpretation of the final scene of *Faust II*, the passage in which she discusses Lipiner's dissertation in the context of Schopenhauer's critique of metaphysics — and more specifically, Schopenhauer's view that we have no access to reality directly, only to representations of reality, except for our own "will" — is particularly relevant.[64] According to Lipiner, Goethe understood our "will" as being directed toward knowledge that consists not of multiple ideas but of "*one* idea" (*eine* Idee; *GSL,* 83). This central idea is closely connected to our will and represents a form of knowledge. Yet its exact nature cannot be defined in a positive sense and according to Lipiner remains an enigma. Nevertheless, it would be wrong to assume that our will has no direction at all. By giving in to our will to gain knowledge of this central idea, we distance ourselves from our individual will and from our material needs and surrender instead to a more general "will."[65] Interestingly, in order to clarify this concept of the will, Lipiner referred to the Dutch-Jewish philosopher Spinoza and his theory of substance (*GSL,* 83).

On the basis of Schein's thesis, one can conclude that Spinoza's work provided Lipiner with one of his dissertation's key arguments. For Lipiner, Goethe's *Faust* was about the philosophical conflict between a materialistic and an idealistic view of the world. The title of Lipiner's thesis, *Homunkulus*, refers to the attempt of Faust's assistant Wagner to create a life form, a homunculus, from inorganic matter alone (*GSL,* 106; see *Faust* vs. 6835–60) — an attempt that of course fails miserably. According to Lipiner, the recognition that our soul is a continuous element, while our body changes all the time, leads us to reject the "myth" of Homunculus (*GSL,* 106). That does not mean, however, that Lipiner was an idealist and believed in the supremacy of the mind over the body. After Schopenhauer and Nietzsche's rigorous debunking of such idealism, that would have been naive. And, much earlier, Spinoza had already offered a way out of this dilemma by presenting a theory of substance, which had acknowledged humans' dependence on the body and on matter while simultaneously claiming that body and mind function as an indivisible unity (for a concise explanation of Spinoza's theory of substance in the context of early-modern Western philosophy, see *SM,* 25–27). In contrast to Schein, who saw Lipiner as an unabashed idealist and who is herself quite critical of the Spinoza analogy — without a doubt because it is in conflict with her image of Lipiner as a deeply religious person in the traditional Protestant sense — I believe that it was Spinoza's monistic theory of mind and body, as an alternative to materialism or idealism, that attracted Lipiner. The second set of references to Spinoza in Schein's dissertation (*GSL,* 104–5) follows a rather vague paragraph in which she discusses Lipiner's view of the principle of "entelechy" in Goethe's *Faust*. The concept of "entelechy" is usually associated with Aristotle or Leibniz, but it also makes sense in a discussion of Spinoza's theory of substance, since he too assumed the existence of a basic drive or tendency in all living beings ("conatus"; see *SM,* 30–31). Our affects are the most substantial manifestation of this basic drive, which is constitutive for human nature (*SM,* 48–49).

Even though the final scene of *Faust* is not mentioned directly in any of the passages of Lipiner's thesis discussed by Schein, and even though his mention of the concept of "entelechy" is only an indirect reference to the final scene of *Faust II*, this scene is clearly on Lipiner's mind in the statements analyzed above. How do Lipiner's references to Spinoza help us understand Mahler's interpretation of this scene? Spinoza's philosophy enables us to synthesize a number of key thoughts articulated in the final scene of *Faust II*. It allows us to make a connection between otherwise heterogeneous elements in Goethe's text. One of Spinoza's major contributions to the history of Western philosophy is the idea that man's dependence on body and matter is, in the end, not a negative thing (*SM*, 51–52).[66] Spinoza does not see a real opposition between what the body and what the mind wants (*SM*, 49, 75, and 80). This is an insight of crucial importance also in Goethe's *Faust*. The idea that man's behavior is driven by a "will" underlying his actions, and that his emotions — or "affect," meaning in this context the general direction behind human emotions — are indicative of this basic drive, is another key element of Spinoza's thinking to be found in Goethe's work. The end of *Faust II* is a powerful articulation of the connection between humankind's emotional life and purpose in the world. However, in spite of the fact that our emotions (according to Spinoza) are indicative of the road we need to take, we do not know our "goal" in life (*SM*, 30)[67] — a thought reflected in Goethe's admission that any knowledge of our driving force can only be incomplete and imperfect.

Both Lipiner and Mahler speak of the principle of "entelechy" that leads our actions and also guarantees some form of further existence of our essence after death (*GSL*, 104; *GR*, 384 and 389). The term refers to a philosophical tradition going back to Aristotle and is associated with the idea that organisms develop in a specific direction, toward a specific goal (*SM*, 30). Interpreting the notion of "entelechy" in the framework of Spinoza's philosophy makes *Faust* a much more radical text than would an Aristotelian or a Leibnizian interpretation of the same notion. An interpretation of the term according to Spinoza's principles emphasizes the openness of man's development, the fact that humans never really know their goal or purpose in life. In this context it is important that for both Mahler and Lipiner the role of art is closely connected to man's dynamic nature, the "will" underlying his actions. For Lipiner, a work of art is an expression of man's will to gain knowledge of the idea (*GSL*, 83–84n1). Mahler states something very similar in his letters to Alma, as I have shown.

There are some other structural reasons why Spinoza is of importance for an understanding of Goethe's *Faust*. Spinoza, like the literary figure Faust, is an icon for the transition from a medieval to a modern view of the world. In fact, some recent research sees Spinoza as a very early and exemplary representative of modernity, the instigator of a radical form of Enlightenment.[68] Spinoza's desire to reconcile man's metaphysical needs with a profoundly modern view of man and of the world that is at the root of the ideas discussed above, must have been appealing to Lipiner and

Mahler. While Spinoza acknowledged the impact of tradition and man's need to be part of a community, his philosophy demonstrates the relativity of traditions by pointing to their historical nature (*SM*, 55, and 62–63)[69] while maintaining a certain universalism. Lipiner's deliberations on the basis of Spinoza's insights about the individual versus the collective help us understand a key insight in Goethe's text. In spite of the fact that humans individually need to make sense of their lives, they are part of a larger collective. The idea that humans need to overcome their own will in order to participate in a more general will is to be understood as an attempt to think of alterity and identity as related. Humans from different parts of the world may be different and represent different values, but in the end they all participate in one project. In Spinoza's terminology our "striving" is simultaneously individual and "ontologically universal" (*SM*, 30).

It is interesting to read Lipiner's idea that Spinoza is crucial for the understanding of Goethe's *Faust* drama in the context of the nineteenth-century Jewish affinity for Goethe discussed above. The thought that a Jewish philosopher stood at the beginning of modernity must have been intriguing to men such as Mahler and Lipiner. The insight into the Spinoza-Goethe nexus therefore constitutes a powerful defense of German-Jewish culture, a component of German culture that had come increasingly under attack in Vienna around 1900. Spinoza also showed that awareness of one's Jewish cultural background could be reconciled with underwriting the basic assumptions of modernity. At a time in which the discourse on the identity of German culture became increasingly nationalistic and xenophobic — a trend that also involved Goethe's legacy in German cultural history — Lipiner and Mahler argued for a very different image of Goethe and German cultural history in general.

Veni Creator Spiritus

At first glance, the pairing of the final scene of *Faust*'s second part and the medieval hymn "Veni Creator Spiritus" in Mahler's Eighth Symphony seems illogical. It seems less so if one knows that Goethe translated the hymn and was fond of it. The two texts show very different sides of Goethe. The second part of *Faust* is a profoundly modern text, full of doubt and with no easy answers. "Veni Creator Spiritus" expresses the confidence of a naive religious faith — a predogmatic faith that believes in the existence of God without backing of religious doctrine — and it also expresses the idea that every human being deserves divine mercy.[70] It is in fact tempting to see "Veni Creator Spiritus" and *Faust II* as the beginning and the end of the German cultural tradition. Around 1900 *Faust II* was, in form and content, without a doubt still one of the most advanced works in German; at least Lipiner saw it that way. Even though written in Latin, the "Veni Creator Spiritus" hymn is one of the first surviving documents from the German-speaking area. In Mahler's time it was attributed to Hrabanus Maurus (ca. 780–856). Today this attribution is in doubt, although the text originated in Maurus's immediate environment around 800. Hrabanus Maurus, the archbishop of Mainz, is commonly known as "praeceptor Germaniae" (teacher of Germany). At a time when Charlemagne's empire was split in three parts and the territory of present-day Germany gained independence for the first time, Hrabanus Maurus was a figure who contributed to shaping an independent German cultural identity; at least, that is how one could see it around 1900.[71]

How did Mahler know about the hymn? One probable source is Goethe's correspondence with Carl Friedrich Zelter (1758–1832), a composer nowadays known mostly as Goethe's friend and as the teacher of Felix Mendelssohn-Bartholdy and Meyerbeer. A first edition of this correspondence was published in 1833 and 1834, shortly after the deaths of Goethe and Zelter in 1832. A second complete edition, with a commentary by Ludwig Geiger, was published by Reclam between 1902 and 1904.[72] Mahler most likely knew of this correspondence, and Zelter's background in music would have interested him. Natalie Bauer-Lechner, one of Mahler's closest intellectual partners, with whom he discussed his literary interests in detail, mentions the correspondence in her *Fragmente*.[73] Goethe added his translation of the hymn to a letter to Zelter, asking him to set the text to music, as he had done with other poems by Goethe, "so that it may be sung by a choir every Sunday in front of my house" (damit solche jeden Sonntags vor meinem Hause chormäßig möge gesungen werden).[74] It is interesting that Mahler again picks up on a musical project of Goethe's that did not materialize.

There is, however, a third and more complex reason why this hymn was attractive to Mahler. The literary scholar Mathias Mayer has pointed out that Goethe discussed the hymn with Zelter in the context of his plans to write a continuation to the *West-östlicher Divan* (West-Eastern Divan), a collection of poems published in 1819, one year before he requested a musical adaptation of the hymn from Zelter.[75] The poems of the *West-östlicher Divan* are based on poems of the medieval Persian poet Hafiz (ca. 1326–90), which Goethe knew in translations, published in 1812–13, by the Austrian Orientalist Joseph von Hammer-Purgstall. Goethe was not interested in a more or less adequate translation of the Persian poems but rather in a renewal of his own poetic production, and he looked to the Orient for inspiration. Goethe's view of the East is full of Orientalist clichés. What appealed to him was not only Hafiz's focus on the here and now, on earthly love and the wisdom of the body, the role of nature, his light rather than dark view of life, but also the poetry's tendency toward mysticism and the religious imagery accompanying it. The materials that Goethe used in his poems in the *West-östlicher Divan* were not all of Eastern origin. Rather, Hafiz's work offered him a new way of looking at Western tradition and a chance to find a new vocabulary for his own philosophy of life. Hafiz clearly appealed to a cosmopolitan trend within Goethe's thinking. The poems of the *West-östlicher Divan* are the product of an imagined dialogue between East and West, but they also tend toward cultural relativism.

What in the text of "Veni creator spiritus" points to the hymn's relevance for the poems of the *West-östlicher Divan*? I would argue that it is the hymn's revalidation of the body and of the senses that makes it a model for a reconciliation of Eastern and Western religious thought. In particular, the verses "Illuminate our senses, / Pour love into our hearts" (Accende lumen sensibus, / Infunde amorem cordibus) express this orientation toward the body as a site of mankind's redemption. Like the introductory stanza, these lines are exclamations: they call for something, demand something, and yet they simultaneously also express doubt by emphasizing that something is being sought. One can understand them as a call for love, but also as asking for the activation of an aesthetic sensibility that will change the subject's relation to the world fundamentally. The music of the Eighth Symphony accents the importance of these lines. Donald Mitchell writes of the "great aspiring cry of 'Accende lumen sensibus' that twice erupts in the [first] movement's central section" and points out that the "Accende" theme returns repeatedly in the second movement of the symphony (*SSLD*, 525, 576, and 579).

The focus on the body as something positive, as the site of love, but also as the location of an aesthetic sensibility toward the world, is the most obvious similarity between the hymn and the final scene of *Faust II*, between the first and second movements of Mahler's symphony. There are two further points of agreement. Both texts evoke a concept of redemption that includes all of mankind, as if there were a contract between God and his people.[76] At least two passages point to this. At the beginning of the hymn, the author speaks of "the hearts of those you created" (quae tu creasti pectora), that is, of *all* those created by God, *all* living beings. Toward the end the hymn evokes a vision of world peace: "Untie the chains of discord, / Fasten the bonds of peace" (Dissolve litis vincula, / Adstringe pacis foedera). The third similarity consists of the central place reserved for the aesthetic act. The first line of the hymn, "Come, creator spirit" (Veni, creator spiritus), is highly ambiguous on a fundamental level. Who is the "creator spirit"? Is it God, creator of the world, or is it the source of the artist's creative powers? It is exactly this ambiguity that attracted Goethe and, I would argue, Mahler. Goethe left us an intriguing aphorism about the text: "The enchanting church song 'Veni creator spiritus' is actually a call to Genius; for that reason it speaks forcefully to spirited and strong humans" (Der herrliche Kirchengesang: Veni creator Spiritus ist ganz eigentlich ein Appell ans Genie; deswegen er auch geist- und kraftreiche Menschen gewaltig anspricht).[77] Goethe does not doubt that the "creator spirit" refers to his own aesthetic brilliance and not the figure of a conventional deity. The idea that aesthetic genius had taken the place of conventional religion certainly also appealed to fin-de-siècle Vienna with its adoration of the artist-hero as represented for instance by the knight in Klimt's Beethoven frieze.

While I initially assumed many discontinuities between the texts of the first and second movements of the Eighth Symphony, a closer look revealed many continuities. The end of the second part of Goethe's drama *postulates* the possibility of a global community characterized both by difference and sameness. The medieval hymn at the beginning of the symphony *demonstrates* the existence of a tradition within Christianity — one could say, in view of the popularity of the hymn in Pentecostal celebrations in particular, at the core of Christianity — that centers on the body and is close to Oriental wisdom. Viewed from this perspective, the end of *Faust II* may not be as heretical as much of the nineteenth century thought. Mahler's primary interest though, I would argue, is not a renewal of the Christian tradition but a counter-reading of the German cultural tradition, a reading that emphasizes those moments within its history that showed openness toward other traditions. In its first and second movements Mahler's symphony seeks to articulate a truly transcultural model, one that aims at a notion of community that is global and inclusive, not exclusive and national. "Veni creator spiritus" and the final scene of *Faust II* illustrate, in different ways, Spinoza's insight that it is in the body, in the affects, and in human emotion that difference and sameness can be found. The above reference to the *West-östlicher Divan* is relevant also because continuity is established between the Eighth Symphony and Mahler's next major musical project, *Das Lied von der Erde* (The Song of the Earth), which incorporates "Oriental" elements in a manner not unlike Goethe's approach in his *West-östlicher Divan*.

On Alterity and Commonality

Even though the Eighth Symphony is one of Mahler's more accessible works — or perhaps precisely because of this — it has remained controversial. Adorno describes the work as a "failed, objectively impossible resuscitation of the cultic" (*MPE*, 138, trans. modified; mißglückte, objektiv unmögliche Wiederbelebung des kultischen: *MP*, 283). After Nietzsche's criticism of metaphysics, Adorno suggests, it is impossible to revive the metaphysical tradition, to act as if Nietzsche had never written (unless one wanted to make the same mistake as Wagner). While the Eighth Symphony suggests a traditional metaphysical frame, it is actually purely self-referential: "In reality it worships itself" (*MPE*, 138; In Wahrheit betet es sich selbst an: *MP*, 283). In other words, Adorno accuses Mahler of substituting an empty aesthetic act for traditional metaphysics, and of mistakenly thinking that the aesthetic act, the act of invention lauded at the beginning of the symphony's first movement, can be a satisfactory substitute for a traditional model of metaphysics.

But if one follows the reading of Goethe's text that I propose here, a very different picture emerges. The aesthetic act is no longer a semi-divine intervention but part of a search for knowledge that is a priori imperfect and incomplete. Tying the aesthetic gesture to a theory of affect makes it clear that this gesture is not privileged. The implied search for knowledge is instead an expression of a general anthropological drive, of something that characterizes the actions of every human being. In contrast to Adorno's claim, Mahler's Eighth Symphony does not search to establish a collective "under the sway of a false consciousness" (*MPE*, 139; im Bann eines falschen Bewußtseins: *MP,* 283). Mahler, in his revision of Goethe's text, accepts the arbitrary and subjective nature of any attempt to make sense of life, while simultaneously acknowledging that mankind is driven by material needs and without a uniform metaphysical framework. In other words, the conceptual structure underlying this work accepts the limits of metaphysics, while all the while attempting to incorporate Nietzsche's anthropological basis for Adorno's criticism, by giving prevalence to the body over the mind. The proof of mankind's desire for knowledge and meaning, for Spinoza, Goethe, Lipiner, and Mahler, resides precisely in that materiality of the body and its desires.

Adorno repeatedly suggests that the canonical status of *Faust* alone, its iconic position in German cultural history, fascinated Mahler rather than the content of Goethe's text. But he misses the possibility of seeing Spinoza, Goethe, and Nietzsche as representing an alternative trajectory of German literary and cultural history. While it is true that Mahler was attracted to Goethe because of his legendary role in German culture, he certainly also was drawn to the specifics of the *Faust* text. A cultural reading of Mahler's symphony proves that it is not just about creating community but also about fostering individuality within this community and about acknowledging what is different among individuals. The work communicates inclusiveness and tolerance rather than the exclusive and intolerant notion of society that the German nationalists among Mahler's contemporaries had in mind. This is the meaning behind Mahler's statement characterizing his symphony as a "gift to the nation." Spinoza's theory of affect makes it possible to conceptualize alterity while simultaneously acknowledging that there is an anthropologically uniform basis for this idea. In other words: human beings are different, but in some respects also the same. In the end, the artist's desire and his search for knowledge or meaning are but one expression of the desire of all mankind.

This desire for a language that reflects humanity's diversity while also acknowledging commonality is also at the roots of Mahler's compositions based on texts by Rückert and, eventually, his *Lied von der Erde.*

6: The Two Faces of German Orientalism

Two essays that Mahler wrote in 1877 as part of his final exams for obtaining his high school diploma have survived. One of them deals with the Duke of Wallenstein (1583–1634), a military hero from the Thirty Years' War (1618–48) best known from a series of plays that Schiller wrote about him. Mahler was clearly not (very) familiar with them and as a consequence received a failing grade. The other essay topic asked him to discuss the impact of the Orient on German literature. For this essay, Mahler received a passing grade, even though it was clearly unfinished.[1] And indeed he has interesting things to say; one might call Mahler's essay cosmopolitan and progressive. It argues unambiguously in favor of cultural cross-pollination: cultures should learn from each other; cultures that isolate themselves risk marginalization (he cites the Chinese as a cautionary example). Mahler links cultural differentiation (entirely in line with the theories of Herder, among others) to differences in climate and geography.[2] The Orient's strangeness is attractive to the West, and in Mahler's view it is the German mind in particular that has sought to assimilate the cultural products of other nations.[3]

The fact that a topic such as "The Influence of the Orient on German Literature" was assigned to high school students in a small town like Iglau is but one proof of the prominent role that Orientalism played in nineteenth-century culture. Mahler's essayistic response also illustrates that the discourse about the East emerging in the late eighteenth and early nineteenth centuries associated the Orient with predominantly positive images. Current scholarship has come to a more nuanced reading. The term "Orientalism" was introduced into Cultural Studies by Edward W. Said's highly influential 1978 study *Orientalism*.[4] Said's approach was innovative in that it pointed to Orientalism's constructed, textual nature. His study stresses that the Western view of what it called the "Orient" had its roots in literary topoi and stereotypes rather than in any form of actual experience of the East. Orientalism sought to reduce the non-Western Other to some form of unchanging "essence," thereby suggesting far more clearly delineated differences between East and West than in fact existed. Said's analysis also calls into question the supposedly positive views of the East constructed by Western Orientalism. It demonstrates that the Western view of the Orient is prejudiced, even if it is meant to be cosmopolitan and open-minded. The East is instrumentalized by the West in part to serve the West's imperial ambitions, but also to flesh out a Western identity (the West as the opposite of the East).

Mahler's opinions on Western European colonialism are quite clear: like Sigmund Freud he was an admirer of Multatuli,[5] the pen name of the Dutch colonial author Eduard Douwes Dekker (1820–87), who wrote the bestseller *Max Havelaar* (1860), a book that was highly critical of the Dutch involvement in the far East. However, concerning the second issue at stake in Said's *Orientalism,* the way in which Mahler viewed the relationship and interactions between Orient and Occident is not so obvious. His high-school essay shows that, early in life, he had what one could consider a relatively sophisticated view of the Orient, one that was clearly informed by German cultural history. In some of his late compositions — in particular *Das Lied von der Erde*, but also the Rückert songs and the *Kindertotenlieder* — Mahler would return to the topic. Adorno has characterized the Orient of *Das Lied von der Erde* as "pseudomorphous" in the sense that it "also" functions as "cover for Mahler's Jewish element" (Pseudomorphose ist dieser Osten auch als Deckbild von Mahlers jüdischem Element), even though he adds immediately that what is Jewish in Mahler's music is intangible in spite of its omnipresence (*MP,* 291; *MPE,* 149). Implicit in Adorno's deliberations is the reproach that Mahler's music lacks authenticity, which is in line with Said's critique of Western Orientalism: Mahler's Orient resembles a "porcelain China" (*MPE,* 149; ein China aus Porzellan: *MP,* 291) rather than the real China. For Adorno, Mahler was not primarily interested in faithfully recreating a different acoustic culture but rather in producing music that would sound alien and irritating to listeners conditioned by European music.

I believe that Adorno is right in claiming that Mahler's interest in the Orient is not free of clichés and is related to his Jewish background.[6] But the question that Adorno does not answer is how exactly Mahler's Orientalism is relevant for his Jewishness. Do Mahler's compositions do more than merely unsettle the expectations of Western listeners? And if so, what kind of knowledge about Jewishness or ethnic diversity in general is contained in *Das Lied von der Erde* and Mahler's other compositions that play with "Oriental" tropes? Here too, text can help to answer these questions. While these compositions clearly participated in constructing a non-Western "Other," they also reflect, I will argue in the following, upon the conditions under which this "otherness" is constructed by Western culture in general and by fin-de-siècle Vienna culture in particular. The latter aspect in particular has not always been recognized.

The Orient in the German Cultural Imagination

In Vienna around 1900 there existed something akin to a popular interest in the Orient that involved literature, music, and the visual arts.

Sometimes the period around 1900 is referred to as the "Second Oriental Renaissance."[7] In the year 1900 the Secession organized a major exhibition on Japanese art — the largest one in Europe until that point, exhibiting approximately 700 objects. In May 1901 a "cherry blossom festival" (Kirschblütenfest) took place in the Rotunde building located in the Vienna Prater; 150,000 people attended, all dressed in Japanese costumes.[8] At the *Kunstschau* exhibition in the spring of 1908 Oskar Kokoschka exhibited illustrations from *Die träumenden Knaben* (The Dreaming Boys) in the style of Japanese woodcuts (discussed in chapter 3).[9] Alma and Gustav Mahler were among the visitors.[10] Gustav Klimt's paintings frequently involved Oriental motifs. And in 1905 Richard Strauss's *Salome* premiered in Dresden; it was an opera that Mahler admired and sought to have performed in Vienna, over the objections of censors and some of his contemporaries. For *Salome* Strauss not only used an Oriental setting but also engaged Jewish history; his intention was to write an opera in the tradition of "Oriental and Jewish operas" (Orient- und Judenopern), but one that was more authentic than those of his contemporaries.[11] These examples are important, because they show that Oriental art started to shed its image of being primarily decorative or ornamental that set it apart from German high art.[12]

German Orientalism was far less homogenous than is sometimes assumed. For someone who was interested in Orientalism around 1900, German cultural history offered two fundamentally different models for looking at the Orient. A key text for understanding German Orientalism is Friedrich Schlegel's *Über die Sprache und Weisheit der Indier* (On the Language and Wisdom of the Indians, 1808). Schlegel built on Herder's idea that human civilization had started in Asia.[13] In his book, however, Schlegel attempts to give a more stable foundation to Herder's theory through what are meant to be precise linguistic and cultural observations. His main thesis is that the ancient Indian language Sanskrit is related to Persian, ancient Greek, Latin, and the Germanic languages, and that this points to a developmental relationship among them.[14] The origins of Germanic culture are consequently to be found in India, according to Schlegel. While Herder believed in a single source from which all civilizations originated,[15] Schlegel in contrast emphasizes the existence of competing linguistic and cultural traditions that originated independently of each other, even though they did have considerable influence on each other.[16] Thus Schlegel distinguishes between two geographical areas of the Orient. One area has its center in India and is seen as being closely related to the Germanic tradition; these are the roots of what later scholars were to call the "Indo-European" or "Indo-Germanic" tradition. Schlegel's other Orient includes everything else: Tibet, China, Arabia, and, to some extent, the Jewish cultural tradition, and is seen as being very different from this "Indo-Germanic" tradition

(115, 297 and 299). While Schlegel emphasizes that all of these traditions are legitimate in their own ways (163), there can be no doubt that he views the "Indo-Germanic" tradition as being superior. Indo-Germanic languages are superior because they know the principle of inflection, in contrast to more "primitive" languages like Chinese, Hebrew, Arabic, and the American-Indian languages.[17] In Schlegel's view, this linguistic superiority is a sign of cultural superiority.

It is precisely this split between a superior and inferior, good and bad Orient that is at the heart of the later distinction between Aryan and non-Aryan (or Semitic) nations that was to have disastrous consequences for Germans' views of other cultures in general, and of Jewish culture in particular.[18] One could say that Schlegel initiated a politicization of German Orientalist discourse in that he made this discourse about the roots of German culture. In his genealogical search, Schlegel was interested in establishing a central trajectory for Germanic culture, and he had a rather negative view of the interactions among divergent traditions that are an unavoidable part of any cultural history.

This is precisely the issue that Goethe addresses in his *West-östlicher Divan* (West-Eastern Divan), the second text of the period that had a paradigmatic function for German thinking about the Orient. This work, which I discussed briefly in chapter 5, is a collection of poems based primarily on the fourteenth-century Persian court poetry of Hafiz and accompanied by a lengthy essay entitled *Noten und Abhandlungen zu besserem Verständnis des West-östlichen Divans* (Notes and Treatises to Further the Understanding of the West-Eastern Divan). It was first published in 1819, roughly a decade after Schlegel's text, and clearly had a polemical function.[19] Goethe's motivation to turn his creative interest eastward is in part explained by the much higher regard for poets that can be found, in his view, in the Orient.[20] But he also quite explicitly looks at the Orient with an interest in alterity. At the very beginning of his commentary Goethe emphasizes how different East and West are. He wants to be seen as a traveler who does his best to adapt to the "unfamiliar way of life" (fremde Landsart) but also realizes that such attempts can be successful only up to a point, that his "own accent" (eignen Akzent) would cause him to be recognized as a "stranger" (Fremdling).[21]

Goethe's view of the Orient, in contrast to Schlegel's, is heterogeneous and yet highly inclusive. At one point he describes Oriental culture as a "mixture" (Gemisch).[22] Hebrews, Arabs, Persians, and Christians are all part of Goethe's Orient, and while Goethe has his preferences among these cultures, he, like Herder, conceives of their relations primarily in developmental terms and not hierarchically. Only once we realize the fundamental differences between East and West do we start to see similarities between East and West, between Horace and Hafiz.[23] Goethe does not intend to collapse the differences between East and West but rather to accept the East and what it stands for as part of his own self-image. Only if we acknowledge the fundamental otherness of the East do we fully appreciate the provocation of Goethe's statement that "what we Germans call *Spirit*" (was wir Deutsche *Geist* nennen[24]) can be found in *Oriental* poetry. At a time when the Napoleonic wars were a recent memory and nationalism was rampant, Goethe reminded his fellow Germans to look elsewhere. For Goethe, in contrast to Schlegel, the Orient represented the other side of the West — of Western rationality — but he wanted this other side also to be part of the West. The Orient allows the West to get back in touch with its repressed Other. Thus he envisions a dialogue that moves beyond geographical and linguistic borders. Even though he did much to counter stereotypes about the Orient, in particular its alleged despotic character, Goethe's view of the Orient is of course not without Orientalist clichés.[25] In the end, Goethe's Orientalism, too, primarily functions as a form of Western self-reflection; the East is instrumentalized in the service of the West's self-improvement. Nevertheless, the polemical potential of Goethe's model of the Orient in the early nineteenth century is considerable.

The aftershocks of the debate between Goethe and Schlegel can be felt throughout nineteenth-century German cultural history, for instance in Arthur Schopenhauer's *Aphorismen zur Lebensweisheit* (Aphorisms on the Wisdom of Life, 1851), which specifically seeks to formulate a non-Christian philosophical ethics and in doing so quotes Goethe's *West-östlicher Divan* extensively,[26] or in Nietzsche's *Also sprach Zarathustra*, a book that is often understood, like Nietzsche's other works, within the framework of Western philosophical history (see chapter 3), but that is in fact framed as an imaginary conversation between one of the oldest documented religions of the East (Zoroastrianism) and the decadent West of the late nineteenth century. Schopenhauer's and Nietzsche's texts had become part of the canon by 1900. One of the more prolific nineteenth-century writers, however, whose work engaged the Orient was the poet Friedrich Rückert (1788–1866). He is largely forgotten today, but his works appear to have been popular in German-speaking countries at the turn of the century. Remarkably, three multi-volume editions of Rückert's collected works were published in the year 1897 alone, each with a different editor;[27] one of them was by Reclam in Leipzig, a publisher instrumental in popularizing the German classics through cheap but generally reliable editions.

Reinventing Culture: The Rückert Songs

Mahler started work on setting a number of Rückert's poems to music during the summer of 1901. While the precise chronology of the so-called "Rückert songs" and of the *Kindertotenlieder*, also based on poems by

Rückert, is not known, it appears that Mahler worked on both groups of songs simultaneously in the summer of 1901; he then composed one more Rückert song in the summer of 1902, and two more *Kindertotenlieder* in the summer of 1904.[28] At the same time, he was working on his entirely instrumental Fifth, Sixth, and Seventh Symphonies. He first published what have now become known as his Rückert songs in 1907 in a collection together with his last two *Wunderhorn* songs, "Revelge" and "Der Tamboursg'sell." It is interesting to note that Mahler chose to publish these songs together. One could argue that "Revelge" and "Der Tamboursg'sell" articulate a kind of culmination. Both songs end with the deaths of their protagonists. They also signal what one could describe as "the end of ideology": Whether one follows the orders of one's superior or rebels against them, in the end the result is the same (see chapter 2). Art may allow us to remember our past or point to the existence of forms of knowledge in our culture that in everyday life are more or less forgotten, but it does not give its audience an ethical framework to live by. The Rückert songs and *Kindertotenlieder* respond to this by seeking out a different basis for art. They no longer evoke the conflict between individual and society that, implicitly or explicitly, was at the core of the *Lieder eines fahrenden Gesellen* and the *Wunderhorn* songs. Language holds a very different status in the Rückert songs in particular. One could say that Rückert's poetry allows Mahler to reinvent himself as a composer (not unlike how the *West-östlicher Divan* allowed Goethe to reinvent himself as a poet).

In contrast to Goethe, Schopenhauer, and Nietzsche, Friedrich Rückert had tangible scholarly credentials in Oriental studies. Suzanne Marchand describes Rückert very correctly as "caught between romanticism and historicism"; from Romanticism he borrowed its "grand political and aesthetic dreams," while increasingly historicist approaches to Oriental languages and cultures were responsible for his desire to be considered as a scholar doing scientifically sound work (138). Rückert had been a professor of Oriental studies, initially in Erlangen and later at a more prestigious post in Berlin, in addition to being a very prolific translator of ancient Oriental texts and a poet in his own right. Interestingly, he is known to have been an industrious reader of *Des Knaben Wunderhorn*, and it has been argued that these poems also served as a model for his own poetry.[29] Rückert had also been an admirer of Jean Paul until the latter author made clear to him that he had little respect for Rückert's work.[30] In contrast to Goethe, Rückert, thanks to his in-depth Oriental studies, had the linguistic knowledge needed for working with original Oriental texts in many different languages. In his own poetry Rückert sought to reproduce Oriental metric and stanza forms; within German literary history he is known for introducing the ghazal (Ghasel) into German poetry.[31] In spite of such high ambitions and an extremely prolific career as a translator, Rückert in his capacity as a scholar frequently reflected on the fact that translations are always imperfect,[32] which was very much in line with Goethe's thinking on the subject. Rückert's poetry inspired by his Oriental scholarship is, however, only one side of his creative work. While pursuing his Oriental studies, Rückert also aimed for a career as a popular — some would say "frivolous" — author who wrote many poems for specific occasions and contributed to and edited popular magazines. This earned him the reputation of someone who was not always able to think critically about his own published output. It also may explain why Rückert, beyond the unquestionably lively interest in his work seen in the late nineteenth century, did not become part of the literary canon over the long term. In fact, he is now mostly known through Mahler's compositions that use his texts.

How does Rückert position himself in the German debate on Orientalism? It is clear that Rückert initially takes Friedrich Schlegel as his model. In his early works he seeks a religious and national revival from studying ancient Indian texts. His dissertation, which he wrote in 1811, was greatly inspired by Schlegel's *Über die Sprache und Weisheit der Indier* and the nationalist tendencies underlying the latter's work; in it he imagines a "reconstructed German version of the divine *Ursprache* emerging as the foundation of German nationhood."[33] In line with this model offered by Schlegel, Rückert actively participates in the nationalistic turn that characterized the work of many Romantics, in particular after 1810. Throughout his life he would combine political leanings toward German unity with an outspoken conservative political agenda. However, there is another side to Rückert as well. When Goethe's *West-östlicher Divan* was published in 1819, Rückert responded very enthusiastically and immediately planned a similar project, which was eventually published as *Östliche Rosen* (Eastern Roses) in 1822.[34] The first poem in this collection is in fact a homage to Goethe's *West-östlicher Divan*; in it, Rückert not only commends Goethe for offering a pure vision of the East but describes his own preoccupation with the Orient as a form of rejuvenation that was akin to the impact of Italy on the younger Goethe.[35] Perhaps not surprisingly, Goethe recommended in a review of the volume that these poems be set to music.[36]

I believe that the impact of Goethe's *West-östlicher Divan* on Rückert was considerable. It is clear that the year 1819 was a kind of turning point in Rückert's life. During the winter of 1818–19 Rückert, returning from a trip to Italy, spent several weeks in Vienna, where he lived in the same house as Friedrich Schlegel and met the famous Orientalist Joseph von Hammer-Purgstall, whose 1812/13 translation *Diwan des Hafis* (Divan of Hafiz) inspired Goethe's *West-östlicher Divan*. These meetings motivated Rückert to turn his attention back to Oriental studies and were followed by a period of intensive study bolstered by the publication of Goethe's *West-östlicher Divan* in late 1819.[37] It was in 1819 that Rückert first wrote poems in an Oriental style.[38]

Before discussing Mahler's individual Rückert songs, the question arises as to whether the composer viewed the songs now known as Rückert songs as being related to Rückert's interests in Orientalism. The clearest answer to this question comes from Donald Mitchell. There are indeed musicological grounds for characterizing the Rückert songs as having been composed in an Orientalist style. These songs use, for instance, a pentatonic scale: a scale that organizes the octave into five pitches, and that is often used to evoke exotic — or more precisely, Oriental — connotations (as by Mahler's contemporaries Debussy and Ravel), but is also associated with folk music, for instance by Bartók (*SSLD,* 60).[39] The use of the pentatonic model links these songs in particular to *Das Lied von der Erde,* in which this model also plays an important role. A second feature characteristic of the Rückert songs is their "heterophony" (*SSLD,* 62): the simultaneous presence of several melodic lines that are rhythmically distinct. This, too, is a characteristic feature of Oriental music. Mahler's friend, musicologist Guido Adler, published an article in 1908 on what he called "heterophony," in which he mentioned "Siamese, Japanese, and Javanese music, as well as Russian folk songs" as examples of polyphonic music, but also pointed to the polyphonic roots of Western music.[40] Adler defines "heterophony" as a more irregular and radical form of polyphony (*SSLD,* 631). Mahler's interest in heterophony seems to have grown out of a renewed interest in the technique of counterpoint, also noticeable in his Fifth and Sixth Symphonies, which were composed simultaneously with the Rückert songs and the *Kindertotenlieder.*

But are there textual reasons, in addition to these musicological reasons, for characterizing the Rückert songs as "Oriental"? The imagery in all the songs based on Rückert's texts is very different from that in Mahler's previous songs. In the words of Donald Mitchell: "Gone are the fanfares, the military signals, the dance and march rhythms and the quasi-folk style of the 'Wunderhorn' songs" (*SSLD,* 68). The attitude toward language in these songs is very different from that in his earlier songs. Interestingly, if one follows the order in which they were initially published in 1907, both the first and second Rückert song involve the phenomenon of semantic ambiguity. Especially if the song is heard and not read, the "Lieder" (songs) of the first song's title "Blicke mir nicht in die Lieder" (Do not look at my songs)[41] could easily be understood to be "Lider" in the sense of "eyelids."[42] The fact that this second interpretation is encouraged is clear from the song's second line "Meine Augen schlag' ich nieder" (I cast down my eyes), which seems to reinforce the impression that we are dealing with "Lider" and not "Lieder" in the first line. Similarly in the second song, "Ich atmet' einen linden Duft" (I was breathing a subtle fragrance),[43] "linden Duft' (subtle fragrance) can also be understood as "Lindenduft" (scent of a linden tree), a term also used in the poem. The first poem, "Blicke mir nicht in die Lieder," is essentially an argument against interfering with or reflecting on the creative process: poets should produce their texts just as bees build their cells, and once they are done, readers should enjoy the product without questioning its background (just as humans enjoy the bees' honey). The second song puts this wisdom into practice: the poem is impressive first and foremost as a play on sounds, in particular *i*, *ei*, and *ie*:

> *I*m Z*i*mmer stand
> *ei*n Zw*ei*g der L*i*nde,
> *ei*n Angeb*i*nde
> von l*ie*ber Hand.
> W*ie* l*ie*bl*i*ch war der L*i*ndenduft!
>
> [In the room stood
> a twig of a linden tree,
> a gift
> from a loving hand.
> How lovely was the scent of the linden tree.]

Semantic content is less important than form in this poem: obviously, the branch of the linden tree is associated with love — it is the memento a lover has left, as the text tells us — but we learn very little else. "Ich atmet' einen linden Duft" is as close as Mahler has ever got to creating a work of art that is interested in art's aesthetic properties alone (an attitude often described as *l'art pour l'art*, or art for art's sake).[44]

Through their reflection on and use of language — unprecedented in Mahler's oeuvre — these first two Rückert songs certainly appear to articulate a new beginning. They formulate an aesthetic ideal that seeks enjoyment and an emotional response unhampered by reflection, an ideal that transcends the (Western) division of mind and body, beyond the schism of the rational from the irrational. Goethe associated the Orient with a language liberated from "the need to represent" (Repräsentationszwänge), a compulsion that, in the West, had resulted in an instrumental way of using poetry ("instrumentelle Dichtungsweise").[45] The fact that the linden tree functions as a symbol of a newfound aesthetic attitude for Mahler is remarkable, not only because he used it in one of his earlier songs ("Die zwei blauen Augen" from the *Lieder eines fahrenden Gesellen*), but also because of the prominent role that the linden tree plays in Schubert's *Winterreise* cycle, which contains a song entitled "Der Lindenbaum" (The Linden Tree; see chapter 2). It is as if Mahler is asking us to interpret an old symbol in a new way. Simultaneously these songs, as I hope to have made clear, live from the ability of language to allow for multiple story lines. This ability is based on the wordplay in these poems, for which Rückert had quite an affinity, an attitude he shared with Oriental poetry in general.[46] It is in their ability to allow for diverging narratives that the words of Rückert's poems assert their autonomy over meaning.

One could also argue that particular sensitivity to the relative power of words over their meanings and attention to the sound of language are typical for non-native speakers of that language. It is as if Rückert steps outside of the German language and asks his reader to do the same.

The next Rückert song, "Ich bin der Welt abhanden gekommen" (I am lost to the world), emphasizes, like "Blicke mir nicht in die Lieder," the separation between the artist and his surrounding environment: The narrator reviews his past and feels that he has "wasted" (verdorben) too much time taking action for or in this world. The line "I live alone [now] in my heaven" (Ich leb' allein in meinem Himmel) can be taken as an intertextual reference to "Das himmlische Leben," the final movement of the Fourth Symphony that also articulated an ideal of art as free play of the imagination (see chapter 3). "Ich bin der Welt abhanden gekommen," like the final Rückert song, "Liebst du um Schönheit," was taken from *Liebesfrühling* (Spring of Love),[47] a collection of love poems that Rückert wrote for his wife in 1821, the year when they first got to know each other, and published as a collection in 1834.[48] Knowing this is relevant, because from its text alone it is not necessarily clear that this poem is a love song. Of the three stanzas, the first two stanzas are dominated by imagery of death, even though it is clear that this imagery is used to explain a mode of being; it is "for the world" (der Welt) that the song's protagonist has died: "For truly for the world I have died, died" (Denn wirklich bin ich gestorben, gestorben der Welt). The word "truly" (wirklich) has a paradoxical function here: while it is meant to emphasize the reality of death, the line simultaneously points to death's metaphorical function for understanding a subjective experience, a feeling. It is not until the song's last two lines that the narrator explains why he is "lost to the world," and even there his answer is ambiguous: it is because of his "love" (Lieben) or "song" (Lied) that he is no longer participating in everyday life. If one takes the song to be about emotions, it tells three different stories: about death, love, and art, but also about loneliness and companionship. The song's point is that all of these stories are equally true.

"Um Mitternacht" (Around Midnight)[49] is one of the Rückert songs in which Mahler's play with heterophony is quite pronounced; the song is therefore representative of Mahler's new style (*SSLD*, 56, 59, and 64). It also anticipates formal aspects of *Das Lied von der Erde* (*SSLD*, 67), Mahler's most prominent experiment with Orientalism. On the other hand, "Um Mitternacht," like "Ich atmet' einen linden Duft" before it, also establishes clear intertextual relationships to other compositions by Mahler: to Zarathustra's "Mitternachtslied" in the fourth movement of the Third Symphony, for instance, or to the nocturnal imagery of the Seventh Symphony (which Mahler would compose several years later). Like these two other compositions, "Um Mitternacht" uses night as an image for illustrating humankind's metaphysical homelessness — symbolized in this poem not only by the invisibility of stars (stanza 1), but also by the absence of "enlightening thought" (Lichtgedanke; stanza 2). Midnight is interpreted as a moment of pain (stanza 3), as a battle for the suffering of humankind (stanza 4), and as a moment between life and death (stanza 5). Much has been made of the autobiographical associations that this poem must have evoked in Mahler: during the night of 24–25 February 1901, six months before Mahler composed this song, he suffered a potentially lethal hemorrhage.[50] This should not detract, however, from the fact that this text also articulates a new philosophy of life in its last stanza: the insight that the decision about life and death is not up to the individual but to a power beyond the individual, and that it is good that way, that this needs to be accepted — even though the music accompanying the final stanza is highly dissonant.[51] This is a philosophy of life that Mahler will work out in much greater detail in *Das Lied von der Erde*.

The last Rückert song, "Liebst du um Schönheit" (If you love for beauty),[52] is, following statements by Alma, often taken as a private gift by Gustav to her, even though it was published (with only a piano score) in the 1907 collection (*SSLD*, 110). It is indeed an unmistakable love song declaring that love is fundamentally indifferent to beauty, youth, or material wealth. When read in context with "Um Mitternacht," this song seeks to give a positive turn to what could be called the dependence of human existence on the body. It is possible to read the song as a rejection of the materialist "Western" world in favor of an "Eastern" attitude that is less concerned with material things while simultaneously acknowledging the physical limits of human life. In terms of atmosphere — short and lighthearted rather than dark and long — the song harks back to the collection's first two songs. This is also true in terms of content: the song argues for the autonomy not only of love but also of art. The text's narrator speaks as an artist who clearly distances himself from what could be interpreted as bourgeois standards in favor of a more insecure but creative existence, but in addition, by presenting itself very explicitly as a love song, the song also turns into a statement about love *and* art. In love the essence of art articulates itself, and vice versa. Both are characterized by autonomy. In addition to acting as a message to Alma, which it certainly was, the song thereby also articulates an artistic program that reaffirms the idea of aesthetic autonomy previously articulated in the first two songs of the cycle.

Mahler's Rückert songs use language differently from all of Mahler's previous songs — a phenomenon that may have something to do with the fact that the texts he used came from a very different source, but that also points to Mahler's rethinking of his aesthetic agenda. The *Wunderhorn* songs are much more worldly in the images they evoke and in the topics they discuss. The Rückert songs, despite the fact that they at times deal with topics familiar from Mahler's other works, not only introduce an alternative aesthetic model (for example, through their use of the pentatonic scale) but also begin to allude to a philosophy of life that Mahler associates with the East (and that he will develop more fully in the *Kindertotenlieder* and *Das Lied von der Erde*). This orientation toward a different view of human existence is especially clear in the way "Ich bin der Welt abhanden gekommen" and "Um Mitternacht" discuss death (also a key topic in the *Kindertotenlieder* and *Das Lied von der Erde*). Finally, the heterophonic treatment of melody in the songs is mirrored by the multiple stories that these songs tell. While many of Mahler's songs, one way or another, are predicated on a certain ambiguity, the Rückert songs go one step further by insisting on multiple narratives simultaneously.

Meditations on the Meaning of Death: Kindertotenlieder

Mahler's *Kindertotenlieder* (Songs on the Death of Children) are based on a collection of poems with the same title that the 45-year-old Friedrich Rückert wrote after the deaths from scarlet fever of his children Luise at age 3 on 31 December 1833 and Ernst at age 5 on 16 January 1834. Rückert's 425 *Kindertodtenlieder* are highly personal texts. At the request of his wife he did not publish these poems but instead, after their completion sometime in late June 1834, gave the autograph manuscript to her.[53] The collection was not printed until 1872, well after the deaths of both Friedrich Rückert and his wife Luise. Mahler composed three of the *Kindertotenlieder* during the summer of 1901, while also working on the first four of his Rückert songs and before starting work on his Fifth Symphony that summer. He composed the remaining two *Kindertotenlieder* three years later, during the summer of 1904.[54]

The key to understanding these songs is, in my view, the cycle's fourth song "Oft denk' ich, sie sind nur ausgegangen" (I often think they just went out walking).[55] This poem starts with the (quite moving) fantasy that the children, who we know have died, have only temporarily gone out into the nearby hills. While the reader would expect some kind of disillusionment, a rejection of the fantasy, the poem actually takes a very different turn: there is some truth to the fantasy in the sense that the children, in a variation of the opening line of the third stanza, "have just gone ahead of us" (sind uns nur vorausgegangen). By reimagining history, we humans can learn something about our future. The children have gone where eventually "we" — a pronoun that may be taken to refer to the poet and his wife but may also be interpreted to include the reader or listener — will also have to go. The poem, in other words, asks us to rethink what we could consider a dark reality in favor of an alternative reality, by offering an image: that of the sun-covered "heights" (Höh'n).[56] This image helps us to work through the absence caused by death and to accept mortality, not just that of others but also *our own*. The poem very explicitly does not refer to Christian imagery or to the promise of an afterlife.[57] It seeks to incorporate the sadness accompanying death without giving in to melancholy. Instead, the poem seeks to work through the experience of death. Nature may be able to help in this, precisely because it does not allow the mourning subject's sadness to carry over into nature: the poem paints a beautiful day with plenty of sunshine, but in the end it is imagination that asserts its autonomy over everyday reality (mimicking the call for aesthetic autonomy in the Rückert songs discussed above). It is through the poem's central image, the image of the children having gone ahead and the parents catching up with them, that the writer/reader/listener can accomplish the difficult operation of accepting mortality as part of life. The instrumental accompaniment, however, which at the very end of the song relates contrapuntally to the sung text, emphasizes that this is a very ambivalent process; the music highlights the deep ambiguity underlying the text.[58]

Nature plays an important role in the other songs as well, particularly in the first and last songs of the cycle. But at no time is nature part of the resolution of the songs' underlying conflict; rather, it functions as a reminder of the chaotic essence of life on earth. The bright sun of "Oft denk' ich, sie sind nur ausgegangen" is also present in the first of the *Kindertotenlieder* entitled "Nun will die Sonn' so hell aufgeh'n" (Now the sun will rise brightly).[59] We discover the narrator at daybreak, but here the world of nature and the mourning subject clash. The narrator reminds himself not to give in to the dark of night, but does so in vain. The poem contrasts a little lamp going out in the narrator's *tent* — reminiscent of the Oriental models that Rückert used for his poetry — used as a symbol of death, with the "light full of joy" (Freudenlicht) outside. There is no way of reconciling the two, a fact also underlined by the song's slow and somber melody. The light referred to in the text is counteracted by a melody that is "unstable in mode — rapidly alternating or combining major and minor — and also in dynamics, which are characteristically intricate, nervous and gusty" (*SSLD*, 93). The second song of the cycle, "Nun seh' ich wohl, warum so dunkle Flammen" (Now I see why such dark flames),[60] can be read as a confirmation of the message underlying the first song. Light plays a role in this poem in the "dark flames" (dunkle Flammen), which the narrator remembers were sometimes visible in the eyes of his children when they were still alive. The poem is structured as an imagined dialogue between narrator and his deceased children. The dark flames in their eyes foreshadow the future: they express a desire to stay nearby but also disclose the knowledge that fate will not allow this. In the poem's last line, only the stars are present to remind the narrator of his children's eyes. The cycle's third song, "Wenn dein Mütterlein"

(When your dear mother),[61] comes closest to "Oft denk' ich, sie sind nur ausgegangen" in terms of its thematical structure: The narrator imagines, for a moment, that in the dark the child is following its mother into the house, as it used to do. As in the preceding poem, this poem is structured as a dialogue with the child. The tension between imagination and reality remains unresolved in this song. The narrator realizes his mistake and in the song's final two lines laments the child's untimely death.

If "Oft denk' ich, sie sind nur ausgegangen" had been the cycle's last song, one could speak of a reconciliatory ending, although an ambiguous one. The cycle's last song "In diesem Wetter, in diesem Braus" (In this weather; in this storm)[62] is a dark footnote to the entire cycle, and in particular to "Oft denk' ich, sie sind nur ausgegangen." This song also imagines the children as having gone out, although against their will and that of their father ("Never would I have let the children out" [Nie hätt' ich gelassen die Kinder hinaus]) — a statement that is repeated, phrased in different ways, in each of the first four stanzas. The father finds some consolation in the idea that the children are now resting "like in their mother's, mother's home" (als wie in der Mutter, der Mutter Haus), suggesting that their death can be seen as a return to their origin,[63] and that they are protected from the storm. The poem's last stanza, in other words, suggests some kind of reconciliation between nature's cruelty and the father's fears, albeit a bitter one, since the text here clearly alludes to the children's graves. This ending is anticipated in the third stanza, in which the father finds some solace in the fact that he does not have to worry about his children dying tomorrow ("sie stürben morgen"), the implication being that since the children are no longer living there is no reason to worry about their future anymore. While "Oft denk' ich, sie sind nur ausgegangen" emphasizes the potentially therapeutic function of imagination, "In diesem Wetter, in diesem Braus" primarily stresses its dark side: it leads the mourning subject to the childrens' graves. To be sure, the music accompanying the poem's last stanza quiets down; not mimicking, however, as has been suggested,[64] a quieting of the storm, but rather (as the text makes clear) the quietness of the newfound "house" amid the storm. Imagination, as the quintessence of all art, does not offer a shelter from life's brutal realities. While in the fourth song of the cycle imagination enabled some form of overcoming death, symbolized by the sunny heights where the parents join their children, the fifth song in contrast ends with a metaphorical evocation of the children's grave. The "als wie" (like) preceding the image of the "mother's house" makes it clear that no real return takes place, only a metaphorical one. By explicitly pointing to the metaphorical status of this image, the poem reflects its own status as a poetic construction.

Again, Mahler's songs offer no easy solutions; at the end of the cycle we are left with conflicted emotions. In the *Kindertotenlieder*, too, we see how Mahler's songs tell multiple stories. This is particularly clear through the juxtaposition of the mourning subject, its emotions, and desires on the one hand, and nature as a cruel entity, exemplifying the chaotic essence of life on earth on the other. Nature is present in all of Mahler's *Kindertotenlieder*, although it moves into the background somewhat in "Oft denk' ich, sie sind nur ausgegangen," the imagery of which is to be read in tandem with the final poem, as I have shown. Many scholars have commented on the strange coincidence whereby Mahler, in his *Kindertotenlieder* (1901–4), appears to anticipate the death of his own daughter Maria Anna (known as Putzi) that occurred several years later in 1907. A number of psychoanalytic critics have sought to explain Mahler's interest in Rückert's *Kindertodtenlieder* through a combination of his brush with death during the night of 24–25 February 1901, half a year before starting work on the *Kindertotenlieder*, his subsequent resolution to marry and have children, and memories of his many brothers and sisters who had not lived to see adulthood.[65] I find these to be plausible readings, even though Mahler had not yet met Alma when he started to conceive his *Kindertotenlieder*. He may have had other motives as well, however. In this context, it is important to be aware of the fact that, for Rückert, the *Kindertodtenlieder* also documented and engaged with a crisis in his *creative* life.

While it is not clear whether Mahler was aware of the chronological framework of the Rückert texts he chose (we do not know which edition of Rückert's texts Mahler used when working on his adaptations), it is quite interesting. The first two Rückert songs that Mahler published in his 1907 collection were taken from the collection *Haus- und Jahreslieder*, and in the 1897 edition of Rückert's works edited by Conrad Beyer, they were dated "Fall 1833" (Herbst 1833) and "May through July 1833" (Mai bis Juli 1833).[66] This means that Rückert wrote these texts just before the *Kindertodtenlieder*, which were written during the first half of 1834 immediately following the deaths of his children Luise and Ernst. Two of the three remaining Rückert songs Mahler took from the collection *Liebesfrühling*, written in 1821 during Rückert's engagement to his future wife but not published as a collection until 1834, when they appeared in volume 1 of the *Gesammelte Gedichte*.[67] Rückert worked on this edition the summer after the deaths of two of his children and after he had finished the *Kindertodtenlieder*. Taken together, Mahler's Rückert songs and the *Kindertotenlieder* offer a sort of psychogram of Friedrich Rückert in 1833 and 1834. The first two Rückert songs reconstruct Rückert's state of mind immediately before the deaths of his children. The *Kindertodtenlieder* document the grieving process. Following this line of thinking, the songs from *Liebesfrühling* could be interpreted as reminiscences of earlier and happier times, to which Rückert sought to return during the summer of 1834.

There is no doubt that, for Rückert, the deaths of his two children challenged his creativity. This confrontation with death led him to question why one should write poetry at all.[68] Some comments that Mahler made during the summer of 1901 to Natalie Bauer-Lechner indicate that he too doubted his ability to sustain his own creativity. Clearly, early in the summer of 1901 Mahler was struggling with some form of composer's block (see *GME,* 188–90 and 192–93; *RGM,* 168, 170, and 172), though Bauer-Lechner downplays his difficulties. Unable to work on a symphony, he took on the Rückert-inspired songs to help him through this crisis (a situation that repeated itself to some extent in 1904).[69] Eventually however, the summer of 1901 would turn out to be quite productive: he composed 7 songs and the middle movement of the Fifth Symphony. One can stipulate that, at least in part, Mahler's creative difficulties were triggered by his brush with mortality in the preceding months. In this context, it may also be relevant that Mahler had started his summer recuperating from an operation resulting from the hemorrhage he had suffered during the night of 24–25 February.[70] The Rückert texts offered an aesthetic model that allowed Mahler to reinvent himself, much as the poetry of Hafiz allowed Goethe to reinvent not simply his poetry but also his philosophy of life in his *West-östlicher Divan.* The first Rückert song, "Blicke mir nicht in die Lieder," not only very explicitly thematizes the issue of creative block but also suggests an ideal of creativity as wholly unproblematic (in the image of the bees building their cells). If Mahler's creative crisis was in fact triggered by being reminded of his own mortality, this certainly would explain why death is an important topic in these poems.

All the songs based on texts by Rückert are composed in an "Oriental" style, as demonstrated by their pentatonic scale and emphasis on polyphony. Most of the texts formally follow a simple folksong pattern with straightforward rhyme schemes, with the exception of "Nun seh' ich wohl, warum so dunkle Flammen," which is a sonnet.[71] The songs do not experiment with the more complex Oriental metric and strophic forms that Rückert uses elsewhere. There are, however, thematic reasons to characterize these poems as "Oriental." Schopenhauer, in his *Aphorismen zur Lebensweisheit,* advises making it a principle to focus not on attaining "the pleasures and comforts of life" (die Genüsse und Annehmlichkeiten des Lebens) but rather on avoiding "the numerous things that are unpleasant" (den zahllosen Uebeln).[72] "Happiness is but a dream; suffering is real" (le bonheur n'est qu'un rêve, et la douleur est réelle), Schopenhauer notes, citing Voltaire (442). Schopenhauer is critical here of a Christian ethical model that assumes that humans will act nobly only if they are promised a reward in the hereafter. Instead, Schopenhauer places human suffering at the center of human ethics; avoiding suffering should be at the core of humanity's efforts. It is not in the West but in the East that Schopenhauer sees a philosophy of life that follows this principle.

This at least partially explains not only the many references in *Aphorismen zur Lebensweisheit* to Goethe's *West-östlicher Divan*, but also Schopenhauer's interest in Brahmanism and Buddhism, which he articulated elsewhere. Schopenhauer found in Indian philosophy an ethical framework without a God.[73] Furthermore, Brahmanism and Buddhism distinguish themselves from other religions by their very different attitude toward suffering and death.[74] Rather than pursue the goal of happiness, humans should acknowledge suffering as the purpose of life.[75] Death is nothing but abandoning our individuality in favor of joining a "primordial being" (Urwesen) or "Brahm";[76] or in Schopenhauer's own terminology, abandoning the general will to live that underlies everything in nature. Both Brahmanism and Buddhism fit Schopenhauer's pessimistic view of life in that they acknowledge the unavoidability of human suffering. However, precisely because of this insight, studying these religions could lead to a reinvented, more authentic Christianity.[77]

In the end, this is what Mahler's *Kindertotenlieder* and Rückert songs seek to accomplish: to find a philosophy of life based in the here-and-now that incorporates the experience of suffering and death and seeks to accept them as an integral part of life. It is the song "Oft denk' ich, sie sind nur ausgegangen" that most clearly articulates this insight. Mahler projected his newfound Schopenhauerian philosophy of life onto the "Orient" and saw it as being fundamentally different from the West. He was not interested in Schlegel's model of appropriating part of the Orient and discarding the rest, but rather in a dialogue between East and West along the lines of Goethe's model in the *West-östlicher Divan*.

Richard Strauss's Orientalism

To understand Mahler's return to Orientalism in his *Lied von der Erde*, composed during the summer of 1908 and not performed until after his death, it is useful to look into his relationship with Richard Strauss and in particular his attitude toward Strauss's opera *Salome*, which seems to have functioned as a catalyst in early-twentieth-century debates about not just Oriental but also anti-Semitic clichés in music.

Race played a role in how contemporaries viewed Mahler and Strauss and compared their compositions. This is made clear, for instance, in a review by Richard Batka of the premiere of Mahler's Seventh Symphony in Prague. The review quotes Arthur Schnitzler (1862–1931), a novelist and playwright of German-Jewish descent living in Vienna who was also an astute observer of Austrian society and culture, in addition to being a great admirer of Mahler's music.

> Arthur Schnitzler apparently said recently in a private conversation that someone who didn't known that Richard Strauss is Aryan and

Gustav Mahler is of Jewish descent would undisputedly observe specifically Semitic characteristics in the composer of *Salome*: the luxuriant, erotic sensuality; the unbridled Oriental imagination; the proclivity toward outward effect; the talent for self-representation, and in general the skill at the economic exploitation of his work. One would contrast him with Gustav Mahler, as a man of mystic rumination, one who storms gigantic boulders, a chaste "Wunderhorn" singer who is able to render the "Wayfarer" music of the *Volk* suited for symphonic form, and an idealist, in short as the paragon of the German artist.

[Arthur Schnitzler soll jüngst in einem Privatgespräch gemeint haben, wenn man nicht wüßte, daß Richard Strauß Arier und Gustav Mahler jüdischer Abstammung ist, würde man bei dem Schöpfer der "Salome" unstreitig die üppige erotische Sinnlichkeit, die orientalische ausschweifende Phantasie, den Hang zum äußeren Effekt und das Talent zur Selbstaufmachung, überhaupt das Geschick zur wirtschaftlichen Verwertung seiner Arbeiten als spezifisch semitische Eigenschaften bemerken und ihm Gustav Mahler, als den Mann der mystischen Vergrübeltheit, als gigantischen Felsblockstürmer, als den keuschen Wunderhornsänger, der die Musik der fahrenden Gesellen aus dem Volke symphoniefähig macht, als Idealisten, kurzum als den Typus des germanischen Künstlers entgegenhalten.][78]

Schnitzler's comments are interesting because they document how steeped the cultural landscape is in racial categories around 1908, when the premiere of Mahler's Seventh Symphony took place. At the same time, he deconstructs the very categories that were used in order to navigate contemporary culture: if one takes them seriously, Schnitzler says, Richard Strauss would have to be Jewish and Gustav Mahler Aryan.[79] Most importantly however, Schnitzler gives an example of what Jewish music in the perception of his contemporaries was supposed to sound like: like Richard Strauss's *Salome*.

Not only the music but also the libretto and imagery of Strauss's opera *Salome* are full of Orientalist clichés. Based on a text by Oscar Wilde, the opera picks up on one of the predominant Orientalist topoi: the association of the East with exuberant, out-of-bounds, and perverse sexuality.[80] Strauss's opera in particular associates sexuality and cruelty in the figure of Salome, daughter of Herodias, who according to an apocryphal tradition was responsible for the death of John the Baptist (in Strauss's opera named *Jochanaan*). She exemplifies the cruel female or femme fatale who is a figure of fascination in fin-de-siècle European culture and who can also be found in some of the works of the Secession artists, for instance in Gustav Klimt's *Judith I* and *Judith II* (1901 and 1909); the first painting was also often referred to as *Salome*.[81] Salome, however, does not merely personify the Oriental woman but also embodies the Jewish woman: she refers to herself as the "princess of Judaea" (Prinzessin von Judäa).[82] In Richard Strauss's opera, clichés about the Orient turn into clichés about Jewish people and their culture, something that is also made clear by Strauss's own characterization of it as an "Oriental and Jewish opera" (Orient- und Judenoper) later in his recollections.[83] In *Salome* we return to the dialectic between a good and bad Orient that we first encountered in the writings of Schlegel. By demanding Jochanaan's head, Salome, and to some extent her mother (who approves of her actions), live out their perverse sexuality and represent the bad Orient. Jochanaan represents the good Orient, along with (at least to some extent) King Herod who, in spite of his promise to Salome that he will fulfill any of her wishes after she has danced for him, is uncomfortable with her request that he give her Jochanaan's head — he would rather give her half of his kingdom.[84]

A second anti-Jewish cliché is that of the Jews quarreling about their religion like "wild animals" (wilde Tiere) at the opera's outset,[85] later epitomized in the so-called "quintet of the Jews," in which five Jews debate what to do with Herod's prisoner, Jochanaan.[86] The music that Strauss composed for this scene mimics their squabbling through the very pronounced use of polyphony and dissonance.[87] The scene can be interpreted as Strauss's reflection on the cultural stereotype that sees Jewish speech (so-called "mauscheln") as a form of deficient or decadent use of German.[88] Such a reference is certainly intended, and anti-Semitic critics did not hesitate to pick up on it.[89] In the context of the German debate on Orientalism, however, it is important to note that the scene is also a comment on a specific model of Orientalism: the dialogic model promoted by Goethe's *West-östlicher Divan* that considered "speaking with an accent" as something positive. What is put into question in Strauss's opera is a dialogic attitude toward one's values. At stake is one of the basic tenets underlying one model of German Orientalism: the willingness to engage in a debate about one's belief system and that of others.

Mahler's response to Richard Strauss's *Salome* was ambivalent. When Strauss told Mahler that he planned to write an opera based on Oscar Wilde's *Salome*, Mahler reacted negatively, but once he had heard the music (when Strauss played it for him at a piano store in Strasbourg during a visit in May 1905), he changed his mind.[90] It is hard to believe that Mahler initially rejected *Salome* on basis of its text alone because of his conservative literary taste, as has been suggested,[91] given his admiration for a play like Frank Wedekind's *Frühlings Erwachen* (Spring Awakening) which he saw in Berlin[92] — a play that dealt very openly with a range of sexual behaviors, not all of which fell within the norms of middle-class society at the time. Mahler did everything he could to get *Salome* to Vienna, but he was not able to convince the censor. He responded very positively to the two performances of Strauss's *Salome* that he attended on 9 and 12 January 1907 in Berlin. In a letter he wrote to Alma on 13 January, he called *Salome* "one of the greatest masterworks of our time" (eines der größten Meisterwerke unserer Zeit); at the same time, however, he admitted some puzzlement as to how Strauss could have composed something like it: "I cannot make sense of it and only suspect that somewhere in this genius the 'spirit of the earth' makes itself heard" (Ich kann es mir nicht zusammenreimen und nur ahnen, daß aus dem Innern des Genies die Stimme des "Erdgeistes" tönt; *GR*, 308). This is a very interesting statement. Mahler clearly thinks that this piece of music is very different from Strauss's other works. His claim that he "cannot make sense" of Strauss's having created a work of art like this should be read in the context of his general opinion on Strauss's artistic output, which is not always positive (*Salome* is the major exception). When speaking of Strauss as a person, Mahler often emphasizes his coldness (see, for example, *GR,* 266–67, and 279). Musically speaking, this translates into an image of Strauss as someone who composes music that is technically advanced but lacking body and soul. The observation that Strauss, in the case of *Salome*, has been touched by the "spirit of the earth" points to a very different creative origin for this opera in comparison to his other works. The "Erdgeist" is a reference to one of the early scenes in Goethe's *Faust I* (vs. 460–513) where Faust seeks to break through his intellectualism, his life of the mind, in order to embrace another reality associated with the "spirit of the earth" and the body. Mahler's reference to the "*Erd*geist" is of course also interesting, because it appears to allude to Mahler's own "Lied von der *Erde*" and suggests that this composition is to be read in tandem with Strauss's *Salome*.

What remains puzzling are Mahler's (well-documented) extraordinary efforts to have *Salome* performed at the Imperial Opera in Vienna.[93] Did Mahler want to have *Salome* performed in Vienna so that he could distance himself from its music and the stereotypes accompanying it, to show that he was not "one of those loud, gesticulating Eastern Jews" that Strauss parodied in his opera?[94] Or did he see it as a chance to engage with the stereotypes that Strauss was promoting? It is not unthinkable that Mahler viewed *Salome* as an opera that Strauss had composed with him in mind. *Salome* is a far more eclectic work than other works by Strauss. Strauss's experiments with polyphony and atonality mirrored Mahler's own interests. At the very least, Strauss' *Salome* created a frame of reference for Mahler that would allow him to pursue his own related interests, although the latter would take him in a very different direction. If we accept that *Salome* plays a catalytic role here, then the role that Strauss plays for Mahler in the first decade of the twentieth century is not that different from that played by Wagner for the younger Mahler.

I argue in the following section that *Das Lied von der Erde* is conceived as a direct dialogue both with Strauss's opera and its libretto and with the Orientalist imagery that both evoke.

The Heterophonic Orient: Das Lied von der Erde

It is possible that Mahler's Rückert adaptations, in particular the *Kindertotenlieder*, were a critical response to a cycle of songs based on texts by Rückert that Richard Strauss had composed in 1899 and 1900,[95] which emphasized the poet's erotic side and his faith in God. However, *Das Lied von der Erde*'s thematic focus on death and suffering creates an atmosphere very different from that of the exuberant "Oriental" sexuality in Strauss's *Salome* (or Klimt's *Judith* series).

More than the Rückert-inspired songs, Mahler's *Lied von der Erde* reproduces a pattern that is typical for Orientalism. In *Das Lied von der Erde* Mahler was not interested in the Orient as it existed in his time; rather, he decided to focus on a classical period within an Oriental literature he conceived of as representing the "good" Orient.[96] While in the seventeenth and eighteenth centuries the German image of China was predominantly positive, in the nineteenth century Germans had mostly negative associations with that country, in part because of its absolutist form of government. It was no longer an object of fascination.[97] Few texts were translated from Chinese into German in the nineteenth century.[98] For Schlegel, China was quite clearly not part of the "good," proto-European Orient but rather prototypical for the "other" Orient that had not contributed to European civilization. Mahler based the texts of *Das Lied von der Erde* on poems from the collection *Die chinesische Flöte* (The Chinese Flute) by Hans Bethge (1876–1946). He had got to know this collection some time in 1907, the year in which the volume was first published, after the death of his daughter.[99] Bethge, who was mostly known for his poetry compilations, presented them as "adaptations of Chinese poetry" (Nachdichtungen Chinesischer Lyrik), but in fact based them on German and French translations of Chinese poetry.[100] The model that Bethge followed was clearly that of Goethe in his *West-östlicher Divan*. Goethe did not know Persian either and "adapted" — a better formulation might be "improvised on" — existing translations. It was a given that such "Nachdichtungen" would by no means be authentic, but they compensate for this lack of authenticity by reflecting explicitly on similarities and differences between Western and Eastern literary traditions (both collections were accompanied by secondary materials).

Several extant letters from Mahler to Bruno Walter dating back to the summer of 1908 document Mahler's work on *Das Lied von der Erde*. The first one is quite negative: Mahler complains about loneliness and about not being able to hike as intensively as he used to because of his heart condition (*Br*, 365–66). Walter's letter replying to Mahler's has been lost, but it is clear Mahler was not particularly happy with it. In a second letter to Walter that summer he gives his suffering a positive turn; in particular, his remark that he "now at the end of life as a beginner must learn to walk and stand again" (nun am Ende eines Lebens als Anfänger wieder gehen und stehen lernen muß) (*Br,* 368) is intriguing. This certainly refers to feelings of mortality evoked by the death of his daughter and the diagnosis of his own heart condition, both of which occurred during the previous summer. But Mahler refuses to psychologize on his condition: he clearly states that he is no hypochondriac and that what he is going through is not something a psychologist ("Geistesarzt") can do anything about. He also rejects Walter's suggestion to take a vacation up north — a suggestion reminiscent of Freud's advice to Walter to take a vacation in Sicily when Walter consulted him for a (psychosomatic?) problem with his right arm that was interfering with his conducting and piano playing.[101] To me, Mahler's comment suggests that he has found a way to integrate his thoughts on mortality into a philosophy of life along the lines of the *Kindertotenlieder.* In *Das Lied von der Erde,* however, these thoughts are more explicitly projected onto the Orient.

An anonymous announcement that was published in the journal *Der Merker* a few weeks before the premiere of *Das Lied von der Erde* speaks of the "expression of a most perfect turning away from and denial of the world" (der Ausdruck vollkommenster Weltabkehr und Weltverneinung) as the cycle's guiding idea.[102] A statement like this certainly suggests a Schopenhauerian view of the Orient. It is possible to read *Das Lied von der Erde* as a meditation on Schopenhauer's insight in the *Aphorismen zur Lebensweisheit,* discussed above, stating that an ethical form of life should focus not on attaining happiness or pleasure but rather on learning to accept and live with the suffering that inevitably accompanies any individual's life. It is precisely these two conflicting perspectives on life that are at the core of Mahler's cycle.

This is illustrated in an exemplary way by the first song, "Das Trinklied vom Jammer der Erde" (The Drinking Song of the Earth's Sorrows), based on a poem by the eighth-century Chinese poet Li Tai Po, 701–62, today also known as Li Bai.[103] The song works with sets of oppositions that are closely linked to the West's Orientalist imagination and that are musically illustrated by the constant presence of upward and downward melodic lines (*SSLD,* 179). At first glance, the song seems to propagate a philosophy that projects onto the Orient a life of pleasure and indulgence, symbolized by the wine lavishly praised by the singer-protagonist in the song's first and second stanzas. Such a life of excess is contrasted with and considered superior to a life of material wealth at the end of the second stanza: "A goblet full of wine at the right moment / is worth more than all the empires in the world!" (Ein voller Becher Weins zur rechten Zeit / ist mehr wert als alle Reiche der Welt!); the importance of the last line is underscored by a "gnashing dissonance."[104] This too alludes to an Orientalist cliché: the Orient as a place of immeasurable riches, although this stereotype is usually associated with the Arabic Orient rather than with the Far East. From

Bethge's afterword, Mahler will have known that Li Tai Po, the poem's author, was an adventurer, vagabond, and drinker.[105] Li Tai Po is, in other words, one of the figures of mobility that had interested Mahler already in the *Lieder eines fahrenden Gesellen* (see chapter 2). In the song's third stanza a second, contrasting perspective appears: the realization that humans are mortal — "Not for a hundred years can you enjoy yourself" (Nicht hundert Jahre darfst du dich ergötzen) — an insight born of the realization that earth and nature's seasonal cycle are timeless while the human lifespan is time-limited. While the first two stanzas presented a world without time, here time suddenly becomes the center of attention.

The third stanza also forces us to revisit the first two stanzas. What is important to realize is that Mahler's song contains what one could call a work-immanent poetics: it reflects on its own status as text. While the singer encourages his audience to embrace a life of pleasure, he also asks it to postpone doing so (briefly) in order to listen to his song. The function of the song is to remind its audience of life's dark side; it is a "song of grief" (Lied vom Kummer) that the singer intends to sing. And yet, simultaneously, the song is also threatened by this grief; if grief approaches, the song and the joy it brings may die. The image that the song's narrator uses to illustrate this point at the end of the first stanza is a comparison of the soul with gardens that have been abandoned and are therefore "wild" (wüst). Poetry, in other words, is to serve as a counterweight to a philosophy of indulgence in the here and now, and to the suffering that goes along with life. The song's fourth stanza is an elaboration of the third. Its dominant image is that of an ape, "wild and haunting" (wild-gespenstisch), howling on the graves in the light of the moon. The accompanying music is highly dissonant.[106] Mahler's contemporaries may have felt reminded of Typhoeus, the giant ape-like creature of Klimt's *Beethoven* frieze from the Secession exhibition of 1902 (see chapter 5), who is accompanied by his daughters, the three Gorgons, representing illness, madness, and death. Clearly the ape in "Das Trinklied" is some kind of counterfigure. He stands for animalistic life, a life that lacks reflection. In the context of the song, this also means giving in to one's dark side, to one's sorrows and anguish. Leaving his audience with this image in mind, the singer returns to the beginning: now it is time to drink the wine. Only now do the full implications of the song's refrain "Dark is life, is death" (Dunkel ist das Leben, ist der Tod) become fully clear: it is impossible to think of life without death; human suffering is but a reminder of death's continual presence in life.

In the end, "Das Trinklied vom Jammer der Erde" is very much centered on the question of what the Orient is about. Is it a place of sensual indulgence or of reflection on life's suffering? This song's answer is, to some extent, that the Orient is both: suffering is nothing but the reverse side of a life that seeks pleasure. From the beginning onward, the joyous atmosphere of the song sounds "strained and out of control," an effect that Mahler also achieves by having the tenor sing almost beyond his range.[107] It is significant that the Orient is depicted in the song as a space without metaphysical consolation: suffering is quite decisively not part of some kind of learning process. The world not only of "Das Trinklied" but also of *Das Lied von der Erde* in general could be called Schopenhauerian, in that it categorically rejects any form of Christian elevation of pain and suffering. In the end the second perspective, that of art as a medium for reflecting on human suffering, dominates. It is not merely the acknowledgement of human suffering as part of "Oriental wisdom," but also the component of reflection, of working through this experience, that sets the Orientalism of *Das Lied von der Erde* apart from that of Strauss's *Salome*.

Like the first song, the cycle's second song, "Der Einsame im Herbst" (The Lonely Man in Autumn), has a first-person narrator. While Bethge's version has a female narrator, Mahler changes her into a male.[108] This allows the audience to assume that we are dealing with the narrator of the preceding song. But while the first song shows the narrator in a social context, the second song thematizes isolation and loneliness. In atmosphere and imagery, the song picks up on the last stanza of the preceding song. Nature is dark and cold; the lotus flowers have withered. This song also reflects on the role of the artist, albeit very indirectly. Contemplating the dreary landscape, the narrator feels as if "an artist has sprinkled dust of jade / over the delicate blossoms" (ein Künstler habe Staub von Jade / über die feinen Blüten ausgestreut). Art, in other words, is perceived not as reconciling humans with their mortality — as the first song's program suggested, if one is inclined to read a program into that song — but rather as adding to the gloominess of life. The line "Now take the wine!" (Jetzt nehmt den Wein!), although accompanied by an ascending melody, sounds "tired and drained," in Mitchell's words (*SSLD,* 204). Only sleep can relieve the narrating subject from its state of mind, although the use of the word "resting place" (Ruhestätte) in this context, already present in Bethge's version of the poem, should make us skeptical; it is often used in the sense of a "final resting place." It is not sleep but death that the narrator desires. While scholarship (not very convincingly, in my opinion) has attempted to read a perpetually returning seasonal progression into the *Lied von der Erde* (*SSLD,* 252),[109] in the second poem, "Autumn" functions explicitly as a metaphor for a state of the human mind: "The autumn in my heart lasts too long" (Der Herbst in meinem Herze währt zu lange). It makes "Der Einsame im Herbst" into a poem about aging, and prepares the way for the third and fourth songs, with their reflections on youth as *reminiscences* of earlier times. The narrator of the second song does not believe that love will ever return.

To a greater extent than Mahler's earlier song cycles, *Das Lied von der Erde* focuses on friendship rather than love as a basis for human association.

The cycle's third song, "Von der Jugend" (Of Youth),[110] depicts an idyllic scene of friends meeting. The song's title is by Mahler and resembles the short chapter titles in Nietzsche's "Orientalist" text *Also sprach Zarathustra*.[111] The youthful scene it depicts is of a group of young men assembled in a pavilion in the middle of a pond, drinking and talking, with some of them writing poetry. Their image and that of their surroundings is mirrored in the pond. The work of art is doubly thematized in this song. When the mirror image is first introduced, in the fifth stanza, the music slows down radically, only to return to the original tempo soon thereafter. Could this be an expression of the desire to stop time?[112] In any case, the image of the friends writing poetry as part of their get-together suggests a concept of art that emphasizes its social functions or sees art as a logical extension of being in society (rather than being separate from society as in "Das Trinklied vom Jammer der Erde"). Beyond that, the song suggests the possibility of a mimetic ideal of art, visualized in the idyllic scene of the friends' meeting being mirrored — "reflected" in a literal sense — in the pond. Nothing in the song is ambivalent; nothing destroys the idyll, except for our knowledge that the mirror image in the water can only be a temporary one. The song is a play on form rather than meaning; Arthur Wenk has suggested that by repeating part of the first three stanzas in the song's second half, the text suggests the shape of an arch, one of the song's major images.[113] The song suggests an ideal of art for art's sake[114] that we also found in the Rückert song "Ich atmet' einen linden Duft," and projects this ideal onto the Orient.[115]

"Von der Schönheit" (Of Beauty),[116] the cycle's fourth song, is to be read in tandem with "Von der Jugend" and depicts a similarly idyllic scene: young girls picking flowers on the bank of a river or lake. Again the song is about friendship, this time friendship between women. And here, too, we find a mirroring scene: the light of the sun[117] behind the girls mirrors their figures and their eyes in the water in front of them. Suddenly, however, this idyllic scene is disturbed: a group of young men appears on wild horses, trampling the flowers. Now it is the image of the young men on horseback that is reflected in the water before they leave. One could say that the appearance of the boys has endangered the girls' friendship. The song's focus of attention is no longer the group of girls but only the most beautiful girl among them. Her eyes longingly follow one of the departing boys (instead of focusing on her own figure in the water as she had done earlier in the poem). An element of sexuality has broken into the idyll: "plaintively" (klagend) the girl's heart longs for the lost love object. In his additions to Bethge's text, Mahler emphasized the text's physical and erotic elements.[118] Interestingly, one critic notes that the music of this song at times appears to allude to Strauss's *Salome*.[119]

"Von der Schönheit" is followed by another drinking song "Der Trunkene im Frühling" (The Drunkard in Spring).[120] The first-person narrator who was absent in the third and fourth songs returns in the first stanza of this song and has not changed his philosophy: "I drink until I can drink no more, / all day long!" (Ich trinke, bis ich nicht mehr kann, / den ganzen lieben Tag!). The song's first line, "If life is but a dream" (Wenn nur ein Traum das Leben ist), is a clear reference, I would argue, to the idyllic "dream-like" sequences of the previous two songs. This also explains the absence of the first-person narrator in these songs. "Von der Jugend" and "Von der Schönheit" function as tableaux, imaginary scenarios, images of desire, playing out in the mind of the narrator, but without his participating in them. The narrator in "Der Trunkene im Frühling" seeks to hold onto the lighthearted, happy atmosphere of the previous two poems. The song's orchestration is marked, however, as was the first movement, by a juxtaposition of "ascending and descending motion" (*SSLD*, 313). The search for happiness is marred by the insight that the earlier tableaux are just figments of his imagination; that is why he seeks drink and sleep (as in the first and second songs). The point is clear: the imaginary scenarios of songs 3 and 4 could have functioned as parts of a learning process, but in reality they do not. Neither does nature. Spring, already alluded to in the first drinking song in one of the changes Mahler made to Bethge's text,[121] finally arrives. Here too, however, the text cautions against finding in nature a metaphysical foundation for life or, more modestly, a medium of consolation. Nature offers no solace or, in the words of the narrator: "What do I care about spring?" (Was geht mich denn der Frühling an?), although there may be food for thought in the fact that the music slows down radically when spring is first mentioned (*SSLD*, 322). Interestingly, this song also thematizes art, in the image in the fifth stanza of the drunkard singing until the moon comes up. Art does not have the communal or social function suggested in "Von der Jugend"; it is nothing but the drunken ruminations of someone who is uninterested in communicating with anyone. Art here, as in the second song, is strongly associated with existential loneliness.

Movements 2 through 5 of *Das Lied von der Erde* develop out of the tension formulated in the very first song: that between the desire to find happiness and the realization that suffering is an integral part of life. This basic dilemma underlying the cycle is linked to the question of what the West can learn from the Orient, and *Das Lied von der Erde*'s answer to that question is decisively heterophonic. The five songs discussed so far offer a variety of perspectives on the Orient. Death and suffering are omnipresent from the cycle's very first song on. Mahler chooses some highly idealizing images of the Orient in songs 3 and 4; while these songs emphasize the pursuit of happiness, they are far from the exuberant sexuality in Richard Strauss's *Salome*. What is remarkable, particularly in the context of Mahler's other song cycles, is *Das Lied von der Erde*'s clear privileging of friendship over love or sexuality, especially in songs three and four; sexual desire threatens the idyll of friendship ("Von der Schönheit"). Friendship is also a major topic in the final song. Another aspect that sets these songs apart from Strauss's *Salome* is their thematic heterophony: their questioning of ideas, their fundamental hesitation to give a *single* answer or privilege a *single* ideology. The East in *Das Lied von der Erde* is not monolithic but a highly diverse entity.

If the song cycle were to provide anything akin to a conclusive answer, it would have to be found in the last song, "Der Abschied" (The Farewell), a song that is equal in length to all of the other songs of *Das Lied von der Erde* combined and is distinctly different in its musical structure — it is much more loosely organized than the preceding movements (*SSLD*, 341, 344–45, and 383) — and narrative. Mahler based the text of his final song on two poems from Bethge's collection: "In Erwartung des Freundes" (In Expectation of a Friend) by Meng Haoran (also known as Mong Kao Yen, 689/691?–740) and "Der Abschied des Freundes" (Goodbye of a Friend) by Wang Wei (701–61), found in Bethge's volume on pages that face each other (18 and 19). While Mahler treats both poems as a single unit — together they provide the text for "Der Abschied" — they are separated in the song by a large orchestral interlude and thus are clearly recognizable as separate sections. What is remarkable here, in comparison to the cycle's other songs with a first-person narrator (songs 1, 2, and 5), is that the narrative has changed mood entirely: the narrator is sober and contemplative. The exuberant Orient is abandoned and yields to something more reflective. The first section of "Der Abschied" describes nature at dawn: sunset in the mountains, the moon over a lake, a breeze, pine trees, a brook, flowers, and so on — indeed, as Adorno notes, a somewhat clichéd image of the Orient, resembling the Dolomites, where Mahler was staying when composing *Das Lied von der Erde* (*MP*, 291; *MPE*, 149). The poem, however, also reflects not only on the impact that these images have on the narrator but on his need for such images as well: "All desire now longs to dream" (Alle Sehnsucht will nun träumen). The sentence originates from Mahler and is at no point implied by Bethge or his sources, and it of course establishes a relationship with the beginning of the previous song. Here, too, we find a work-immanent poetics, poetry-about-poetry; Mahler thinks through the imagery he uses far more consciously than is often assumed.

The narrator longs for sleep — reminiscent, of course, of "Der Einsame im Herbst" with its evocation of the (final) "resting place" (Ruhestätte). But it is the desire to see his friend that keeps him from giving in to sleep and dreams. This is the second time that the narrative "I" is mentioned explicitly in this context: "I stand here and wait for my friend" (Ich stehe hier und harre meines Freundes). The protagonist walks back and forth and is overcome by beauty, love, and life. The term used in this context, "trunken," is interesting. Here it should be translated as "intoxicated," but its literal meaning is "drunk"; it establishes a (weak) link to songs 1, 2, and 5 as a sort of reminiscence or afterthought of earlier exuberance. These final three stanzas of the first section, together with a major orchestral interlude, function as a transition to the song's second section.

While Mahler made considerable changes to Bethge's texts in general, at the beginning of the second section he does something that would strike even a superficial reader or listener as inconsistent. Rather than continuing the poem's narrative from a first-person perspective, as in Bethge's original, Mahler consciously changes to a third-person narrative, as the beginning of the second section makes clear: "*He* dismounted from the horse and gave *him* / a farewell drink" (*Er* stieg vom Pferd und reichte *ihm* den Trunk / des Abschieds dar; my italics). This third-person narrative on the farewell between two friends, in turn, gives way to a dialogue between the two friends that reintroduces two first-person narratives. This shifting between first- and third-person narrative perspectives could be interpreted as a shift between a statement of the speaking subject's direct articulation of his feelings and a search for a different style, in which the narrator produces images but functions only as an outside observer. It reproduces something we found earlier in *Das Lied von der Erde*: the interruption of songs with a first-person narrator (1, 2, and 5) by songs offering more distanced imaginary scenarios in the form of tableaux that do without a first-person narrator (songs 3 and 4). Instead of seeing this as an inconsistency, Mahler's decision to change the narrative perspective of the last song is clearly an intentional manipulation of the cycle's narrative structure. What follows after section 1 is a tableau or imaginary scenario, consisting in part of a dialogue between the two friends that never took place. The poem gives at least an implied reason for this: the friend is not coming, as is clear from the words of the narrator toward the end of the first section. "Where are you lingering? You are leaving me alone for a long time!" (Wo bleibst du? Du läßt mich lang allein!). The suggestion is that the narrator sings a song; at the end of the first poem we find him pacing back and forth (another sign of the friend not arriving) with his lute. The narrator imagines a farewell, which we assume to be imaginary.

In stylistic terms, these last four stanzas are highly elliptical. It is as if language is leaving the narrator at the moment of his demise. One sign of this elliptical style is the trouble we have in assigning different personae to the pronouns used in the poem, although doing so is certainly not impossible.[122] The event that can be articulated only through imagination is the experience of death as something deeply contradictory (incidentally, the music at the end of "Der Abschied" is among the most heterophonic that Mahler ever composed). The two friends stand for different aspects of the song's protagonist. "Death" is imagined through the image of the friend giving the farewell drink, speaking about the mountains — not unlike the "heights" in "Oft denk' ich, sie sind nur ausgegangen" and the mountains of the final scene of Goethe's *Faust* — to which he will travel, and about his seeking rest for his "lonely heart" (einsam Herz). "Death" is imagined as an irrevocable separation between human beings, as a trip to other places from which one will not return. It is precisely this image of the friend leaving for other places that allows the narrator to go home in the knowledge that his time will also (soon) come: "My heart is quiet and waits for its hour" (Still ist mein Herz und harret seiner Stunde). The imagery used comes close to suggesting peace and resignation. Death is imagined as a form of homecoming, not unlike "In diesem Wetter, in diesem Braus," and as a return to a sleeplike form of existence, to one's place (Stätte), reminiscent, of course, of the "resting place" (Ruhestätte) in "Der Einsame im Herbst." What we see here is the difference between death as a promise of a life elsewhere — evoking associations with Christianity and the West,[123] although the text and music here remain firmly embedded in the Orient — and a view of death as a purely immanent event, accepted but not celebrated,[124] that was projected onto the Orient, at least within the Schopenhauerian framework in which Mahler was working.

Das Lied von der Erde is about the existential loneliness of human beings when facing death; the fundamental inability to imagine what is happening within the dying person; and the need or desire to invent images in order to make the process understandable. In the last stanza we find the narrator imagining the earth blooming again in spring and the eternally blue horizon (behind which we assume his friend has disappeared), a clear reference to the blue sky of the cycle's first song, with the protagonist mumbling "forever . . . forever" (ewig . . . ewig). The nature imagery undoubtedly has positive connotations, but how does it relate to the dying protagonist? This is not the first time in Mahler's work that a narrative becomes fragmented, its syntactic structure breaks down, and a gradual dissolution of the narrative frame takes place (for example, in the final lines of "Die zwei blauen Augen," the final song of the *Lieder eines fahrenden Gesellen*; see chapter 2). The breakdown simulates the moment of dying as if the narrator were falling asleep; the narrative dissolution dramatizes the inadequacy of language to describe what is going on. It is highly significant that the final stanza of "Der Abschied" does not consist of material taken from Bethge's collection but was written by Mahler himself and evokes associations with poetry that Mahler wrote himself much earlier. The lines

> The dear earth blossoms everywhere in spring
> and turns green again
>
> [Die liebe Erde überall blüht auf im Lenz
> und grünt auf's Neu]

show at least some similarity to

> the spring has come
> and flowers blossom everywhere
>
> [der Lenz gezogen
> und Blumen blühn ja überall]

from the poem "Vergessene Liebe" (Forgotten Love) that Mahler wrote in 1880.[125] Of course references to spring in nature poetry are not uncommon, but what counts here is that spring fulfills very similar functions in both texts. Moreover, this is not the only instance in the text of "Der Abschied" where Mahler revisits his own poetry. Earlier in "Der Abschied" Mahler quoted from an untitled poem he wrote for the *Lieder eines fahrenden Gesellen* cycle in 1884 but never used (see chapter 2 for a discussion of this poem in the context of that cycle). The following lines in "Der Abschied"

> the tired people go home,
> to learn anew in sleep forgotten happiness
> and youth!
>
> [die müden Menschen gehn heimwärts,
> um im Schlaf vergeß'nes Glück
> und Jugend neu zu lernen!]

resemble the lines

> And tired people close their eyelids
> in their sleep, to learn anew forgotten happiness
>
> [Und müde Menschen schließen ihre Lider
> Im Schlaf, auf's neu vergessnes Glück zu lernen]

from the 1884 *Gesellen* poem.[126] At the very end of *Das Lied von der Erde*, the last of Mahler's compositions for which he used text, it is not merely spring that returns. Mahler also revisits his own beginnings as a composer: the *Lieder eines fahrenden Gesellen* and the closely related First Symphony. One can take these lines as another instance of work-immanent poetics: the need to produce (dream-like) images, images of nature and past happiness, in the face of death. Mahler is telling us something here about the roots of his creativity. At the same time, by placing these lines in a new context, he is also rewriting and reinterpreting his own work. Precisely the ability to produce alternative visions is a red thread throughout Mahler's oeuvre.

The question then remains as to what exactly the word "ewig" and the references to spring and nature blossoming again in *Das Lied von der Erde*'s final stanza mean. "Ewig" can mean "in eternity," suggesting something like the "eternal life" after death — a suggestion so self-evident to some scholars that they do not even feel they have to discuss alternatives to it. Scholars have speculated that Mahler is embracing a vision of "divine nature," in which human essence would live on — a vision supposedly inspired by the works of Fechner.[127] "Ewig," however, can also mean something like "forever," in the sense of a perpetually returning process. The term "ewig" in fin-de-siècle Vienna would certainly have evoked associations with Nietzsche's "eternal return of the same" (ewige Wiederkehr des Gleichen), one of the key concepts in *Also sprach Zarathustra* and in Nietzsche's philosophy in general; the concept also stands at the heart of Nietzsche's criticism of metaphysics (see chapter 3). For Nietzsche it represents the autonomy of nature: the perpetual recurrence of natural phenomena, independent of and indifferent to any human action or need for transcendence.

Perhaps it is the ambiguous nature of the term "ewig" that prompted Mahler to use it in the final lines of *Das Lied von der Erde*. The term lives off the tension between the desire to find something eternal beyond the here and now and the realization that it is precisely life on earth that will carry on perpetually. "Ewig" in the context of the end of *Das Lied von der Erde* is expressive of the protagonist's effort to accept the fact that life goes on without him. In spite of its religious etymology, it does not in any way contain a *promise* that anything like a divine order or ongoing spiritual essence of nature exists.[128] The song's final stanza refers to a renewal of life (spring), but it leaves entirely unresolved the issue of how this is meaningful for the main character, particularly since in the previous movement, "Der Trunkene im Frühling," spring had left him indifferent. *Das Lied von der Erde*, as do many of Mahler's other compositions, ends with a question rather than an answer. Ultimately, the question is what these images and this music mean to the listener, what emotions and thoughts s/he associates with them.

From World Literature to World Culture

A primary characteristic of Mahler's view of the Orient is an insight into the body's primacy over the mind — echoing the philosophies of Schopenhauer, Nietzsche, Freud, and fin-de-siècle Viennese culture in general — combined with a strong need to contemplate human dependency on the corporeal. *Das Lied von der Erde* is very much the product of a reflection on human dependence on the body, but this reflection is an inquisitive one. If the song cycle provides any answer to the question of how to make sense of human mortality, the answer itself is full of ambiguities.

One could call this Mahler's acknowledgement that in matters of life and death humankind will always be searching for answers, and no answer is definitive. *Das Lied von der Erde* tells many stories. It constructs the Orient in many different ways. Mahler's vision of the Orient is a highly heterophonic and dialogic one. In it, as we have seen, the "ability to doubt" has an unequivocally positive connotation. In the end, it is a vision that seeks to incorporate diversity rather than to exclude and discard it. This is in line with Goethe's thinking in the *West-östlicher Divan* and very different from the model proposed by Friedrich Schlegel in *Über die Sprache und Weisheit der Indier.*

In Mahler's late works, such as the Eighth Symphony and *Das Lied von der Erde*, pre-Nietzschean thinkers such as Goethe and Schopenhauer function as points of reference, and the influence of Nietzsche is much less visible than was the case, for instance, in the Second, Third, and Fourth Symphonies. And yet the persistence of the body, along with the profound skepticism toward metaphysics also seen in these late works, has something very Nietzschean about it. While Mahler's intellectual interests had certainly moved beyond Nietzsche at this point in his life, I do not believe that he had discarded Nietzsche's cultural and philosophical diagnosis; he still held to his insight that humankind was living after the death of God, in an eternal return of the same, and that any kind of future ethical theory or practice would need to take this insight into account. The fact that Mahler returns to Nietzsche at the end of *Das Lied von der Erde* is of more than symbolic significance in this context.

Musically speaking, Mahler strongly emphasized the Oriental nature of *Das Lied von der Erde*. In addition to the pentatonism and heterophony that had already characterized the Rückert songs and the *Kindertotenlieder*, the lack of a bass function in the traditional sense and the fact that the tenor has to sing in an exceptionally high register can be said to contribute to an Oriental atmosphere.[129] Mahler also uses specific instruments (bass drum, cymbals, harps, glockenspiel, piccolo, tamtam, and triangle) to create an Oriental impression.[130] In general, the very noticeable presence of woodwinds adds to the Oriental impression (the oboe, which plays such a prominent role in "Der Abschied," is also used prominently by Richard Strauss at the beginning of the very Oriental "Dance of the Seven Veils" of *Salome*). It is clear that in *Das Lied von der Erde* the Orient serves as a model for reflecting cultural otherness, albeit in a thoroughly German-Austrian context. Text is very much a part of this Orientalism. In what is a definite attempt to boost his own creativity, Mahler was interested in creating fundamentally new perspectives on things, even though he simultaneously makes it abundantly clear (quite intentionally in my opinion) that similarities exist between *Das Lied* and his earlier works. The Oriental character of *Das Lied von der Erde*, however, raises the question of which models of cultural diversity were available in German cultural history when Mahler sat down in the summer of 1908 to create this work of art.

One of these models was Goethe's idea of a "world literature" (Weltliteratur). Late in life, Goethe developed this concept in order to find a formula for some of the ideas first expressed in the notes accompanying the *West-östlicher Divan*. One of the most succinct descriptions of the idea of a "world literature" can be found in a letter from Goethe to Thomas Carlyle dated 20 July 1827:

> A truly general tolerance will be reached most certainly if one leaves intact what is unique about individual people and nations while simultaneously maintaining the conviction that what deserves true merit distinguishes itself by the fact that it belongs to all of humankind. Germans have contributed to such a mediation and reciprocal recognition for a long time. A person who understands and studies German finds himself in a marketplace where all nations offer their goods; he acts as the interpreter while he enriches himself.
>
> [Eine wahrhaft allgemeine Duldung wird am sichersten erreicht, wenn man das Besondere der einzelnen Menschen und Völkerschaften auf sich beruhen läßt, bey der Überzeugung jedoch festhält, daß das wahrhaft Verdienstliche sich dadurch auszeichnet, daß es der ganzen Menschheit angehört. Zu einer solchen Vermittlung und wechselseitigen Anerkennung tragen die Deutschen seit langer Zeit schon bey. Wer die deutsche Sprache versteht und studirt befindet sich auf dem Markte wo alle Nationen ihre Waren anbieten, er spielt den Dolmetscher indem er sich selbst bereichert.][131]

The concept of "world literature" is often mentioned in relation to Rückert's writings.[132] In many respects these writings represent the epitome of what Goethe had in mind, with the added benefit of of Rückert's knowledge of many Oriental languages — a knowledge that Goethe did not possess. The idea underlying Goethe's idea of "world literature," in line with Herder's ideas discussed in chapter 2, is, on the one hand, that through studying the literature of other nations one gets to know and respect their ideas and values, their culture.[133] True tolerance means respecting what is unique about other peoples and their cultures. On the other hand, however, in spite of the great differences between cultural traditions, there is also something in them that belongs to "all of mankind" (der ganzen Menschheit). Literatures from very different traditions appeal to ideas or emotions that are common to all of humanity. In the Rückert adaptations, *Das Lied von der Erde,* and in the Goethean second movement of the Eighth Symphony, Mahler seeks this commonality in alterity. This is not unlike Rückert himself, one of whose goals was to show that the great human emotions are the same everywhere.[134] The idea that certain emotions can be similar throughout space and time is — quite intentionally, I would argue — also what motivates Mahler's borrowing from his own early poetry in the final movement of *Das Lied von der Erde*.

Today, the "inauthenticity" of the "Oriental" texts with which Mahler was working, noted by Adorno, may strike us as problematic. The idea of a "marketplace" (Markt) of ideas may appear to us outdated and naively optimistic. And despite the truly cosmopolitan intentions informing these ideas, one should not overlook a certain German nationalism resonating in these statements. By letting German intellectuals and the German language play a privileged role in the process of mediating world literature, Goethe, through the back door, reintroduces an element of German patriotism, if not nationalism — something we encountered in Mahler's high school essay discussed at the beginning of this chapter, which is clearly informed by Goethe's ideas of a "world literature." And yet Goethe's narcissistic privileging of German culture (and European culture[135]) is perhaps less important than the message that his deliberations contain about cultures in general: we should conceive of cultures as being open toward each other rather than closed; borders between cultures are permeable, and there is something to be learned from a dialogue between cultures. There is a polemical impetus behind these ideas that may hold some validity today as well. On the one hand, the awareness that we are always dealing with our own constructions when looking at other cultures; on the other hand, that it is not only what differentiates humans that counts, but also what they have in common. Ultimately the question is whether it is possible to experience what we perceive as different as a potential in ourselves as well.

Conclusion: Beyond Mahler

> I am deeply fascinated by musical ideas which manage to develop a polyphony of different formations of meaning — ideas that do not reject the possibility of dealing with specific and concrete instrumental gestures which then set up a whole range of distant echoes and memories, allowing us to establish a dialogue of specific presences and absences: a musical space inhabited by the significant presence of absences and by the echo of absent presences. (Luciano Berio, *Remembering the Future*)

THE IMAGE OF MAHLER THAT HAS EMERGED from this study is neither that of a nostalgic modernist nor that of a neoromanticist. Mahler was not melancholically looking backward in the sense that he longed to reinstate traditions presumably lost or mourned values associated with earlier times — an image that was in part created by Alma Mahler and Bruno Walter, but that, in a far more sophisticated way, also underlies Adorno's ideas about Mahler. What is sometimes called Mahler's "eclecticism" — a term I am not entirely comfortable with, because it has associations with a passive borrowing and an implied lack of creativity, while Mahler's music is also highly original when it refers to tradition — is one aspect of Mahler's work that is far closer to the aesthetic strategies of the avant-garde version of modernism, which considered all of the means that cultural history had in stock as potential tools (see "Introduction"), than to the nostalgic modernism of some of Mahler's contemporaries. Mahler chose to use traditions selectively and in a critical way, and in doing so showed that German cultural history was far more diverse than the nationalistic mobilization of German cultural heritage that occurred around 1900 would suggest. It is important to realize that he did not simply mimic the cultural and literary preferences of his time but rather made determined and conscious choices. In doing so, he reconstructed German cultural history in ways very different from those of the composers before him in whose tradition he worked (Wagner, Bruckner) as well as those of his contemporaries (Hugo Wolf, Richard Strauss).

To some extent Mahler viewed cultural history, as did many of his contemporaries, as a conversation between great men — a conversation in which he himself would participate. Accordingly, he was very interested in positioning his own creative works within cultural tradition, musical and otherwise. This may partially account for his privileging of earlier writers and thinkers over his contemporaries. And yet despite this approach to the German cultural canon, Mahler's use of text is emancipatory and critical of ideological investments. Initially, this critical agenda manifests itself in Mahler's insistence on a notion of crisis that does not allow for easy resolution. The First Symphony can be read as a critique of the *Bildungsroman* and, more broadly, of notions of *Bildung* that the nineteenth-century German middle class sought to read into its literary and cultural history. Similarly, in his *Lieder eines fahrenden Gesellen* and the *Wunderhorn* songs Mahler takes apart notions of the "Volk" that were beginning to play an increasingly important role in nationalistic politics. The Second, Third, and Fourth Symphonies seek to keep alive the radical, modern impulse of Nietzsche's critique of metaphysics — his sense that Western culture is in a crisis to which there are no easy solutions — not only in contrast to the reactionary modernism of the later Wagner, but also in reaction to the kitsch industry developing around Nietzsche. Later Mahler actively searches for alternative readings of German culture. In the Seventh Symphony Rembrandt stands for an alternative way to look at German cultural history, one that focuses on the marginal and repressed. The Eighth Symphony searches for a sense of community that is tolerant toward alterity and historical difference, while arguing that human emotions shape a form of commonality among different cultures. Mahler's most radical attempt to deal with different cultures and their views and value systems is his Rückert adaptations (including the *Kindertotenlieder*) and *Das Lied von der Erde*. It is very much a dialogic perspective on cultural difference that Mahler promotes, but the dialogue focuses both on difference and on what humans have in common. Again, emotions play a key role.

The writers and thinkers who interested Mahler represented a way of engaging with German cultural history that was deeply critical toward normative ambitions. They were, in their way, radical thinkers. It is because of their texts and the way they were situated in the cultural contexts of their time that we can understand Mahler's radical side as well — despite his skepticism toward text. Texts were of great importance to him, in spite of their fallibility and inability to provide final answers.

Text and Music

One of the most interesting musical responses to Mahler's oeuvre is *Sinfonia* (1968/69) by Italian composer Luciano Berio (1925–2003), the third movement of which is based on the scherzo of Mahler's Second Symphony but augmented by a plethora of heterophonic textual and musical references. The musical references include Schoenberg's *Fünf Orchesterstücke*, Debussy's *La Mer*, Hindemith's *Kammermusik*, Berg's Violin Concerto, Ravel's *La Valse* and *Daphnis et Chloé*, Stravinsky's *Le*

Sacre du Printemps and *Agon*, Strauss's *Der Rosenkavalier*, Brahms's Fourth Symphony, Bach's First Brandenburg Concerto, Beethoven's Sixth Symphony, and Boulez's *Pli selon pli*, along with numerous references to Mahler's symphonies. The textual references are to Beckett's *L'innommable* (The Unnamable) — a clear reference to Mahler's distrust of programs — one of Berio's own essays, Joyce's *Ulysses*, and Valéry's *Le cimetière marin* (The Marine Cemetery).[1] Berio added also texts specifically designed for *Sinfonia*. While the quotations that Berio used were not entirely random, his choice was limited to the materials he had brought with him on vacation in Sicily, where he composed the piece, and to what was available in the Catania Public Library.[2] In addition to being a highly original piece of music on its own, *Sinfonia*'s third movement also offers us a way of looking at Mahler. If one follows Berio's lead, the problem with Mahler's music is not that text is a fallible and imperfect medium for expressing thoughts (and emotions), but rather that there is not enough text and there are not enough musical references in it to do justice to its complexity. By making both more complex — that is, by adding more text and more quotations from Western musical history rather than questioning the value of both — we come to a closer approximation of what Mahler's music has to tell its audiences.

For Berio, what I described in my "Introduction" as the problem of Mahler's anti-programmatic programs is a predicament facing musical history in general. According to Berio, Western musical history since Boethius (475/480?–524/526?) has conceived of music as having a cognitive function, as a means or instrument of knowledge, rather than as being solely a medium of pleasure.[3] The problem is, however, that when we think of cognition we think of language; it is very hard to conceive of forms of knowledge that cannot be captured, one way or another, in language. According to Berio, we feel a need to translate music (31). But music does not work this way. Any effort to get to the cognitive essence of a piece of music through language is doomed to fail or to be, at the very least, incomplete; eventually such attempts will be confronted with "an elusive *elsewhere*" or an "empty space" not accessible through textual analysis (51 and 137). And yet Berio is by no means ready to give up on language or text as a means for understanding music. For him the key is that the functioning of language and text offers a model for understanding how music and its cognitive contents affect its listeners. He is interested in "open forms" of art;[4] this openness is the result of the many "intertextual" references that a work of art contains. According to Berio, "great works invariably subsume an incalculable number of other texts, not always identifiable on the surface — a multitude of sources, quotations, and more or less hidden precursors that have been assimilated, not always on a conscious level, by the author himself" (126). It is only through reconstructing implicit or explicit references that we can get to the layers of meaning that a musical piece can have, without necessarily arriving at any final conclusions about it. It is with this context in mind that I understand Berio's statement that analyzing a work of art is an invitation to "renew our perception of history, maybe to re-invent it" (45). The third movement of *Sinfonia* is constructed according to this principle and, as such, represents the best possible analysis of the Scherzo of Mahler's Second Symphony (40), without however, one might add, damaging its "unnamable" core.

The idea of the existence of such forms of cognition that are not language-bound as Berio posits plays a important role in Martha Nussbaum's deliberations on Mahler. Her work unquestionably figures among the most interesting examples of Mahler scholarship published in recent years. In her study *Upheavals of Thought* Nussbaum is interested in music because it is an example of "forms of cognitive/intentional activity, embodying ideas of salience and urgency, that are not linguistic."[5] The cognitive content of music, for Nussbaum, is linked to the fact that it expresses emotions. It should immediately be added that it is not a simplistic view of emotions as a momentary state of our psychic life that Mahler is after. Rather, the main thesis of Nussbaum's book is that emotions are "forms of evaluative judgment that ascribe to certain things and persons outside a person's own control great importance for the person's own flourishing" (22). Emotions are, in other words, about much more than feelings: they are experiences that tell us something about our values, about what we think is important or not, about intuitions of a better life, whether we are conscious of this or not. For Nussbaum, too, text does not necessarily stand in the way of understanding such experiences as long as we realize that their essence cannot be captured by language (265).

The idea that emotions are of crucial importance to humans' functioning as social beings, for their sense of value, is very much in line with the readings I have developed in the preceding chapters. In particular, the final movements of Mahler's Second, Third, and Eighth Symphonies are reflections on the value of emotions for human life. Here Mahler comes close to saying that, by paying attention to our emotions, we not only learn something about our values but also experience an intuition that an ethical life is possible in this world. By reflecting on the value of emotions, these symphonies indirectly meditate on their own impact and importance as works of art. But where the nexus is less obvious or explicit, emotions appear to play a key role for understanding Mahler's music as well. Text can help us to understand how complex, perhaps even paradoxical, emotions can be. From a literary/cultural historical perspective, the *Trauermarsch* of the First Symphony is one of the most intensively thought-out pieces of music that Mahler composed. At the core of the images and texts that Mahler evoked to explain this movement is precisely its emotional ambiguity: it is sad and mournful, and yet at the same time an expression of the joy of life (along with the many emotions falling between these two poles). It is thanks to the piece's multi-layered intertextual references that we understand the music's many dimensions. A similar observation can be made about the final movement of the Fourth Symphony, the conclusion of *Das Lied von der Erde*, "Der Abschied," and many other pieces in which multiple layers of emotions seem to be determinative for the music's cognitive content.

For Berio, text is closely connected to the avant-garde side of Mahler's work, which he finds fascinating. Text and the mode of cognition to which it alludes are very much part of this fascination, even though in the end they teach us to live with a certain openness, an "elusive *elsewhere*." Both Berio and Nussbaum are interested in text in their analyses of Mahler, not because it can give final answers but because it can provide us with an intuition of what is at stake and how complex and ambiguous this music is. But what does this multiplicity and ambiguity mean in the context of modernist cultural discourse in Vienna around 1900?

Jewishness and Modernism

If Mahler's Jewishness is part of his current fascination for us, as Leon Botstein suggested (see "Introduction"), then we need to ask how Mahler's work and its reception history relate to the authoritarian regimes that paved the way for the Third Reich and the Holocaust.[6] This may seem a simple or perhaps even superfluous question, but it is not. When we think of Mahler and the Third Reich, we tend to think of performances of Mahler's music by Jewish orchestras in Berlin in early 1941[7] or in Amsterdam during the German occupation[8] — events to which only Jews were admitted. These were highly symbolic happenings that could be interpreted as (desperate) attempts to hold onto the viability of a European-Jewish cultural tradition under the direst of circumstances. Leonard Bernstein's efforts in the 1960s and 1970s to introduce Viennese audiences to a "new" Mahler could be considered critical attempts at revitalizing this tradition. In a sense, Bernstein was attempting to bring back the "old," more authentic Mahler through a performance practice reflecting the musical and cultural diversity of Vienna around 1900, as opposed to the rather homogenous cultural landscape of Austria after the Second World War.

If there exists something like a counterpoint to Bernstein's efforts, it must be the attempts to make Mahler into a national icon during the authoritarian regime that ruled Austria from 1934 and 1938, a period known today as "Austrofascism" — a little-known chapter in the history of Mahler's reception. In contrast to Germany, where Jewish music was forbidden and Jewish musicians could no longer perform (except under exceptional circumstances), and despite the anti-Semitic undertones of the new Austrian regime,[9] Mahler became a figure that this regime promoted,[10] in part to consolidate an independent cultural identity but also to foster the image that Austria (unlike Germany) was an open-minded, tolerant, and liberal country.[11] This was possible because of the close friendship among Alma Mahler, Bruno Walter, and Kurt Schuschnigg,[12] the new chancellor of the deeply Catholic, autocratic, anti-parliamentarian Austrofascist regime that envisioned a state modeled after Mussolini's Italy. Efforts were undertaken to erect a monument to Mahler at the *Grinzingerplatz*;[13] they failed, mostly because Alma had a falling-out with the sculptor, Fritz Wotruba.[14] On the twenty-fifth anniversary of Mahler's death in 1936, Bruno Walter and the Vienna Philharmonic performed the Second and Eighth Symphonies (Mahler's most affirmative works), as well as *Die Lieder eines fahrenden Gesellen*, and *Das Lied von der Erde*.[15] This was followed later by performances of the Fifth Symphony (in late 1937) and finally the Ninth in January 1938, also conducted by Walter, weeks before the Nazis invaded Austria (a recording of this last performance is extant). In his efforts to make Mahler acceptable to the new regime and new audience, Walter filed away the music's sharp edges and aimed for an interpretation that showed the similarities between Mahler and the nineteenth-century symphonic tradition.[16] In his autobiography, *Theme and Variations*, first published in 1946, Walter describes Schuschnigg in exceptionally positive terms as someone whose "quiet, serious, firm personality made a deeply sympathetic and powerful impression" on him (317; see also 319). While recognizing the regime's "authoritarian constitution," the Schuschnigg government "proved friendly to the world of the spirit and tried to further Austria's cultural mission," something that was especially clear, according to Walter, in the flourishing of the *Salzburger Festspiele*.[17] Alma Mahler is reported, by her daughter, to have occasionally worn a swastika on her coat collar during this period, even though she was not a member of the NSDAP.[18]

To be sure, both Bruno Walter and Alma Mahler later rethought their political alliances of the Austrofascist period. But the question raised by this rather unfortunate episode in Mahler's reception history is whether something in his music catered to this kind of affirmative ideological (ab)use, or whether using Mahler's music for legitimizing an authoritarian regime was a fundamental misunderstanding of what his music is about, of the critical intentions that were meant to resist this kind of appropriation.

The answer to this question is that, to some extent, both statements are true. Of course, as someone writing in the early twenty-first century I would like to affirm that there indeed is an element of resistance in Mahler that immunizes his music, once and for all, against its uncritical, affirmative mobilization for anti-humanitarian purposes. To some extent, the problem sketched out here is not specific to Mahler's music alone but encompasses music in general. Because music is the most abstract (and the most German) of the arts, it may appear defenseless against ideological abuse. The problem I have attempted to describe here is also a problem of modernism in general. Neither the Nietzschean vocabulary of cultural decline and renewal,[19] which Mahler and his circle utilized, and which is so important for understanding Vienna modernism, nor the modernist concept of culture underlying his work, which emphasized autonomy and followed a broader pattern in German culture by conceiving of it as substitute for political action (see "Introduction"), was necessarily immune from appropriation by authoritarian regimes. But the problem is also specific to Mahler's work. There is a fundamental ambiguity underlying Mahler's musical and literary language. The religious imagery used at the end of the Second and Eighth symphonies, the symphonies Walter performed with the Vienna Philharmonic in 1936, may have appeared to many audience members to fit in neatly with the new regime's Catholic identity. But in order to do so it had to be taken at face value, while what the music and texts of these symphonies actually did was to deconstruct the imagery and traditions that they quoted. What, then, in Mahler's work resists its ideological abuse?

The critical dimension of Mahler's work has something to do with his Jewishness; and it is precisely in order to identify the critical dimension in Mahler's compositions that we need to look at them from this perspective. One does find, in Mahler's works, traces of a discourse that sought to link together Jewishness, the Enlightenment, and modernity.[20] I would argue against reading Mahler and his work as examples of the attempt to assimilate into German culture that has often been associated with this discourse: Mahler's investment was not in adapting to German cultural standards, not in acculturation, but rather in reinventing the German cultural tradition differently. As I said at the outset of this chapter, he made determined and conscious choices that were different from those of his contemporaries. And he was invested in a modern way of looking at the world, in humans' ability to invent their own norms and values, rather than their need to rely on others for those norms and values. Mahler was interested in what Michael P. Steinberg has called "the emancipatory potential of the modern," in "interrogating past absolutes, by making the marginal central."[21] The thinkers who dominate Mahler's thought have in common that they propagated a clearly modern view of life, in the sense that they did not believe in an authoritative tradition and believed in human autonomy as a means of establishing one's own norms and leading an ethical life. Mahler, in other words, sought to keep modernity's critical potential alive, rooted in its secularism, without buying into its pressure to conform.

Mahler's readings of German cultural history focus on those moments when this tradition turns critical and self-reflective. This explains his insistence on the notion of crisis seen throughout his work. While the notion of crisis is a genuine aspect of *fin-de-siècle* Vienna modernism (see "Introduction") — and perhaps, even more broadly, of late nineteenth-century German culture in general — many of his generation interpreted this notion in very different ways. Some of his contemporaries tended to resolve it with a nostalgia for times past, but not Mahler. His insistence on a notion of crisis that cannot be easily resolved is, in my view, to be understood as a response to Wagner. It involved uneasiness with the normative and political ambitions underlying Wagner's later works, particularly *Parsifal*. This discomfort was at the time most prominently articulated by Nietzsche. Mahler appropriated Wagner in that he picked up on some of the issues that had been brought into German cultural discourse by Wagner, but simultaneously he sought, with Nietzsche's help, to be smarter than Wagner. And more importantly, through his readings he wanted to show that German cultural history was on his side rather than Wagner's. Wagner's theoretical writings formulated a strictly normative framework stipulating specifically what Jewish composers could and could not do. Mahler countered such a framework by continually reinventing himself, taking the greatest possible liberty with German musical and cultural history, and ultimately by showing that he could do whatever he wanted to do.

A third critical aspect of Mahler's works, especially his later works, is their emphasis on difference and diversity, on the need of his music to be heterophonic, to tell many different stories. Karen Painter has pointed out that the polemics surrounding Mahler's music (and, to some extent, that of Schoenberg and Richard Strauss as well) in the first decade of the twentieth century were not about harmonics (atonality and dissonance) — Adorno's model! — but rather about counterpoint and polyphony.[22] Within this debate, Mahler chose a radical position: his technique of orchestration aimed for a "maximum independence of lines" (203), a proliferation of thematic and melodic material. This is a highly interesting observation for several reasons: First, it helps us understand how Mahler's music, in its insistence on heterophony, was perceived as radical within the musicological and journalistic discourses of *fin-de-siècle* Vienna. As Painter reports, within anti-Semitic discourse during the latter period, this kind of heterophony was associated with the stereotype of the assimilated Jew (202 and 207) who could not master pure (German) counterpoint. Second, Painter's observation also enables a different way of looking at musical history. If we look at Mahler from the perspective of a history of music focused on increasingly complex harmonic configurations (Adorno's model), Mahler lags behind in comparison to some of his contemporaries. But if we look at musical history as a movement toward increasingly heterogeneous melodic patterns and narratives, not only do we have the tools for describing the complex nature of Mahler's music but we can also reconceive the relationship of Mahler's oeuvre to the music of Schoenberg and Stravinsky,[23] for instance, who in their respective ways also aimed for more diverse narratives. In early-twentieth-century music, there is a link between the musical heterophony Mahler was interested in and the textual dimension of his music. In the so-called Jews' Quintet from Strauss's *Salome*, which, as Painter observes, seems to have served as a matrix for stereotypes about Jewish heterophony (202), the music's heterophony is mimicked by a highly polyphonic proliferation of text and an inability to come to consensus. Here too, text helps to illustrate what music is about.

While I have argued that there is a link between Mahler's Jewishness and the critical ambitions of his music in *fin-de-siècle* Vienna, this does not mean that there is an automatic connection between modernist or avant-gardist art and Jewishness.[24] In fact, Jewish artists made many different choices, as the examples of Mahler, Schoenberg, Schreker, and Zemlinsky show. But did the critical ambitions of Mahler's music matter? One could point out that, even for Mahler himself, it was not at all clear that the critical paradigm he proposed was going to work. As we saw in our readings of the later *Wunderhorn* songs (chapter 2) and of the Seventh Symphony (chapter 4), Mahler was often highly skeptical in his reflections about the use, functioning, and value of art — a skepticism he shared with many of his modernist contemporaries. Such reservations should not, however, keep us from looking for a critical or radical gesture in his music. Even Schuschnigg's Austrofascist regime sought to use Mahler, as I have explained above, to showcase its independence and cosmopolitanism in comparison to Nazi Germany; it sought, in other words, to capitalize on the critical dimension associated with Mahler's name.

Reading Cultural History — Differently

In this book I have argued that the cultural choices that Mahler made were clearly connected to his Jewish heritage. He did not wish to assimilate into German culture but rather sought to assert his own voice and to construct German cultural history in ways that diverged from the mainstream and that were indisputably at odds with the nationalistic and anti-Semitic cultural critics among his contemporaries. Rather than speaking of "assimilation" or "acculturation"[25] when characterizing Mahler's ties to German culture, it would therefore be more accurate to speak of Mahler's "reading" of German cultural history. It is important to realize that he was not primarily interested in a genealogical reconstruction of Jewish contributions to "German" cultural history, even though some of his findings may have ended up doing exactly that. He did, however, pay a price for his rereading of German musical and cultural history. Many of the polemics surrounding his works seem to have their roots in his highly individual way of reading German culture, which nationalistic, conservative, or anti-Semitic critics deemed inappropriate. Furthermore, the occasional presence of masochistic imagery in Mahler's texts (for instance in the novel *Titan*, so important for the First Symphony, in the song "Ich hab' ein glühend Messer," and in the *Faust* excerpt in the second movement of the Eighth) may be indicative of the fact that Mahler's relationship to German culture on some level was more conflict-ridden than a more superficial reading would suggest.[26]

The attitude that Mahler proposes toward one's own culture and the cultures of others could be more precisely described as a specific modality — a mode of dealing with texts, cultures, and the history within and underlying them. Part of the ethics underpinning Mahler's work as a composer is to engage with absolutely everything, canonical or otherwise, but also to pay attention to elements of heterogeneity and crisis in cultural material. Mahler's point is that such a dialogue should not concern merely our rational faculties but our emotions as well. It is through our affect that we learn about our values and investments. But what is the cultural meaning of the heterogeneity in Mahler's music today? This is one of the issues that Berio alludes to when he reminds his readers that "heterogeneity and pluralism have to translate themselves into processes and ideas, not into forms and manners" (30). Mahler teaches us to read differently. It is part of Mahler's aesthetics that it accepts no final answers. The relation between language and music becomes a metaphor for humankind's metaphysical homelessness, for its longing to find something that makes sense, a stable relation between the two and its inability to do so — or at least to find any final answers. But this metaphysical homelessness is also an opportunity.

While the ability to read differently, to discover heterogeneity and diversity, is constitutive of Mahler's music, it is not necessarily its final answer. When engaging rationally and emotionally with the diversity in our own cultural history or that of others, we may actually find that the investments of others appeal to us more than those of what we perceive to be our own culture. We may find commonality rather than alterity, along the lines of Goethe's concept of "world literature" (see chapter 6), but only after we have gone through the process of rethinking our investments, of trying to conceive of ourselves differently. Music can function this way because different cognitive dimensions work together in it. Music, as Mahler saw it, is designed as an interaction between narrative or text on the one hand and a sensual experience that appeals to our emotions and the values, intuitions, and priorities we associate with them on the other. Reading cultural history while listening to music is both a creative and a critical endeavor, even though it may be a fragile form of resistance against the totalitarian, homogenizing powers at work in society then and now. Rather than conceiving of Mahler's relationship to past cultural traditions as that of an "untimely modernism," emphasizing that Mahler's "conservative worldview"[27] may be relevant for us today, I see Mahler's attitude toward cultural history as a form of "remembering the future" — the title of Berio's lecture series and a formula that offers the most concise summary of his views on the contemporary relevance of cultural history.[28] It is Mahler's consistent sense of crisis, his need to bring to the surface what has been left out, and the interest in heterogeneity and otherness seen in his readings of literary and cultural history that may be anticipatory of future thinking and are very much part of his relevance today (and far from conservative).

Today Mahler is part of the canon, no doubt as he wanted to be. Canonicity, however, never stopped him from taking apart and rethinking the past. And perhaps it is precisely in his complex model of engaging with the past — our past and that of others — that his legacy is most clear to us. It is the hope of finding a secular approach to (cultural) history that seeks to learn from the problematic moments (crises) in that history, accepts living in a chaotic world, but is simultaneously interested in rethinking that history and discovering not only diversity but commonality. Ultimately this is a vision that has also political relevance.[29] To approach Mahler as he himself approached cultural history means paying attention to moments of crisis in his music and to the music's heterogeneity. It means looking for those instants in his music that are ironic or humorous, but also for moments that are uncomfortable, uncanny, disruptive, or heterophonic. It entails finding a performance practice that articulates and reflects on those moments, and one that therefore may still challenge our ideas about him and his time. However, if we take his model seriously, we should also dare to move *beyond* him and construct new contexts for his work that may include *fin-de-siècle* Vienna — the names Korngold (Erich Wolfgang), Křenek, Rathaus, Schreker, Ullmann, Wellesz, and Zemlinsky come to mind — but may also go much further than that and seek a global sense of how culture and identity can be thought and experienced together. We need to break open our view of musical and cultural history, and open our minds to those traditions that have been discarded or are ignored. It is not simply that Mahler's music is among the most complex and engaging in existence; his views on text and culture allow us, in Berio's words (29), to look at cultural history, our own and that of others, as being "inhabited by the significant presence of absences and by the echo of absent presences."

Notes

Introduction

[1] See Gerhard Scheit and Wilhelm Svoboda, *Feindbild Gustav Mahler: Zur antisemitischen Abwehr der Moderne in Österreich* (Vienna: Sonderzahl, 2002).

[2] Leon Botstein, "Whose Gustav Mahler?" in *Mahler and His World*, ed. Karen Painter (Princeton, NJ, and London: Princeton UP, 2002), 1–53; here 14.

[3] Botstein, "Whose Gustav Mahler?" 6.

[4] See in this context Walter's introduction to the 1957 edition of *Gustav Mahler: Ein Porträt* (Berlin and Frankfurt am Main: Fischer, 1957), in which he states that Mahler's work "with all its boldness nevertheless belongs to the healthy period that developed under the influence of our great classical music, and even in our ailing present maintains its vitality" ("mit all seinen Kühnheiten doch der gesunden Epoche angehört, die sich unter dem Einfluß unserer großen klassischen Musik entwickelt hat, noch im kranken Heute seine Lebenskraft bewährt"; 10). All translations are my own, unless otherwise noted. See also Scheit and Svoboda, *Feindbild*, esp. 85–87. Regarding the "authenticity" of Walter's approach to Mahler, see K. Kropfinger's comparison of Walter's performances of the Fourth Symphony with those of Willem Mengelberg in "Gerettete Herausforderung: Mahlers 4. Symphonie — Mengelbergs Interpretation," in *Mahler-Interpretation: Aspekte zum Werk und Wirken von Gustav Mahler*, ed. R. Stephan (Mainz: Schott, 1985), 111–75; here 173–75. Kropfinger argues that the great liberties Mengelberg takes with the score and the greater contrasts in his performance of the Fourth, in particular regarding tempo and dynamics, may be more authentic (that is, similar to Mahler's own performance practice) than Walter's balanced, classical reading. This is confirmed by Scheit and Svoboda's analysis of a review from 1934 that compared the two conductors' approaches to that same symphony (Scheit and Svoboda, *Feindbild*, 82–84).

[5] See, for example, Constantin Floros, *Die geistige Welt Gustav Mahlers in systematischer Darstellung*, vol. 1 of *Gustav Mahler*, 2nd ed. (Wiesbaden: Breitkopf & Härtel, 1987), 122–25.

[6] Botstein, "Whose Gustav Mahler?" 3.

[7] See Eric Hobsbawm, "Mass-Producing Traditions: Europe, 1870—1914," in *The Invention of Tradition*, ed. Eric Hobsbawm and Terence Ranger (Cambridge: Cambridge UP, 1992), 263–307; here 263.

[8] Hobsbawm, "Mass-Producing Traditions," 278.

[9] A collection of quotations from Mahler about musical programs can be found in Floros, *Die geistige Welt*, 19–20 and 22–24. I do not share Floros's view that

Mahler changed his ideas in 1900, but rather believe that Mahler was ambivalent about programs throughout his career.

[10] Bruno Walter, letter to Ludwig Schiedermair, 6 Dec. 1901, in *Briefe, 1894–1962* (Frankfurt am Main: S. Fischer, 1969), 48. Further references to this work are given in the text using page numbers alone.

[11] See Morten Solvik, "The Literary and Philosophical Worlds of Gustav Mahler," 27, in *The Cambridge Companion to Mahler*, ed. Jeremy Barham (Cambridge: Cambridge UP, 2007), 21–34.

[12] See Jens Malte Fischer, "Gustav Mahler und das 'Judentum in der Musik,'" *Merkur* 51 (1997): 665–80; here 668. Adorno is of course aware of this anti-Semitic cliché and refers to it in his essay "Mahler heute" (*Gesammelte Werke* 18:226–34; here 226).

[13] See Botstein, "Whose Gustav Mahler?" 20–33. For a similar problematization of Adorno's concept of culture, see Marc Weiner, "Hans Pfitzner and the Anxiety of Nostalgic Modernism," in *Legacies of Modernism: Art and Politics in Northern Europe, 1890–1950*, ed. Patrizia C. McBride, Richard W. McCormick, and Monika Žagar (New York: Palgrave MacMillan, 2007), 17–28; here 27.

[14] Alfred Roller, *Die Bildnisse von Gustav Mahler* (Leipzig and Vienna: E. P. Tal, 1922), 25; In English, "Alfred Roller" (excerpt), in *Mahler Remembered*, ed. Norman Lebrecht (New York and London: Norton, 1988), 149–65; here 163–64; see also Botstein, "Whose Gustav Mahler?" 21.

[15] Max Paddison, *Adorno's Aesthetics of Music* (Cambridge: Cambridge UP, 1997), 262.

[16] Paddison, *Adorno's Aesthetics*, 262. The following summary is based primarily on Adorno's overview of musical development in *Philosophie der neuen Musik*, in *Gesammelte Schriften*, vol. 12 (Frankfurt am Main: Suhrkamp, 1997), 55–63.

[17] Botstein, "Whose Gustav Mahler?" 19; see also 3.

[18] See, for instance, *Philosophie der neuen Musik*, 60–61. Richard Leppert speaks in this context of a "progressive core in Wagner." "Commentary," 538, in Adorno, *Essays on Music*, ed. Richard Leppert (Berkeley: U of California P, 2002).

[19] This observation is made by Dieter Borchmeyer, in his book *Richard Wagner: Ahasvers Wandlungen* (Frankfurt am Main and Leipzig: Insel, 2002), 14–15.

[20] Adorno, "Zu einem Streitgespräch über Mahler," in *Gesammelte Schriften* (Frankfurt am Main: Suhrkamp, 1997), 18:244–50; here 247.

[21] See for instance Adorno, *Versuch über Wagner*, 17–25, in *Gesammelte Schriften* 13:7–148, in particular his discussion of Wagner's relationship with the conductor Hermann Levi.

[22] Carl E. Schorske, *Fin-de-Siècle Vienna: Politics and Culture* (New York: Vintage, 1981), "Introduction," xxvii. For a discussion and critique of the ways in which Schorske's views shaped scholarship on fin-de-siècle Vienna, see Steven Beller's introduction to *Rethinking Vienna, 1900*, ed. Steven Beller (New York and Oxford: Berghahn, 2001), 1–25.

[23] See Steven Beller, *Rethinking Vienna*, in particular Beller's introduction, 1–25, and Allan Janik's "Vienna 1900 Revisited: Paradigms and Problems," 27–56.

[24] See for instance chapter 3, "Politics in a New Key," in Schorske, *Fin-de-Siècle Vienna*, 116–80.

[25] Ernst Křenek, "Gustav Mahler," in Bruno Walter, *Gustav Mahler: With a Biographical Essay by Ernst Křenek*, trans. James Galston (New York: Greystone, 1941), 155–220; here 159.

[26] See for instance Hans Rudolf Vaget's response to Paul Lawrence Rose, *Wagner: Race and Revolution* (New Haven, CT, and London: Yale UP, 1992), in "Wagner, Anti-Semitism, and Mr. Rose: *Merkwürd'ger Fall!*" *German Quarterly* 66 (1993): 222–36. For a counterperspective, see Marc Weiner, "Über Wagner sprechen: Ideologie und Methodenstreit," in *Richard Wagner im Dritten Reich*, ed. Saul Friedländer and Jörn Rüsen (Munich: Beck, 2000), 342–62.

[27] See in this context also Paul Reitter's criticism of "backshadowing" in the discourse on Jewish self-hatred: "The Jewish Self-Hatred Octopus," *German Quarterly* 82.3 (2009): 356–72; here 359.

[28] See Charles Maier, "Mahler's Theater: The Performative and the Political in Central Europe, 1890–1910," in Painter, *Mahler and his World*, 55–85; here 71–72.

[29] This is argued by David J. Levin in *Unsettling Opera: Staging Mozart, Verdi, Wagner, and Zemlinsky* (Chicago and London: Chicago UP, 2007), 44 (see also fn. 17). For a detailed discussion of the *Tristan* production of 1903 see Patrick Carnegy, *Wagner and the Art of the Theatre* (New Haven, CT, and London: Yale UP, 2006), 165–70.

[30] See for instance his letter of 29 June 1896: "Unfortunately I have to go to Bayreuth again this year. (I received again a letter from Cosima, in which she declares that she expects to see me there)" (Ich muß heuer leider nach Bayreuth [Ich habe wieder einen Brief von Cosima bekommen, in dem sie die Erwartung ausspricht, mich dort zu sehen]). Gustav Mahler, *"Mein lieber Trotzkopf, meine süße Mohnblume": Briefe an Anna von Mildenburg* (Vienna: Paul Zsolnay, 2006), 133; see also 112 and 231.

[31] Jens Malte Fischer, *Gustav Mahler: Der fremde Vertraute* (Vienna: Paul Zsolnay, 2003), 672.

[32] See Richard Wagner, "Das Kunstwerk der Zukunft," 97–98, in *Sämtliche Schriften und Dichtungen*, vol. 3 (Leipzig: Breitkopf & Härtel, [1911]), 42–178; in English, "The Art-Work of the Future," in *The Art-Work of the Future and Other Works*, trans. William Aston Ellis (Lincoln: Nebraska UP, 1993), 69–213; here 127–28. See also Esteban Buch, *Beethoven's Ninth: A Political History*, trans. Richard Miller (Chicago and London: U of Chicago P, 2003), 160.

[33] See Jens Malte Fischer, *Der fremde Vertraute*, 87; see also Donald Mitchell, *Gustav Mahler: The Early Years* (1958; repr., Woodbridge, UK: Boydell, 2003), 249, fn. 35.

[34] See Henry-Louis de La Grange, *Mahler*, vol. 1 (Garden City, NJ, and New York: Doubleday, 1973), 33; and Jens Malte Fischer, *Der fremde Vertraute*, 88.

[35] Jens Malte Fischer, *Der fremde Vertraute*, 88.

[36] See Dietrich Fischer-Dieskau, *Hugo Wolf: Leben und Werk* (Berlin: Henschel, 2003), 106 and 126.

37 Fischer-Dieskau, *Hugo Wolf,* 124–25.

38 Fischer-Dieskau, *Hugo Wolf,* 126; de La Grange, 1:72.

39 In a recent essay Leon Botstein has shown that Jewish responses to Wagner's work and its anti-Semitic agenda were highly diverse in fin-de-siècle Vienna. See "German Jews and Wagner," in *Richard Wagner and His World,* ed. Thomas S. Grey (Princeton, NJ, and Oxford: Princeton UP, 2009), 151–97; here 162–77. Interestingly, Botstein's essay also proves that there was a lively debate about Wagner's anti-Semitism in Vienna around 1900.

40 See Sander L. Gilman, *Jewish Self-Hatred: Anti-Semitism and the Hidden Language of the Jews* (Baltimore and London: Johns Hopkins UP, 1990), 139: "[*Mauscheln*] is the use of altered syntax and bits of Hebrew vocabulary and a specific pattern of gestures to represent the spoken language of the Jews. What is stressed is the specifically 'Jewish' intonation, the mode of articulation as well as the semantic context." Mahler's remarks also confirm Gilman's insight that "*Mauscheln* was a quality of language and discourse that Jews perceived as a major problem in their true and total acceptance within the German community" (141).

41 On Mime as a personification of anti-Semitic stereotypes, see Marc Weiner, *Richard Wagner and the Anti-Semitic Imagination* (Lincoln, NE, and London: Nebraska UP, 1997), 144–45 and 169–72.

42 Siegfried Lipiner, quoted in Natalie Bauer-Lechner, *Fragmente: Gelerntes und Gelebtes* (Vienna: Rudolf Lechner & Sohn, 1907), 235.

43 See Donald Mitchell's list of Mahler's early works, which includes a fairy-tale opera *Rübezahl* and an opera project with the title *Die Argonauten;* texts for these projects may have existed, but the assumption is that very little of the actual music was composed (*Gustav Mahler: The Early Years,* 116–20). On the question as to why Mahler did not write operas, see also Křenek, "Gustav Mahler," 177–78.

44 Barbara Jelavich, *Modern Austria: Empire & Republic, 1800–1986* (Cambridge: Cambridge UP, 1987), 87. See also Steven Beller, *A Concise History of Austria* (Cambridge: Cambridge UP, 2006), 155–57.

45 For a detailed discussion of the importance of the Enlightenment's legacy for Jewish emancipation in Vienna around 1900 see Steven Beller, *Vienna and the Jews, 1867—1938: A Cultural History* (Cambridge: Cambridge UP, 1989), 122–43. Concerning the highly ambiguous feelings of many Jews regarding the ideal of assimilation, see also Ritchie Robertson, *The "Jewish Queston" in German Literature, 1749–1939: Emancipation and Its Discontents* (Oxford and New York: Oxford UP, 2002), 233–378.

46 Beller, *Vienna and the Jews,* 147–48.

47 Beller, *Vienna and the Jews,* 155–62.

48 See, for example, William McGrath, *Dionysian Art and Populist Politics in Austria* (New Haven, CT, and London: Yale UP, 1974), 12–13, 53–54, and 69.

49 McGrath, *Dionysian Art,* 89.

50 This argument has been made by Schorske, *Fin-de-Siècle Vienna,* xxvi; Beller, *Vienna and the Jews, 1867—1938,* 156 and 158; and Maier, "Mahler's Theater," 68.

51 McGrath, *Dionysian Art,* 208.

⁵² Beller, *Vienna and the Jews,* 162. Charles Maier points out that, at the time, "not all nationalist trends appeared menacing. Cultural nationalism and ethnic diversity could appear as progressive forces . . . nonetheless, such nationalism with a human face or incipient multiculturalism remained a precarious and vulnerable stance" ("Mahler's Theater," 68).

⁵³ Alma Mahler reports that on 1 May 1905 Mahler ran into a workers' demonstration and enthusiastically joined them. See *Gustav Mahler: Erinnerungen und Briefe* (Amsterdam: Allert de Lange, 1940), 104–5; see also McGrath, *Dionysian Art,* 243–44).

⁵⁴ See Michael Brenner, *The Renaissance of Jewish Culture in Weimar Germany* (New Haven, CT, and London: Yale UP, 1996), in particular "Pre-Weimar Origins," 19–21; quote from 20.

⁵⁵ Roller, *Die Bildnisse von Gustav Mahler,* 25; *Mahler Remembered,* 163.

⁵⁶ See the detailed reconstruction of the many anti-Semitic incidents surrounding Mahler's tenure as director of the Court Opera in volumes 2 and 3 of Henry Louis de La Grange's biography on Mahler.

⁵⁷ Talia Pecker Berio, "Mahler's Jewish Parable," in Painter, *Mahler and His World,* 87–110; here 89.

⁵⁸ See Botstein, "Sozialgeschichte und die Politik des Ästhetischen: Juden und Musik in Wien, 1870–1938," in *quasi una fantasia: Juden und die Musikstadt Wien,* ed. Leon Botstein and Werner Hanak (Vienna: Wolke, 2003), 43–63; here 49–50.

⁵⁹ Patrizia C. McBride, "Introduction: The Future's Past — Modernism, Critique, and the Political," in McBride, McCormick, and Žagar, *Legacies of Modernism,* 1–13; here 6. For an approach that understands Vienna modernism as centered around the notion of "crisis," see Jacques Le Rider, *Modernity and Crises of Identity: Culture and Society in Fin-de-Siècle Vienna,* trans. Rosemary Norris (New York: Continuum, 1993), esp. 30–45.

⁶⁰ Křenek, "Gustav Mahler," 193 and 219. The following quotes are from 193. The reference to the avant-garde is cryptic and yet highly relevant, since it can be found in the last paragraph of Křenek's essay and therefore can be seen as (part of) the essay's conclusion.

⁶¹ Peter Bürger, *Theorie der Avantgarde* (Frankfurt am Main: Suhrkamp, 1974), 23. In English, *Theory of the Avant-Garde,* trans. Michael Shaw, forew. Jochen Schulte-Sasse (Minneapolis: U of Minnesota P, 1989), 18.

⁶² See Hermann Bahr, "Das junge Oesterreich," in *Studien zur Kritik der Moderne* (Frankfurt am Main: Rütten & Loening, 1894), 73–96; here 75.

⁶³ Bürger, *Theorie der Avantgarde,* 28–29; *Theory of the Avant'Garde,* 22–23.

⁶⁴ See the DVD with the excerpts from Bernstein's Vienna rehearsals of the first movement of Mahler's Fifth (Leonard Bernstein, *Mahler Rehearsals: Symphonies Nos. 5 & 9; Das Lied von der Erde.* DVD. Hamburg: Deutsche Grammophon, 2005), in particular 1:29–34:35; see also Scheit and Svoboda, *Feindbild,* 248–57.

⁶⁵ See, for an exemplary illustration of this point, Bernstein's analysis of the *Trauermarsch* (third movement) of the First Symphony in his video essay *The Little*

Drummer Boy: An Essay on Gustav Mahler (DVD. Hamburg: Deutsche Grammophon, 2007), 6:42–12:42. Philip V. Bohlman has recently argued that Jewishness was an integral part of popular music in Vienna around 1900; the identification of specific Jewish elements in Mahler's music, however, suggests specific borders between traditions where these did not exist and presupposes therefore a model of tradition that does not adequately describe cultural realities. See Bohlman, *Jewish Music and Modernity* (Oxford and New York: Oxford UP, 2008), 184.

[66] Wolf Lepenies, *The Seduction of Culture in German History* (Princeton, NJ, Oxford: Princeton UP, 2006), 9.

[67] See Lepenies, *The Seduction of Culture*, 15–16, 23, 27, 39–41, and 54.

[68] See Esteban Buch, *Beethoven's Ninth*, 260–62.

[69] See Buch, *Beethoven's Ninth*, 157. It is unlikely that this is true, even though there exists a version of Schiller's poem "An die Freude" that is earlier than the one Beethoven decided to use and is considerably more political (see Buch, *Beethoven's Ninth*, 47). From Bernstein's program notes for the performance, it is clear that he was aware of the nineteenth-century controversy (Buch, *Beethoven's Ninth*, 261–62).

[70] For a critical discussion of the political meanings of this concert, see James Schmidt, "'Not these Sounds': Beethoven at Mauthausen," *Philosophy and Literature* 29 (2005): 146–63, esp. 147–48, 153, and 156; and Josef Haslinger, "Klasse Burschen," in *Klasse Burschen: Essays* (Frankfurt am Main: Fischer, 2001), 27–36.

Chapter 1

[1] See Donald Mitchell, *Gustav Mahler: The Wunderhorn Years* (Woodbridge, UK: Boydell, 2005), 157–59.

[2] Bruno Walter, *Gustav Mahler: Ein Porträt* (Berlin and Frankfurt am Main: S. Fischer, 1957), 102–3; In English, *Gustav Mahler: With a Biographical Essay by Ernst Křenek*, trans. James Galston (New York: Greystone, 1941), 137–38.

[3] Bruno Walter, letter to Ludwig Schiedermaier, 6 Dec. 1901, in Bruno Walter, *Briefe, 1894–1962* (Frankfurt am Main: S. Fischer, 1969), 51. Bauer-Lechner's remarks above are based on a letter she wrote on 16 Nov. 1900 at Mahler's request to the critic Ludwig Karpath. A little more than a year later Walter wrote his letter, also on behalf of Mahler, directly contradicting Bauer-Lechner!

[4] Mahler's statement was recorded by Robert Holtzmann in 1918 (quoted in Mitchell, *The Wunderhorn Years*, 226).

[5] A concise overview of the nineteenth-century history of the *Bildungsroman* can be found in Todd Kontje, *The German Bildungsroman: History of a National Genre* (Columbia SC: Camden House, 1993), 15–30. Kontje discusses the gendered agenda associated with the genre (17 and 27). Regarding the *Bildungsroman* as a genre focused on love and work, see Friedrich A. Kittler, "Über die Sozialisation Wilhelm Meisters," in Gerhard Kaiser and Friedrich A. Kittler, *Dichtung als Sozialisationsspiel: Studien zu Goethe und Gottfried Keller* (Göttingen: Vandenhoeck & Ruprecht, 1978), 13–24; here 14–15.

⁶ This translation is proposed by W. H. Bruford in his classic study *The German Tradition of Self-Cultivation: "Bildung" from Humboldt to Thomas Mann* (London and New York: Cambridge UP, 1975). Bruford in particular highlights the term's association with Germanness (see for instance his introduction, vii–x). For a chronological overview of the development of the concept "Bildung" in German intellectual history, see Ursula Franke, "Bildung/Erziehung, ästhetische," in *Ästhetische Grundbegriffe*, ed. Karlheinz Barck, vol. 1 (Stuttgart and Weimar: J. B. Metzler, 2000), 696–727.

⁷ Peter Sprengel, "Einleitung," lxix, in *Jean Paul im Urteil seiner Kritiker: Dokumente zur Wirkungsgeschichte Jean Pauls in Deutschland*, ed. Peter Sprengel (Munich: C. H. Beck, 1980), xv–xcii.

⁸ Sprengel, "Einleitung," lxix.

⁹ See Gert Ueding, *Jean Paul* (Munich: C. H. Beck, 1993), 50.

¹⁰ The similarities between the biographies of Jean Paul and Mahler have been noted by Jost Hermand in his chapter "Deutsch-jüdische Zerrissenheit: Gustav Mahlers I. Symphonie," in *Judentum und deutsche Kultur: Beispiele einer schmerzhaften Symbiose* (Cologne, Weimar, and Vienna: Böhlau, 1996), 71–84; here 75. More recent biographical research has shown that the conditions in Mahler's parental home were less severe than is usually assumed and that the family was actually somewhat well-off; see Jonathan Carr, *Mahler: A Biography* (Woodstock, NY and New York: Overlook, 1998), 10–11; and Jens Malte Fischer, *Gustav Mahler: Der fremde Vertraute* (Vienna: Paul Zsolnay, 2003), 30–31.

¹¹ For an example of Jean Paul's strategy of turning a negative experience into something positive, see his discussion of the hunger he suffered during childhood in his autobiographical text *Selbsterlebensbeschreibung*, in *Werke*, vol. 6, 4th ed., ed. Norbert Miller (Munich: Hanser, 1987), 1037–1103; here 1044; see also Ueding, *Jean Paul*, 11–22.

¹² Alma Mahler, *Gustav Mahler: Erinnerungen und Briefe* (Amsterdam: Allert de Lange, 1940), 14.

¹³ See Jürgen Fohrmann, "Jean Pauls 'Titan': Eine Lektüre," *Jahrbuch der Jean-Paul-Gesellschaft* 20 (1985): 7–32; here 9.

¹⁴ See Hugo von Hofmannsthal, "Blick auf Jean Paul," in *Gesammelte Werke*, vol. 8, ed. Bernd Schoeller (Frankfurt am Main: Fischer, 1979), 434–37; here 434. Herta Blaukopf argues that Jean Paul experienced a renaissance in Vienna around 1880, but she produces very little evidence to support her claim. Blaukopf, "Jean Paul, die erste Symphonie und Dostojewski," in *Gustav Mahler: Werk und Wirken*, ed. Erich Wolfgang Partsch (Vienna: Vom Pasqualatihaus, 1996), 35–42; here 35.

¹⁵ Goethe's poem "Der Chinese in Rom" can be found in *Goethes Werke*, vol. 1, ed. Erich Trunz (Munich: C. H. Beck, 1982), 206. See also Sprengel, "Einleitung," xxx–xxxiii; and Hendrik Birus, "Der 'Orientale' Jean Paul: Versuch über Goethes 'Vergleichung,'" *Jahrbuch der Jean-Paul-Gesellschaft* 20 (1985): 103–26; here 108–10.

¹⁶ See Sprengel, "Einleitung," xxxii–xxxiii. Goethe's characterization of Jean Paul can be found in the annotations to his *West-östlicher Divan*, in *Werke*, vol. 2, ed. Erich Trunz (Munich: C. H. Beck, 1982), 184–86.

[17] Birus, "Der 'Orientale' Jean Paul," 113.

[18] See Peter Sprengel, "Zur Wirkungsgeschichte von Jean Pauls 'Titan,' *Jahrbuch der Jean-Paul-Gesellschaft* 17 (1982): 11–30; here 20.

[19] Jean Paul, *Titan*, in *Werke*, vol. 3, 6th ed., ed. Norbert Miller (Munich and Vienna: Hanser, 1999). Further references to this work are given in the text using the page number alone.

[20] The third edition of Eucharius Ferdinand Christian Oertel's *Gemeinnütziges Wörterbuch zur Erklärung und Verteutschung der im gemeinen Leben vorkommenden fremden Ausdrükke* . . . (Ansbach: Gassertsche Buchhandlung, 1816) defines "Schnurrer"/"Schnurrjude" as a Jewish beggar (2:783). The *Jewish Encyclopedia* defines the "Schnorrer" as a Jewish beggar having some pretensions to respectability; examples given are someone collecting money to provide a dowry for his daughter or someone who needs money in order to reestablish himself after his house has been burned down "in a general conflagration." See http://www.jewishencyclopedia.com/view.jsp?artid=344&letter=S&search=schnorrer (accessed 26 Oct. 2009).

[21] The most prominent among them is of course Gotthold Ephraim Lessing, whose drama *Nathan der Weise*, with its emphasis on tolerance, is a homage to his friend the Enlightenment philosopher Moses Mendelssohn. In *Titan*, Moses Mendelssohn is also respectfully mentioned once (299).

[22] See Jean Paul, *Selbsterlebensbeschreibung*, 1090–91, and Richard Otto Spazier, *Jean Paul Friedrich Richter: Ein biographischer Commentar zu dessen Werken*, 5 vols. (Leipzig: C. Brüggemann & O. Wigand, 1833), 1:93, and 99–100.

[23] Spazier, *Jean Paul Friedrich Richter*, 3:195–98; see also Ueding, *Jean Paul*, 85.

[24] For example, in his letter to Friedrich Heinrich Jacobi, 8 Sept. 1803, in *Die Briefe Jean Pauls*, vol. 4, ed. Eduard Berend (Munich: Georg Müller, 1926), 263–66; here 264. Jutta Schönberg makes Jean Paul's statement the point of departure for her analysis of *Titan*, which seeks to reflect the text's heterogeneity and the conflicts and tension in Jean Paul's conceptualization of subjectivity. See Schönberg, *Anti-Titan: Subjektgenese und Subjektkritik bei Jean Paul im psychokulturellen Kontext* (Frankfurt am Main: Peter Lang, 1994), 10 and 11, esp. fn. 2.

[25] While many nineteenth-century critics sought to read normative ideals into the genre, more critical views emphasizing "irony" were by no means absent (e.g., Kontje, *The German Bildungsroman*, 11, 16, and 29–30).

[26] Ralph-Rainer Wuthenow, "Verführung durch Phantasie," *Jahrbuch der Jean-Paul-Gesellschaft* 26/27 (1991/92): 92–107; here 98.

[27] Wuthenow, "Verführung durch Phantasie," 94.

[28] See also Fohrmann, "Jean Pauls 'Titan,'" 17.

[29] See Ralf Berhorst, *Anamorphosen der Zeit: Jean Pauls Romanästhetik und Geschichtsphilosophie* (Tübingen: Max Niemeyer, 2002), 314.

[30] For a concise overview of Freud's theory of masochism, see Michael C. Finke, "Introduction," in *One Hundred Years of Masochism: Literary Texts, Social and Cultural Contexts*, ed. Michael C. Finke and Carl Niekerk (Amsterdam and Atlanta: Rodopi, 2000), 1–13; here 5–10.

[31] Bruno Walter, *Theme and Variations: An Autobiography*, trans. James A. Galston (New York: Afred A. Knopf, 1966), 105. See also Erik Ryding and Rebecca Pechefsky, *Bruno Walter: A World Elsewhere* (New Haven, CT, and London: Yale UP, 2001), 28.

[32] This thought is expressed by Lipiner when he states: "We have the experience of nature; the old generation had *nature*." ("Wir haben Naturgefühl, die Alten aber hatten *die Natur*.") Lipiner, quoted in Natalie Bauer-Lechner, *Fragmente: Gelerntes und Gelebtes* (Vienna: Rudolf Lechner & Sohn, 1907), 157.

[33] Berhorst, *Anamorphosen der Zeit*, 334.

[34] Berhorst, *Anamorphosen der Zeit*, 344–45.

[35] Fohrmann, "Jean Pauls 'Titan,'" 9.

[36] See Bruno Walter, *Gustav Mahler: Ein Porträt*, 82; *Gustav Mahler: With a Biographical Essay by Ernst Křenek*, 105: "He does not illustrate in sound that which he had experienced — that would be 'program music.' But the mood of his soul, engendered by memory and present feeling, produces themes and influences the general direction of their development without, however, introducing itself forcibly into the musical issue. In that manner, a compact composition is born which, at the same time, is an avowal of the soul." (Er schildert nicht etwa Erlebtes in Tönen — das wäre Programmusik; aber die Stimmung seiner Seele, von Erinnerung und gegenwärtigem Gefühl hervorgerufen, produziert Themen, wirkt auf die Gesamtrichtung ihrer musikalichen Entwicklung ein, ohne sich jemals in den musikalischen Ablauf gewaltsam einzuschalten, und so entsteht eine geschlossene Komposition, die zugleich Seelenbekenntnis ist.)

[37] Mitchell, *The Wunderhorn Years*, 158.

[38] See Constantin Floros, *Gustav Mahler: The Symphonies* (Pompton Plains, NJ, and Cambridge: Amadeus, 2000), 36.

[39] See Jean Paul, *Blumen-, Frucht- und Dornenstücke oder Ehestand, Tod und Hochzeit des Armenadvokaten F. St. Siebenkäs*, in *Werke*, ed. Norbert Miller, vol. 2 (Munich and Vienna: Carl Hanser, 1999), 7–576.

[40] See Floros, *Gustav Mahler: The Symphonies*, 28.

[41] See Jean Paul Friedrich Richter, "Vorrede," in *Fantasiestücke in Callots Manier*, in *E. T. A. Hoffmanns sämtliche Werke; Historisch-kritische Ausgabe*, vol. 1, ed. Carl Georg von Maassen, 2nd ed. (Munich and Leipzig: Georg Müller, 1912), 3–9.

[42] Jost Hermand assumes that the notes accompanying Walter's last recording of Mahler's First Symphony refer specifically to the thirty-second book of *Titan* (see *Judentum und deutsche Kultur*, 78); I agree, even though there is no specific reference to Jean Paul's novel in Walter's text. See "Bruno Walter on Mahler's Symphony No. 1"; essay accompanying Walter's last recording of the First Symphony: *Mahler: Symphony No. 1 in D ("The Titan")*, Bruno Walter/Columbia Symphony Orchestra, Columbia Masterworks 1962, Stereo LP MS 6394.

[43] See Wolfgang Amadeus Mozart, *Il dissoluto punito ossia il Don Giovanni* [score], 225–31, in *Sämtliche Werke: Neue Ausgabe*, 2:17 (Kassel: Bärenreiter, 1968).

⁴⁴ See Francien Markx, *Der Kritiker als Magier: E. T. A. Hoffmanns Musikererzählungen im Kontext der Allgemeinen Musikalischen Zeitung* (PhD diss., U of Illinois at Urbana-Champaign, 2003), 116–17.

⁴⁵ Susanne Vill links this expression to Dante's *Divina Commedia*, with which it is often associated, even though it is not used in Dante's text itself. Vill, *Vermittlungsformen verbalisierter und musikalischer Inhalte in der Musik Gustav Mahlers* (Tutzing, Germany: Hans Schneider, 1979), 213.

⁴⁶ Floros, *Gustav Mahler: The Symphonies*, 48.

⁴⁷ Bruno Walter, *Gustav Mahler: Ein Porträt*, 82; *Gustav Mahler: With a Biographical Essay*, 105.

⁴⁸ For the biographical information discussed here about Mahler's relationship with Marion von Weber and its relevance to the First Symphony, see Jonathan Carr, *Mahler: A Biography*, 44–47, and Jens Malte Fischer, *Gustav Mahler: Der fremde Vertraute*, 207–9.

⁴⁹ Alma Mahler, *Erinnerungen und Briefe*, 137–38; *Memories and Letters*, 110–11.

⁵⁰ Goethe, *Aus meinem Leben: Dichtung und Wahrheit*, in *Werke*, vol. 9 (Munich: Beck, 1982), 587.

⁵¹ Willem Mengelberg in a letter to his wife, Dresden, 10 Jul. 1907, in *Gustav Mahler und Holland: Briefe*, ed. Eduard Reeser (Vienna: Universal Edition, 1980), 90. The Dutch original of this letter is printed in E. Bysterus Heemskerk, *Over Willem Mengelberg* (Amsterdam: Heuff, 1971), 55–57.

⁵² For an analysis that views Jean Paul's *Titan* as critical of the tradition of the *Bildungsroman*, see Jürgen Jacobs and Markus Krause, *Der deutsche Bildungsroman: Gattungsgeschichte vom 18. bis zum 20. Jahrhundert* (Munich: C. H. Beck, 1989), 129, and 137–38.

⁵³ Jacobs and Krause, *Der deutsche Bildungsroman*, 143 and 149.

⁵⁴ Kontje, *The German Bildungsroman*, 31–32, and 35.

⁵⁵ See Wilhelm Dilthey, *Das Erlebnis und die Dichtung: Lessing, Goethe, Novalis, Hölderlin*, 16th ed. (Göttingen: Vandenhoeck & Ruprecht, 1985), 272–73. Regarding Dilthey's importance for the nineteenth-century history of the term, see Kontje, *The German Bildungsroman*, 27–30.

⁵⁶ For two contrasting perspectives, which both, however, incorporate elements critical of the tradition of *Bildung*, see Kontje, *The German Bildungsroman*, 77–79, and Jacobs and Krause, *Der deutsche Bildungsroman*, 99–102.

⁵⁷ See Umberto Eco's classic study of the open work of art, *The Open Work*, trans. Anna Cancogni (Cambridge, MA: Harvard UP, 1989).

⁵⁸ See also Donald Mitchell, who argues that Jean Paul's "handling of his materials" and the "nature of his imagery" are the main connection between novel and symphony (Mitchell, *The Wunderhorn Years*, 227).

⁵⁹ Alphons Diepenbrock, letter to Johanna Jongkindt, 17 Oct. 1909. Diepenbrock, *Brieven en Documenten*, ed. Eduard Reeser ('s-Gravenhage, Netherlands: Martinus Nijhoff, 1991), 152–57, quote 155; see also Reeser, *Gustav Mahler und Holland*, 32.

[60] In my view this is a decisively modernist feature of Mahler's aesthetics, and one that also differentiates his music from Wagner's: "One could say that in [Wagner's] works there is a mode of address, a kind of voice speaking to the audience that brooks no discussion and refuses to recognize the autonomy of the listening subject." Marc A. Weiner, "Primal Sounds," *Opera Quarterly* 23.2/3 (2007): 217–46; here 217.

[61] The original German versions of both programs were taken from Henry-Louis de La Grange, *Mahler*, vol. 1 (Garden City, NJ, and New York: Doubleday, 1973), 747–48. All translations are mine.

Chapter 2

[1] See Renate Stark-Voit, "'Bild — Symbol — Klang': Zu Gustav Mahlers Wunderhorn-Vertonungen," in *Mahler-Gespräche: Rezeptionsfragen — literarischer Horizont — musikalische Darstellung*, ed. Friedbert Aspetsberger and Erich Wolfgang Partsch (Innsbruck: Studien Verlag, 2002), 118–43; here 120.

[2] Stark-Voit, "'Bild — Symbol — Klang,'" 120.

[3] See Ludwig Achim von Arnim, "Von Volksliedern," in *Des Knaben Wunderhorn: Alte deutsche Lieder*, ed. Achim von Arnim and Clemens Brentano, vol. 1 (Stuttgart: Reclam, 1987), 377–414.

[4] Johann Gottfried Herder, *Volkslieder*, 2 vols. (Leipzig: Weigandsche Buchhandlung, 1778/79).

[5] Philip V. Bohlman, *World Music: A Very Short Introduction* (Oxford: Oxford UP, 2002), 39, 40.

[6] See Philip V. Bohlman, "Landscape — Region — Nation — Reich: German Folk Song in the Nexus of National Identity," in *Music and German National Identity*, ed. Celia Applegate and Pamela Potter (Chicago and London: Chicago UP, 2002), 105–27.

[7] See Reinhart Koselleck, "Volk, Nation, Nationalismus, Masse," in *Geschichtliche Grundbegriffe. Historisches Lexikon zur politisch-sozialen Sprache in Deutschland*, ed. Otto Brunner, Werner Conze, and Reinhart Koselleck, vol. 7 (Stuttgart: Klett-Cotta, 1992), 141–431; here 316.

[8] See Johann Gottfried Herder, *Ideen zur Philosophie der Geschichte der Menschheit*, in *Werke in zehn Bänden*, vol. 6 (Frankfurt am Main: Deutscher Klassiker Verlag, 1989), 347.

[9] Johann Gottfried Herder, *Briefe zu Beförderung der Humanität*, vol. 7 (Frankfurt am Main: Deutscher Klassiker Verlag, 1991), 575.

[10] This explains Herder's interest in Germany as a "cultural nation" (Kulturnation), that is, a nation unified through its cultural production. See Bernd Fischer, *Das Eigene und das Eigentliche: Klopstock, Herder, Fichte, Kleist; Episoden aus der Konstruktionsgeschichte nationaler Intentionalitäten* (Berlin: Erich Schmidt, 1995), 200. This concept would prove to be highly influential for German intellectuals' self-perception in the nineteenth and twentieth centuries.

[11] Koselleck, "Volk, Nation, Nationalismus, Masse," 317–18.

[12] See Alexander von Bormann, "Volk als Idee: Zur Semiotisierung des Volksbegriffs," in *Volk — Nation — Europa: Zur Romantisierung und Entromantisierung politischer Begriffe,* ed. Alexander von Bormann (Würzburg: Königshausen & Neumann, 1998), 35–56; here 52.

[13] Von Arnim, "Von Volksliedern," 381 and 384. Page numbers in the following paragraphs refer to this volume of this edition.

[14] For a discussion of the roots of the *Völkische Bewegung* in nineteenth-century culture, see Roger Griffin, *Modernism and Fascism: The Sense of a Beginning under Mussolini and Hitler* (New York: Palgrave MacMillan, 2007), for example, 139–40, and 175. Supporters of the *Völkische Bewegung* believed in the "Volk" not as a concrete but as an abstract category: a "mystical entity above, apart from, and outside social class or political party." George L. Mosse, *Germans and Jews: The Right, the Left, and the Search for a "Third Force" in Pre-Nazi Germany* (New York: Howard Fertig, 1970), 117. When looking at Mahler's folk songs, it is advisable to remember that although it was predominantly after the First World War that the *Völkische Bewegung* gained popularity, its roots were in the late nineteenth century even though at that time its political ambitions may not have been recognized as such.

[15] See Dieter Borchmeyer, *Richard Wagner: Ahasvers Wandlungen* (Frankfurt am Main and Leipzig: Insel, 2002), 143.

[16] Richard Wagner, "Was ist Deutsch?" 46, 49, in *Sämtliche Schriften und Dichtungen,* vol. 10, 36–54; here 46, 49. English version: "What is German" 161, 164, in *Art and Politics* (Lincoln/London: Nebraska UP, 1995), 149–69; here 161, 164 (translation modified).

[17] With that characterization he refers to the central concepts of his book, namely the division between Apollonian and Dionysian forms of art. Apollonian art, according to Nietzsche, is rational and individual; it is associated with light, and it seeks higher truth and calm wisdom. Dionysian art, in contrast, is irrational and orgiastic; it is associated with the body, the abandonment of individuality, and the goal of repairing the bond between mankind and nature (see *SW* 1:25–30; *BT,* 14–19).

[18] Jens Malte Fischer has pointed to Baumbach's text as one of the possible sources of inspiration for Mahler's cycle (*Gustav Mahler: Der fremde Vertraute,* 217).

[19] See Mitchell, *Gustav Mahler: The Wunderhorn Years,* 119–22; Mahler refers to the importance of this relationship for his songs in his letter to Friedrich Löhr of 1 January 1885 (*Br,* 57). The assumption is that he wrote the texts shortly before the letter. Two of the poems are dated 15 and 19 Dec. 1884; the songs were probably orchestrated in 1892. See de La Grange, *Mahler,* vol. 1 (Garden City, NJ, and New York: Doubleday, 1973), 741–42.

[20] While "Geselle" has historically assumed many different meanings, the element of travel has been important from the term's origins onward; the word originally referred to someone who traveled as part of the entourage of a nobleman (it was also used in a military sense, as we will see below). For the etymological history of "Geselle," see Jacob and Wilhelm Grimm, *Deutsches Wörterbuch,* vol. 5 (Munich: DTV, 1991), 4025–37.

[21] The song is based on an untitled poem in *Des Knaben Wunderhorn*. See Arnim and Brentano, *Des Knaben Wunderhorn*, vol. 3 (Stuttgart: Reclam, 1987), 119–21. See Henry-Louis de La Grange, *Mahler* 1:743 for a detailed comparison of the two texts.

[22] Mitchell, *The Wunderhorn Years*, 124.

[23] A comprehensive bibliography of eighteenth- and nineteenth-century German *Wanderliteratur* can be found in *Wanderzwang — Wanderlust: Formen der Raum- und Sozialerfahrung zwischen Aufklärung und Frühindustrialismus*, ed. Wolfgang Albrecht and Hans-Joachim Kertscher (Tübingen: Niemeyer, 1999), 239–309.

[24] See Andrew Cusack, *The Wanderer in Nineteenth-Century German Literature: Intellectual History and Cultural Criticism* (Rochester, NY: Camden House, 2008) 15, 34, and 50.

[25] Cusack, *The Wanderer in Nineteenth-Century German Literature*, 195.

[26] See Peter Revers, *Mahlers Lieder: Ein musikalischer Werkführer* (Munich: C. H. Beck, 2000), 61.

[27] Revers, *Mahlers Lieder*, 65.

[28] Revers, *Mahlers Lieder*, 61.

[29] See Revers, *Mahlers Lieder*, 58.

[30] See *Lieder eines fahrenden Gesellen für eine Singstimme mit Orchester* [score], 47, in *Sämtliche Werke: Kritische Gesamtausgabe*, vol. 14.1 (Vienna, Frankfurt am Main, and London: Josef Weinberger, 1982).

[31] See Jonathan Carr, *Mahler: A Biography* (Woodstock, NY, and New York: Overlook, 1998), 10, and Jens Malte Fischer, *Gustav Mahler, Der fremde Vertraute*, 30–32.

[32] See Jacob and Wilhelm Grimm, *Deutsches Wörterbuch* (Munich: DTV, 1991), 26:454–55.

[33] Ida Dehmel, Diary, cited in Alma Mahler, *Gustav Mahler: Erinnerungen und Briefe* (Amsterdam: Allert de Lange, 1940), 117.

[34] Martina Vordermayer, *Antisemitismus und Judentum bei Clemens Brentano* (Frankfurt am Main: Lang, 1999), 135. Other texts in *Des Knaben Wunderhorn* speak about Jews in more neutral terms (Vordermayer, *Antisemitismus*, 135–36).

[35] For a brief discussion of this text, see my essay "The Romantics and Other Cultures," in *The Cambridge Companion to German Romanticism*, ed. Nicholas Saul (Cambridge: Cambridge UP, 2009), 147–61. I do believe that Mahler was aware of the anti-Semitic undertone in Brentano's work, since he knew Brentano's *Märchen von Gockel, Hinkel und Gackeleia* (*Fairy Tale of Gockel, Hinkel, and Gackeleia*); see my discussion of this text in chapter 3.

[36] See George L. Mosse, *The Image of Man: The Creation of Modern Masculinity* (New York and Oxford: Oxford UP, 1996), 57. The German reception of the figure of the "wandering Jew" was influenced in particular by a pamphlet dating from 1602. A comprehensive collection of materials on the "wandering Jew" in Western culture can be found in Galit Hasan-Rokem and Alan Dundes, eds., *The*

Wandering Jew: Essays in the Interpretation of a Christian Legend (Bloomington: Indiana UP, 1986).

[37] Mosse, *The Image of Man*, 57.

[38] Mahler, letter to Josef Steiner, 17–19 June 1879, in *Br*, 32. For a very detailed analysis of this letter, see Hans Heinrich Eggebrecht, *Die Musik Gustav Mahlers* (Munich and Zurich: Piper, 1986), 11–38.

[39] See Mitchell, *The Wunderhorn Years*, 140–43. Before composing these orchestral settings, between 1888 and 1891, Mahler had composed piano versions of a series of nine (different) songs from *Des Knaben Wunderhorn*.

[40] See the two 1905 programs reprinted in Renate Stark-Voit, "Bild — Symbol — Klang: Zu Mahlers Wunderhorn-Vertonungen," in *Mahler-Gespräche*, ed. Aspetsberger and Partsch, 118–43; here 122 and 125. Also in this context, see Henry-Louis de La Grange's question whether the songs constitute a collection or a cycle (De La Grange, *Gustav Mahler:* vol. 2: *Vienna; The Years of Challenge (1897–1904)*, 731.

[41] Niklas Luhmann, *Liebe als Passion: Zur Codierung von Intimität* (Frankfurt am Main: Suhrkamp, 1984), 73, and 150–51.

[42] Von Arnim and Brentano, *Des Knaben Wunderhorn* 1:182.

[43] See Revers, *Mahlers Lieder*, 83. For Paul Hamburger, the status of the girl is open ("Mahler and *Des Knaben Wunderhorn*," in *Mahler Companion*, 62–83; here 72), but the last few lines make it clear that the entire song is sung by the sentinel.

[44] See von Arnim and Brentano, *Des Knaben Wunderhorn* 1:334–35.

[45] Based on von Arnim and Brentano, 1:189–90.

[46] Hamburger, "Mahler and *Des Knaben Wunderhorn*," 75.

[47] Hamburger, "Mahler and *Des Knaben Wunderhorn*," 75.

[48] The original version in von Arnim and Brentano's collection is much more cynical. We learn that the girl can be had for 1,000 Thaler and the promise never to indulge in wine again or to spend the parental inheritance; that is, the man will have to marry her and be a good husband.

[49] There is some folkloric evidence that associates white geese with fertility, as illustrated by the saying: "A white goose breeds well" (Eine weiße Gans brütet gut). Heinrich Lessmann, *Der deutsche Volksmund im Licht der Sage* (Berlin and Leipzig: Haude & Spenersche Buchhandlung Max Paschke, 1922), 364.

[50] See von Arnim and Brentano, *Des Knaben Wunderhorn*, 2:17–18; in the collection the song is entitled "Verspätung" (Delay) and is located immediately before "Urlicht" (18).

[51] See Goethe, *Werke*, vol. 1, ed. Erich Trunz (Munich: Beck, 1982), 154–55.

[52] See de La Grange, *Mahler*, vol. 1, 768 for a discussion of the different designations Mahler used for these songs.

[53] See Hans Heinrich Eggebrecht, *Die Musik Gustav Mahlers*, 2nd ed. (Munich: Piper, 1986), 222–23.

54 See von Arnim and Brentano, *Des Knaben Wunderhorn* 2:39–40. The original title is "Wettstreit des Kukuks mit der Nachtigal" (Contest of the Cuckoo and Nightingale). The fact that the song is Mahler's response to his critics is reported by Bauer-Lechner, *GME*, 56 (*RGM*, 58). An unfinished sketch shows that the song's original title was "Lob der Kritik" (de La Grange, *Mahler* 1:778).

55 See Dieter Borchmeyer, *Richard Wagner: Ahasvers Wandlungen*, 255–56.

56 Borchmeyer, *Ahasvers Wandlungen*, 251.

57 See Marc Weiner, *Richard Wagner and the Anti-Semitic Imagination*, 118–24; for a counterargument, see Borchmeyer, *Ahasvers Wandlungen*, 255–75. Borchmeyer does not address Weiner's arguments directly.

58 Von Arnim and Brentano, *Des Knaben Wunderhorn* 2:22–23. The Rhine frequently functions as a symbol of Germany in folk songs (see Bohlmann, "Landscape — Region — Nation — Reich," 111).

59 This is the (archaic) meaning of the word "grasen" that Mahler's text uses and also explains the reference to the sickle in the poem. He is not a shepherd, in other words, as has been suggested (Hamburger, "Mahler and *Des Knaben Wunderhorn*," 80).

60 See the final section of my "Introduction" and Wolf Lepenies, *The Seduction of Culture in German History* (Princeton, NJ, and Oxford: Princeton UP, 2006), in particular chapter 1, "Culture: A Noble Substitute" (9–26), for a brief history of this idea.

61 Von Arnim and Brentano, *Des Knaben Wunderhorn* 3:109.

62 Hamburger, "Mahler and *Des Knaben Wunderhorn*," 81.

63 See von Arnim and Brentano, *Des Knaben Wunderhorn*, 1:67–69 and 72. For the dating of these songs, see *GME* 135 and 193 (*RGM*, 173) and Mitchell, *The Wunderhorn Years*, 142.

64 Donald Mitchell, "Mahler's 'Kammermusikton,'" in *The Mahler Companion*, 217–35; here 232.

65 "Gesell" in "Tamboursg'sell" goes back to an older meaning of "Geselle": someone who is part of an army troop (see note 20 above).

66 On militarism and anti-militarism in the *Wunderhorn* collection, see Heinz Rölleke, "'Des Knaben Wunderhorn' — eine romantische Liedersammlung: Produktion — Distribution — Rezeption," in *Das "Wunderhorn" und die Heidelberger Romantik: Mündlichkeit, Schriftlichkeit, Performanz*, ed. Walter Pape (Tübingen: Niemeyer, 2005), 3–19; here 11–12.

67 Eric Hobsbawm: "Mass-Producing Traditions; Europe, 1870—1914," in *The Invention of Tradition*, ed. Hobsbawm and Ranger (Cambridge: Cambridge UP, 1992), 263–307; here 263.

68 See Klaus von See, *Freiheit und Gemeinschaft: Völkisch-nationales Denken in Deutschland zwischen Französischer Revolution und Erstem Weltkrieg* (Heidelberg: Universitätsverlag C. Winter, 2001), 11–15.

69 Hobsbawm, "Introduction," in Hobsbawm and Ranger, *The Invention of Tradition*, 1–14; here 7.

[70] Hobsbawm, "Mass-Producing Traditions," 278; Hobsbawm sees both the less-precise historical references and the importance of the image of an enemy as being characteristics of late-nineteenth-century German Nationalism (278–79; see also 274–75).

[71] Hobsbawm, "Introduction," 6.

[72] Weissberg, "Introduction," 15, in *Cultural Memory and the Construction of Identity*, ed. Dan Ben-Amos and Liliane Weissberg (Detroit: Wayne State UP, 1999), 7–26.

[73] Weissberg, "Introduction," 12.

[74] Azade Seyhan, *Writing outside the Nation* (Berkeley, CA, Los Angeles, and Oxford: U of California P, 1992), 15. For a historical overview of the concept of "cultural memory" see Weissberg, "Introduction," 12–18.

[75] For a discussion of the anthropological view of "culture," see Adam Kuper, *Culture: The Anthropologists' Account* (Cambridge, MA, and London: Harvard UP, 1999), 98.

[76] See Mitchell, *Gustav Mahler: The Early Years* (Woodbridge, UK: Boydell, 2003), 142–44, for a comparison of Mahler's, Bechstein's, and the Grimms' versions. The following summary is based on the original version of the cantata in three parts.

[77] See Klaus von See, *Barbar, Germane, Arier: Die Suche nach der Identität der Deutschen* (Heidelberg: Universitätsverlag C. Winter, 1994), 97–107, and also *Freiheit und Gemeinschaf*, 29–40 and 93–100.

[78] Von See, *Freiheit und Gemeinschaft*, 112 and 130.

[79] Mosse, *The Image of Man*, 133.

[80] See Mosse, *The Image of Man*, 119–32.

[81] See Mosse, *The Image of Man*, 56–76, for a history of the countermodel to existing ideals of masculinity.

[82] See my essay "The Romantics and Other Cultures," in *The Cambridge Companion to German Romanticism*, ed. Nicholas Saul (Cambridge: Cambridge UP, 2009), 147–61.

Chapter 3

[1] See Raymond Furness: *Zarathustra's Children: A Study of a Lost Generation of German Writers* (Rochester, NY, and Woodbridge, UK: Camden House, 2000), 3; and Steven E. Aschheim, *The Nietzsche Legacy in Germany, 1890–1990* (Berkeley, CA, Los Angeles, and Oxford: California UP, 1992), 18–19.

[2] See Hillebrand, "Einführung," in *Nietzsche und die deutsche Literatur: Texte zur Nietzsche-Rezeption, 1873–1963*, vol. 1 (Tübingen: Niemeyer, 1978), 1–55; here 6; see also Aschheim, *Nietzsche Legacy*, 23.

[3] Aschheim, *Nietzsche Legacy*, 52.

[4] For a comprehensive chronological overview of Nietzsche's impact on Mahler and the many thematic similarities in their thinking, see Eveline Nikkels, "O

Mensch! Gib Acht!" Friedrich Nietzsches Bedeutung für Gustav Mahler (Amsterdam and Atlanta: Rodopi, 1989).

5 William J. McGrath, *Dionysian Art and Populist Politics in Austria* (New Haven, CT, and London: Yale UP, 1974), 53–54.

6 See Manfred Frank, *Der kommende Gott: Vorlesungen über die Neue Mythology* (Frankfurt am Main: Suhrkamp, 1982), 188–89.

7 Frank, *Der kommende Gott*, 197–98.

8 The fact that this statement is also important to Nietzsche is seen in his repetition of it later in his text (*SW* 1:152; *BT*, 113), and also in the new introduction he added in 1886 (*SW* 1:17; *BT*, 8).

9 Frank, *Der kommende Gott*, 194.

10 See Aristotle, *Poetics*, trans. Malcolm Heath (London: Penguin, 1996), 10.

11 It is interesting to note in this context that the Greek god Dionysos had Oriental origins. It should be no surprise, then, that Nietzsche twice characterizes this view of nature as being close to a Buddhist vision of life (*SW* 1:116 and 133; *BT*, 85 and 98). Nietzsche associates Buddhism with a vision of nature that is beyond space, time, and individuality. This Oriental imagery returns in Nietzsche's later works, most prominently in *Also sprach Zarathustra*, and also, for instance, in Mahler's *Lied von der Erde* (see chapter 6).

12 See Stefan Lorenz Sorgner, "Nietzsche," 125–26, in *Musik in der deutschen Philosophie: Eine Einführung*, ed. Stefan Lorenz Sorgner and Oliver Fürbeth (Stuttgart and Weimar: Metzler, 2003), 115–34.

13 See Hillebrand, "Einführung," 1; Jens Malte Fischer, *Gustav Mahler: Der fremde Vertraute* (Vienna: Paul Zsolnay, 2003), 104; and Aschheim, *Nietzsche Legacy*, 32–34.

14 See McGrath, *Dionysian Art and Populist Politics*, 62 and 64; regarding the correspondence between Lipiner and Nietzsche, see 69–71.

15 See Nietzsche, *Briefwechsel: Kritische Gesamtausgabe*, section 2, vol. VI 6/2, ed. Giorgio Colli and Mazzino Montinari (Berlin and New York: de Gruyter, 1980), 737–38. See also William J. McGrath, "Dionysian Art: Crisis and Creativity in Turn-of-the-Century Vienna," in *Nietzsche and the Austrian Culture/Nietzsche und die österreichische Kultur*, ed. Jacob Golomb (Vienna: WUV, 2004), 23–41; here 25; and McGrath, "Mahler and the Vienna Nietzsche Society," in Golomb, *Nietzsche and Jewish Culture* (London and New York: Routledge, 1997), 218–32; here 220.

16 For a detailed reconstruction of the relationship between Nietzsche and Wagner, see Dieter Borchmeyer and Jörg Salaquarda, "Nachwort: Legende und Wirklichkeit einer epochalen Begegnung," in *Nietzsche und Wagner: Stationen einer epochalen Begegnung* (Frankfurt am Main and Leipzig: Insel, 1994), 2:1271–1386.

17 See, for example, Kurt Blaukopf, *Gustav Mahler oder der Zeitgenosse der Zukunft*, 2nd ed. (Vienna, Munich, and Zurich: Fritz Molden, 1969), 142–43; Constantin Floros, *Die geistige Welt Gustav Mahlers in systematischer Darstellung*, 2nd ed. (Wiesbaden: Breitkopf & Härtel, 1987), 70; and Nike Wagner, "Nietzsche komponieren," 278 and 281, in Golomb, *Nietzsche and the Austrian Culture/Nietzsche und die österreichische Kultur*, 271–88.

[18] See Siegfried Lipiner, *Über die Elemente einer Erneuerung religiöser Ideen in der Gegenwart* (Vienna: Selbstverlag des Vorstandes des Lesevereines der deutschen Studenten Wiens, 1878), 2–3. Further references to this work are given in the text using page numbers alone,

[19] Malwina von Meysenbug, *Memoiren einer Idealistin*, vol. 3, 6th ed. (Berlin and Leipzig: Schuster & Loeffler, 1900), 166.

[20] Fischer, *Der fremde Vertraute*, 107.

[21] See Lipiner's letter of 15 Oct. 1877 to Nietzsche (Nietzsche, *Briefwechsel*, 6/2:738–40, esp. 739) and Aldo Venturelli, "Nietzsche in der Berggasse 19: Über die erste Nietzsche-Rezeption in Wien," *Nietzsche-Studien* 13 (1984): 448–80; here 459.

[22] Cosima Wagner, *Die Tagebücher*, ed. Martin Gregor-Dellin and Dietrich Mack (Munich: Piper, 1976, 1977), 2:173 and 179 (10 and 20 Sept. 1878).

[23] Richard Wagner, "Religion und Kunst," in *Sämtliche Schriften und Dichtungen*, Volksausgabe, vol. 10 (Leipzig: Breitkopf & Härtel, [1911]), 211–85; here 211; in English, "Religion and Art," in *Prose Works*, vol. 6, trans. William Ashton Ellis (New York: Broude Brothers, 1966), 211–52; here 213. Parenthetical references to Wagner's essay in the following will refer to these two editions, abbreviated as *RK* and *RA*, respectively. Manfred Frank has called this sentence a "concise summary of early-Romantic ideas about Art-Religion" (gedrängtes Résumé der frühromantischen Ideen zur Kunstreligion). See Manfred Frank, *Gott im Exil: Vorlesungen über die Neue Mythologie*, vol. 2 (Frankfurt am Main: Suhrkamp, 1988), 73.

[24] Goethe, *Maximen und Reflexionen*, in *Werke*, Hamburger Ausgabe in 14 Bänden, ed. Erich Trunz (1948–1952; repr., Munich: Beck, 1982), 12:470–71.

[25] Wagner quotes Schiller's letter of 17 Aug. 1795 to Goethe. See *Briefwechsel zwischen Schiller und Goethe in den Jahren 1794 bis 1805*, vol. 1, ed. Manfred Beetz (Munich: Hanser, 1990), 98 (= vol. 8.1 of *Sämtliche Werke nach Epochen seines Schaffens*, Munich edition, ed. Karl Richter).

[26] Frank, *Gott im Exil*, 65 and 74.

[27] See Willi Goetschel, *Spinoza's Modernity: Mendelssohn, Lessing, and Heine* (Madison: U of Wisconsin P, 2004), 12, 16, 259, 275, and 321, fn. 23.

[28] See Henry-Louis de La Grange, *Mahler*, vol. 1 (Garden City, NJ, and New York: Doubleday, 1973), 781.

[29] See Peter Franklin, "'Funeral Rites': Mahler and Mickiewicz," *Music & Letters* 55.2 (Apr. 1974): 203–8; here 206.

[30] See Stephen E. Hefling, "Mahler's 'Todtenfeier' and the Problem of Program Music," *Nineteenth-Century Music* 12. 1 (Summer 1988): 27–53, for a discussion of these parallels and the link with *Werther* (esp. 29–30), which is also noted in Lipiner's foreword to his translation of Mickiewicz's *Todtenfeier (Dziady)*, in *Poetische Werke*, by Adam Mickiewicz, vol. 2, trans. Siegfried Lipiner (Leipzig: Breitkopf & Härtel, 1887), "Einleitung: Zur Erklärung der 'Todtenfeier,'" xiii, xiv, xviii, and xx.

[31] Jean Paul, *Titan*, in *Werke*, vol. 3, 6th ed., ed. Norbert Miller (Munich and Vienna: Hanser, 1999), 825.

³² Lipiner, "Einleitung," xvii.

³³ Lipiner, "Einleitung," xvii.

³⁴ A very similar summary of the symphony's program can be found in Bauer-Lechner, *GME,* 40 (*RGM,* 43–44).

³⁵ Donald Mitchell, *Gustav Mahler: The Wunderhorn Years* (Woodbridge, UK: Boydell, 2005), 271–72.

³⁶ Hans Heinrich Eggebrecht, *Die Musik Gustav Mahlers,* 2nd ed. (Munich: Piper, 1986), 224.

³⁷ See von Arnim and Brentano, *Des Knaben Wunderhorn: Alte deutsche Lieder,* kritische Ausgabe, ed. Heinz Rölleke, vol. 2 (Stuttgart: Reclam, 1987), 18.

³⁸ See Mitchell, *The Wunderhorn Years,* 183; German original in Gustav Mahler, *GR,* 89. In her edition of Mahler's letters, Alma writes "in our ear" (an unser Ohr), making the song into a defense of a naive form of religion rather than a stage in the development of the symphony's protagonist. Alma Mahler, *Gustav Mahler: Erinnerungen und Briefe* (Amsterdam: Allert de Lange, 1940), 262.

³⁹ Adolf Nowak, "Zur Deutung der Dritten und Vierten Sinfonie Gustav Mahlers," in *Gustav Mahler,* ed. Hermann Danuser (Darmstadt: Wissenschaftliche Buchgesellschaft, 1992), 191–205; here 194.

⁴⁰ Mahler makes a point here about programs, claiming that they lead, not unlike revealed religions, to misunderstandings and simplification. In the scholarship on Mahler's Second Symphony, Edward R. Reilly has picked up on the importance of this reference in Mahler's letter for understanding his concept of religion. Reilly, "Todtenfeier and the Second Symphony," in *The Mahler Companion,* ed. Donald Mitchell and Andrew Nicholson (Oxford and New York: Oxford UP, 1999), 84–125; here 95, and 120–21.

⁴¹ See for instance Jack Tresidder, *The Complete Dictionary of Symbols* (San Francisco: Chronicle Books, 2005), 417–18.

⁴² The editor of Brentano's collected works assumes that the text is based on several *Wunderhorn* songs; see Brentano, *Werke,* ed. Friedhelm Kemp, vol. 2 (Munich: Hanser, 1963), 1198.

⁴³ See Clemens Brentano, *Geschichte vom braven Kasperl und dem schönen Annerl,* in *Werke* 2:774–806; here 779. All parenthetical page references in the following refer to this edition.

⁴⁴ See the score reproduced in Renate Stark-Voit, "'Bild — Symbol — Klang': Zu Gustav Mahlers Wunderhorn-Vertonungen," in *Mahler-Gespräche: Rezeptionsfragen — literarischer Horizont — musikalische Darstellung,* ed. Friedbert Aspetsberger and Erich Wolfgang Partsch (Innsbruck: Studien Verlag, 2002), 118–43; here 131.

⁴⁵ See Stark-Voit, "'Bild — Symbol — Klang,'" 130 and 132.

⁴⁶ See Clemens Brentano, *Das Märchen von Gockel, Hinkel und Gackeleia,* in *Werke,* vol. 3 (Munich: Hanser, 1965), 661, 671, 694, 797, 809, 811, 814–15, 829, 831, 857, 871, 917, 922, and 930; the maxim's origin is explained on 856–57; see also 694.

[47] See Stark-Voit, "'Bild — Symbol — Klang,'" 137. That the seal makers are Jews becomes gradually clear in the text; in an earlier version of the text, not published until 1924, the fairy tales' antagonists are introduced as "three Jewish philosophers of nature" (drei jüdische Naturphilosophen) and later simply called "the three Jews" (die drei Juden). Brentano, *Das Märchen von Gockel und Hinkel*, 484–565; here 504–5.

[48] Martha C. Nussbaum, *Upheavals of Thought: The Intelligence of Emotions* (Cambridge: Cambridge UP, 2001), 628–29.

[49] See Leonard Bernstein, *The Little Drummer Boy: An Essay on Gustav Mahler*. DVD (Hamburg: Deutsche Grammophon, 2007), 56:08–57:14.

[50] See Vladimír Karbusicky, "Gustav Mahler's Musical Jewishness," in *Perspectives on Gustav Mahler*, ed. Jeremy Barham (Aldershot, UK, and Burlington, VT: Ashgate, 2005), 195–216; here 199.

[51] See Gerhard Kaiser, *Aufklärung, Empfindsamkeit, Sturm und Drang*. 3rd ed. (Munich: Francke, 1979), 106–7.

[52] Kaiser, *Aufklärung*, 109.

[53] English translation in Donald Mitchell, *Gustav Mahler: The Wunderhorn Years*, 184 (organization of text modified according to the facsimile reprint of the original document, 179–82, trans. modified). The fact that Mahler's version is critical of biblical accounts is also implied, as Martha Nussbaum argues, by his famous remark in a letter to Arthur Seidl (*Br*, 223) that he went through all of world literature, including the Bible, only to decide in the end to develop his own version of Klopstock's poem (Nussbaum, *Upheavals of Thought: The Intelligence of Emotions*, 615).

[54] Mahler suppresses the "Halleluja" at the end of both stanzas and uses the word "called" (rief) instead of "created" (schuf) to express life's origin. See Friedrich Klopstock, *Sämmtliche Werke* (Leipzig: Göschen, 1840), 540–41.

[55] In *Ecce Homo* Nietzsche describes this as the key thought of *Also sprach Zarathustra* (*SW* 6:335; *AC*, 123); see also *Also sprach Zarathustra* (*SW* 4:275–77; *TSZ*, 177–79).

[56] See William J. McGrath, "Dionysian Art: Crisis and Creativity in Turn-of-the-Century Vienna," 36–37, and also "Mahler and the Vienna Nietzsche Society," 230.

[57] Mahler to Friedrich Löhr, 29 Aug. 1895 (*Br*, 151). By the summer of 1896 Mahler had already abandoned the idea of incorporating "Das himmlische Leben"; he also started to use the subtitle "Ein Sommermittagstraum" (see *Br*, 188 and 196).

[58] Bauer-Lechner transcribes Mahler's letter incorrectly; see the reproduction on page 37 (translation modified).

[59] The link between Mahler's symphony and the "chain of being" was first made by Donald Mitchell in his essay "The Twentieth Century's Debt to Mahler: Our Debt to Him in the Twenty-First," in *Discovering Mahler: Writings on Mahler, 1955–2005* (Woodbridge, UK: Boydell, 2007), 556–96; here 566. For the roots of the idea of a "chain of being" in ancient Greek philosophy, see Arthur O. Lovejoy, *The Great Chain of Being: A Study of the History of an Idea* (New York:

Harper & Row, 1960), 24–66. For its adaptation by Christianity, see the same work, 67–98. This hierarchical view of nature leads Constantin Floros to interpret the symphony from a religious standpoint, even though he admits that the idea of a hierarchy of being can, for instance, be found in Schopenhauer, who was by no means a traditional religious thinker. Floros, *Gustav Mahler: The Symphonies* (Pompton Plains, NJ, and Cambridge: Amadeus, 2000), 88–91, esp. 90,

[60] Lovejoy, *The Great Chain of Being*, 242–87.

[61] See, for instance, Mahler's first remarks, made during the summer of 1895, on the Third Symphony, in *GME*, 35 (*RGM*, 40). See also Franklin, "'Funeral Rites,'" 203–8; here 206.

[62] Mahler, letter to Richard Batka, 18 Nov. 1896 (*Br*, 202–3).

[63] See the lemma "Pan," in *Brill's New Pauly: Encyclopedia of the Ancient World*, vol. 10, ed. Hubert Cancik and Helmuth Schneider (Leiden and Boston: Brill, 2007), 420–22. Pan is often associated with Dionysos (421).

[64] Lipiner, *Über die Elemente*, 11.

[65] According to one of Alma Mahler's footnotes accompanying the 1924 edition of Mahler's letters, Mahler dropped the programmatic title "Die fröhliche Wissenschaft" because audiences might think of Nietzsche's text with the same title (*Br*, 149).

[66] On the role of "chaos" in Nietzsche, see John A. McCarthy, *Remapping Reality: Chaos and Creativity in Science and Literature (Goethe — Nietzsche — Grass)* (Amsterdam and New York: Rodopi, 2006), 159–60 and 252–54.

[67] See Furness, *Zarathustra's Children*, 4.

[68] This is consistent with other ideas that Mahler discusses in relation to the Third Symphony: in a conversation with Natalie Bauer-Lechner about the symphony's first movement Mahler envisioned the movement as the struggle of a young man trying to break away from lifeless nature, as in Hölderlin's poem "Der Rhein" (*GME*, 56; *RGM*, 59 and 200). Mahler refers to the second stanza of the poem. Interestingly, the last two stanzas use the juxtaposition of noon and midnight/day and night; the poem ends with the evocation of night as a time of disorder and uncertainty. See Friedrich Hölderlin, *Gedichte: Sämtliche Werke und Briefe*, vol. 1, ed. Jochen Schmidt (Frankfurt am Main: Deutscher Klassiker Verlag, 1992), 328–34.

[69] See Zarathustra's explanation of the poem: "Have you ever said Yes to one joy? Oh my friends, then you also said Yes to *all* pain. All things are enchained, entwined, enamored —" (Sagtet ihr jemals Ja zu einer Lust? Oh, meine Freunde, so sagtet ihr Ja auch zu *allem* Wehe. Alle Dinge sind verkettet, verfädelt, verliebt, —; *SW* 4:402; *TSZ*, 263).

[70] Arnim and Brentano, *Des Knaben Wunderhorn* 3:80–81.

[71] That the element of play is important for Nietzsche is also clear from another passage in *Zarathustra* (see *SW* 4:85; *TSZ*, 48–49).

[72] See, for instance, Kurt Blaukopf, *Gustav Mahler oder der Zeitgenosse der Zukunft*, 142–43; and Nike Wagner, "Nietzsche komponieren," 282.

[73] Parsifal is the "pure fool" who knows through "compassion" (durch Mitleid wissend / der reine Thor). See *Parsifal*, in *Sämtliche Schriften und Dichtungen*

10:324–75, here 333 and 342; see also 328. Wagner's concept of compassion in *Parsifal* is based on the philosophy of Schopenhauer; see Ulrike Kienzle, "*Parsifal* and Religion: A Christian Music Drama?" 91–93, and 106, in *A Companion to Wagner's Parsifal*, ed. William Kinderman and Katherine R. Syer (Rochester, NY, and Woodbridge, UK: Camden House, 2005), 81–130.

[74] Franklin, *Mahler: Symphony No. 3* (Cambridge: Cambridge UP, 1991), 98–99; see also Mahler's letter to Löhr and a letter of 1 Jul. 1896 to Anna von Mildenburg (*Br*, 151 and 189).

[75] The complete text of the poem is as follows (see Arnim and Brentano, *Des Knaben Wunderhorn* 3:192):

> Erlösung
> Maria
> Mein Kind, sieh an die Brüste mein,
> Kein Sünder laß verloren sein.
> Christus
> Mutter, sieh an die Wunden,
> Die ich für dein Sünd trag alle Stunden.
> Vater, laß dir die Wunden mein
> Ein Opfer für die Sünde sein.
> Vater
> Sohn, lieber Sohn mein,
> Alles was du begehrst, das soll seyn.

[76] Gustav Mahler, *Unbekannte Briefe*, ed. Herta Blaukopf (Vienna and Hamburg: Paul Zsolnay, 1983), 127.

[77] The last words of *Ecce homo* are: "Have I been understood? — *Dionysus versus the crucified*" (Hat man mich verstanden? — *Dionysos gegen den Gekreuzigten*; *SW* 6:374; *AC*, 151). Earlier in the same text he states that "overman" stands in opposition to "Christians and other nihilists" (Christen und andren Nihilisten) (*SW* 6:300; *AC*, 101).

[78] Aschheim, *The Nietzsche Legacy*, 203–5; Furness, *Zarathustra's Children*, 9–10.

[79] Aschheim, *The Nietzsche Legacy*, 247–49; Hillebrand, "Einführung," 13.

[80] Bernard Reginster, *The Affirmation of Life: Nietzsche on Overcoming Nihilism* (Cambridge, MA, and London: Harvard UP, 2006), 251. The potential for ideological abuse made possible by the concept's relatively obscure contours (see Hillebrand, "Einführung," 9 and 12) may have led Nietzsche to abandon the term relatively quickly after introducing it; the term had a "rather brief career in his writings" (Reginster, *Affirmation of Life*, 250).

[81] McCarthy, *Remapping Reality*, 234.

[82] See Aschheim, *The Nietzsche Legacy*, 107–8.

[83] Franklin, *Mahler: Symphony No. 3*, 71.

[84] William McGrath, "Mahler and the Vienna Nietzsche Society," 229.

[85] See John Lippitt, "Nietzsche, Zarathustra and the Status of Laughter," *British Journal of Aesthetics* 32.1 (Jan. 1992): 39–49; here esp. 39–40, and 43.

[86] James L. Zychowicz, *Mahler's Fourth Symphony* (Oxford and New York: Oxford UP, 2000), 47.

[87] Zychowicz, *Mahler's Fourth Symphony*, 37.

[88] See Donald Mitchell, "'Swallowing the Programme': Mahler's Fourth Symphony," in *The Mahler Companion*, 187–216; here 194. Mitchell bases his observation on Adorno, *MP*, 207–8 (*MPE*, 58).

[89] Arnim and Brentano, *Des Knaben Wunderhorn* 1:275–77.

[90] The most comprehensive overview is given by Zychowicz in *Mahler's Fourth Symphony*, 18–25.

[91] For a brief history of the origins of the "Schellenkappe," see Maurice Lever, *Zepter und Schellenkappe: Zur Geschichte des Hofnarren*, trans. Kathrina Menke (Frankfurt am Main: Fischer, 1992), 42–45.

[92] Mahler used this formula to characterize the first movement in the original, 6-movement, design of the Fourth Symphony (see Zychowicz, *Mahler's Fourth Symphony*, 48).

[93] Bruno Walter, letter to Ludwig Schiedermaier, 6 Dec. 1901, in *Briefe, 1894–1962* (Frankfurt am Main: S. Fischer, 1969), 51–52.

[94] Mahler had already noted this (see *GME*, 202; *RGM*, 183).

[95] See Constantin Floros, *Gustav Mahler: The Symphonies*, 117–18; Zychowicz, *Mahler's Fourth Symphony*, 12–13.

[96] Zychowicz, *Mahler's Fourth Symphony*, 55. See also Mitchell, "Swallowing the Programme," 206.

[97] This would be my answer to Donald Mitchell's rhetorical question asking whether the movement demonstrates the impossibility of a return to the "simplicities" of the past ("Swallowing the Programme," 204).

[98] Walter, *Briefe*, 52. The "Grim Reaper" has, of course, a very different cultural iconographic archaeology from "Freund Hein," but is the closest equivalent to that figure in the Anglo-American tradition. For a discussion of the figure of "Freund Hein" in German cultural history and in relation to Mahler's symphony, see Raymond Knapp, "Perspectives on Innocence and Vulnerability in Mahler's Fourth Symphony," *Nineteenth-Century Music* 22.3 (1999): 233–67; here 256–57.

[99] The reference to Holbein in Mengelberg's score is reported by Henry-Louis de La Grange, *Gustav Mahler*, vol. 2: *Vienna: The Years of Challenge (1897–1904)* (Oxford and New York: Oxford UP, 1995), 764. Knapp discusses Mahler's visual sources for the scherzo in great detail (252–56), and he also shows that one of Holbein's woodcuts portrays death as a fiddler.

[100] Mitchell, "Swallowing the Programme," 215.

[101] See Jonathan Carr, *Mahler: A Biography* (Woodstock, NY, and New York: Overlook, 1998), 12; and Jens Malter Fischer, *Der fremde Vertraute*, 34.

[102] Walter, *Briefe*, 52.

[103] The English version of Bauer-Lechner's memoirs translates "Heiterkeit" as "serenity"; while this is a possible translation of "Heiterkeit," it constructs, in my view, a narrative for the Fourth Symphony very different from the one

Mahler envisions in his many documented statements, which consistently mention "humor" as its main component.

[104] Donald Mitchell, "Swallowing the Programme," 216; see also 214.

[105] See Mitchell, "Swallowing the Programme," 208–9, and 216.

[106] See Arnim and Brentano, *Des Knaben Wunderhorn* 1:276–77; in addition to suppressing four verses, Mahler consolidated the third and fourth stanzas into one new and longer stanza.

[107] Zychowicz, *Mahler's Fourth Symphony*, 48.

[108] See for example, Peter Singer, "Preface," in *Animal Philosophy: Essential Readings in Continental Thought*, ed. Peter Atterton and Matthew Calarco (London and New York: Continuum, 2004), xi, xii; here xi.

[109] See von Arnim and Brentano, *Des Knaben Wunderhorn*, vol. 1, commentary 304.

[110] See the lemma on "St. Ursula and the Eleven Thousand Virgins," in the *Catholic Encyclopedia* (http://www.newadvent.org/cathen/15225d.htm).

[111] See Adolf Nowak, "Zur Deutung der Dritten und Vierten Sinfonie Gustav Mahlers," 202; see also Stephen E. Hefling, "Techniques of Irony in Mahler's Oeuvre," in *Gustav Mahler et l'ironie dans la culture viennoise au tournant du siècle*, ed. André Castagné, Michel Chalon, and Patrick Florençon (Montpellier, France: Climats, 2001), 99–142; here 113–17. In my own essay "Mahler contra Wagner: The Philosophical Legacy of Romanticism in Mahler's Third and Fourth Symphonies," *German Quarterly* 77.2 (2004): 189–210, esp. 201, I support such a reading and also point to the early-Romantic discussions of the concept of irony. In the following, I will develop Jean Paul's understanding of "humor" as an alternative paradigm to understand this movement's ambiguities.

[112] Jean Paul, *Vorschule der Ästhetik*, in *Werke*, vol. 5 (Munich: Carl Hanser, 1963), 9–456; here 148.

[113] See de La Grange, *The Years of Challenge*, 310.

[114] See *Symphonie Nr. 4, Kritische Ausgabe*, ed. International Gustav Mahler Society (London: Universal Edition, 1963), [score] 102; see also Zychowicz, *Mahler's Fourth Symphony*, 150.

[115] Jean Paul, *Vorschule der Ästhetik*, 129. Jean Paul here seeks to illustrate his claim that humor is the "reversed sublime" (das umgekehrte Erhabene; *Vorschule der Ästhetik*, 125).

[116] Simon Critchley points out that there is a long tradition of understanding humor as a form of incongruity that includes, among others, Hutcheson, Kant, Schopenhauer, and Kierkegaard. Critchley, *On Humour* (London and New York: Routledge, 2002), 3.

[117] Critchley, *On Humour*, 5.

[118] Jean Paul, *Vorschule der Ästhetik*, 139–40. See also Critchley, *On Humour*, 41–52.

[119] See Jean Paul's ideas about humor as an "annihilating" (vernichtende) force (*Vorschule der Ästhetik*, 129).

[120] See Adolf Nowak, "Zur Deutung der Dritten und Vierten Sinfonie Gustav Mahlers," 204, 205.

[121] See Sigmund Freud, *Die Traumdeutung*, 127–38, in *Gesammelte Werke*, vol. 2/3, ed. Anna Freud (Frankfurt am Main: Fischer, 1999). Mahler would not necessarily have to have read *Die Traumdeutung* in order to be aware of these ideas; someone in his environment may well have discussed the book with him. Mahler's awareness of Freud's work, would explain why in the summer of 1910, when he was analyzed by Freud during a walk in Leyden, he exhibited an "intuitive understanding" of Freud's ideas. Mary Bonaparte, quoting Freud in her unpublished diaries; reprinted in Stuart Feder, *Gustav Mahler: A Life in Crisis* (New Haven and London: Yale UP, 2004), 229.

[122] See Freud, "Der Dichter und das Phantasieren," in *Gesammelte Werke* 7:213–23.

[123] Oskar Kokoschka, *Die träumenden Knaben und Der weiße Tiertöter* (Frankfurt am Main and Leipzig: Insel, 1998), 25. See Mitchell, "The Twentieth Century's Debt," 561–62, for a discussion on Mahler's innovative use of percussion instruments.

[124] See Peter Vergo, *Art in Vienna, 1898–1918: Klimt, Kokoschka, Schiele and Their Contemporaries* (London and New York: Phaidon, 2001), 190.

[125] Kokoschka, *Die träumenden Knaben*, 9.

[126] Vergo, *Art in Vienna*, 190.

[127] Kokoschka, *Die träumenden Knaben*, 9.

[128] For a discussion of the biographical circumstances under which Kokoschka produced *Die träumenden Knaben*, see Heinz Spielmann, *Oskar Kokoschka: Leben und Werk* (Cologne: Dumont, 2003), 38–45.

[129] Bruno Walter, *Gustav Mahler: Ein Porträt* (Berlin and Frankfurt am Main: S. Fischer, 1957), 102; in English, *Gustav Mahler: With a Biographical Essay by Ernst Křenek*, trans. James Galston (New York: Greystone, 1941), 136–37.

[130] Alma Mahler, *Erinnerungen und Briefe*, 28.

[131] Nikkels, *"O Mensch! Gib Acht!"* 101.

[132] A typical statement in this respect can, for instance, be found in Mahler's letter of 14 Dec. 1901 to Alma: "That I will love about you forever: that you are so *real* and *simple*" (Das ist mir so ewig lieb an Dir, daß Du so *echt*, so *schlicht* bist; GR, 92).

[133] Walter, *Ein Porträt*, 101 (quote), and also 102; *Gustav Mahler: With a Biographical Essay*, 135–36, trans. modified.

[134] Aschheim mentions the year 1890 as a turning point (see, for instance, *Nietzsche Legacy*, 1, 11, 13, and 18). Before him, Bruno Hillebrand had noted the same phenomenon ("Einführung," 1).

[135] Aschheim, *Nietzsche Legacy*, 33, 36.

[136] See for instance Elisabeth Förster-Nietzsche, *Das Leben Friedrich Nietzsche's*, vol. 2.1 (Leipzig: C. G. Naumann, 1897), 268–69, 309, and 322–23. If one reads Wagner's essay "Publikum und Popularität" (Public and Popularity) of 1878 as

his (only) public response to the break with Nietzsche, even though the latter is not mentioned by name, then Wagner too believed that Nietzsche's break had something to with his own popularity. Wagner's defense is that he never aimed for this, that Bayreuth rather was designed to break with the normal dynamics of the opera world, but that no artist can ultimately prevent his own popularity. See "Publikum und Popularität," in *Sämtliche Schriften und Dichtungen*, vol. 10 (Leipzig: Breitkopf & Härtel, 1911), 61–90; here 63–64 and 77–78.

[137] An earlier version of this statement (minus the first two sentences, i.e. the statement on Wagner's anti-Semitism) can be found in the second volume of *Menschliches, Allzumenschliches*, in *Sämtliche Werke: Kritische Studienausgabe*, ed. Giorgio Colli and Mazzino Montinari (Munich: DTV; Berlin: de Gruyter, 1999), 2: 372; in English, *Human, All Too Human: A Book for Free Spirits*, trans. R. J. Hollingdale (Cambridge: Cambridge UP, 2002), 210–11 — the first text in which Nietzsche clearly distanced himself from Wagner.

[138] Sander L. Gilman, "Heine, Nietzsche, and the Idea of the Jew," in Golomb, *Nietzsche and Jewish Culture*, 76–100; here 79.

[139] For a reconstruction of the turn-of-the-century debate on Wagner's anti-Semitism, see Leon Botstein "German Jews and Wagner," in *Richard Wagner and His World*, ed. Thomas S. Grey (Princeton, NJ, and Oxford: Princeton UP, 2009), 151–97; here 162–78. For an overview of the reception of Wagner's anti-Semitic essay, see Jens Malte Fischer's excellent book *Richard Wagners "Das Judentum in der Musik"* (Frankfurt am Main and Leipzig: Insel, 2000), esp. 121–33; an overview of the essay's different editions can also be found there (134–35). The *Jubiläumsausgabe* of Wagner's *Dichtungen und Schriften* (Frankfurt am Main: Insel, 1983), edited by Dieter Borchmeyer, is the first edition to leave the essay out.

[140] See Elisabeth Förster-Nietzsche, *Das Leben Friedrich Nietzsche's*, 2.1:208, 232, 307, and 322. This is remarkable, because Nietzsche's criticism of Wagner's anti-Semitism does not fit the patriotic and nationalist images of Nietzsche that Förster-Nietzsche had sought to create of her brother (see Aschheim, *Nietzsche Legacy*, 47, 118, and 120).

[141] See, for instance, the final line of the "Foreword": "An intelligent people can only ever enter into a *mésalliance* with the 'Reich' . . ." (Mit dem "Reich" macht ein intelligentes Volk immer nur eine mésalliance . . .) *Sämtliche Werke: Kritische Studienausgabe* 6:415; *AC*, 265.

[142] "The Jewish musician mixes up the different forms and styles of all masters and all times" (der jüdische Musiker wirft . . . die verschiedenen Formen und Stilarten aller Meister und Zeiten durch einander). Richard Wagner, "Das Judentum in der Musik," in Jens Malte Fischer, *Richard Wagners "Das Judentum in der Musik,"* 141–96; here 161.

[143] Jean Paul, *Vorschule der Ästhetik*, for example, 104, 125, 127, and 132.

[144] Judith Norman, "Nietzsche and Early Romanticism," *Journal of the History of Ideas* 63.3 (2002): 501–19; here 502. Regarding Nietzsche's affinity for early Romantic thinking, see also Ernst Behler, "Nietzsche und die frühromantische Schule," *Nietzsche-Studien: Internationales Jahrbuch für die Nietzsche-Forschung* 7 (1978): 59–96, especially 65 and 69, and Rüdiger Görner, "'[. . .] das letzte grosse Ereigniss im Schicksal unserer Cultur' Oder: Nietzsche 'liest' die Romantik," in

Die Lesbarkeit der Romantik: Material, Medium, Diskurs, ed. Erich Kleinschmidt (Berlin: De Gruyter, 2009), 83–102; here 100–101.

[145] On the increasing role of anti-Semitism in Romanticism, see my essay "The Romantics and Other Cultures," in *The Cambridge Companion to German Romanticism*, ed. Nicholas Saul (Cambridge: Cambridge UP, 2009), 147–61.

[146] Dieter Borchmeyer and Jörg Salaquarda argue that Nietzsche was intellectually more indebted to Wagner's thinking than is generally assumed; see their "Nachwort: Legende und Wirklichkeit einer epochalen Begegnung," 1274, 1288, 1296, and 1298–99, in *Nietzsche und Wagner: Stationen einer epochalen Begegnung*, vol. 2 (Frankfurt am Main and Leipzig: Insel, 1994), 1271–1386. They also claim that Nietzsche's break with Wagner was never entirely wholehearted (see, for instance, 1275, 1344, 1353, 1377, and 1383). While Borchmeyer and Salaquarda do allude to the role of Wagner's anti-Semitism in Nietzsche's estrangement from Wagner (see 1287, 1310, 1328–29, 1330–32, and 1365), the aspect of Wagner's new political affiliations is categorically downplayed (instead, both authors seem to be convinced that purely personal dynamics played a decisive role in Nietzsche's break with Wagner).

[147] Ernst Decsey, "Stunden mit Mahler: Notizen," *Die Musik* 10.18 (1910/11): 352–56 (Gustav Mahler-Heft); here 354.

[148] See, for example, a passage on Wagner's *Tristan* in *Ecce homo* (*SW* 6:289–90; *AC*, 93–94).

[149] Patrick Carnegy, *Wagner and the Art of the Theatre* (New Haven, CT, and London: Yale UP, 2006), 164–65; see also David Levin, *Unsettling Opera: Staging Mozart, Verdi, Wagner, and Zemlinsky* (Chicago and London: U of Chicago P, 2007), 44, and Charles S. Maier, "Mahler's Theater: The Performative and the Political in Central Europe, 1890–1910," in *Mahler and His World*, ed. Karen Painter (Princeton, NJ, and London: Princeton UP, 2002), 55–85; here 69–75.

[150] One example is Richard Dehmel, whom Mahler knew superficially (see Hillebrand, *Nietzsche und die deutsche Literatur*, 1:15–16, and 136).

[151] See Richard Wagner, "Autobiographische Skizze (bis 1842)," in *Sämtliche Schriften und Dichtungen*, 1:4–19; here 15.

[152] Ernst Křenek, "Gustav Mahler," in Walter, *Gustav Mahler: With a Biographical Essay by Ernst Křenek*, 198. It would, however, be wrong to read a progressive political agenda into Křenek's statement; Křenek was a supporter of the austrofascist "Ständestaat" (1934–38); see Gerhard Scheit and Wilhelm Svoboda: *Feindbild Gustav Mahler: Zur antisemitischen Abwehr der Moderne in Österreich* (Vienna: Sonderzahl, 2002), 92 and 96. Ironically, the "Ständestaat" was a period characterized by increased interest in Mahler's music in the context of Austrian history.

Chapter 4

[1] See Alma Mahler, *Erinnerungen und Briefe* (Amsterdam: Allert de Lange, 1940), 113. In English, *Gustav Mahler: Memories and Letters*, rev. ed., ed. Donald Mitchell (New York: Viking, 1969), 89.

² Bruno Walter, *Gustav Mahler: Ein Porträt* (Berlin and Frankfurt am Main: S. Fischer, 1957), 92. In English, *Gustav Mahler: With a Biographical Essay by Ernst Křenek*, trans. James Galston (New York: Greystone, 1941), 121.

³ This is reported in Donald Mitchell, "Mahler on the Move: His Seventh Symphony," in *Discovering Mahler: Writings on Mahler, 1955—2005* (Woodbridge: Boydell, 2007) 394–410; here 406.

⁴ See, for example, Peter Davison, "Nachtmusik I: Sound and Symbol," 69 and 71, in *The Seventh Symphony of Gustav Mahler: A Symposium*, ed. James L. Zychowicz (Cincinnati: U. of Cincinnati College-Conservatory of Music, 1990), 68–73.

⁵ The essay can be found in Robert A. Kann, ed., *Theodor Gomperz: Ein Gelehrtenleben im Bürgertum der Franz-Josefs-Zeit* (Vienna: Verlag der österreichischen Akademie der Wissenschaften, 1974), 384–89. Gomperz published frequently in prominent newspapers and scholarly journals; his essay gives the impression of having been written for such a publication, but it is not clear whether it was published during his lifetime. On Gomperz's essay, see also Steven Beller, *Vienna and the Jews, 1867–1938: A Cultural History* (Cambridge: Cambridge UP, 1989), 210.

⁶ Michael Brenner, "Pre-Weimar Origins," in *The Renaissance of Jewish Culture in Weimar Germany* (New Haven, CT, and London: Yale UP, 1996), 11–35; here 30. George Mosse remarks that Jews are seen as being "devoid of spirituality and feeling" in nineteenth-century Germany. Mosse, *Germans and Jews: The Right, the Left, and the Search for a "Third Force" in Pre-Nazi Germany* (New York: Howard Fertig, 1970), 35.

⁷ Brenner, "Pre-Weimar Origins," 29.

⁸ The questions Gomperz raises may have been triggered by Otto Weininger's notorious text *Geschlecht und Charakter: Eine prinzipielle Untersuchung* (Sex and Character: An Investigation of Fundamental Principles), first published in 1903 — the year before Gomperz wrote his essay. Weininger, who was Jewish himself, indeed asks why the Jews have not been able to produce great men; like Gomperz, he sees Spinoza as one of the few exceptions. See Weininger, *Geschlecht und Charakter: Eine prinzipielle Untersuchung*, 9th ed. (Vienna and Leipzig: Wilhelm Braumüller, 1907), 430.

⁹ Karen Painter, "Contested Counterpoint: 'Jewish' Appropriation and Polyphonic Liberation," *Archiv für Musikwissenschaft* 58.3 (2001): 201–30; here 207.

¹⁰ Jens Malte Fischer, *Gustav Mahler: Der fremde Vertraute* (Vienna: Paul Zsolnay, 2003), 604.

¹¹ Frits Zwart, *Willem Mengelberg, 1871–1951: Een biografie, 1871–1920*, vol. 1 (Amsterdam: Prometheus, 1999), 205.

¹² See also Jens Malte Fischer, *Der fremde Vertraute*, 603.

¹³ The following is based on Eduard Reeser, *Alphons Diepenbrock* (Amsterdam: Bigot and van Rossum, [1936]), 21–38, and *De muzikale handschriften van Alphons Diepenbrock* (Amsterdam: G. Alsbach, 1933).

¹⁴ See J. van der Veen, "Diepenbrock, Alphonsus Joannes Maria (1862–1921)," in *Biografisch Woordenboek van Nederland*, vol. 1 (The Hague 1979); http://www.inghist.nl/Onderzoek/Projecten/BWN/lemmata/bwn1/diepenbrock (accessed 17 Jun. 2008).

[15] Diepenbrock, "Schemeringen," *De Nieuwe Gids* 8.2 (1893): 449–64; here 449.

[16] Zwart, *Willem Mengelberg*, 196–97.

[17] The following summary is based on Nietzsche, "Im grossen Schweigen," in *Morgenröthe*, in *Sämtliche Werke: Kritische Studienausgabe*, ed. Giorgio Colli and Mazzino Montinari (Munich: DTV; Berlin: de Gruyter, 1980–99), 3:259–60; in English, in *Daybreak: Thoughts on the Prejudices of Morality* (Cambridge: Cambridge UP, 2003), 181.

[18] "In Genoa at the time of evening twilight I heard coming from a tower a long peal of bells. It seemed it would never stop, resounding as though it could never have enough of itself over the noise of the streets out into the evening sky and the sea breeze, so chilling and at the same time so childlike, so melancholy. Then I recalled the words of Plato and suddenly they spoke to my heart: nothing human is worthy of being taken very seriously; nonetheless." (In Genua hörte ich zur Zeit der Abenddämmerung von einem Thurme her ein langes Glockenspiel. Das wollte nicht enden und klang, wie unersättlich aus sich selber, über das Geräusch der Gassen in den Abendhimmel und die Meerluft hinaus, so schauerlich, so kindisch zugleich, so wehmuthsvoll. Da gedachte ich der Worte Platons und fühlte sie auf einmal im Herzen: alles Menschliche insgesamt ist des grossen Ernstes nicht werth; trotzdem.) Nietzsche, *Menschliches, Allzumenschliches*, 2:354; in English: *Human, All Too Human: A Book for Free Spirits* (Cambridge: Cambridge UP, 2002), 198. See also Reeser, *De muzikale handschriften van Alphons Diepenbrock*, 24–25.

[19] Diepenbrock, letter to Johanna Jongkindt, 17 Oct. 1909, quoted in Reeser, *Gustav Mahler und Holland: Briefe* (Vienna: Universal Edition, 1980), 31.

[20] Mahler, letter of 8 Jun. 1910 to Alma (no. 303). *GR*, 423–25; here 424.

[21] Henry-Louis de La Grange, *Gustav Mahler*, vol 3: *Vienna: Triumph and Disillusion (1904–1907)* (Oxford and New York: Oxford UP, 1999), 854–55.

[22] Regarding the extent to which the first movement can be interpreted within traditional notions of structure, see John G. Williamson, "Mahler and Episodic Structure: The First Movement of the Seventh Symphony," in Zychowicz, *The Seventh Symphony of Gustav Mahler*, 27–46; here 36.

[23] De La Grange, *Vienna: Triumph and Disillusion*, 852.

[24] See Diepenbrock to Jongkindt, in Reeser, *Gustav Mahler und Holland*, 31–32.

[25] Robert Musil, *Tagebücher*, vol. 1, ed. Adolf Frisé (Reinbek bei Hamburg: Rowohlt, 1983), 386.

[26] Herta Blaukopf, "Mahler an der Universität: Versuch, eine biographische Lücke zu schließen," in *Neue Mahleriana: Essays in Honour of Henry-Louis de La Grange on His Seventieth Birthday*, ed. Günther Weiß (Bern: Peter Lang, 1997), 1–16; here 5.

[27] Paul Nathorp, "Vorwort," in *Adam. Ein Vorspiel. Hyppolytos. Tragödie*, by Siegfried Lipiner (Stuttgart: W. Spemann, 1913), 3–13; here 7.

[28] See Pauline Micheels, "Gustav Mahler in Amsterdam (1903–1909)," in *Mahler in Amsterdam van Mengelberg tot Chailly*, ed. Johan Giskes and Ester L. Woudhuysen (Bussum and Amsterdam: THOTH/Gemeentearchief Amsterdam, 1995), 24–36; here 25.

[29] On the history of Amsterdam's Jewish neighborhood and the Breestraat, where Rembrandt's house was situated, see Steven Nadler, *Rembrandt's Jews* (Chicago and London: Chicago UP, 2003), 14–16. Regarding the history of Rembrandt's image as a philo-Semite, see 44–57.

[30] Diary of H. de Booy, quoted in Micheels, *Mahler in Amsterdam*, 32 (German spelling corrected).

[31] Simon Schama, *Rembrandt's Eyes* (New York: Knopf, 1999), 487–89.

[32] Diepenbrock, letter to Jongkindt, in Reeser, *Gustav Mahler und Holland: Briefe*, 32.

[33] Simon Schama, *Rembrandt's Eyes*, 481–82.

[34] See A. Roger Ekirch, *At Day's Close: Night in Times Past* (New York and London: W. W. Norton, 2005), 81–82.

[35] Cf. Fritz Stern, *The Politics of Cultural Despair: A Study in the Rise of the Germanic Ideology* (Garden City, NJ: Doubleday, 1965), 199. For a discussion of the immense impact of Langbehn's book, see Stern, *Cultural Despair*, 197–227. In the following I will quote the fortieth edition: Julius Langbehn, *Rembrandt als Erzieher: Von einem Deutschen* (Leipzig: C. L. Hirschfeld, 1892).

[36] Stern, *Cultural Despair*, 200.

[37] During the winter of 1889–90 Langbehn acted as Nietzsche's guardian after his collapse (Stern, *Cultural Despair*, 143).

[38] Stern, *Cultural Despair*, 146.

[39] See Bernd Behrendt, "August Julius Langbehn, der 'Rembrandtdeutsche,'" in *Handbuch zur "Völkischen Bewegung," 1871–1918*, ed. Uwe Puschner, Walter Schmitz, and Julius H. Ulbricht (Munich: K. G. Saur, 1996), 94–113; here 99.

[40] See Peter Ulrich Hein's thesis that Langbehn (at least initially) goes to some lengths in his text to avoid alienating his Jewish readers. Hein, *Transformation der Kunst: Ziele und Wirkungen der deutschen Kultur- und Kunsterziehungsbewegung* (Cologne and Vienna: Böhlau, 1991), 66.

[41] Langbehn, *Rembrandt als Erzieher*, 43. For Michael Brenner, this passage shows that Jews have come to represent the "antithesis of the neo-Romantic ideals of the time" (Brenner, "Pre-Weimar Origins," 30).

[42] The following references are taken from Langbehn, *Rembrandt als Erzieher*, 52–54.

[43] "Rembrandt and Spinoza resituated . . ., in opposition to tradition, the center of their artistic and secular outlook into the individual and the world themselves" (Rembrandt und Spinoza verlegten, . . . der Tradition entgegen, den Schwerpunkt der künstlerischen und weltlichen Anschauung in das Individuum und die Welt selbst; *Rembrandt als Erzieher*, 53).

[44] See Klaus L. Berghahn, *Grenzen der Toleranz: Juden und Christen im Zeitalter der Aufklärung* (Cologne: Böhlau, 2000), 195–205.

[45] See Peter Pulzer, "The Return of the Old Hatreds," in *Integration in Dispute*, ed. Michael A. Meyer, vol. 3 of *German-Jewish History in Modern Times*, ed. Michael A. Meyer (New York: Columbia UP, 1997), 196–251; here 241. For Pulzer, Langbehn plays a key role in the resurgence of political anti-Semitism in the 1890s.

⁴⁶ See Mitchell, "Mahler's 'Kammermusikton,'" in *The Mahler Companion*, ed. Mitchell and Andrew Nicholson (Oxford and New York: Oxford UP, 1999), 217–35; here 226–31.

⁴⁷ Mahler, letter to Richard Strauss, May 1905; Gustav Mahler and Richard Strauss, *Briefwechsel, 1888–1911*, ed. Herta Blaukopf (Munich and Zurich: R. Piper, 1980), 95; see also Mitchell, "Mahler's 'Kammermusikton,'" 231.

⁴⁸ Langbehn, *Rembrandt als Erzieher*, 22–23, quote 22. The following quotes in the text are, unless otherwise indicated, from the section "Musikalisches" (Musical Matters), 22–23. Langbehn emphasizes the importance of this observation by returning to it much later in his book.

⁴⁹ The following quotes are taken from Langbehn, *Rembrandt als Erzieher*, 276–78, unless otherwise indicated.

⁵⁰ See James Zychowicz, "Ein schlechter Jasager: Considerations on the Finale to Mahler's Seventh Symphony," in Zychowicz, *The Seventh Symphony of Gustav Mahler*, 98–106; here 98.

⁵¹ Diepenbrock, letter to Johanna Jongkindt. Reeser, *Gustav Mahler und Holland*, 32.

⁵² Diepenbrock, letter to Jongkindt. Reeser, *Gustav Mahler und Holland*, 31.

⁵³ Peter Revers, "The Seventh Symphony," in Mitchell and Nicholson, *The Mahler Companion*, 377.

⁵⁴ See de La Grange, *Triumph and Disillusion*, 881; see also Zychowicz, *The Seventh Symphony*, 102.

⁵⁵ De La Grange, *Triumph and Disillusion*, 877–78; Zychowicz, *The Seventh Symphony*, 103.

⁵⁶ Revers, "The Seventh Symphony," 377; see also Adorno, *MP*, 281; *MPE*, 137.

⁵⁷ See Mahler's statement, quoted in Josefine von Kralik's diary: "Don't many people do useless things? Play tarot; perform the 'Merry Widow'!" (Thun die Leute nicht auch viel, was unnütz ist? Tarock spielen; die "lustige Witwe" aufführen!; diary entry quoted in *GR*, 426). Mahler, however, appears to have enjoyed a performance of *Die lustige Witwe* that took place during the winter when he was revising his Seventh Symphony (de La Grange, *Triumph and Disillusion*, 473–74).

⁵⁸ See Marc Weiner, *Richard Wagner and the Anti-Semitic Imagination*, 2nd ed. (Lincoln, NE, and London: Nebraska UP, 1997), 117–22. Since Mahler was well aware of the Jewish traits of Mime (see the introduction in this volume) in the *Ring des Nibelungen*, the Jewish character of Beckmesser in the *Meistersinger* will not have escaped him.

Chapter 5

¹ Richard Specht, *Gustav Mahlers VIII. Symphonie: Thematische Analyse* (Leipzig: Universal-Edition, 1912), 6; see also Specht, *Gustav Mahler*, 5th–8th ed. (Berlin: Schuster & Loeffler, [1918]), 252.

[2] Engelbert Pernerstorfer and Victor Adler, for instance, became prominent leaders of the Social-Democratic Party; see McGrath, *Dionysian Art and Populist Politics in Austria* (New Haven: Yale UP, 1974), chapters 7 and 8 (182–237). Georg von Schönerer, in contrast, became a leader of the conservative, nationalist, and increasingly anti-Semitic pan-Germanic movement (165–66). There are indications that Mahler and Adler later in life felt affinity for each others' goals (243–245). A preference for German over Austrian culture is quite typical in Vienna's educated, cosmopolitan Jewish families, as Steven Beller has shown in *Vienna and the Jews, 1867–1938: A Cultural History* (Cambridge: Cambridge UP, 1989), 144.

[3] See for instance Esteban Buch's recent reconstruction of this tradition in *Beethoven's Ninth: A Political History* (Chicago: U of Chicago P, 2003), esp. chapters 1 and 2 (11–44).

[4] Within the Pernerstorfer Circle, however, some members were more interested in aesthetics and others more in politics (McGrath, *Dionysian Art*, 87–99 and also 246; see also chapter 3 in this volume). Membership in the Circle did not necessarily mean, in other words, a whole-hearted subscription to a nationalistic and conservative political philosophy, even though this was paradoxically an important part of the group's identity.

[5] Wolfgang Menzel, *Die deutsche Literatur*, vol. 2 (Stuttgart: Franckh, 1828), 209 and 214–216. Further references to this work will be given in the text using page numbers alone. For a detailed discussion of Menzel's text and its impact on nineteenth-century thinking, see Jeffrey L. Sammons, "Schiller vs. Goethe: Revisiting the Conflicting Reception Vectors of Heinrich Heine, Ludwig Börne, and Wolfgang Menzel," *Goethe Yearbook* 13 (2005): 1–17.

[6] See Karl Robert Mandelkow, *Goethe in Deutschland: Rezeptionsgeschichte eines Klassikers*, vol. 1: *1773–1918* (Munich: C. H. Beck, 1980), 134.

[7] Mandelkow, *Goethe in Deutschland* 1:135.

[8] Among them Börne and Heine, as Sammons has shown; Heine was one of the first intellectuals to problematize his contemporaries' preference for Schiller over Goethe. See Sammons, "Schiller vs. Goethe," 6–7 and 9.

[9] See Hans Joachim Kreutzer, *Faust: Mythos und Musik* (Munich: Beck, 2003) for a comprehensive overview of musical adaptations based on *Faust*.

[10] See Hans Schwerte [= Hans Schneider], *Faust und das Faustische: Ein Kapitel deutscher Ideologie* (Stuttgart: Ernst Klett, 1962), chap. 5 (94–147); quote from 119.

[11] Schwerte, *Faust und das Faustische*, 161–62; Mandelkow, *Goethe in Deutschland*, 1:229 and 253.

[12] The following summary of a nationalistic interpretation of *Faust* is based on texts by the famous and very influential literary scholar Heinrich Düntzer and by August Spieß. See Schwerte, *Faust und das Faustische*, 76 and 105.

[13] Schwerte, *Faust und das Faustische*, 167.

[14] Schwerte, *Faust und das Faustische*, 103; Mandelkow, *Goethe in Deutschland* 1:245.

[15] Mandelkow, *Goethe in Deutschland* 1:245.

[16] For more information on Gustav von Loeper's biography and his Goethe editions, see Schwerte, *Faust und das Faustische,* 149.

[17] The following is based on the "Vorbemerkung des Herausgebers," in *Faust: Eine Tragödie,* by Goethe, ed. Gustav von Loeper (Berlin: Gustav Hempel, 1870), xxx. See also Schwerte, *Faust und das Faustische,* 150–51.

[18] See Schwerte, *Faust und das Faustische,* 117, 191, 193, and 196.

[19] See Heinrich Heine, *Die romantische Schule,* in *Sämtliche Schriften,* vol. 3 (Munich: DTV, 2005), 357–504; here 400–402. See also Schwerte, *Faust und das Faustische,* 54–55, and Mandelkow, *Goethe in Deutschland* 1:242. Heine's ambivalent attitude toward Goethe is discussed in Wilfried Barner, *Von Rahel Varnhagen bis Friedrich Gundolf: Juden als deutsche Goethe-Verehrer* (Göttingen: Wallstein, 1992), 14 and 16.

[20] Nietzsche, *Nachgelassene Fragmente, 1887–1889,* in *Sämtliche Werke: Kritische Studienausgabe,* ed. Giorgio Colli and Mazzino Montinari (Munich: DTV; Berlin: de Gruyter, 1980–99), 13:411.

[21] Richard Wagner, "Beethoven," in *Sämtliche Schriften und Dichtungen,* Volksausgabe, vol. 9 (Leipzig: Breitkopf & Härtel, [1911]), 61–127; here 66. The idea that Goethe, in contrast to Schiller, was unsuccessful as a dramatist, in particular also in *Faust,* can also be found in the work of Hans Pfitzner, "Der zweite Teil Faust ist ganz und gar Lesedrama," in *Werk und Wiedergabe,* in *Gesammelte Schriften,* vol. 3 (Augsburg: Dr. Benno Filser Verlag, 1929), 115–19; here 118).

[22] Nietzsche, *Der Fall Wagner: Ein Musikanten-Problem,* in *Kritische Studienausgabe* 6:9–54; here 18; *AC,* 238.

[23] See Barner, *Von Rahel Varnhagen bis Friedrich Gundolf,* 12; see also Barbara Hahn, "Demarcations and Projections: Goethe in the Berlin Salons," in *Goethe in German-Jewish Culture,* ed. Klaus L. Berghahn and Jost Hermand (Columbia SC: Camden House, 2001), 31–43.

[24] See, for instance, Nietzsche, *Nachgelassene Fragmente, 1884–1885,* in *Kritische Studienausgabe* 11:472; and Nietzsche, *Nachgelassene Fragmente, 1885–1887,* in *Kritische Studienausgabe* 12:90.

[25] See Barner, *Von Rahel Varnhagen bis Friedrich Gundolf,* 30–33. Among them was Albert Bielschowsky, whose Goethe biography Mahler knew; see Herta Blaukopf, "Bücher fresse ich immer mehr und mehr": Gustav Mahler als Leser," in *Mahler-Gespräche: Rezeptionsfragen — literarischer Horizont — musikalische Darstellung,* ed. Friedbert Aspetsberger and Erich Wolfgang Partsch (Innsbruck: Studien Verlag, 2002), 96–116; here 102.

[26] George L. Mosse, *German Jews beyond Judaism* (Cincinnati, OH: Hebrew Union College P, 1997), 44.

[27] For a critical discussion of the place of Goethe in German-Jewish culture see Erhard Bahr, "Goethe and the Concept of Bildung in Jewish Emancipation," in Berghahn and Hermand, *Goethe in German-Jewish Culture,* 16–28; in the same volume Klaus L. Berghahn discusses Goethe's very ambivalent views of Jews ("Patterns of Childhood: Goethe and the Jews" 3–15).

[28] Alma Mahler, *Gustav Mahler: Erinnerungen und Briefe* (Amsterdam: Allert de Lange, 1940), 37; see also *Memories and Letters*, 26: "he was a bogus Goethe in his writing and a haggling Jew in his talk."

[29] See Sander Gilman, *Jewish Self-Hatred: Anti-Semitism and the Hidden Language of the Jews* (Baltimore: Johns Hopkins UP, 1990), 139.

[30] Nietzsche, *Nachgelassene Fragmente, 1884–1885*, 11:688–89; and Nietzsche, *Götzen-Dämmerung*, in *Kritische Studienausgabe* 6:55–162; here 151; *AC*, 222.

[31] For a description of the façade in the context of the architectural history of the Burgtheater, see Josef Bayer, *Das neue k. k. Hofburgtheater als Bauwerk mit seinen Sculpturen und Bilderschmuck* (Vienna: Gesellschaft für vervielfältigende Kunst, 1894), 69.

[32] Such a monumental privileging of Goethe over Schiller in the nineteenth century is not uncommon. Rietschel's Goethe-Schiller monument in Weimar from 1859, for instance, shows Goethe as slightly taller than Schiller, something that in real life was most likely not the case (see Sammons, "Schiller vs. Goethe," 1).

[33] Detailed factual information on the history of these monuments can be found in Gerhardt Kapner, *Die Denkmäler der Wiener Ringstrasse* (Vienna: Jugend & Volk, 1969), 29–37 (page numbers in this paragraph refer to this work) and at the following website: http://www.suf.at/wien/ringstr_uebers.htm (accessed 24 Jan. 2010).

[34] Kapner, *Denkmäler*, 36.

[35] See *Neue Freie Presse*, 27 Aug. 1899; in the following I refer to pages 1 and 2. See also Beller's analysis of this material in *Vienna and the Jews*, 152–53.

[36] In the issue of Monday, 28 Aug., however, there was a detailed report on the Goethe celebration in the Hofoper, where Mahler performed Beethoven's *Egmont* overture and Mozart's *Zauberflöte*: "Das Haus war nur mäßig gut besucht. Diejenigen aber, die gekommen waren, hatten einen großen, ungetrübten Genuß" (2).

[37] See Marian Bisanz-Prakken, *Gustav Klimt: Der Beethovenfries; Geschichte, Funktion und Bedeutung* (Munich: DTV, 1980), 26. Alfred Roller would later collaborate with Mahler on his Wagner stagings at Vienna's Court Opera.

[38] The exhibition catalogue contained a detailed description of the frieze and the artist's intention; the text is reprinted in Bisanz-Prakken, *Gustav Klimt*, 47–48.

[39] A leading motive behind the establishment of the Secession was its desire to open up Vienna for art from outside Austria and to participate fully in European modernism. See Peter Vergo, *Art in Vienna, 1898–1918: Klimt, Kokoschka, Schiele and Their Contemporaries* (London: Phaidon, 2001), 23 and 26.

[40] See Bisanz-Prakken, *Gustav Klimt*, 49–51. Klimt used Richard Wagner's explanatory notes in his "Bericht über die Aufführung der neunten Symphonie von Beethoven im Jahre 1846 in Dresden," in *Sämtliche Schriften und Dichtungen*, Volksausgabe, vol. 2 (Leipzig: Breitkopf & Härtel, [1911]), 50–65.

[41] Richard Wagner, "Beethoven," in *Sämtliche Schriften und Dichtungen* 9:61–127; here 120; see also Bisanz-Prakken, *Gustav Klimt*, 49. (Wagner actually uses the term "our kingdom" [unser Reich].)

[42] See Wagner, "Beethoven," 66.

[43] See also Klimt's painting *Nuda Veritas* of 1899, which also quotes Schiller: "If you cannot please all through your deeds and work of art — do justice to a few. To please many is bad. Schiller." ("Kannst du nicht allen gefallen durch deine That und dein Kunstwerk — mach es wenigen recht. Vielen gefallen ist schlimm. Schiller."). The source is Friedrich Schiller, *Votivtafeln*, in *Werke und Briefe*, vol. 1 (Frankfurt am Main: Deutscher Klassiker Verlag, 1992), 174–82; here 181.

[44] Jens Malte Fischer, *Gustav Mahler: Der fremde Vertraute* (Vienna: Zsolnay, 2003), 435.

[45] Michael P. Steinberg calls the second movement of Mahler's Eighth "a kind of unstageable metaopera," in *The Meaning of the Salzburg Festival: Austria as Theater and Ideology, 1890–1938* (Ithaca, NY: Cornell UP, 1990), 214.

[46] Bisanz-Prakken, *Gustav Klimt*, 48.

[47] Siegfried Lipiner saw Goethe's *Faust* stylistically as a model for a "new" form of literature. See Ida Schein, *Die Gedanken- und Ideenwelt Siegfried Lipiners* (PhD diss., University of Vienna, 1936), 63. A copy of this dissertation can be found in the archives of the *Deutsches Literaturarchiv Marbach*.

[48] "I was reading around in 'Eckermann,' like I usually do during the summer" (Ich las wie meistens im Sommer im "Eckermann"), Mahler writes to his old Hamburg friend Adele Marcus in August 1908 from Toblach (*Br*, 370).

[49] Johann Peter Eckermann, *Gespräche mit Goethe in den letzten Jahren seines Lebens* (Frankfurt am Main: Deutscher Klassiker Verlag, 1999), 306.

[50] Eckermann, *Gespräche mit Goethe*, 219–20. For a detailed discussion of Goethe's statements and his knowledge of musical history, see Kreutzer, *Faust: Mythos und Musik*, 59–61.

[51] See Marc Weiner, *Richard Wagner and the Anti-Semitic Imagination*. 2nd ed. (Lincoln: Nebraska UP, 1997), 52–53.

[52] Another source of reflection about a musical adaptation of *Faust* is Goethe's correspondence with the composer Zelter. In a letter to Goethe of 21 Jun. 1829 Zelter harshly criticized Berlioz's adaptation of *Faust*, because of its extreme use of orchestral instrumentation. It is likely that Goethe would have agreed with him. See Goethe, *Briefwechsel zwischen Goethe und Zelter in den Jahren 1799 bis 1832*, ed. Hans-Günter Ottenberg and Edith Zehm, 2 vols. (Munich: Carl Hanser, 1991), 2:1244.

[53] "Übrigens werden Sie zugeben, daß der Schluß, wo es mit der geretteten Seele nach oben geht, sehr schwer zu machen war, und daß ich, bei so übersinnlichen, kaum zu ahnenden Dingen, mich sehr leicht im Vagen hätte verlieren können, wenn ich nicht meinen poetischen Intentionen, durch die scharf umrissenen christlich-kirchlichen Figuren und Vorstellungen, eine wohltätig beschränkende Form und Festigkeit gegeben hätte." Eckermann, *Gespräche mit Goethe*, 489.

[54] See Albrecht Schöne, *Faust*, vol. 2: *Kommentare* (Frankfurt am Main: Deutscher Klassiker Verlag, 1999), 779. See Wilhelm von Humboldt, "Der Montserrat bei Barcelona," in *Gesammelte Schriften*, vol. 3: *1799–1818*, ed. Albert Leitzmann (Berlin: B. Behr, 1904), 30–57. (The text is dedicated to Goethe.)

⁵⁵ The complete passage reads as follows: "Like the abyss of rock at my feet / Rests on a deeper abyss still, / Like thousands of streams flow brightly / Into the horrific foaming waterfall, / As straight as, through its own strong force / The tree's stem rises into the sky, / So is the omnipotent love / That shapes and cherishes everything." (Wie Felsenabgrund mir zu Füßen / Auf tiefem Abgrund lastend ruht, / Wie tausend Bäche strahlend fließen / Zum grausen Sturz des Schaums der Flut, / Wie strack, mit eignem kräftigen Triebe, / Der Stamm sich in die Lüfte trägt, / So ist es die allmächtige Liebe, / Die alles bildet, alles hegt"; vs. 11866–73). For my translations I have consulted the *Faust* translations of Stuart Atkins; in general, however, I provide a translation that follows the German text as closely as possible.

⁵⁶ Scholarship has shown that Goethe based his concept of heaven on the works of the third-century theologian Origen (see Schöne, *Faust: Kommentare* 2:788–93). He learned about Origen from Gottfried Arnold's book *Unparteyische Kirchen- und Ketzer-Historie* (Impartial History of Church and Heresy) published in two volumes in 1699 and 1700. There is no doubt that Origen's ideas were still considered heretical within the theological framework of Goethe's time. Gottfried Arnold (1666–1714) was a theologian and church historian and was highly critical of the church as an institution. The *Unparteyische Kirchen- und Ketzer-Historie* was also one of Goethe's sources of knowledge about Spinoza. In the following, I will argue that Spinoza can be seen as a key figure for Mahler's understanding of *Faust*.

⁵⁷ See Schöne, *Faust: Kommentare* 2:804.

⁵⁸ What "of it" ("daran") exactly refers to, is not clear from the context (Alma blacked out one-and-a-half lines immediately preceding this quote); see Mahler, *GR,* 388.

⁵⁹ "Gleichnis" is very hard to translate. Atkins uses the term "symbol" (*Faust I & II,* ed. and trans. Stuart Atkins, 305). I prefer "simile" because the German term "Gleichnis" emphasizes the aspect of similarity (not necessarily inherent to symbols) and not the aspect of a tradition of understanding that is specific for symbols.

⁶⁰ See Goethe, *Faust,* ed. Albrecht Schöne, vol. 1 (Frankfurt am Main: Deutscher Klassiker Verlag, 1999), 733. In the following, I will refer to this edition.

⁶¹ Floros speaks of a religion of art (Kunstreligion) in relation to the end of the Eighth Symphony. See Constantin Floros, "Die 'Symphonie der Tausend' als Botschaft an die Menschheit," in *A "Mass" for the Masses: Proceedings of the Mahler VIII Symposium Amsterdam 1988,* ed. Eveline Nikkels and Robert Becqué (The Hague: Nijgh & Van Ditmar Universitair, 1992), 121.

⁶² In a letter written to Lipiner in the summer before the Eighth's premiere in Munich (7 Jul. 1910), Mahler writes to Lipiner that he will certainly find some of his own ideas in the Eighth (see *Br,* 412).

⁶³ Siegfried Lipiner's dissertation file in the archive of the University of Vienna does not contain a copy of the dissertation. According to a hand-written note accompanying a letter from Lipiner's widow, Clementine Lipiner, in this file, the copy of his dissertation that used to be part of the file was given to her after

Lipiner's death in 1911. Schein's dissertation shows that in the 1930s this copy was still in the possession of Lipiner's relatives.

⁶⁴ The following summary is based on Schein, *GSL*, 83–84.

⁶⁵ Robert Zimmermann also makes this point in relation to Goethe's *Faust* in *Über das Tragische und die Tragödie* (Vienna: Wilhelm Braumüller, 1856), 293. Zimmermann was one of Mahler's university teachers and Lipiner's main dissertation advisor; see Herta Blaukopf, "Mahler an der Universität: Versuch, eine biographische Lücke zu schließen," in *Neue Mahleriana: Essays in Honour of Henry-Louis de La Grange on His Seventieth Birthday*, ed. Günther Weiß (Berne: Peter Lang, 1997), 1–16; here 13, and Siegfried Lipiner's dissertation file.

⁶⁶ See also Jonathan Israel, *Radical Enlightenment: Philosophy and the Making of Modernity, 1650–1750* (Oxford: Oxford UP, 2001), 162 and 231.

⁶⁷ See also Israel, *Radical Enlightenment*, 233.

⁶⁸ See Israel, *Radical Enlightenment*, "Introduction," 11; see also Goetschel, *SM*, 4 and 6; and Adam Sutcliffe, *Judaism and Enlightenment* (Cambridge: Cambridge UP, 2003), 13 and 134. Spinoza, however, also played a prominent role in nineteenth-century scholarship on Goethe. Albert Bielschowsky in his popular two-volume monograph on Goethe which Mahler knew discusses Spinoza extensively in his chapter "Goethe und die Philosophie." Bielschowsky, *Goethe: Sein Leben und seine Werke*, vol. 2, 10th ed. (Munich: Beck, 1906), 77–101). The only philosopher with a similar impact on Goethe was, according to Bielschowsky, Kant, even though Goethe also sought an interpretation of Kant's philosophy that would confirm what he had learned from Spinoza (99).

⁶⁹ See also Sutcliffe, *Judaism and Enlightenment*, 119.

⁷⁰ See Alexander von Bormann, "Metaphysik der Unmöglichkeit? Zum Text von Mahlers VIII. Symphonie," in Nikkels and Becqué, *A "Mass" for the Masses*, 92–99; here 95–96.

⁷¹ See Dietrich Türnau, *Rabanus Maurus, der praeceptor Germaniae: Ein Beitrag zur Geschichte der Pädagogik des Mittelalters* (Munich: J. Lindauersche Buchhandlung, 1900), 51 and 60.

⁷² See Thomas Richter, *Die Dialoge über Literatur im Briefwechsel zwischen Goethe und Zelter* (Stuttgart: Metzler, 2000), 13.

⁷³ Bauer-Lechner, *Fragmente: Gelerntes und Gelebtes* (Vienna: Rudolf Lechner & Sohn, 1907), 95.

⁷⁴ Letter from Goethe to Zelter, 12 April 1820. See Goethe, *Briefwechsel zwischen Goethe und Zelter in den Jahren 1799 bis 1832*, 596.

⁷⁵ See Mathias Mayer, "Islamisiertes Christentum, poetisierte Religion: Goethes Übersetzung eines spätlateinischen Pfingsthymnus," *Neue Zürcher Zeitung*, 29 May 2004, 35. To prove that Goethe thinks about the "Veni creator spiritus" in the context of a continuation of the *West-östlicher Divan*, Mayer refers to a letter of 11 May 1820 from Goethe to Zelter.

⁷⁶ Von Bormann, "Metaphysik," 95.

⁷⁷ Goethe, *Maximen und Reflexionen*, in *Werke*, ed. Erich Trunz, vol. 12 (Munich: Beck, 1982), 472, fragment 762.

Chapter 6

[1] For information on both essays, see the materials reproduced in Donald Mitchell, *Gustav Mahler: The Early Years* (Woodbridge, UK: Boydell, 2003), 287–90. Mahler's poor performance at these exams may be partially explained by the fact that he was a day student: he prepared for his exams on his own, since he was already participating in classes at the conservatory in Vienna while still having to take these exams in Iglau. See Jens Malte Fischer, *Gustav Mahler: Der fremde Vertraute* (Vienna: Paul Zsolnay, 2003), 53–55. An overview of all exam topics can be found in Henry-Louis de La Grange, *Mahler*, vol. 1 (Garden City, NJ, and New York: Doubleday, 1973), 50–51.

[2] See Herder, *Ideen zur Philosophie der Geschichte der Menschheit,* in *Werke in zehn Bänden,* vol. 6 (Frankfurt am Main: Deutscher Klassiker Verlag, 1989), 251–85.

[3] Mitchell, *The Early Years,* 289.

[4] Edward W. Said, *Orientalism* (New York: Vintage, 1994). Said's ideas have been criticized for not recognizing Orientalism's diversity and the specific cultural and historical settings in which interest in the Orient arose. See, for instance, Edmund Burke III and David Prochaska, "Introduction: Orientalism from Postcolonial Theory to World History," in *Genealogies of Orientalism: History, Theory, Politics* (Lincoln, NE, and London: U of Nebraska P, 2008), 1–71; here 8–9, 18, and 22; and, with German cultural history in mind, Suzanne L. Marchand, *German Orientalism in the Age of Empire* (Cambridge: Cambridge UP, 2009), xviii–xxiii.

[5] At a dinner with the board of the Concertgebouw in March 1906, Mahler caused a scene by defending Multatuli. See Pauline Micheels, "Gustav Mahler in Amsterdam," in *Mahler in Amsterdam van Mengelberg tot Chailly,* ed. Johan Giskes and Ester L. Woudhuysen (Bussum and Amsterdam: THOTH/Gemeentearchief Amsterdam, 1995), 24–36; here 25. *Max Havelaar* is mentioned in Mahler's letter to Alma dated 21 Oct. 1903 (Mahler, *GR,* 169).

[6] In the chapter "Fin de Siècle Orientalism, the *Ostjuden,* and the Aesthetics of Jewish Self-Affirmation" of his book *Divided Passions: Jewish Intellectuals and the Experience of Modernity* (Detroit: Wayne State UP, 1991), Paul Mendes-Flohr points to a renewed interest around 1910 among Jewish intellectuals in Oriental languages and cultures (84–89); this can be documented, for instance, in Martin Buber's writings.

[7] See Marchand, *German Orientalism,* 158 and 160. According to this same logic the period around 1800 (Herder, Schlegel) represents the First Oriental Rennaissance.

[8] See Manfred Wagner, "Wien grüßt den fernen Osten," in *Die liebe Erde allüberall: Proceedings of Das Lied von der Erde Symposium Den Haag 2002,* ed. Robert Becqué and Eveline Nikkels (Den Haag: Stichting rondom Mahler, 2005), 20–33; here 27.

[9] See Peter Vergo, *Art in Vienna, 1898–1918: Klimt, Kokoschka, Schiele and Their Contemporaries* (London and New York: Phaidon, 2001), 189.

[10] Herta Blaukopf, "Kunstschau Wien 1908," in Becqué and Nikkels, *Die liebe Erde allüberall,* 34–48; here 41.

[11] Richard Strauss, *Betrachtungen und Erinnerungen*, 3rd ed., ed. Willi Schuh (Zurich: Atlantis, 1981), 224. See also Sander L. Gilman, "Strauss, the Pervert, and Avant Garde Opera of the Fin de Siècle," in *New German Critique* 43 (Winter, 1988): 35–68; here 38–39.

[12] Marchand, *German Orientalism*, 388; see also 392.

[13] Herder, *Ideen*, 386 and 390.

[14] Friedrich Schlegel, *Über die Sprache und Weisheit der Indier*, in *Kritische Friedrich-Schlegel-Ausgabe*, vol. 8 (Munich: Schöningh and Thomas, 1975), 105–380; here 115.

[15] Herder, *Ideen*, 390–97.

[16] Schlegel, *Über die Sprache*, 161 and 163.

[17] See Tuska Benes, "From Indo-Germans to Aryans: Philology and the Racialization of Salvationist National Rhetoric, 1806–30," in *The German Invention of Race*, ed. Sara Eigen and Mark Larrimore (Albany: State U of New York P, 2006), 167–81; here 169–70. See also Andrea Polaschegg, *Der andere Orientalismus: Regeln deutsch-morgenländischer Imagination im 19. Jahrhundert* (Berlin and New York: Walter de Gruyter, 2005), 191.

[18] On the genesis of the concept of an Aryan affinity of German and Indian cultures in the nineteenth century, see Benes, "From Indo-Germans to Aryans," 175–77. Todd Kontje also discusses the dualistic construction of the Orient in German intellectual and cultural history; Kontje, *German Orientalisms* (Ann Arbor: Michigan UP, 2004). 109–10). So does Marchand, *German Orientalism*, (61, and 126–27), who also points out that Schlegel's division results in "lining up lighter peoples with Indo-European languages and casting darker peoples into cultural-linguistic outer circles" (127).

[19] Kontje, *German Orientalisms*, 121–24; see also Polaschegg, *Der andere Orientalismus*, 368–71.

[20] Letter to Voigt, 10 Jan. 1805, in Polaschegg, *Der andere Orientalismus*, 330.

[21] Johann Wolfgang von Goethe, *West-östlicher Divan*, in *Werke*, ed. Erich Trunz, vol. 2 (Munich: Beck, 1982), 7–210; here 127. On the importance of "traveling" for understanding Goethe's attitude toward the Orient, see also Polaschegg, *Der andere Orientalismus*, 307–8.

[22] Goethe, *Noten und Abhandlungen zu besserem Verständnis des West-östlichen Divans*, essay accompanying the poems in *West-östlicher Divan*, 42; see also 150.

[23] Goethe, *Noten*, 183.

[24] Goethe, *Noten*, 165.

[25] Kontje, *German Orientalisms*, 119.

[26] See Arthur Schopenhauer, *Aphorismen zur Lebensweisheit*, in vol. 8 of *Werke: Zürcher Ausgabe*, ed. Arthur Hübscher (Zurich: Diogenes, 1977), 348, 384, 406, and 430–31. In spite of his respect for the *West-östlicher Divan*, Schopenhauer is, however, critical of Goethe for selling out his ideals for worldly gain (see 365).

[27] *Friedrich Rückerts Werke in sechs Bänden*, ed. Conrad Beyer (Leipzig: Gustav Fock [1897]); *Rückerts Werke*, 2 vols., ed. Georg Ellinger (Leipzig and Vienna:

Bibliographisches Institut, [1897]); and *Friedrich Rückerts ausgewählte Werke in sechs Bänden.* ed. Philipp Stein (Leipzig: Reclam, 1897). In addition, a one-volume selection was published: *Friedrich Rückerts Werke: Auswahl in einem Bande*, ed. Oskar Linke (Halle: Otto Hendel [1897]). See Rüdiger Rückert and Max-Rainer Uhrig, *Friedrich-Rückert-Literaturen, 1813 bis 2007*, MS Word document. [Rückert bibliography] http://www.rueckert-gesellschaft.de/bibliographie.html (accessed 16 May 2008). Regarding this "sudden and intense interest" in Rückert's poetry in the late nineteenth century, see also Peter Russell, *Light in Battle with Darkness: Mahler's Kindertotenlieder* (Bern: Peter Lang, 1991), 30–31. One should add that this interest did not last beyond the final years of the nineteenth century.

[28] See Donald Mitchell, *Gustav Mahler: Songs and Symphonies of Life and Death* (Woodbridge, UK: Boydell, 2002), 57 and 111.

[29] Annemarie Schimmel, *Friedrich Rückert: Lebensbild und Einführung in sein Werk* (Freiburg: Herder, 1987), 15.

[30] Schimmel *Friedrich Rückert*, 18.

[31] Polaschegg, *Der andere Orientalismus*, 151–52; also 391.

[32] Schimmel, *Friedrich Rückert*, 72.

[33] Benes, "From Indo-Germans to Aryans," 179; see also 170.

[34] See Leopold Magon, "Goethes 'West-östlicher Divan' und Rückerts 'Östliche Rosen': Zur Vorgeschichte der 'Östlichen Rosen,'" in *Friedrich Rückert im Spiegel seiner Zeitgenossen und der Nachwelt: Aufsätze aus der Zeit zwischen 1827 und 1986*, ed. Wolfdietrich Fischer (Wiesbaden: Harrassowitz, 1988), 310–30, esp. 310, 313, 316, and 318; see also Schimmel, *Friedrich Rückert*, 23.

[35] Friedrich Rückert, "Zu Goethe's west-östlichem Diwan," in *Oestliche Rosen*, in *Gesammelte poetische Werke*, vol. 5 (Frankfurt am Main: J. D. Sauerländer's Verlag, 1868), 286–367; here 286–87.

[36] Goethe, "Über Kunst und Alterthum: Mittheilungen im ersten bis dritten Bande," in *Werke: Weimarer Ausgabe* (Weimar: Böhlau, 1887–1919), section 1, vol. 41 (1902), 372–73; here 373. See also Magon, "Goethes 'West-östlicher Divan,'" 310.

[37] See Magon, "Goethes 'West-östlicher Divan,'" 320-21; see also Helmut Prang, *Friedrich Rückert: Geist und Form der Sprache* (Wiesbaden: Harrassowitz, 1963), 82–85.

[38] Magon, "Goethes 'West-östlicher Divan,'" 328.

[39] For a concise definition of the pentatonic scale and its importance in musical history, see Jeremy Day O'Connell's article "Pentatonic," in *Grove Music Online*, ed. L. Macy, http://www.grovemusic.com.proxy2.library.uiuc.edu (accessed 13 May 2008).

[40] See Guido Adler, "Heterophony," repr. in Mitchell, *SSLD*, 624–31; here 626 (originally published as "Über Heterophonie," *Jahrbuch der Musikbibliothek Peters* 14 [1908]: 17–27).

[41] See Friedrich Rückert, *Haus und Jahr*, in *Gesammelte poetische Werke*, vol. 2 (Frankfurt am Main: J. D. Sauerländer, 1868), 4, where the poem is entitled

"Verbotener Blick" (Forbidden Look). In the following I will discuss the songs in the order in which Mahler first published them in 1907 (see Mitchell, *SSLD*, 110). Mahler changed little about Rückert's texts; an overview of his modifications can be found in Henry-Louis de La Grange, *Gustav Mahler*, vol. 2: *Vienna: The Years of Challenge (1897–1904)* (Oxford and New York: Oxford UP, 1995), 787, 789–92, and 798.

[42] See de La Grange, *The Years of Challenge*, 788.

[43] See Rückert, *Haus und Jahr*, 337. In his version, Mahler moved around some of the lines in the first stanza and replaced "friendship of the heart" (Herzensfreundschaft) with "love" (Liebe) in the last line.

[44] See also in this context Hermann Danuser's reading of "Ich atmet' einen linden Duft" as a "rejection of a conventional mimetic ideal" (Absage an das tradierte Mimesis-Ideal). Danuser, *Gustav Mahler und seine Zeit*, 2nd ed. (Laaber: Laaber-Verlag, 1996), 60.

[45] See Lutz Köpnick, "Goethes Ikonisierung der Poesie: Zur Schriftmagie im *West-östlichen Divan*," *Deutsche Vierteljahrsschrift für Literaturwissenschaft und Geistesgeschichte* 66 (1992): 361–89; here 361. See also Polaschegg, *Der andere Orientalismus*, 322–23.

[46] Schimmel, *Friedrich Rückert*, 114.

[47] Rückert, *Liebesfrühling*, in *Gesammelte poetische Werke* 1:281–639; here 567.

[48] See Hubert Grimme, "Liebesfrühlings Entstehung," in Wolfdietrich Fischer, *Friedrich Rückert im Spiegel*, 292–300, for a history of *Liebesfrühling*'s origins.

[49] See Rückert, *Haus und Jahr*, vol. 2 of *Gesammelte poetische Werke*, 465–66. In contrast to Henry-Louis de La Grange's claim (de La Grange, *The Years of Challenge*, 794), the poem is not part of the *Liebesfrühling* collection.

[50] See Stuart Feder, "Gustav Mahler um Mitternacht," in *International Review of Psycho-Analysis* 7 (1980): 11–26; here 17–18.

[51] See Stephen E. Hefling, "The Rückert Lieder," 352, in *The Mahler Companion*, ed. Donald Mitchell and Andrew Nicholson (Oxford and New York: Oxford UP, 1999), 338–65.

[52] Rückert, *Liebesfrühling*, in *Gesammelte poetische Werke*, 1:572. That the song has often been seen as being very different from the other Rückert songs may also be explained by the fact that it was composed a year later, during the summer of 1902 (see de La Grange, *The Years of Challenge*, 796).

[53] The biographical background for these songs and their publication history can be found in the new critical edition of the text, Rückert, *Kindertodtenlieder und andere Texte des Jahres 1834: Historisch-kritische Ausgabe "Schweinfurter Edition"*, ed. Hans Wollschläger und Rudolf Kreutner (Göttingen: Wallstein, 2007), commentary 7–12 and 565–66 (henceforth called "critical edition"). In the following I will refer to Rückert's texts as *Kindertodtenlieder* and to Mahler's songs as *Kindertotenlieder* (in line with the author's and composer's own spelling of the titles).

[54] Henry-Louis de La Grange assumes that the second and fifth songs were composed in 1904 (de La Grange, *The Years of Challenge*, 827).

⁵⁵ See Rückert, *Kindertodtenlieder: Aus seinem Nachlasse* (Frankfurt am Main: J. D. Sauerländer, 1872), 311 (critical edition 377).

⁵⁶ This depiction of the transition from life to death being accomplished through the climbing of a hill or small mountain anticipates the "mountain gorges" scene from *Faust II*, at the beginning of Mahler's excerpt from that text in the second movement of the Eighth Symphony (see chapter 5).

⁵⁷ See Reinhard Gerlach, *Strophen von Leben, Traum und Tod: Ein Essay über Rückert-Lieder von Gustav Mahler* (Wilhelmshaven: Heinrichshofen, 1983), 88. See also Peter Russell's comment that Rückert's poetry, in spite of using imagery affiliated with the Christian tradition, does not promote a Christian worldview (*Light in Battle with Darkness*, 52; see also 41 and 46).

⁵⁸ See Hans Heinrich Eggebrecht's very detailed musicological analysis of the song's final passage in *Die Musik Gustav Mahlers* (Munich: Piper, 1986), 245–46. For Eggebrecht, the song articulates a "belief as desire to believe" (Glauben als Glaubenwollen; 246). Russell comes to a similar conclusion (92).

⁵⁹ Rückert, *Kindertodtenlieder* (1872), 369 (critical edition, 451). While the song is situated late in Rückert's posthumous collection, it alludes to the death of the child as a recent event (which has taken place in the night). One could say that Mahler, by making this into the first song of his cycle, reinstates the chronological order ignored by the editor of the 1872 edition of Rückert's *Kindertodtenlieder* (see Russell, *Light in Battle with Darkness*, 35 and 45). The imagery of light and darkness can be found throughout the *Kindertotenlieder*, as Mitchell has shown (*SSLD*, 141–42).

⁶⁰ Rückert, *Kindertodtenlieder* (1872), 70 (critical edition, 91).

⁶¹ Rückert, *Kindertodtenlieder* (1872), 59 (critical edition, 77).

⁶² Rückert, *Kindertodtenlieder* (1872), 341 (critical edition, 416).

⁶³ In a manuscript version of the song, Mahler replaced the word "Haus" with "Schoss" (lap or womb); see Edward F. Kravitt, "Mahler's Dirges for His Death: 24 February 24, 1901," *The Musical Quarterly* 64.3 (1978): 329–53; here 335, 337, and 339. This is certainly interesting from a psychoanalytical perspective: it portrays, in line with Freud's theories, death as a return to the mother's womb (339). I do not, however, believe that Mahler's use of the word "Schoss" in this context legitimizes a reading of the song as illustrating "a concept of life as eternal renewal mystically conceived," as Kravitt posits (345). While one can say that the song illustrates life returning to its original state, the text, I would argue, offers no indication that this is a new beginning. The image of a return to the womb is also used by Nietzsche and in Wagner's *Tristan und Isolde;* see Stephen E. Hefling, *Mahler: Das Lied von der Erde* (Cambridge, New York, and Melbourne: Cambridge UP, 2000), 118–19. The visit of the mothers (depicted as archaic matriarchal goddesses) is one of the key episodes in the second part of Goethe's *Faust* (see vs. 6212–6306).

⁶⁴ See E. Mary Dargie, *Music and Poetry in the Songs of Gustav Mahler* (Bern: Peter Lang, 1981), 329, and also Mitchell, *SSLD,* 142. Mahler's view of nature in the songs based on texts by Rückert is therefore not different from, for instance, that in the Third Symphony: nature is chaotic and does not lend itself to the projection of a divine instance but rather illustrates the lawlessness of all life. In

contrast to Dargie, I therefore also do not believe that the cycle's conflicts are resolved in this final song (324).

65 See Theodor Reik, *The Haunting Melody: Psychoanalytic Experiences in Life and Music* (New York: Farrar, Straus, & Young, 1953), 315–20 (Reik does not mention Mahler's own near-death experience in February); Stuart Feder, "Gustav Mahler, Dying," *International Review of Psycho-Analysis* 5 (1978): 125–48; here 130–31, and "Gustav Mahler um Mitternacht," *International Review of Psycho-Analysis* 7 (1980): 11–26; here 14, 17–18, and 22; and Kravitt, "Mahler's Dirges," 333–39.

66 See Friedrich Rückert, *Werke in sechs Bänden* 3:196 ("Blicke mir nicht in die Lieder") and 169 ("Ich atmet' einen linden Duft," which here has the title "Dank für den Lindenzweig"). Information regarding the timeline of these collections is on 187 and 152). In this same edition, "Um Mitternacht" is the very first poem of the first volume (see 1:39–40) at the beginning of a collection called "Pantheon."

67 See *Liebesfrühling, 1821*, in *Gesammelte Gedichte*, vol. 1, 5th ed. (1834; repr., Erlangen: Carl Heyder, 1840), 221–480.

68 See, for instance, *Kindertodtenlieder* (1872) 150–51, 153, and 156–57 (critical edition, 194, 199, and 203); the lines "Have I also written poetry in vain, / Why then did I live?" (Hab' ich auch umsonst gedichtet, / Wozu hab' ich dann gelebt?) exemplify this creative crisis (151; critical edition, 194). Regarding Rückert's crisis, see also Schimmel, *Friedrich Rückert*, 34.

69 See de La Grange, *The Years of Challenge*, 362 and 709–10.

70 See Feder, "Gustav Mahler, Dying," 130, and "Gustav Mahler um Mitternacht," 18.

71 See Dargie, *Music and Poetry*, 307; Russell, *Light in Battle with Darkness*, 46–47.

72 Schopenhauer, *Aphorismen*, 442.

73 Marchand, *German Orientalism*, 300.

74 See, for example, Schopenhauer, *Werke* 4:543, 589, and 737.

75 Schopenhauer, *Werke* 4:684–85.

76 Schopenhauer, *Werke* 4:543 and 596; see also 589–92. Insights like these may very well be the basis for a belief in reincarnation, occasionally attributed to Mahler (see de La Grange, *Gustav Mahler*, vol. 3: *Triumph and Disillusion (1904–1907)* (Oxford and New York: Oxford UP, 1999), 930–31), although one needs to add that Schopenhauer considers any attempt to capture this process in some form of religious system as being necessarily flawed.

77 Schopenhauer, *Aphorismen*, 743. See also Bryan Magee, "A Note on Schopenhauer and Buddhism," in *The Philosophy of Schopenhauer*, rev. ed. (Oxford and New York: Clarendon and Oxford UP, 1997), 340–45; here 345.

78 Richard Batka, "Gustav Mahlers 'Siebente,'" in the *Prager Tagblatt*, 20 Sept. 1908, 16; English translation (slightly modified) from Karen Painter, ed., *Mahler and His World* (Princeton, NJ, and London: Princeton UP, 2002), 322. See also Donald Mitchell, "Reception," 44, in *Facsimile Edition of the Seventh Symphony*,

by Gustav Mahler, 2 vols., ed. Donald Mitchell and Edward Reilly (Amsterdam: Rosbeek, 1995), Commentary volume, 31–74.

[79] Mahler himself draws this conclusion as well in a conversation with Alphons Diepenbrock: since Strauss is an "utterly earthly human being" (ein durchaus irdischer Mensch) one would have to consider him Semitic, while he, Mahler, as "homo religiosus" — Mahler here is talking about his public image associated with the Second Symphony, I would argue — would have to be considered non-Semitic; see Diepenbrock, letter to W. G. Hondius van den Broek, 3 Nov. 1909, in *Brieven en Documenten*, vol. 6, ed. Eduard Reeser ('s-Gravenhage, Netherlands: Martinus Nijhoff, 1991), 164. In van den Broek's reply he talks about Goethe's interest in Spinoza as another example of the flexibility of these categories (166). Could this also have been part of the conversation with Mahler?

[80] See Said, *Orientalism*, 180–90.

[81] See Susanna Partsch, *Gustav Klimt: Painter of Women* (Munich: Prestel, 2006), 74–75 and 78–79; see also Bram Dijkstra, *Idols of Perversity: Fantasies of Feminine Evil in Fin-de-Siècle Culture* (New York and Oxford: Oxford UP, 1986), 376–401.

[82] See Richard Strauss, *Salome: Drama in One Act after Oscar Wilde's Poem*, English and German; trans. Hedwig Lachmann (Berlin: Adolph Fürstner; New York: Breitkopf & Härtel, 1905), 22.

[83] Strauss, *Betrachtungen und Erinnerungen*, 224. See also Gilman, "Strauss, the Pervert," 38–39.

[84] Strauss, *Salome*, 19.

[85] Strauss, *Salome*, 4, trans. modified.

[86] Strauss, *Salome*, 13–15.

[87] See Karen Painter, "Contested Counterpoint: 'Jewish' Appropriation and Polyphonic Liberation," *Archiv für Musikwissenschaft* 58.3 (2001): 201–30; here 215–16; see also, by the same author, *Symphonic Aspirations: German Music and Politics, 1900–1945* (Cambridge, MA, and London: Harvard UP, 2007), 59. The point of the scene is that the five Jews are unable to grasp the truth of the more advanced religion (Christianity). This stereotype of Judaism as primitive and of Jews as longing to be part of Christianity can also be found in an unpublished diary note by Strauss on the occasion of Mahler's death. While Strauss calls this "a great loss" (ein schwerer Verlust), he responds rather negatively to Mahler's Jewish background: "The Jew Mahler could still find elevation in Christianity. / The heroic Wagner as an old man descended to it because of Schopenhauer's influence." (Der Jude Mahler konnte im Christentum noch Erhebung gewinnen. / Der Held Richard Wagner ist als Greis durch den Einfluß Schopenhauers wieder zu ihm herabgestiegen.) Richard Strauss, quoted in Herta Blaukopf, "Rivalität und Freundschaft: Die persönlichen Beziehungen zwischen Gustav Mahler und Richard Strauss," in *Briefwechsel, 1888–1911*, by Gustav Mahler and Richard Strauss (Munich and Zurich: R. Piper, 1980), 129–225; here 211.

[88] See Gilman, "Strauss, the Pervert," 56–58. Gilman's reading is supported by Painter's musicological analysis in "Contested Counterpoint," 216.

[89] See Painter, "Contested Counterpoint," 217.

90 See Alma Mahler, *Gustav Mahler: Erinnerungen und Briefe* (Amsterdam: Allert de Lange, 1940) 111–12; in English, *Gustav Mahler: Memories and Letters*, 88–89.

91 Blaukopf, "Rivalität und Freundschaft," 198.

92 See Mahler's letter of 12 Jan. 1907 to Alma (Mahler, *GR*, 307). This was during the same visit that Mahler saw Strauss's *Salome* twice.

93 For a comprehensive summary of these efforts, see Herta Blaukopf, "Rivalität und Freundschaft," 186–88, and de La Grange, *Triumph and Disillusion*, 249–52.

94 Gilman, "Strauss, the Pervert," 68.

95 See James L. Zychowicz, "The Lieder of Mahler and Richard Strauss," in *The Cambridge Companion to the Lied*, ed. James Parsons (Cambridge: Cambridge UP, 2004), 245–72; here 264, and 268–69.

96 See Said, *Orientalism*, 99, for a discussion of this strategy of privileging a "classical" period over the present in Western thinking on the Orient. The poems that Mahler chose are from the Golden Age of Chinese poetry during the Tang Dynasty (618–907), a period when Buddhism was very influential (see de La Grange, *Gustav Mahler*, vol. 4: *A New Life Cut Short (1907–1911)* (Oxford and New York: Oxford UP, 2008), 1305 and 1309–10; see also Bethge, *Die chinesische Flöte*, 20th ed. (Kelkheim, Germany: YinYang Media, 2001), 107).

97 Polaschegg, *Der andere Orientalismus*, 106–7, and 120.

98 Polaschegg, *Der andere Orientalismus*, 148.

99 See Alma Mahler, *Gustav Mahler: Erinnerungen und Briefe*, 152; *Memories and Letters*, 123. Alma here appears to think that the collection had been around for some time. The exact time of publication of Bethge's collection is not known; it was announced in a Berlin periodical on 5 Oct. 1907 but may have been circulating before that date (see de La Grange, *A New Life*, 1294).

100 See Hans Bethge, *Die chinesische Flöte*, 1. Bethge mentions his sources in his afterword (103–4).

101 See Erik Ryding and Rebecca Pechefsky, *Bruno Walter: A World Elsewhere* (New Haven, CT, and London: Yale UP, 2001), 61.

102 *Der Merker: Österreichische Zeitschrift für Musik und Theater* 27.1 November-Heft (1911): iii; see also Hefling, *Mahler: Das Lied von der Erde*, 58.

103 See Bethge, *Die chinesische Flöte*, 21–22. For a line-by-line overview of Mahler's changes to Bethge's texts in *Das Lied von der Erde*, see Stephen E. Hefling, *Mahler: Das Lied von der Erde*, 120–31, and de La Grange, *A New Life*, 1333–34, 1340, 1345–46, 1352-53, 1358–59, and 1370–72. In the following, I will discuss only those changes that are relevant for my analysis.

104 Hefling, *Mahler: Das Lied von der Erde*, 89.

105 Bethge, *Die chinesische Flöte*, 107.

106 See Hermann Danuser, *Gustav Mahler: Das Lied von der Erde* (Munich: Wilhelm Fink, 1986), 48.

107 Hefling, *Lied von der Erde*, 88 and 86.

[108] Bethge's title for the poem is "Die Einsame im Herbst" (The Lonely Woman in Autumn; 59). The poem is attributed to Tchang Tsi (ninth century), possibly incorrectly (see de La Grange, *A New Life*, 1336). Mahler's changes, in comparison with Bethge's version, are minimal.

[109] However, as Mitchell notes, most songs do not specify any season, and the time of year must be inferred. This and the actual contexts in which the different seasons are mentioned in the text argue against making nature's cyclical progression the core of the *Lied*'s message.

[110] In Bethge's text the poem is entitled "Der Pavillon aus Porzellan" (The Porcelain Pavilion; 23–24) and attributed to Li Tai Po. It immediately follows "Das Trinklied vom Jammer der Erde."

[111] See Eveline Nikkels, *"O Mensch! Gib Acht!" Friedrich Nietzsches Bedeutung für Gustav Mahler* (Amsterdam and Atlanta, GA: Rodopi, 1989), 151.

[112] For an alternative interpretation see Danuser, for whom the mysteriousness ("Rätselhaftigkeit") of this moment indicates that the image of youth can only be illusory (*Gustav Mahler: Das Lied von der Erde*, 66).

[113] See Arthur B. Wenk, "The Composer as Poet in 'Das Lied von der Erde,'" *Nineteenth-Century Music* 1.1 (1977): 33–47; here 36–37.

[114] The implication is, paradoxically, that precisely because art refuses to comment on society and is just aesthetic "play" it can have the social function described above.

[115] Donald Mitchell, arguing from a musicological point of view, characterizes the third and fourth movements as being the most Oriental in *Das Lied von der Erde* (*SSLD*, 276 and 286). Similar observations are made by de La Grange (*A New Life*, 1342 and 1348); see also Danuser, *Gustav Mahler und seine Zeit*, 228–29.

[116] Based on Bethge, *Die chinesische Flöte*, "Am Ufer" (26–27). The author is assumed to be Li Tai Po. In Bethge's collection, the poem precedes "Der Trunkene im Frühling."

[117] It is possible to link this "sun" to the narrator's desire in the second song to see the "sun of love" (Sonne der Liebe) shine again. Another similarity between both songs is the use of the word "Blüten" (blossoms or flowers) in both songs.

[118] See Wenk, "The Composer as Poet," 38.

[119] Hefling, *Mahler: Das Lied von der Erde*, 99.

[120] See Bethge, *Die chinesische Flöte*, 28–29.

[121] See de La Grange, *A New Life*, 1334.

[122] See Wenk's diagram (43); I disagree with Wenk's view that the second and third stanzas of the second section should be attributed to the same first-person narrator. The line "I will never stray abroad" (Ich werde niemals in die Ferne schweifen) in the third stanza is clearly meant to indicate that we are dealing with a narrator who is different from the friend wandering in the mountains (second stanza).

[123] If one accepts this reading, however, it should noted that "the beyond," here and in the Eighth Symphony, is a highly anthropomorphic construction; in order to imagine the "beyond," humans necessarily rely on images from the "here and now."

[124] Here I disagree with Donald Mitchell's otherwise extremely insightful analysis of the last movement of *Das Lied von der Erde*. Mitchell describes "Der Abschied" as an example of death "conquered through ecstatic acceptance" (*SSLD*, 355); I disagree, both on basis of the text and music, with the "ecstatic" part of Mitchell's interpretation, which to me suggests some form of celebrative aspect. Certainly the music accompanying the natural imagery is meant to provide reprieve; but does this also go for the segment following it, the final section with its multiple repetition of the word "ewig"? The conductor Bernard Haitink, in an interview on *Das Lied von der Erde*, suggests that what the finale intends is more complex than consolation: "I don't know if the end of *Das Lied von der Erde* is a consolation. I don't know. It is just more than that. Humanity dissolves into the air and nothing is left. A sort of emptiness — which is very moving." Frank Scheffer, *Conducting Mahler*, DVD (Paris: Idéale Audience, 2005), 1:01:43–1:01:59. In my view this is precisely the point: Mahler is searching for a philosophy of life and death that is decidedly postmetaphysical and heterophonic, and therefore more complex than any scenario that seeks to read some form of redemption into the end of *Das Lied von der Erde*. Haitink's view is in line with that of Adorno, who opposes a pantheistic reading of the end of *Das Lied* and a reconciliatory reading in general (*MP*, 296; *MPE*, 154).

[125] See de La Grange, *A New Life*, 1364–65; the complete poem can be found in de La Grange, *Mahler* 1:824-25.

[126] See Hefling, *Mahler: Das Lied von der Erde*, 110, and de La Grange, *A New Life*, 1363–64. The complete poem is reprinted in Mitchell, *SSLD*, 124 and in de La Grange, *Mahler* 1:831–32.

[127] On Fechner's dogma of the continued existence of the soul after death in relation to *Das Lied von der Erde*, see Hefling, *Mahler: Das Lied von der Erde*, 116–17; Stuart Feder, *Gustav Mahler: A Life in Crisis* (New Haven, CT, and London: Yale UP, 2004), 150–51; and de La Grange, *A New Life*, 1382–84. Little is known about Mahler's knowledge of Fechner or to what extent Mahler agreed with Fechner's thinking. In the case of *Das Lied von der Erde*, it is important to remember that the idea of the existence of some form of striving, of will, embodied by nature and lasting beyond humans' individual lives was extremely common in nineteenth-century German philosophy and was also embraced by Goethe, Schopenhauer, and Nietzsche (without, however, assuming some kind of spiritual similarity between man and nature). The assumption of Fechner's importance for Mahler's *Lied von der Erde* is often based on the similar imagery that both use. However, one needs to take into account that using natural imagery in order to design a philosophical ethics is extremely common in nineteenth-century German intellectual discourse in general, not only in relation to religious philosophy but also often in developing a *secular* philosophy of life as well. A concise summary of Fechner's ideas as they relate to Mahler's work and thinking can be found in Jens Malte Fischer, *Gustav Mahler: Der fremde Vertraute*, 485–88; and de La Grange, *A New Life*, 1693–95.

[128] See in this context also Hermann Danuser's observation that *Das Lied von der Erde* ends with a dissonant accord (*Gustav Mahler: Das Lied von der Erde*, 110).

[129] Hefling, *Mahler: Das Lied von der Erde*, 84, 86, and 88.

[130] See de La Grange, *A New Life,* 1326, 1342 and 1348.

[131] Goethe, letter to Thomas Carlyle dated 20 Jul. 1827, in *Werke: Weimarer Ausgabe,* section 4, vol. 42 (Weimar: Hermann Böhlaus Nachfolger, 1907), 267–72; here 270. See also "Goethes wichtigste Äusserungen über 'Weltliteratur,'" in *Werke,* vol. 12, ed. Erich Trunz, 361–64. The term "Weltliteratur" is also used in Goethe's Conversations with Eckermann, which Mahler knew well. Johann Peter Eckermann, *Gespräche mit Goethe in den letzten Jahren seines Lebens* (Frankfurt am Main: Deutscher Klassiker Verlag, 1999), 362.

[132] See Schimmel, who also discusses the above passage (*Friedrich Rückert,* 69–70), and, for instance, Robert Boxberger, "Rückerts Stellung zur Weltliteratur," in *Friedrich Rückert im Spiegel seiner Zeitgenossen und der Nachwelt: Aufsätze aus der Zeit zwischen 1827 und 1986,* ed. Wolfdietrich Fischer (Wiesbaden: Harrassowitz, 1988), 111–24. A discussion of the nineteenth- and early-twentieth-century reception of Goethe's concept of *Weltliteratur* can be found in John Pizer, *The Idea of World Literature: History and Pedagogical Practice* (Baton Rouge: Louisiana State UP, 2006), 46–72.

[133] Reinhard Meyer-Kalkus points out that interest in the idea of *Weltliteratur* consequently faded in the later nineteenth century when the idea of competing national literatures became more prominent, even though it can be argued that the two ideas complement each other in productive ways. See Meyer-Kalkus, "World Literature beyond Goethe," in *Cultural Mobility: A Manifesto,* ed. Stephen Greenblatt (Cambridge and New York: Cambridge UP, 2010), 96–121; here 111–12.

[134] Schimmel, *Friedrich Rückert,* 96.

[135] See Pizer, *The Idea of World Literature,* 25.

Conclusion

[1] See David Osmond-Smith, *Playing on Words: A Guide to Luciano Berio's Sinfonia.* (London: Royal Music Association, 1985), 54–71. According to Berio, *Sinfonia* was inspired by a 1967 performance of Mahler's Second Symphony by the New York Philharmonic under the direction of Leonard Bernstein and was subsequently commissioned by the New York Philharmonic. See Thomas Schäfer, *Modellfall Mahler: Kompositorische Rezeption in zeitgenössischer Musik* (Munich: Fink, 1999), 125.

[2] Osmond-Smith, *Playing on Words,* 39.

[3] Luciano Berio, *Remembering the Future: The Charles Eliot Norton Lectures* (Cambridge, MA, and London: Harvard UP, 2006), 6 and 136.

[4] Berio, *Remembering the Future,* 82. Interestingly, Berio bases his theory of semantic openness in music on Umberto Eco's semiotic study *Opera aperta;* in English, *The Open Work,* trans. Anna Cancogni (Cambridge MA: Harvard UP, 1989).

[5] Martha C. Nussbaum, *Upheavals of Thought: The Intelligence of Emotions* (Cambridge: Cambridge UP, 2001), 263.

⁶ See also Joshua Cohen's provocative essay "Purist of the Self: Did Mahler Get the Biographer He Deserves?" *Harper's Magazine*, July 2008, 88–94: "Any true biography or program intending to describe Mahler's 'world-era' should engage with the Holocaust, which sounded the last discordant cadence of Mitteleuropean culture" (94).

⁷ See Gerhard Scheit and Wilhelm Svoboda, *Feindbild Gustav Mahler: Zur antisemitischen Abwehr der Moderne in Österreich* (Vienna: Sonderzahl, 2002), 116. The piece performed was the Second Symphony.

⁸ See Johan Giskes, "Van triomf naar tragedie (1920–1942)," in *Mahler in Amsterdam van Mengelberg tot Chailly*, ed. Johan Giskes and Ester L. Woudhuysen (Bussum and Amsterdam: THOTH/Gemeentearchief Amsterdam, 1995), 57–72; here 71–72. Performances included the First and Fourth Symphonies, *Die Lieder eines fahrenden Gesellen*, and excerpts from other works.

⁹ For examples see Hilmes, *Witwe im Wahn: Das Leben der Alma Mahler-Werfel* (Munich: Siedler, 2004), 241 and 286. See also Hilmes, *Im Fadenkreuz: Politische Gustav-Mahler-Rezeption, 1919–1945. Eine Studie über den Zusammenhang von Antisemitismus und Kritik an der Moderne* (Frankfurt am Main: Peter Lang, 2003), 177–78.

¹⁰ See Scheit and Svoboda, *Feindbild*, 56–60.

¹¹ Hilmes, *Witwe im Wahn*, 282.

¹² Regarding Alma's close ties to Schuschnigg, see Oliver Hilmes, *Witwe im Wahn*, 276–78; Bruno Walter discusses his friendship with Schuschnigg in his autobiography, *Theme and Variations: An Autobiography*, trans. James A. Galston (1946; repr., New York: Alfred A. Knopf, 1966), 317 and 319. The paradox underlying Schuschnigg's regime was that he was "never quite sure whether to oppose Nazism outright, or compete with Hitler for the loyalty of Austria's fascist and German nationalist elements, while reaching some *modus vivendi* with the Third Reich." Steven Beller, *A Concise History of Austria* (Cambridge: Cambridge UP, 2006), 224–25.

¹³ Scheit and Svoboda, *Feindbild*, 72–74.

¹⁴ See Hilmes, *Witwe im Wahn*, 279–80; for a more detailed analysis of the discussions about the Mahler monument, see also *Im Fadenkreuz*, 200–213.

¹⁵ Scheit and Svoboda, *Feindbild*, 57; Hilmes, *Im Fadenkreuz*, 190.

¹⁶ Scheit and Svoboda, *Feindbild*, 79 and 86. Křenek at the time published an essay that was very critical of Walter's views of "modern" music. See *Im Atem der Zeit: Erinnerungen an die Moderne*, trans. Friedrich Saathen and Sabine Schulte (Hamburg: Hoffmann & Campe, 1998), 903–4. In Walter's case, one could say, his "classical" reading of Mahler mirrored the cultural priorities of the regime for which it was performed. Willem Mengelberg's far more radical readings of Mahler's scores — emphasizing the music's contrasts, discontinuities, and dissonances (see "Introduction," n. 4) — however did not keep him from collaborating with the German occupiers after the German invasion of the Netherlands in May 1940.

[17] Walter, *Theme and Variations*, 303–4; see also Erik Ryding and Rebecca Pechefsky, *Bruno Walter: A World Elsewhere* (New Haven, CT, and London: Yale UP, 2001), 233.

[18] Hilmes, *Witwe im Wahn*, 288–89.

[19] For example, see Roger Griffin, *Modernism and Fascism: The Sense of a Beginning under Mussolini and Hitler* (New York: Palgrave MacMillan, 2007), 58–61 and 94–95.

[20] For a recent critical analysis of this discourse in German cultural and intellectual history, including a discussion of current scholarship on the topic, see, for example, Jonathan M. Hess, *Germans, Jews and the Claims of Modernity* (New Haven, CT, and London: Yale UP, 2002), 7–11 and 19–20.

[21] Michael P. Steinberg, *Judaism Musical and Unmusical* (Chicago and London: Chicago UP, 2007), 8.

[22] See Karen Painter, "Contested Counterpoint: 'Jewish' Appropriation and Polyphonic Liberation," *Archiv für Musikwissenschaft* 58.3 (2001): 201–30; here 201–2. The page numbers in parentheses in the text in this paragraph refer to this work. Karen Painter works out these ideas in more detail in her recent book *Symphonic Aspirations: German Music and Politics, 1900–1945* (Cambridge, MA, and London: Harvard UP, 2007), in particular 51–68.

[23] In *Remembering the Future* Berio speaks of Stravinsky and Schoenberg's neo-classicism as being "very different sides of a musical journey that wants to exorcise and at the same time come to terms with memory and diversities. . . . The seeds of this conflicting relationship with memories and diversities are also present in Mahler. Breaking conventional stylistic codes, he solitarily developed within himself a musical discourse made of contrasting yet complementary forces where, in the same breath, trite melodic signals and compelling ideas, though 'institutionally' incompatible with each other, interact" (73–74). The Stravinsky piece that Berio has in mind here is *Agon*, with its wide range of references (75). Elsewhere Berio states that Adorno has problems in "dealing with diversities" (57), meaning that his theories are not equipped to deal with the trajectory of twentieth-century musical history Berio envisions.

[24] For an impression of the diversity of ideological responses to modernism among Jewish artists and intellectuals see, for example, Leon Botstein, *Judentum und Modernität: Essays zur Rolle der Juden in der deutschen und österreichischen Kultur, 1848 bis 1938* (Vienna and Cologne: Böhlau, 1991), 136–48. See also Steinberg's critique of the "derivation of critical modernism from an essential Jewish 'identity,'" (*Judaism Musical and Unmusical*, 254n42). For an earlier discussion of this issue, see Peter Gay, *Freud, Jews and other Germans: Masters and Victims in Modernist Culture* (New York: Oxford UP, 1978), for example, 101, 131, 153, 157–59, and 161.

[25] For a recent critique of the use of this term in German-Jewish cultural history, see Steinberg, *Judaism Musical and Unmusical*, 3.

[26] Sander L. Gilman interprets masochism in the context of conflicting cultural expectations as the "acting out of the conflict felt between the claims lodged against the individual and the ability of that individual to counter these claims

completely." "Preface," in *One Hundred Years of Masochism: Literary Texts, Social and Cultural Contexts*, ed. Michael C. Finke and Carl Niekerk (Amsterdam and Atlanta: Rodopi, 2000), v–viii; here v–vi.

[27] Morten Solvik, "Mahler's Untimely Modernism," in *Perspectives on Gustav Mahler*, ed. Jeremy Barham (Aldershot, UK, and Burlington, VT: Ashgate, 2005), 152–71; here 171.

[28] See Berio, *Remembering the Future*, 24, 45. Independently of Berio, this dialectical formula of characterizing modernism's double relationship with time has also been picked up by Patrizia C. McBride in a recent volume on the legacies of modernism. See "Introduction: The Future's Past — Modernism, Critique, and the Political," in *Legacies of Modernism. Art and Politics in Northern Europe, 1890–1950*, ed. Patrizia C. McBride, Richard W. McCormick, and Monika Żagar, 1–13. New York: Palgrave MacMillan, 2007.

[29] See in this context, for instance, the increased emphasis on musical "Germanness" in writings on music after the First World War, which has been identified by Pamela M. Potter in *Most German of the Arts: Musicology and Society from the Weimar Republic to the End of Hitler's Reich* (New Haven, CT, and London: Yale UP, 1998), for example, 203–4.

Works Consulted

Adorno, Theodor W. *Essays on Music.* Edited by Richard Leppert. Berkeley: U of California P, 2002.

———. *Gesammelte Schriften.* 20 vols. Frankfurt am Main: Suhrkamp, 1997.

———. *Mahler: Eine musikalische Physiognomik.* In *Gesammelte Schriften* 13:149–319. In English, *Mahler: A Musical Physiognomy.* Translated by Edmund Jephcott. Chicago and London: U of Chicago P, 1996.

———. "Mahler heute." In *Gesammelte Schriften* 18:226–34.

———. *Philosophie der neuen Musik.* Vol. 12 of *Gesammelte Schriften.*

———. *Versuch über Wagner.* In *Gesammelte Schriften* 13:7–148.

———. "Zu einem Streitgespräch über Mahler." In *Gesammelte Schriften* 18:244–50.

Alali-Huseinat, Mahmoud. *Rückert und der Orient: Untersuchungen zu Friedrich Rückerts Beschäftigung mit arabischer und persischer Literatur.* Frankfurt am Main: Peter Lang, 1993.

Albrecht, Wolfgang, and Hans-Joachim Kertscher, eds. *Wanderzwang — Wanderlust: Formen der Raum- und Sozialerfahrung zwischen Aufklärung und Frühindustrialismus.* Tübingen: Niemeyer, 1999.

Amerongen, Martin van, and Philo Bregstein. *Willem Mengelberg tussen licht en donker.* Baarn, Netherlands: de Prom, 2001.

Applegate, Celia, and Pamela Potter, eds. *Music and German National Identity.* Chicago and London: U of Chicago P, 2002.

Aristotle. *Poetics.* Translated by Malcolm Heath. London: Penguin, 1996.

Arnim, Achim von. "Von Volksliedern." In *Des Knaben Wunderhorn. Alte deutsche Lieder* 1:377–414.

Arnim, Achim von, and Clemens Brentano, eds. *Des Knaben Wunderhorn: Alte deutsche Lieder.* 3 vols. Kritische Ausgabe. Edited by Heinz Rölleke. Stuttgart: Reclam, 1987.

Aschheim, Steven E. *The Nietzsche Legacy in Germany, 1890–1990.* Berkeley, CA, Los Angeles, and Oxford: U of California P, 1992.

Aspetsberger, Friedbert, and Erich Wolfgang Partsch, eds. *Mahler-Gespräche: Rezeptionsfragen — literarischer Horizont — musikalische Darstellung.* Innsbruck: Studien Verlag, 2002.

Bahr, Erhard. "Goethe and the Concept of Bildung in Jewish Emancipation." In Berghahn and Hermand, *Goethe in German-Jewish Culture,* 16–28.

Bahr, Hermann. "Das junge Oesterreich." In *Studien zur Kritik der Moderne,* 73–96.

———. *Studien zur Kritik der Moderne.* Frankfurt am Main: Rütten & Loening, 1894.

Barham, Jeremy, ed. *The Cambridge Companion to Mahler*. Cambridge: Cambridge UP, 2007.

———, ed. *Perspectives on Gustav Mahler*. Aldershot, UK, and Burlington, VT: Ashgate, 2005.

Barner, Wilfried. *Von Rahel Varnhagen bis Friedrich Gundolf: Juden als deutsche Goethe-Verehrer*. Göttingen: Wallstein, 1992.

Bauer-Lechner, Natalie. *Fragmente: Gelerntes und Gelebtes*. Vienna: Rudolf Lechner & Sohn, 1907.

———. *Gustav Mahler in den Erinnerungen von Natalie Bauer-Lechner*. Edited by Herbert Killian. Rev. ed. Hamburg: Verlag der Musikalienhandlung Karl Dieter Wagner, 1984. In English, *Recollections of Gustav Mahler*. Translated by Dika Newlin. Edited by Peter Franklin. Cambridge: Cambridge UP, 1980.

Baumbach, Rudolf. *Lieder eines fahrenden Gesellen*. 1878. Reprint, Leipzig: A. G. Liebeskind, 1898.

Bayer, Josef. *Das neue k.k. Hofburgtheater als Bauwerk mit seinen Sculpturen und Bilderschmuck*. Vienna: Gesellschaft für vervielfältigende Kunst, 1894.

Becqué, Robert, and Eveline Nikkels, eds. *Die liebe Erde allüberall: Proceedings of Das Lied von der Erde Symposium Den Haag 2002*. Den Haag: Stichting rondom Mahler, 2005.

Behler, Ernst. "Nietzsche und die frühromantische Schule." *Nietzsche-Studien: Internationales Jahrbuch für die Nietzsche-Forschung* 7 (1978): 59–96.

Behrendt, Bernd. "August Julius Langbehn, der 'Rembrandtdeutsche.'" In *Handbuch zur "Völkischen Bewegung," 1871–1918*, edited by Uwe Puschner, Walter Schmitz, and Julius H. Ulbricht, 94–113. Munich: K. G. Saur, 1996.

Beller, Steven. *A Concise History of Austria*. Cambridge: Cambridge UP, 2006.

———, ed. *Rethinking Vienna, 1900*. New York and Oxford: Berghahn, 2001.

———. *Vienna and the Jews, 1867–1938: A Cultural History*. Cambridge: Cambridge UP, 1989.

Ben-Amos, Dan, and Liliane Weissberg, eds. *Cultural Memory and the Construction of Identity*. Detroit: Wayne State UP, 1999.

Benes, Tuska. "From Indo-Germans to Aryans: Philology and the Racialization of Salvationist National Rhetoric, 1806–30." In Eigen and Larrimore, *The German Invention of Race*, 167–81.

Berghahn, Klaus L. *Grenzen der Toleranz: Juden und Christen im Zeitalter der Aufklärung*. Cologne: Böhlau, 2000.

———. "Patterns of Childhood: Goethe and the Jews." In Berghahn and Hermand, *Goethe in German-Jewish Culture*, 3–15.

Berghahn, Klaus L., and Jost Hermand, eds. *Goethe in German-Jewish Culture*. Columbia, SC: Camden House, 2001.

Berhorst, Ralf. *Anamorphosen der Zeit: Jean Pauls Romanästhetik und Geschichtsphilosophie.* Tübingen: Max Niemeyer, 2002.
Berio, Luciano. *Remembering the Future: The Charles Eliot Norton Lectures.* Cambridge, MA, and London: Harvard UP, 2006.
Berio, Talia Pecker. "Mahler's Jewish Parable." In Painter, *Mahler and His World*, 87–110.
Bernstein, Leonard. *The Little Drummer Boy: An Essay on Gustav Mahler.* DVD. Hamburg: Deutsche Grammophon, 2007.
———. *Mahler Rehearsals: Symphonies Nos. 5 & 9; Das Lied von der Erde.* DVD. Hamburg: Deutsche Grammophon, 2005.
Bethge, Hans. *Die chinesische Flöte.* 20th ed. Kelkheim: YinYang Media, 2001.
Bielschowsky, Albert. *Goethe: Sein Leben und seine Werke.* 2 vols. 10th and 11th eds. Munich: Beck, 1906.
Birus, Hendrik. "Der 'Orientale' Jean Paul: Versuch über Goethes 'Vergleichung.'" *Jahrbuch der Jean-Paul-Gesellschaft* 20(1985): 103–26.
Bisanz-Prakken, Marian. *Gustav Klimt: Der Beethovenfries; Geschichte, Funktion und Bedeutung.* Munich: DTV, 1980.
Blaukopf, Herta. "'Bücher fresse ich immer mehr und mehr': Gustav Mahler als Leser." In Aspetsberger and Partsch, *Mahler-Gespräche*, 96–116.
———. "Jean Paul, die erste Symphonie und Dostojewski." In *Gustav Mahler: Werk und Wirken; Neue Mahler-Forschung aus Anlaß des vierzigjährigen Bestehens der Internationalen Gustav Mahler Gesellschaft*, edited by Erich Wolfgang Partsch, 35–42. Vienna: Vom Pasqualatihaus, 1996.
———. "Mahler an der Universität: Versuch, eine biographische Lücke zu schließen." In *Neue Mahleriana: Essays in Honour of Henry-Louis de La Grange on His Seventieth Birthday*, edited by Günther Weiß, 1–16. Bern: Peter Lang, 1997.
———. "Rivalität und Freundschaft: Die persönlichen Beziehungen zwischen Gustav Mahler und Richard Strauss." In Mahler and Strauss, *Briefwechsel*, 129–225.
Blaukopf, Kurt. *Gustav Mahler oder der Zeitgenosse der Zukunft.* 2nd ed. Vienna, Munich, and Zurich: Fritz Molden, 1969.
———. *Mahler: Sein Leben, sein Werk und seine Welt in zeitgenössischen Bildern und Texten.* Mit Beiträgen von Zoltan Roman. Vienna: Universal Edition, 1976.
Bohlmann, Philip V. *Jewish Music and Modernity.* Oxford and New York: Oxford UP, 2008.
———. "Landscape — Region — Nation — Reich: German Folk Song in the Nexus of National Identity." In Applegate and Potter, *Music and German National Identity*, 105–27.
———. *World Music: A Very Short Introduction.* Oxford: Oxford UP, 2002.
Borchmeyer, Dieter. "Gustav Mahler's Goethe and Goethe's Holy Ghost: Marginalia on the Eighth Symphony in Light of a Recent Event." *News about Mahler Research* 32 (1994): 18–20.

———. *Richard Wagner: Ahasvers Wandlungen.* Frankfurt am Main and Leipzig: Insel, 2002.
Borchmeyer, Dieter, and Jörg Salaquarda. "Nachwort: Legende und Wirklichkeit einer epochalen Begegnung." In *Nietzsche und Wagner: Stationen einer epochalen Begegnung,* 2:1271–1386. 2 vols. Frankfurt am Main and Leipzig: Insel, 1994.
Bormann, Alexander von. "Metaphysik der Unmöglichkeit? Zum Text von Mahlers VIII. Symphonie." In Nikkels and Becqué, *A "Mass" for the Masses: Proceedings of the Mahler VIII Symposium, Amsterdam 1988,* 92–99.
———. "Volk als Idee. Zur Semiotisierung des Volksbegriffs." In *Volk — Nation — Europa. Zur Romantisierung und Entromantisierung politischer Begriffe,* 35–56.
———, ed. *Volk — Nation — Europa: Zur Romantisierung und Entromantisierung politischer Begriffe.* Würzburg: Königshausen & Neumann, 1998.
Botstein, Leon. "German Jews and Wagner." In *Richard Wagner and His World,* edited by Thomas S. Grey, 151–97. Princeton, NJ, and Oxford: Princeton UP, 2009.
———. *Judentum und Modernität: Essays zur Rolle der Juden in der deutschen und österreichischen Kultur, 1848 bis 1938.* Vienna and Cologne: Böhlau, 1991.
———. "Sozialgeschichte und die Politik des Ästhetischen: Juden und Musik in Wien 1870–1938." In Botstein and Hanak, *quasi una fantasia. Juden und die Musikstadt Wien,* 43–63.
———. "Whose Gustav Mahler?" In Painter, *Mahler and His World,* 1–53.
Botstein, Leon, and Werner Hanak, eds. *quasi una fantasia: Juden und die Musikstadt Wien.* Vienna: Wolke, 2003.
Bouillon, Jean-Paul. *Klimt: Beethoven. The Frieze for the Ninth Symphony.* Translated by Michael Heron. New York: Rizzoli International Publications, 1987.
Boxberger, Robert. "Rückerts Stellung zur Weltliteratur." In Wolfdietrich Fischer, *Friedrich Rückert im Spiegel seiner Zeitgenossen und der Nachwelt,* 111–24.
Brenner, Michael. "Pre-Weimar Origins." In *The Renaissance of Jewish Culture in Weimar Germany,* 11–35.
———. *The Renaissance of Jewish Culture in Weimar Germany.* New Haven, CT, and London: Yale UP, 1996.
Brentano, Clemens. *Geschichte vom braven Kasperl und dem schönen Annerl.* In *Werke* 2:774–806.
———. *Das Märchen von Gockel, Hinkel und Gackeleia.* In *Werke* 3:617–930.
———. *Das Märchen von Gockel und Hinkel.* In *Werke* 3:484–565.
———. *Werke.* Edited by Friedhelm Kemp. Vols. 2 and 3. Munich: Hanser, 1963 and 1965.
Bruford, W. H. *The German Tradition of Self-Cultivation: "Bildung" from Humboldt to Thomas Mann.* London and New York: Cambridge UP, 1975.

Buch, Esteban. *Beethoven's Ninth: A Political History.* Translated by Richard Miller. Chicago and London: U of Chicago P, 2003.
Bürger, Peter. *Theorie der Avantgarde.* Frankfurt am Main: Suhrkamp, 1974. In English, *Theory of the Avant-Garde.* Translated by Michael Shaw. Foreword by Jochen Schulte-Sasse. Minneapolis: U of Minnesota P, 1989.
Burke III, Edmund, and David Prochaska, eds. *Genealogies of Orientalism: History, Theory, Politics.* Lincoln, NE, and London: U of Nebraska P, 2008.
———. "Introduction: Orientalism from Postcolonial Theory to World History." In *Genealogies of Orientalism: History, Theory, Politics,* 1–71.
Burton, Humphrey. *Leonard Bernstein.* London: Faber & Faber, 1995.
Carnegy, Patrick. *Wagner and the Art of the Theatre.* New Haven, CT, and London: Yale UP, 2006.
Carr, Jonathan. *Mahler: A Biography.* Woodstock NY and New York: Overlook, 1998.
Cloot, Julia. *Geheime Texte: Jean Paul und die Musik.* Berlin and New York: Walter de Gruyter, 2001.
Cohen, Joshua. "Purist of the Self: Did Mahler Get the Biographer He Deserves?" *Harper's Magazine,* July 2008, 88–94.
Critchley, Simon. *On Humour.* London and New York: Routledge, 2002.
Cusack, Andrew. *The Wanderer in Nineteenth-Century German Literature: Intellectual History and Cultural Criticism.* Rochester, NY: Camden House, 2008.
Dahlhaus, Carl. *Richard Wagners Musikdramen.* 1971/85. 2nd ed., Stuttgart: Reclam, 1996.
Danuser, Hermann. *Gustav Mahler: Das Lied von der Erde.* Munich: Wilhelm Fink, 1986.
———, ed. *Gustav Mahler.* Wege der Forschung 653. Darmstadt: Wissenschaftliche Buchgesellschaft, 1992.
———. *Gustav Mahler und seine Zeit.* 2nd ed. Laaber, Germany: Laaber-Verlag, 1996.
———. "Natur-Zeiten in transzendenter Landschaft: Gustav Mahlers *Faust*-Komposition in der *Achten Symphony.*" In *Goethe und die Verzeitlichung der Natur,* edited by Peter Matussek, 301–25. Munich: Beck, 1998.
Dargie, E. Mary. *Music and Poetry in the Songs of Gustav Mahler.* Bern: Peter Lang, 1981.
Davison, Peter. "Nachtmusik I: Sound and Symbol." In Zychowicz, *The Seventh Symphony of Gustav Mahler: A Symposium,* 68–73.
Decsey, Ernst. "Stunden mit Mahler: Notizen." *Die Musik* 10.18 (1910/11): 352–56 (Gustav Mahler-Heft).
Diepenbrock, Alphons: *Brieven en Documenten.* Edited by Eduard Reeser. Vol. 6. 's-Gravenhage, Netherlands: Martinus Nijhoff, 1991.
———. "Schemeringen." *De Nieuwe Gids* 8.2 (1893): 449–64.
Dijkstra, Bram. *Idols of Perversity: Fantasies of Feminine Evil in Fin-de-Siècle Culture.* New York and Oxford: Oxford UP, 1986.
Dilthey, Wilhelm. *Das Erlebnis und die Dichtung: Lessing, Goethe, Novalis, Hölderlin.* 16th ed. Göttingen: Vandenhoeck & Ruprecht, 1985.

Eckermann, Johann Peter. *Gespräche mit Goethe in den letzten Jahren seines Lebens.* Frankfurt am Main: Deutscher Klassiker Verlag, 1999.

Eco, Umberto. *The Open Work.* Translated by Anna Cancogni. Cambridge MA: Harvard UP, 1989.

Eggebrecht, Hans Heinrich: *Die Musik Gustav Mahlers.* 2nd ed. Munich: Piper, 1986.

Eigen, Sara, and Mark Larrimore, eds. *The German Invention of Race.* Albany: State U of New York P, 2006.

Ekirch, A. Roger. *At Day's Close: Night in Times Past.* New York and London: W. W. Norton, 2005.

Feder, Stuart. "Gustav Mahler, dying." *International Review of Psycho-Analysis* 5 (1978): 125–48.

———. *Gustav Mahler: A Life in Crisis.* New Haven, CT, and London: Yale UP, 2004.

———. "Gustav Mahler um Mitternacht." *International Review of Psycho-Analysis* 7 (1980): 11–26.

Finke, Michael C. "Introduction." In Finke and Niekerk, *One Hundred Years of Masochism: Literary Texts, Social and Cultural Contexts,* 1–13.

Finke, Michael C., and Carl Niekerk, eds. *One Hundred Years of Masochism: Literary Texts, Social and Cultural Contexts.* Amsterdam and Atlanta: Rodopi, 2000.

Fischer, Bernd. *Das Eigene und das Eigentliche: Klopstock, Herder, Fichte, Kleist. Episoden aus der Konstruktionsgeschichte nationaler Intentionalitäten.* Berlin: Erich Schmidt, 1995.

Fischer, Jens Malte. "Ahnung und Aufbruch: Der junge Gustav Mahler und das Wien um 1870." *Neue Zürcher Zeitung,* 2 June 2001. http://www.nzz.ch/2001/06/02/li/page-article79J2Q.html.

———. *Gustav Mahler: Der fremde Vertraute.* Vienna: Paul Zsolnay, 2003.

———. "Gustav Mahler und das "Judentum in der Musik." *Merkur* 51(1997): 665–80.

———. *Richard Wagners "Das Judentum in der Musik."* Frankfurt am Main and Leipzig: Insel, 2000.

Fischer, Wolfdietrich, ed. *Friedrich Rückert im Spiegel seiner Zeitgenossen und der Nachwelt: Aufsätze aus der Zeit zwischen 1827 und 1986.* Wiesbaden: Harrassowitz, 1988.

Fischer-Dieskau, Dietrich. *Hugo Wolf: Leben und Werk.* Berlin: Henschel, 2003.

Fleming, Paul. *The Pleasures of Abandonment: Jean Paul and the Life of Humor.* Würzburg: Königshausen & Neumann, 2006.

Fliedl, Gottfried. *Gustav Klimt, 1862–1918: The World in Female Form.* Cologne: Taschen, 1998.

Floros, Constantin. *Die geistige Welt Gustav Mahlers in systematischer Darstellung.* Vol. 1 of *Gustav Mahler.* 2nd ed. Wiesbaden: Breitkopf & Härtel, 1987.

———. *The Symphonies.* Vol. 3 of *Gustav Mahler.* Translated by Vernon and Jutta Wicker. Pompton Plains, NJ, and Cambridge: Amadeus, 2000.

———. "Die 'Symphonie der Tausend' als Botschaft an die Menschheit." In Nikkels and Becqué, *A "Mass" for the Masses: Proceedings of the Mahler VIII Symposium Amsterdam 1988*, 121–30.
Fohrmann, Jürgen. "Jean Pauls 'Titan': Eine Lektüre." *Jahrbuch der Jean-Paul-Gesellschaft* 20(1985): 7–32.
Förster-Nietzsche, Elisabeth. *Das Leben Friedrich Nietzsche's*. 3 vols. Leipzig: C. G. Naumann, 1894, 1897, and 1904.
Frank, Manfred. *Einführung in die frühromantische Ästhetik: Vorlesungen*. Frankfurt am Main: Suhrkamp, 1989.
———. *Gott im Exil*. Vol. 2 of *Vorlesungen über die Neue Mythologie*. Frankfurt am Main: Suhrkamp, 1988.
———. *Der kommende Gott*. Vol. 1 of *Vorlesungen über die Neue Mythologie*. Frankfurt am Main: Suhrkamp, 1982.
Franke, Ursula. "Bildung/Erziehung, ästhetische," in *Ästhetische Grundbegriffe*, edited by Karlheinz Barck, vol. 1, 696–727. Stuttgart and Weimar: J. B. Metzler, 2000.
Franklin, Peter. "'Funeral Rites': Mahler and Mickiewicz." *Music & Letters* 55.2 (April 1974): 203–8.
———. *Mahler: Symphony No. 3*. Cambridge: Cambridge UP, 1991.
Freud, Sigmund. "Der Dichter und das Phantasieren." In *Gesammelte Werke*, edited by Anna Freud, 7:213–23. Frankfurt am Main: Fischer, 1999.
———. *Die Traumdeutung*. In *Gesammelte Werke*, 2/3:1–642.
Furness, Raymond. *Zarathustra's Children: A Study of a Lost Generation of German Writers*. Rochester, NY: Camden House, 2000.
Gay, Peter. *Freud, Jews and Other Germans: Masters and Victims in Modernist Culture*. New York: Oxford UP, 1978.
Gerlach, Reinhard: *Strophen von Leben, Traum und Tod: Ein Essay über Rückert-Lieder von Gustav Mahler*. Wilhelmshaven: Heinrichshofen, 1983.
Gilman, Sander L. "Heine, Nietzsche, and the Idea of the Jew." In Golomb, *Nietzsche and Jewish Culture*, 76–100.
———. *Jewish Self-Hatred: Anti-Semitism and the Hidden Language of the Jews*. Baltimore and London: Johns Hopkins UP, 1990.
———. "Preface." In *One Hundred Years of Masochism: Literary Texts, Social and Cultural Contexts*, edited by Michael C. Finke and Carl Niekerk, v–viii. Amsterdam and Atlanta: Rodopi, 2000.
———. "Strauss, the Pervert, and Avant Garde Opera of the Fin de Siècle." *New German Critique* 43 (Winter, 1988): 35–68.
Giskes, Johan. "Van triomf naar tragedie (1920–1942)." In Giskes and Woudhuysen, *Mahler in Amsterdam van Mengelberg tot Chailly*, 57–72.
Giskes, Johan, and Ester L. Woudhuysen, eds. *Mahler in Amsterdam van Mengelberg tot Chailly*. Bussum and Amsterdam: THOTH/Gemeentearchief Amsterdam, 1995.
Goethe, Johann Wolfgang von. *Aus meinem Leben: Dichtung und Wahrheit*. Vol. 9 of *Werke*. Hamburger Ausgabe.
———. *Briefwechsel zwischen Goethe und Zelter in den Jahren 1799 bis 1832*. Edited by Hans-Günter Ottenberg and Edith Zehm. 2 vols. Munich:

Carl Hanser, 1991. [= vols. 20.1 and 20.2 of *Sämtliche Werke nach Epochen seines Schaffens. Münchner Ausgabe*, edited by Karl Richter]

———. *Briefwechsel zwischen Schiller und Goethe in den Jahren 1794 bis 1805.* 2 vols. Edited by Manfred Beetz. Munich: Hanser, 1990. [= vols. 8.1 and 8.2 of *Sämtliche Werke nach Epochen seines Schaffens. Münchner Ausgabe*, edited by Karl Richter]

———. *Faust.* Edited by Albrecht Schöne. 2 vols. Sonderausgabe. Frankfurt am Main: Deutscher Klassiker Verlag, 1999.

———. *Faust I & II.* Edited and translated by Stuart Atkins. In *Collected Works in 12 Volumes*, vol. 2. Princeton, NJ: Princeton UP, 1994.

———. *Faust: Der Tragödie erster und zweiter Teil; Urfaust.* Edited by Erich Trunz. Sonderausgabe. Munich: Beck, 1987.

———. *Faust: Eine Tragödie.* Edited by Gustav von Loeper. Berlin: Gustav Hempel, 1870.

———. *Gespräche mit Goethe in den letzten Jahren seines Lebens*, see Eckermann, Johann Peter.

———. *Maximen und Reflexionen.* In *Werke. Hamburger Ausgabe* 12:365–547.

———. "Über Kunst und Alterthum: Mittheilungen im ersten bis dritten Bande." In *Werke. Weimarer Ausgabe*, section 1, 41:372–73. Weimar: Böhlau, 1902.

———. *Werke. Hamburger Ausgabe.* Edited by Erich Trunz. 14 vols. 1948–1952. Reprint, Munich: Beck, 1982.

———. *West-östlicher Divan.* In *Werke. Hamburger Ausgabe* 2:7–270.

Goetschel, Willi. *Spinoza's Modernity: Mendelssohn, Lessing, and Heine.* Madison: U of Wisconsin P, 2004.

Golomb, Jacob, ed. *Nietzsche and Jewish Culture.* London and New York: Routledge, 1997.

———, ed. *Nietzsche and the Austrian Culture/Nietzsche und die österreichische Kultur.* Wiener Vorlesungen: Konversatorien und Studien 17. Vienna: WUV, 2004.

Golomb, Jacob, and Robert S. Wistrich, eds. *Nietzsche, Godfather of Fascism? On the Uses and Abuses of a Philosophy.* Princeton, NJ, and Oxford: Princeton UP, 2002.

Gomperz, Theodor. 'Über die Grenzen der jüdischen intellectuellen Begabung." In Kann, *Theodor Gomperz. Ein Gelehrtenleben im Bürgertum der Franz-Josefs-Zeit*, 384–89.

Görner, Rüdiger "'[. . .] das letzte grosse Ereigniss im Schicksal unserer Cultur' Oder: Nietzsche 'liest' die Romantik." In *Die Lesbarkeit der Romantik: Material, Medium, Diskurs*, edited by Erich Kleinschmidt, 83–102. Berlin: De Gruyter, 2009.

Griffin, Roger. *Modernism and Fascism: The Sense of a Beginning under Mussolini and Hitler.* New York: Palgrave MacMillan, 2007.

Hahn, Barbara. "Demarcations and Projections: Goethe in the Berlin Salons." In *Goethe in German-Jewish Culture*, edited by Klaus L. Berghahn and Jost Hermand, 31–43. Columbia, SC: Camden House, 2001.

Hasan-Rokem, Galit, and Alan Dundes, eds. *The Wandering Jew: Essays in the Interpretation of a Christian Legend*. Bloomington: Indiana UP, 1986.
Haslinger, Josef. *Klasse Burschen: Essays*. Frankfurt am Main: Fischer, 2001.
Hefling, Stephen E. *Mahler: Das Lied von der Erde*. Cambridge, New York, and Melbourne: Cambridge UP, 2000.
———. "Mahler's 'Todtenfeier' and the Problem of Program Music." *Nineteenth-Century Music* 12.1 (Summer 1988): 27–53.
———. "The Rückert Lieder." In Mitchell and Nicholson, *The Mahler Companion*, 338–65.
———. "Techniques of Irony in Mahler's Oeuvre." In *Gustav Mahler et l'ironie dans la culture viennoise au tournant du siècle*, edited by André Castagné, Michel Chalon, and Patrick Florençon, 99–142. Montpellier: Climats, 2001.
Hein, Peter Ulrich. *Transformation der Kunst: Ziele und Wirkungen der deutschen Kultur- und Kunsterziehungsbewegung*. Cologne and Vienna: Böhlau, 1991.
Heine, Heinrich. *Die romantische Schule*. In *Sämtliche Schriften*, vol. 3:357–504. Munich: DTV, 2005.
Herder, Johann Gottfried. *Briefe zu Beförderung der Humanität*. Vol. 7 of *Werke in zehn Bänden*.
———. *Ideen zur Philosophie der Geschichte der Menschheit*. Vol. 6 of *Werke in zehn Bänden*.
———. *Volkslieder*. 2 vols. Leipzig: Weigandsche Buchhandlung, 1778–79.
———. *Werke in zehn Bänden*. Edited by Günter Arnold. Frankfurt am Main: Deutscher Klassiker Verlag, 1985–2000.
Hermand, Jost. *Judentum und deutsche Kultur: Beispiele einer schmerzhaften Symbiose*. Cologne, Weimar, and Vienna: Böhlau, 1996.
Hess, Jonathan M. *Germans, Jews and the Claims of Modernity*. New Haven, CT, and London: Yale UP, 2002.
Hillebrand, Bruno. "Einführung." In *Nietzsche und die deutsche Literatur: Texte zur Nietzsche-Rezeption, 1873–1963*, 1:1–55.
———. *Nietzsche und die deutsche Literatur: Texte zur Nietzsche-Rezeption, 1873–1963*. Vol. 1. Tübingen: Niemeyer, 1978.
Hilmes, Oliver. *Im Fadenkreuz: Politische Gustav-Mahler-Rezeption, 1919–1945. Eine Studie über den Zusammenhang von Antisemitismus und Kritik an der Moderne*. Frankfurt am Main: Peter Lang, 2003.
———. *Witwe im Wahn: Das Leben der Alma Mahler-Werfel*. Munich: Siedler, 2004.
Hirsch, Leo. "'Beinahe echt?' Nietzsche und der jüdische Prometheus." *Central Verein Zeitung*, 20 June 1935.
Hobsbawm, Eric. "Introduction." In Hobsbawm and Ranger, *The Invention of Tradition*, 1–14.
———. "Mass-Producing Traditions: Europe, 1870–1914." In Hobsbawn and Ranger, *The Invention of Tradition*, 263–307.
Hobsbawm, Eric, and Terence Ranger, eds. *The Invention of Tradition*. Cambridge: Cambridge UP, 1992.

Hoffmann, E. T. A. *Fantasiestücke in Callots Manier.* Vol. 1 of *E. T. A. Hoffmanns sämtliche Werke.* Edited by Carl Georg von Maassen. 2nd ed. Munich and Leipzig: Georg Müller, 1912.

Hofmannsthal, Hugo von. "Blick auf Jean Paul." In *Gesammelte Werke*, vol. 8, edited by Bernd Schoeller, 434–37. Frankfurt am Main: Fischer, 1979.

Hölderlin, Friedrich. *Gedichte.* Vol. 1 of *Sämtliche Werke und Briefe*, edited by Jochen Schmidt. Frankfurt am Main: Deutscher Klassiker Verlag, 1992.

Humboldt, Wilhelm von. "Der Montserrat bei Barcelona." In *Gesammelte Schriften*, vol. 3: *1799–1818*, edited by Albert Leitzmann, 30–57. Berlin: B. Behr, 1904.

Israel, Jonathan. *Radical Enlightenment: Philosophy and the Making of Modernity, 1650–1750.* Oxford: Oxford UP, 2001.

Jacobs, Jürgen, and Markus Krause. *Der deutsche Bildungsroman: Gattungsgeschichte vom 18. bis zum 20. Jahrhundert.* Munich: C. H. Beck, 1989.

Janik, Allan. "Vienna 1900 Revisited: Paradigms and Problems." In Beller, *Rethinking Vienna, 1900,* 27–56.

Jean Paul. *Blumen-, Frucht- und Dornenstücke oder Ehestand, Tod und Hochzeit des Armenadvokaten F. St. Siebenkäs.* In *Werke* 2:7–576.

———. *Die Briefe Jean Pauls.* Vol. 4. Edited by Eduard Berend. Munich: Georg Müller, 1926.

———. *Selbsterlebensbeschreibung.* In *Werke* 6:1037–1103.

———. *Titan.* In *Werke* 3:7–1010.

———. "Vorrede." In *Fantasiestücke in Callots Manier*, in *E. T. A. Hoffmanns sämtliche Werke: Historisch-kritische Ausgabe* 1:3–9.

———. *Vorschule der Ästhetik.* In *Werke* 5:9–456.

———. *Werke.* Edited by Norbert Miller. 6 vols. 1st–6th ed. Munich: Carl Hanser, 1959–1999.

Jelavich, Barbara. *Modern Austria: Empire & Republic, 1800–1986.* Cambridge: Cambridge UP, 1987.

Jiang, Yimin. "*Die chinesische Flöte* von Hans Bethge und *Das Lied von der Erde* von Gustav Mahler: Vom Textverständnis bei der Rückübersetzung." In *Ostasienrezeption zwischen Klischee und Innovation: Zur Begegnung zwischen Ost und West um 1900*, edited by Walter Gebhard, 331–54. Munich: Iudicium, 2000.

Kaiser, Gerhard. *Aufklärung, Empfindsamkeit, Sturm und Drang.* 3rd ed. Munich: Francke, 1979.

Kann, Robert A., ed. *Theodor Gomperz: Ein Gelehrtenleben im Bürgertum der Franz-Josefs-Zeit.* Vienna: Verlag der österreichischen Akademie der Wissenschaften, 1974.

Kapner, Gerhardt. *Die Denkmäler der Wiener Ringstrasse.* Vienna: Jugend & Volk, 1969.

Karbusicky, Vladimír. "Gustav Mahler's Musical Jewishness." In *Perspectives on Gustav Mahler*, edited by Jeremy Barham, 195–216. Aldershot, UK, and Burlington, VT: Ashgate, 2005.

Kienzle, Ulrike. "*Parsifal* and Religion: A Christian Music Drama?" In *A Companion to Wagner's Parsifal*, edited by William Kinderman and Katherine R. Syer, 81–130. Rochester, NY: Camden House, 2005.
Kittler, Friedrich A. "Über die Sozialisation Wilhelm Meisters." In Gerhard Kaiser and Friedrich A. Kittler, *Dichtung als Sozialisationsspiel: Studien zu Goethe und Gottfried Keller,* 13–124. Göttingen: Vandenhoeck & Ruprecht, 1978.
Klemperer, Otto. *Meine Erinnerungen an Gustav Mahler und andere autobiographische Skizzen.* Freiburg i. Br. and Zurich: Atlantis, 1960.
Klopstock, Friedrich. *Sämmtliche Werke.* Leipzig: Göschen, 1840.
Knapp, Raymond. "Perspectives on Innocence and Vulnerability in Mahler's Fourth Symphony." *Nineteenth-Century Music* 22.3 (1999): 233–67.
Kokoschka, Oskar. *Die träumenden Knaben und Der weiße Tiertöter.* Frankfurt am Main and Leipzig: Insel, 1998.
Kontje, Todd. *The German Bildungsroman: History of a National Genre.* Columbia, SC: Camden House, 1993.
———. *German Orientalisms.* Ann Arbor: U of Michigan P, 2004.
Köpnick, Lutz. "Goethes Ikonisierung der Poesie: Zur Schriftmagie des *Westöstlichen Divans*." *Deutsche Vierteljahrsschrift für Literaturwissenschaft und Geistesgeschichte* 66.2 (1992): 361–89.
———. *Nothungs Modernität: Wagners 'Ring' und die Poesie der Macht.* Munich: Fink, 1994.
Koselleck, Reinhart. "Volk, Nation, Nationalismus, Masse." In *Geschichtliche Grundbegriffe: Historisches Lexikon zur politisch-sozialen Sprache in Deutschland,* edited by Otto Brunner, Werner Conze, and Reinhart Koselleck, 7:141–431. Stuttgart: Klett-Cotta, 1992.
Kravitt, Edward F. "Mahler's Dirges for his Death: February 24, 1901." *Musical Quarterly* 64.3 (1978): 329–53.
Křenek, Ernst. "Gustav Mahler." In Walter, *Gustav Mahler: With a Biographical Essay by Ernst Křenek,* 155–220.
———. *Im Atem der Zeit: Erinnerungen an die Moderne.* Translated by Friedrich Saathen and Sabine Schulte. Hamburg: Hoffmann & Campe, 1998.
Kreutzer, Hans Joachim. *Faust: Mythos und Musik.* Munich: Beck, 2003.
Kropfinger, K. "Gerettete Herausforderung: Mahlers 4. Symphonie — Mengelbergs Interpretation." In *Mahler-Interpretation: Aspekte zum Werk und Wirken von Gustav Mahler,* edited by R. Stephan, 111–75. Mainz: Schott, 1985.
Kuper, Adam. *Culture: The Anthropologists' Account.* Cambridge, MA, and London: Harvard UP, 1999.
Lacoue-Labarthe, Philippe, and Jean-Luc Nancy. *The Literary Absolute: The Theory of Literature in German Romanticism.* Albany: State U of New York P, 1988.
La Grange, Henry-Louis de. *Mahler.* Vol. 1. Garden City, NJ, and New York: Doubleday, 1973.

———. *Gustav Mahler*. Vol. 2: *Vienna: The Years of Challenge (1897–1904)*. Oxford and New York: Oxford UP, 1995.
———. *Gustav Mahler*. Vol. 3: *Vienna: Triumph and Disillusion (1904–1907)*. Oxford and New York: Oxford UP, 1999.
———. *Gustav Mahler*. Vol. 4: *A New Life Cut Short (1907–1911)*. Oxford and New York: Oxford UP, 2008.
Langbehn, Julius. *Rembrandt als Erzieher: Von einem Deutschen*. 40th ed. Leipzig: C. L. Hirschfeld, 1892.
Lebrecht, Norman, ed. *Mahler Remembered*. New York and London: Norton, 1988.
Lepenies, Wolf. *The Seduction of Culture in German History*. Princeton, NJ, and Oxford: Princeton UP, 2006.
Leppert, Richard. "Compositions, Composers, and Works: Commentary." In *Essays on Music*, by Theodor W. Adorno, edited by Richard Leppert, 513–63. Berkeley: U of California P, 2002.
Le Rider, Jacques. *Modernity and Crises of Identity: Culture and Society in Fin-de-Siècle Vienna*. Translated by Rosemary Morris. New York: Continuum, 1993.
Lever, Maurice. *Zepter und Schellenkappe: Zur Geschichte des Hofnarren*. Translated by Kathrina Menke. Frankfurt am Main: Fischer, 1992.
Levin, David J. *Richard Wagner, Fritz Lang, and the Nibelungen: The Dramaturgy of Disavowal*. Princeton, NJ: Princeton UP, 1998.
———. *Unsettling Opera: Staging Mozart, Verdi, Wagner, and Zemlinsky*. Chicago and London: U of Chicago P, 2007.
Lipiner, Siegfried *Adam. Ein Vorspiel. Hyppolytos. Tragödie*. Stuttgart: W. Spemann, 1913.
———. *Der entfesselte Prometheus: Eine Dichtung in fünf Gesängen*. Leipzig: Breitkopf & Härtel, 1876.
———. *Über die Elemente einer Erneuerung religiöser Ideen in der Gegenwart*. Vienna: Selbstverlag des Vorstandes des Lesevereines der deutschen Studenten Wiens, 1878.
Lippitt, John. "Nietzsche, Zarathustra and the Status of Laughter." *British Journal of Aesthetics* 32.1 (January 1992): 39–49.
Lovejoy, Arthur O. *The Great Chain of Being: A Study of the History of an Idea*. New York: Harper & Row, 1960.
Luhmann, Niklas. *Liebe als Passion: Zur Codierung von Intimität*. Frankfurt am Main: Suhrkamp, 1984.
Magee, Bryan. *The Philosophy of Schopenhauer*. Rev. ed. Oxford and New York: Clarendon and Oxford UP, 1997.
Magon, Leopold. "Goethes 'West-östlicher Divan' und Rückerts 'Östliche Rosen': Zur Vorgeschichte der 'Östlichen Rosen.'" In Fischer, *Friedrich Rückert im Spiegel seiner Zeitgenossen und der Nachwelt: Aufsätze aus der Zeit zwischen 1827 und 1986*, 310–30.
Mahler, Alma. *And the Bridge Is Love*. In collaboration with E. B. Ashton. New York: Harcourt, Brace, 1958.

——. *Diaries, 1898–1902*. Translated and edited by Antony Beaumont. Ithaca, NY: Cornell UP, 2000.

——. *Gustav Mahler: Erinnerungen und Briefe*. Amsterdam: Allert de Lange, 1940. In English, *Gustav Mahler: Memories and Letters*. Rev. ed. Translated by Basil Creighton. Edited by Donald Mitchell. New York: Viking, 1969.

——. *Mein Leben*. Frankfurt am Main: Fischer, 1998.

Mahler, Gustav. *Briefe*. Edited by Herta Blaukopf. 2nd rev. ed. Vienna: Paul Zsolnay Verlag, 1996.

——. *Ein Glück ohne Ruh': Die Briefe Gustav Mahlers an Alma*. Edited by Henry-Louis de La Grange and Günther Weiß. Berlin: Siedler, 1995.

——. *"Mein lieber Trotzkopf, meine süße Mohnblume": Briefe an Anna von Mildenburg*. Vienna: Paul Zsolnay, 2006.

——. *Sämtliche Werke: Kritische Gesamtausgabe* [score]. Edited by the International Gustav Mahler Society, Vienna. Wasserburg am Bodensee: C. F. Kahnt; Frankfurt am Main: C. F. Peters; and Vienna: Universal Edition, 1960–2002.

——. *Unbekannte Briefe*. Edited by Herta Blaukopf. Vienna and Hamburg: Paul Zsolnay, 1983.

Mahler, Gustav, and Richard Strauss. *Briefwechsel, 1888–1911*. Edited by Herta Blaukopf. Munich and Zurich: R. Piper, 1980.

Maier, Charles. "Mahler's Theater: The Performative and the Political in Central Europe, 1890–1910." In Painter, *Mahler and His World*, 55–85.

Mandelkow, Karl Robert, ed. *Goethe im Urteil seiner Kritiker: Dokumente zur Wirkungsgeschichte Goethes in Deutschland. Vol. 2: 1832–1870*. Munich: Beck, 1977.

——. *Goethe in Deutschland: Rezeptionsgeschichte eines Klassikers*. Vol. 1: *1773–1918*. Munich: C. H. Beck, 1980.

Marchand, Suzanne L. *German Orientalism in the Age of Empire*. Cambridge: Cambridge UP, 2009.

Markx, Francien. *Der Kritiker als Magier: E. T. A. Hoffmanns Musikerzählungen im Kontext der Allgemeinen Musikalischen Zeitung*. PhD diss., U of Illinois at Urbana-Champaign, 2003.

McBride, Patrizia C. "Introduction: The Future's Past — Modernism, Critique, and the Political." In McBride, McCormick, and Žagar, *Legacies of Modernism*, 1–13.

McBride, Patrizia C., Richard W. McCormick, and Monika Žagar, eds. *Legacies of Modernism: Art and Politics in Northern Europe, 1890–1950*. New York: Palgrave MacMillan, 2007.

McCarthy, John A. *Remapping Reality: Chaos and Creativity in Science and Literature (Goethe — Nietzsche — Grass)*. Amsterdam and New York: Rodopi, 2006.

McGrath, William J. *Dionysian Art and Populist Politics in Austria*. New Haven, CT, and London: Yale UP, 1974.

———. "Dionysian Art: Crisis and Creativity in Turn-of-the-Century Vienna." In Golomb, *Nietzsche and the Austrian Culture/Nietzsche und die österreichische Kultur*, 23–41.

———. "Mahler and the Vienna Nietzsche Society." In Golomb, *Nietzsche and Jewish Culture*, 218–32.

Mendes-Flohr, Paul. *Divided Passions: Jewish Intellectuals and the Experience of Modernity*. Detroit: Wayne State UP, 1991.

Menzel, Wolfgang. *Die deutsche Literatur*. Vol. 2. Stuttgart: Franckh, 1828.

Meyer, Michael A., ed. *German-Jewish History in Modern Times*. Vol. 3: *Integration in Dispute*. New York: Columbia UP, 1997.

Meyer-Kalkus, Reinhart. "Richard Wagners Theorie der Wort-Tonsprache in 'Oper und Drama' und 'Der Ring des Nibelungen.'" *Athenäum: Jahrbuch für Romantik* 6 (1996): 153–95.

———. "World Literature beyond Goethe." In *Cultural Mobility: A Manifesto*, ed. by Stephen Greenblatt, 96–121. Cambridge and New York: Cambridge UP, 2010.

Meysenbug, Malwina. *Memoiren einer Idealistin*. Vol. 3. 6th ed. Berlin and Leipzig: Schuster & Loeffler, 1900.

Micheels, Pauline. "Gustav Mahler in Amsterdam (1903–1909)." In Giskes and Woudhuysen, *Mahler in Amsterdam van Mengelberg tot Chailly*, 24–36.

Mickiewicz, Adam. *Todtenfeier (Dziady). Poetische Werke*, vol. 2, translated by Siegfried Lipiner. Leipzig: Breitkopf & Härtel, 1887.

Mitchell, Donald. *Discovering Mahler: Writings on Mahler, 1955—2005*. Woodbridge, UK: Boydell, 2007.

———. *Gustav Mahler: The Early Years*. 1958. Repr., Woodbridge, UK: Boydell, 2003.

———. *Gustav Mahler: Songs and Symphonies of Life and Death*. 1985. Repr., Woodbridge, UK: Boydell, 2002.

———. *Gustav Mahler: The Wunderhorn Years*. 1975. Repr., Woodbridge, UK: Boydell, 2005.

———. "Mahler on the Move: His Seventh Symphony." In *Discovering Mahler: Writings on Mahler, 1955—2005*, 394–410.

———. "Mahler's 'Kammermusikton.'" In Mitchell and Nicholson, *The Mahler Companion*, 217–35.

———. "Reception." In *Facsimile Edition of the Seventh Symphony*, by Gustav Mahler, 2 vols., edited by Donald Mitchell and Edward Reilly, Commentary volume, 31–74. Amsterdam: Rosbeek, 1995.

———. "'Swallowing the Programme': Mahler's Fourth Symphony." In Mitchell and Nicholson, *The Mahler Companion*, 187–216.

———. "The Twentieth Century's Debt to Mahler: Our Debt to Him in the Twenty-First." In *Discovering Mahler*, 556–96.

Mitchell, Donald, and Andrew Nicholson, eds. *The Mahler Companion*. Oxford and New York: Oxford UP, 1999.

Mosse, George L. *German Jews beyond Judaism*. Cincinnati, OH: Hebrew Union College P, 1997.

———. *Germans and Jews: The Right, the Left, and the Search for a "Third Force" in Pre-Nazi Germany.* New York: Howard Fertig, 1970.

———. *The Image of Man: The Creation of Modern Masculinity.* New York and Oxford: Oxford UP, 1996.

Mozart, Wolfgang Amadeus. *Il dissoluto punito ossia il Don Giovanni* [score]. In *Sämtliche Werke. Neue Ausgabe*, vol. II, 17. Kassel: Bärenreiter, 1968.

Müller, Karl-Josef. *Mahler: Leben — Werke — Dokumente.* Mainz and Munich: Schott and Piper, 1988.

Musil, Robert. *Tagebücher.* Edited by by Adolf Frisé. 2 vols. Reinbek bei Hamburg: Rowohlt, 1983.

Nadler, Steven. *Rembrandt's Jews.* Chicago and London: U of Chicago P, 2003.

Nathorp, Paul. "Vorwort." In Lipiner, *Adam. Ein Vorspiel. Hyppolytos. Tragödie*, 3–13.

Néret, Gilles. *Gustav Klimt, 1862—1918.* Cologne: Taschen, 2003.

Niekerk, Carl. "Mahler contra Wagner: The Philosophical Legacy of Romanticism in Mahler's Third and Fourth Symphonies." *German Quarterly* 77.2 (2004): 189–210.

———. "The Romantics and Other Cultures." In *The Cambridge Companion to German Romanticism*, edited by Nicholas Saul, 147–61. Cambridge: Cambridge UP, 2009.

———. "Sexual Imagery in Goethe's *Faust II*." *Seminar* 33.1 (1997): 1–21.

Nietzsche, Friedrich. *Also sprach Zarathustra.* Vol. 4 of *Sämtliche Werke: Kritische Studienausgabe.* In English, *Thus Spoke Zarathustra: A Book for All and None.* Translated by Adrian Del Caro. Cambridge: Cambridge UP, 2006.

———. *Briefwechsel: Kritische Gesamtausgabe.* Edited by Giorgio Colli and Mazzino Montinari. Section 2, vol. VI 6/2. Berlin and New York: de Gruyter, 1980.

———. *Ecce Homo.* In *Sämtliche Werke: Kritische Studienausgabe* 6:255–349. In English, *Ecce Homo: How to Become What you Are.* In *The Anti-Christ, Ecce Homo, Twilight of the Idols. And Other Writings*, translated by Josefine Nauckhoff and Adrian Del Caro, 69–151. Cambridge: Cambridge UP, 2005.

———. *Der Fall Wagner: Ein Musikanten-Problem.* In *Sämtliche Werke: Kritische Studienausgabe* 6:9–54. In English, *The Case of Wagner: A Musician's Problem.* In *The Anti-Christ, Ecce Homo, Twilight of the Idols: And Other Writings*, 231–62.

———. *Die fröhliche Wissenschaft.* In *Sämtliche Werke, Kritische Studienausgabe* 3:343–651. In English, *The Gay Science. With a Prelude in German Rhymes and an Appendix of Songs.* Translated by Josefine Nauckhoff and Adrian Del Caro. Cambridge: Cambridge UP, 2001.

———. *Die Geburt der Tragödie.* In *Sämtliche Werke, Kritische Studienausgabe* 1:9–156. In English, *The Birth of Tragedy and Other Writings.* Translated by Ronald Speirs. Cambridge: Cambridge UP, 2004.

———. *Götzen-Dämmerung*. In *Sämtliche Werke: Kritische Studienausgabe* 6:55–162. In English, *Twilight of the Idols*. In *The Anti-Christ, Ecce Homo, Twilight of the Idols. And Other Writings*, translated by Josefine Nauckhoff and Adrian Del Caro, 153–229. Cambridge: Cambridge UP, 2005.

———. *Menschliches, allzu Menschliches*. Vol. 2 of *Sämtliche Werke: Kritische Studienausgabe*. In English, *Human, All Too Human: A Book for Free Spirits*. Translated by R. J. Hollingdale. Cambridge: Cambridge UP, 2002.

———. *Morgenröthe*, in *Sämtliche Werke: Kritische Studienausgabe* 3:9–331. In English, *Daybreak: Thoughts on the Prejudices of Morality*. Translated by R. J. Hollingdale. Cambridge: Cambridge UP, 2003.

———. *Nachgelassene Fragmente, 1884–1885*. Vol. 11 of *Sämtliche Werke: Kritische Studienausgabe*.

———. *Nachgelassene Fragmente, 1885–1887*. Vol. 12 of *Sämtliche Werke: Kritische Studienausgabe*.

———. *Nachgelassene Fragmente, 1887–1889*. Vol. 13 of *Sämtliche Werke: Kritische Studienausgabe* 13.

———. *Sämtliche Werke: Kritische Studienausgabe in 15 Bänden*. Edited by Giorgio Colli and Mazzino Montinari. Munich: DTV; Berlin: de Gruyter, 1999.

Nikkels, Eveline. *Gustav Mahler: Een leven in tien symfonieën*. Leeuwarden, Netherlands: Bluestone, 2003.

———."O Mensch! Gib Acht!" *Friedrich Nietzsches Bedeutung für Gustav Mahler*. Amsterdam and Atlanta: Rodopi, 1989.

Nikkels, Eveline, and Robert Becqué, eds. *A "Mass" for the Masses. Proceedings of the Mahler VIII Symposium Amsterdam 1988*. The Hague: Nijgh & Van Ditmar Universitair, 1992.

Norman, Judith. "Nietzsche and Early Romanticism." *Journal of the History of Ideas* 63.3 (2002): 501–19.

Nowak, Adolf. "Zur Deutung der Dritten und Vierten Sinfonie Gustav Mahlers." In Danuser, *Gustav Mahler*, 191–205. Darmstadt: Wissenschaftliche Buchgesellschaft, 1992.

Nussbaum, Martha C. *Upheavals of Thought: The Intelligence of Emotions*. Cambridge: Cambridge UP, 2001.

O'Connell, Jeremy Day. "Pentatonic." In *Grove Music Online*, edited by L. Macy. http://www.grovemusic.com.proxy2.library.uiuc.edu (accessed 13 May 2008).

Osmond-Smith, David. *Playing on Words: A Guide to Luciano Berio's Sinfonia*. London: Royal Music Association, 1985.

Paddison, Max. *Adorno's Aesthetics of Music*. Cambridge: Cambridge UP, 1997.

Painter, Karen. "Contested Counterpoint: 'Jewish' Appropriation and Polyphonic Liberation." *Archiv für Musikwissenschaft* 58.3 (2001): 201–30.

———, ed. *Mahler and His World*. Princeton, NJ, and London: Princeton UP, 2002.

———. "The Sensuality of Timbre: Responses to Mahler and Modernity at the 'Fin de Siècle.'" *Nineteenth-Century Music* 18.3 (Spring 1995): 236–56.

———. *Symphonic Aspirations: German Music and Politics, 1900–1945*. Cambridge, MA, and London: Harvard UP, 2007.

Pape, Walter, ed. *Das "Wunderhorn" und die Heidelberger Romantik: Mündlichkeit, Schriftlichkeit, Performanz*. Tübingen: Niemeyer, 2005.

Partsch, Susanna. *Gustav Klimt: Painter of Women*. Munich: Prestel, 2006.

Pfitzner, Hans. "Werk und Wiedergabe." In *Gesammelte Schriften*, 3:115–19. Augsburg: Dr. Benno Filser Verlag, 1929.

Pizer, John. *The Idea of World Literature: History and Pedagogical Practice*. Baton Rouge: Louisiana State UP, 2006.

Polaschegg, Andrea. *Der andere Orientalismus: Regeln deutsch-morgenländischer Imagination im 19. Jahrhundert*. Berlin and New York: Walter de Gruyter, 2005.

Potter, Pamela M. *Most German of the Arts: Musicology and Society from the Weimar Republic to the End of Hitler's Reich*. New Haven, CT, and London: Yale UP, 1998.

Prang, Helmut. *Friedrich Rückert: Geist und Form der Sprache*. Wiesbaden: Harrassowitz, 1963.

Pulzer, Peter. "The Return of the Old Hatreds." In Meyer, *Integration in Dispute*, vol. 3 of *German-Jewish History in Modern Times*, 196–251.

Puschner, Uwe. *Die völkische Bewegung im wilhelminischen Kaiserreich: Sprache — Rasse — Religion*. Darmstadt: Wissenschaftliche Buchgesellschaft, 2001.

Reeser, Eduard. *Alphons Diepenbrock*. Amsterdam: Bigot & van Rossum, 1936.

———, ed. *Gustav Mahler und Holland: Briefe*. Vienna: Universal Edition, 1980.

———. "Die Mahler-Rezeption in Holland, 1903–1911." In *Mahler-Interpretation*, edited by Rudolph Stephan, 81–103. Mainz: Schott's Söhne, 1985.

———. *De muzikale handschriften van Alphons Diepenbrock*. Amsterdam: G. Alsbach, 1933.

Reginster, Bernard. *The Affirmation of Life: Nietzsche on Overcoming Nihilism*. Cambridge, MA, and London: Harvard UP, 2006.

Reik, Theodor. *The Haunting Melody: Psychoanalytic Experiences in Life and Music*. New York: Farrar, Straus, & Young, 1953.

Reilly, Edward R. "Sketches, Text Sources, Dating of Manuscripts — Unanswered Questions." *News about Mahler Research* 30 (October 1993): 3–9.

———. "Todtenfeier and the Second Symphony." In Mitchell and Nicholson, *The Mahler Companion*, 84–125.

Reitter, Paul. *The Anti-Journalist: Karl Kraus and Jewish Self-Fashioning in Fin-de-Siècle Europe*. Chicago: U of Chicago P, 2008.

———. "The Jewish Self-Hatred Octopus." *German Quarterly* 82.3 (2009): 356–72.

Revers, Peter. *Mahlers Lieder: Ein musikalischer Werkführer*. Munich: C. H. Beck, 2000.

———. "The Seventh Symphony." In Mitchell and Nicholson, *The Mahler Companion*, 376–99.

Richter, Thomas. *Die Dialoge über Literatur im Briefwechsel zwischen Goethe und Zelter*. Stuttgart and Weimar: Metzler, 2000.

Robertson, Ritchie. *The "Jewish Queston" in German Literature, 1749–1939: Emancipation and Its Discontents*. Oxford and New York: Oxford UP, 2002.

Rölleke, Heinz. "Gustav Mahlers 'Wunderhorn'-Lieder: Textgrundlagen und Textauswahl." *Jahrbuch des freien deutschen Hochstifts* 20 (1981): 370–78.

———. "'Des Knaben Wunderhorn' — eine romantische Liedersammlung: Produktion — Distribution — Rezeption." In *Das "Wunderhorn" und die Heidelberger Romantik: Mündlichkeit, Schriftlichkeit, Performanz*, edited by Walter Pape, 3–19. Tübingen: Niemeyer, 2005.

Roller, Alfred. *Die Bildnisse von Gustav Mahler*. Leipzig and Vienna: E. P. Tal, 1922. In English, "Alfred Roller" (excerpt). In Lebrecht, *Mahler Remembered*, 149–65.

Rose, Paul Lawrence. *Wagner: Race and Revolution*. New Haven, CT, and London: Yale UP, 1992.

Rosenberg, Wolf. "Mahler und die Avantgarde: Kompositionstechnisches Vorbild oder geistige Sympathie?" In *Gustav Mahler: Sinfonie und Wirklichkeit*, edited by Otto Kolleritsch, 81–92. Graz: Universal Edition, 1977.

Rückert, Friedrich. *Gesammelte Gedichte*. 6 vols. Erlangen: Carl Heyder, 1834–38.

———. *Gesammelte poetische Werke*. 12 vols. Frankfurt am Main: J. D. Sauerländer, 1868, 1869.

———. *Haus und Jahr.* Vol. 2 of *Gesammelte poetische Werke*.

———. *Kindertodtenlieder. Aus seinem Nachlasse*. Frankfurt am Main: J. D. Sauerländer, 1872.

———. *Kindertodtenlieder und andere Texte des Jahres 1834. Historisch-kritische Ausgabe "Schweinfurter Edition."* Edited by Hans Wollschläger und Rudolf Kreutner. Göttingen: Wallstein, 2007.

———. *Liebesfrühling*. In *Gesammelte poetische Werke* 1:281–639.

———. *Werke in sechs Bänden*. Vol. 3. Edited by Conrad Beyer. Leipzig: Gustav Fock, 1897.

Rückert, Rüdiger, and Max-Rainer Uhrig. *Friedrich-Rückert-Literaturen, 1813 bis 2007*. Microsoft Word document. [Rückert-bibliography] http://www.rueckert-gesellschaft.de/bibliographie.html (accessed 16 May 2008).

Russell, Peter. *Light in Battle with Darkness: Mahler's Kindertotenlieder*. Bern: Peter Lang, 1991.

Ryding, Erik, and Rebecca Pechefsky. *Bruno Walter: A World Elsewhere*. New Haven, CT, and London: Yale UP, 2001.
Said, Edward W. *Orientalism*. New York: Vintage, 1994.
Sammons, Jeffrey L. "Schiller vs. Goethe: Revisiting the Conflicting Reception Vectors of Heinrich Heine, Ludwig Börne, and Wolfgang Menzel." *Goethe Yearbook* 13 (2005): 1–17.
Schäfer, Thomas. *Modellfall Mahler: Kompositorische Rezeption in zeitgenössischer Musik*. Munich: Fink, 1999.
Schama, Simon. *Rembrandt's Eyes*. New York: Knopf, 1999.
Scheffer, Frank. *Gustav Mahler: Attrazione d'Amore/Voyage to Cythera: Luciano Berio*. DVD. Paris: Idéale Audience, 2005.
———. *Gustav Mahler: Conducting Mahler/I Have Lost Touch with the World*. DVD. Paris: Idéale Audience, 2005.
Schein, Ida. *Die Gedanken- und Ideenwelt Siegfried Lipiners*. PhD diss., University of Vienna, 1936.
Scheit, Gerhard, and Wilhelm Svoboda. *Feindbild Gustav Mahler: Zur antisemitischen Abwehr der Moderne in Österreich*. Vienna: Sonderzahl, 2002.
Schiller, Friedrich. *Gedichte*. Vol. 1 of *Werke und Briefe*. Frankfurt am Main: Deutscher Klassiker Verlag, 1992.
———. *Votivtafeln*. In *Werke und Briefe* 1:174–82.
Schimmel, Annemarie. *Friedrich Rückert: Lebensbild und Einführung in sein Werk*. Freiburg: Herder, 1987.
Schlegel, Friedrich. *Über die Sprache und Weisheit der Indier*. In *Kritische Friedrich-Schlegel-Ausgabe* 8:105–380. Munich: Schöningh & Thomas, 1975.
Schmidt, James. "'Not these Sounds': Beethoven at Mauthausen." *Philosophy and Literature* 29 (2005): 146–63.
Schönberg, Jutta. *Anti-Titan: Subjektgenese und Subjektkritik bei Jean Paul im psychokulturellen Kontext*. Frankfurt am Main: Peter Lang, 1994.
Schopenhauer, Arthur. *Aphorismen zur Lebensweisheit*. Vol. 8 of *Werke: Zürcher Ausgabe*.
———. *Werke: Zürcher Ausgabe in zehn Bänden*. Edited by Arthur Hübscher. Zurich: Diogenes, 1977.
Schorske, Carl E. *Fin-de-Siècle Vienna: Politics and Culture*. New York: Vintage, 1981.
———. *Eine österreichische Identität: Gustav Mahler*. Vienna: Picus, 1996.
Schwerte, Hans [= Hans Schneider]. *Faust und das Faustische: Ein Kapitel deutscher Ideologie*. Stuttgart: Ernst Klett, 1962.
See, Klaus von. *Barbar, Germane, Arier: Die Suche nach der Identität der Deutschen*. Heidelberg: Universitätsverlag C. Winter, 1994.
———. *Freiheit und Gemeinschaft: Völkisch-nationales Denken in Deutschland zwischen Französischer Revolution und Erstem Weltkrieg*. Heidelberg: Universitätsverlag C. Winter, 2001.
Seyhan, Azade. *Representation and Its Discontents: The Critical Legacy of German Romanticism*. Berkeley, CA, Los Angeles, and Oxford: U of California P, 1992.

———. *Writing outside the Nation*. Princeton, NJ, and Oxford: Princeton UP, 2001.
Singer, Peter. "Preface." In *Animal Philosophy: Essential Readings in Continental Thought*, edited by Peter Atterton and Matthew Calarco. London and New York: Continuum, 2004.
Sloterdijk, Peter. *Der Denker auf der Bühne: Nietzsches Materialismus*. Frankfurt am Main: Suhrkamp, 1986.
Solvik, Morten. "The Literary and Philosophical Worlds of Gustav Mahler." In Barham, *The Cambridge Companion to Mahler*, 21–34.
———. "Mahler's Untimely Modernism." In Barham, *Perspectives on Gustav Mahler*, 152–71.
Sorgner, Stefan Lorenz. "Nietzsche." In Sorgner and Fürbeth, *Musik in der deutschen Philosophie: Eine Einführung*, 115–34.
Sorgner, Stefan Lorenz, and Oliver Fürbeth, eds. *Musik in der deutschen Philosophie: Eine Einführung*. Stuttgart and Weimar: Metzler, 2003.
Spazier, Richard Otto. *Jean Paul Friedrich Richter: Ein biographischer Commentar zu dessen Werken*. 5 Vols. Leipzig: C. Brüggemann and O. Wigand, 1833. [= Vols. 61–65 of *Jean Paul's Sämmtliche Werke*]
Specht, Richard. *Gustav Mahler*. 5th–8th ed. Berlin: Schuster & Loeffler, 1918.
Spielmann, Heinz. *Oskar Kokoschka: Leben und Werk*. Cologne: Dumont, 2003.
Sprengel, Peter, ed. "Einleitung." In *Jean Paul im Urteil seiner Kritiker*, xv–xcii.
———. *Jean Paul im Urteil seiner Kritiker: Dokumente zur Wirkungsgeschichte Jean Pauls in Deutschland*. Munich: C. H. Beck, 1980.
———. "Zur Wirkungsgeschichte von Jean Pauls 'Titan.'" *Jahrbuch der Jean-Paul-Gesellschaft* 17 (1982): 11–30.
Stark-Voit, Renate. "'Bild — Symbol — Klang': Zu Gustav Mahlers Wunderhorn-Vertonungen." In Aspetsberger and Partsch, *Mahler-Gespräche: Rezeptionsfragen — literarischer Horizont — musikalische Darstellung*, 118–43.
Steffen, Hans, ed. *Nietzsche: Werk und Wirkungen*. Göttingen: Vandenhoeck & Ruprecht, 1974.
Steinberg, Michael P. *Judaism Musical and Unmusical*. Chicago and London: U of Chicago P, 2007.
———. *Listening to Reason: Culture, Subjectivity, and Nineteenth-Century Music*. Princeton, NJ, and Oxford: Princeton UP, 2004.
———. *The Meaning of the Salzburg Festival: Austria as Theater and Ideology, 1890–1938*. Ithaca, NY: Cornell UP, 1990.
Stern, Fritz. *The Politics of Cultural Despair: A Study in the Rise of the Germanic Ideology*. Garden City, NJ: Doubleday & Co., 1965.
Strauss, Richard. *Betrachtungen und Erinnerungen*. 3rd ed. Edited by Willi Schuh. Zurich: Atlantis, 1981.
———. *Salome: Drama in One Act after Oscar Wilde's Poem*. English and German. Translated by Hedwig Lachmann. Berlin: Adolph Fürstner; New York: Breitkopf & Härtel, 1905.

Strohschneider-Kohrs, Ingrid. "Zur Poetik der deutschen Romantik II: Die romantische Ironie." In *Die deutsche Romantik: Poetik, Formen und Motive*, edited by Hans Steffen, 75–97. Göttingen: Vandenhoeck & Ruprecht, 1967.

Sutcliffe, Adam. *Judaism and Enlightenment*. Cambridge: Cambridge UP, 2003.

Türnau, Dietrich. *Rabanus Maurus, der praeceptor Germaniae: Ein Beitrag zur Geschichte der Pädagogik des Mittelalters*. Munich: J. Lindauersche Buchhandlung (Schöpping), 1900.

Ueding, Gert. *Jean Paul*. Munich: C. H. Beck, 1993.

Vaget, Hans Rudolf. "Wagner, Anti-Semitism, and Mr. Rose: *Merkwürd'ger Fall!*" *German Quarterly* 66 (1993): 222–36.

Venturelli, Aldo. "Nietzsche in der Berggasse 19: Über die erste Nietzsche-Rezeption in Wien." *Nietzsche-Studien* 13 (1984): 448–80.

Vergo, Peter. *Art in Vienna, 1898–1918: Klimt, Kokoschka, Schiele and Their Contemporaries*. London and New York: Phaidon, 2001.

Vill, Susanne. "Mahler und Wagner — sichtbares und unsichtbares Theater." In *Richard Wagner und die Juden*, edited by Dieter Borchmeyer, Ami Maayani, and Susanne Vill, 296–309. Stuttgart and Weimar: Metzler, 2000.

———. *Vermittlungsformen verbalisierter und musikalischer Inhalte in der Musik Gustav Mahlers*. Tutzing, Germany: Hans Schneider, 1979.

Vordermayer, Martina. *Antisemitismus und Judentum bei Clemens Brentano*. Frankfurt am Main: Lang, 1999.

Wagner, Cosima. *Die Tagebücher*. 2 vols. Edited by Martin Gregor-Dellin and Dietrich Mack. Munich: Piper, 1976, 1977.

Wagner, Manfred. "Wien grüßt den fernen Osten." In *Die liebe Erde allüberall: Proceedings of Das Lied von der Erde Symposium Den Haag 2002*, edited by Eveline Nikkels and Robert Becqué, 20–33. Den Haag: Stichting rondom Mahler, 2005.

Wagner, Nike. "Nietzsche komponieren." In Golomb, *Nietzsche and the Austrian Culture/Nietzsche und die österreichische Kultur*, 271–88.

———. *Wagner Theater*. Frankfurt am Main and Leipzig: Insel, 1998.

Wagner, Richard. "Autobiographische Skizze (bis 1842)." In *Sämtliche Schriften und Dichtungen* 1:4–19.

———. "Beethoven." In *Sämtliche Schriften und Dichtungen* 9:61–127.

———. "Bericht über die Aufführung der neunten Symphonie von Beethoven im Jahre 1846 in Dresden." In *Sämtliche Schriften und Dichtungen* 2:50–65.

———. *Dichtungen und Schriften: Jubiläumsausgabe in zehn Bänden*. Edited by Dieter Borchmeyer. Frankfurt am Main: Insel, 1983.

———. "Das Kunstwerk der Zukunft." In *Sämtliche Schriften und Dichtungen* 3:42–178. In English, "The Art-Work of the Future." In *The Art-Work of the Future and Other Works*, translated by William Aston Ellis, 69–213. Lincoln: Nebraska UP, 1993.

———. *Parsifal*. In *Sämtliche Schriften und Dichtungen* 10:324–75.

———. "Publikum und Popularität." In *Sämtliche Schriften und Dichtungen* 10:61–90.

———. "Religion und Kunst" In *Sämtliche Schriften und Dichtungen* 10:211–85. In English, "Religion and Art." In *Prose Works*, vol. 6, translated by William Ashton Ellis, 211–52. New York: Broude Brothers, 1966.

———. *Sämtliche Schriften und Dichtungen*. Volksausgabe. 16 vols. Leipzig: Breitkopf & Härtel, 1911.

Walter, Bruno. *Briefe, 1894–1962*. Frankfurt am Main: S. Fischer, 1969.

———. "Bruno Walter on Mahler's Symphony No. 1." Essay accompanying Walter's last recording of the First Symphony: *Mahler: Symphony No. 1 in D ("The Titan")*. Bruno Walter/Columbia Symphony Orchestra, Columbia Masterworks 1962, Stereo LP MS 6394.

———. *Gustav Mahler: Ein Porträt*. Berlin and Frankfurt am Main: S. Fischer, 1957. In English, *Gustav Mahler: With a Biographical Essay by Ernst Křenek*. Translated by James Galston. New York: Greystone, 1941.

———. *Theme and Variations: An Autobiography*. Translated by James A. Galston. 1946. Reprint, New York: Alfred A. Knopf, 1966.

Weiner, Marc A. "1903 Gustav Mahler launches a new production of *Tristan und Isolde*, Otto Weininger commits suicide shortly after his *Geschlecht und Charakter* is published, and Max Nordau advocates the development of a 'muscle Jewry.'" In *Yale Companion to Jewish Writing and Thought in German Culture, 1096–1996*, edited by Sander L. Gilman and Jack Zipes, 255–61. New Haven, CT, and London: Yale UP, 1997.

———. "Hans Pfitzner and the Anxiety of Nostalgic Modernism." In McBride, McCormick, and Žagar, *Legacies of Modernism*, 17–28.

———. "Mahler and America: A Paradigm of Cultural Reception." *Modern Austrian Literature* 20.3/4 (1987): 155–69.

———. "Primal Sounds." *Opera Quarterly* 23.2/3 (2007): 217–46.

———. *Richard Wagner and the Anti-Semitic Imagination*. 2nd ed. Lincoln, NE, and London: Nebraska UP, 1997.

———. "Über Wagner sprechen: Ideologie und Methodenstreit." In *Richard Wagner im Dritten Reich*, edited by Saul Friedländer and Jörn Rüsen, 342–62. Munich: Beck, 2000.

———. *Undertones of Insurrection: Music, Politics, & the Social Sphere in the Modern German Narrative*. Lincoln, NE, and London: Nebraska UP, 1993.

Weininger, Otto. *Geschlecht und Charakter: Eine prinzipielle Untersuchung*. 9th ed. Vienna and Leipzig: Wilhelm Braumüller, 1907.

Weissberg, Liliane. "Introduction." In Ben-Amos and Weissberg, *Cultural Memory and the Construction of Identity*, 7–26.

Wenk, Arthur B. "The Composer as Poet in 'Das Lied von der Erde.'" *Nineteenth-Century Music* 1.1 (1977): 33–47.

Williamson, John G. "Mahler and Episodic Structure: The First Movement of the Seventh Symphony." In Zychowicz, *The Seventh Symphony of Gustav Mahler*, 27–46.

Wuthenow, Ralph-Rainer. "Verführung durch Phantasie." *Jahrbuch der Jean-Paul-Gesellschaft* 26/27 (1991/92): 92–107.
Zimmermann, Robert. "Leibnitz bei Spinoza: Eine Beleuchtung der Streitfrage." In *Sitzungsberichte der philosophisch-historischen Classe der kaiserlichen Akademie der Wissenschaften* 122:9–64. Vienna: F. Tempsky, 1890.
———. *Über das Tragische und die Tragödie*. Vienna: Wilhelm Braumüller, 1856.
Zwart, Frits. *Willem Mengelberg, 1871–1951: Een biografie, 1871–1920*. Vol. 1. Amsterdam: Prometheus, 1999.
Zychowicz, James L. "The Lieder of Mahler and Richard Strauss." In *The Cambridge Companion to the Lied*, edited by James Parsons, 245–72. Cambridge: Cambridge UP, 2004.
———. *Mahler's Fourth Symphony*. Studies in Musical Genesis and Structure, edited by Malcolm Gillies. Oxford and New York: Oxford UP, 2000.
———. "Ein schlechter Jasager: Considerations on the Finale to Mahler's Seventh Symphony." In *The Seventh Symphony of Gustav Mahler*, 98–106.
———, ed. *The Seventh Symphony of Gustav Mahler: A Symposium*. Cincinnati, OH: The U. of Cincinnati College-Conservatory of Music, 1990.

Index

Adler, Guido, 13, 185, 262
Adler, Victor, 18, 254
Adorno, Theodor W., 6–11, 21, 39, 66–67, 151, 163, 176–77, 179, 204, 211–12, 219, 224, 245, 253, 269, 272
Adorno, Theodor W., works by: *Mahler: Eine musikalische Physiognomik* (*Mahler: A Musical Physiognomy*), 6–8, 10–11, 39, 66–67, 151, 176–77, 179, 204, 245, 253, 269; "Mahler heute" ("Mahler today"), 224; *Philosophie der neuen Musik* (*Philosophy of New Music*), 8, 224; "Versuch über Wagner" ("Essay on Wagner"), 224; "Zu einem Streitgespräch über Mahler" ("Regarding a Disputation on Mahler"), 224
aesthetic immanence, 11–12, 75, 125, 144, 186, 188, 190, 268
alterity. *See* otherness
animals, 30, 43, 54, 72–73, 90–92, 120–21, 124, 196, 200
anti-programmatic statements, 5–6, 30, 52–53, 115, 135, 147, 214
anti-Semitic stereotypes, 14, 67, 74, 151, 196, 253
anti-Semitism, 7–8, 10–12, 14–15, 17, 19–21, 67–68, 82, 96, 127–29, 145–47, 154, 159, 194, 196, 216, 219–20, 224–27, 235, 237, 248–49, 252–54
Aristotle, 85, 100, 108, 118, 171–72, 239
Arnim, Achim von, 56–57, 59–63, 66–69, 71, 76, 81, 109, 115, 233–37, 241, 243–46

Arnim, Achim von, works by: "Von Volksliedern," 56, 59, 233–34
Arnim, Achim von, and Clemens Brentano, works by: *Des Knaben Wunderhorn* (*The Boy's Magic Horn*), 18, 56–57, 59, 61, 63, 66–68, 71, 76, 78, 82, 94–95, 102, 108–9, 111–13, 115, 120, 124, 128, 183, 235–37, 241, 243–46
Arnold, Gottfried, 258
art for art's sake (l'art pour l'art), 186
Aryan race, theory of, 181, 194–95, 261, 266
Aschheim, Steven E., 238–39, 244, 247–48
assimilation, 17, 19–20, 137, 147, 159, 178, 218–20, 226
atheism, 83, 90
Atkins, Stuart, 258
Austria, 3, 131, 154, 217
Austrofascism, 216, 220
avant-garde, 6, 21–23, 150, 161, 212, 216, 220, 227

Bach, Johann Sebastian, 86, 214
Bahr, Erhard, 255
Bahr, Hermann, 227
Barner, Wilfried, 255
Bartók, Béla, 185
Batka, Richard, 103–5, 194, 243, 265
Bauer-Lechner, Natalie, 14, 19–20, 29–31, 34–35, 41, 47–49, 94, 102, 105, 115, 117–18, 123, 127, 193, 226, 228, 231, 237, 242–43, 245, 259
Baumbach, Rudolf, 62
Bayer, Josef, 256

Bayreuth, 13–15, 32, 34, 89, 126, 130–31, 156, 225, 248
Bechstein, Ludwig, 80
Bechstein, Ludwig, works by: *Der singende Knochen* (*The Singing Bone*), 80–81
Beethoven, Ludwig van, 13, 15, 20, 24, 75, 86, 135, 144, 149, 155, 158, 161–62, 169–70, 176, 200, 214, 225, 228, 254–57
Beethoven, Ludwig van, works by: *Egmont* overture, 256; *Fidelio*, 75–76; *Symphony No. 6*, 214; *Symphony No. 9*, 13, 20, 24, 155, 161, 170, 228
Behrendt, Bernd, 252
Beller, Steven, 224, 226–27, 250, 254, 256, 271
Benes, Tuska, 261–62
Berg, Alban, 6–7
Berghahn, Klaus L., 252, 255
Berhorst, Ralf, 230–31
Berio, Luciano, 212–16, 221–22, 270, 272–73
Berio, Luciano, works by: *Remembering the Future*, 212, 214–16, 221–22, 270, 272–73; *Sinfonia*, 213–15, 270
Berio, Talia Pecker, 20, 227
Berlioz, Hector, 155, 257
Bernstein, Leonard, 3, 22–25, 97, 216, 227–28, 242, 270
Bethge, Hans, 198, 200–206, 267–68
Bethge, Hans, works by: *Die chinesische Flöte* (*The Chinese Flute*), 198, 200–206, 267–68
Bielschowsky, Albert, 255, 259
Bildung, 19, 31, 46, 152, 159, 213, 229, 232
Bildungsroman, 17, 31, 33, 35, 38–40, 42–43, 46–47, 50–52, 64, 68, 118–19, 128, 152, 213, 228, 230, 232
Birus, Hendrik, 229–30
Bisanz-Prakken, Marian, 256–57
Blaukopf, Herta, 229, 251, 255, 259–60, 266–67
Blaukopf, Kurt, 239, 243

Böckling, Arnold, 117
Bohlman, Philip V., 228, 233, 237
Bonaparte, Mary, 247
Booy, Hendrik de, 252
Borchmeyer, Dieter, 224, 237, 239, 248–49
Bormann, Alexander von, 234, 259
Börne, Ludwig, 254
Botstein, Leon, 2–4, 8–9, 25, 216, 223–24, 226–27, 248, 272
Boulez, Pierre, 214
Boxberger, Robert, 270
Brahmanism, 90, 194
Brahms, Johannes, 214
Brenner, Michael, 19, 227, 250, 252
Brentano, Clemens, 56–57, 61, 67, 69, 71, 76, 95–96, 109, 115, 233, 235–37, 241–46
Brentano, Clemens, works by: *Die Geschichte vom braven Kasperl und dem schönen Annerl* (*The Story of Brave Kasperl and Lovely Annerl*), 95–96, 241; *Märchen von Gockel, Hinkel und Gackeleia* (*Fairy Tale of Gockel, Hinkel, and Gackeleia*), 96, 235, 241–42; *Der Philister vor, in und nach der Geschichte* (*The Philistine before, in, and after History*), 67. See also Arnim, Achim von
Brockhoff, Ferdinand, 156–57
Bruckner, Anton, 117, 212
Bruford, Walter Horace, 229
Buch, Esteban, 225, 228, 254
Buddhism, 90, 194, 239, 265, 267
Bürger, Peter, 21–22, 227
Burgtheater, 160
Burke, Edmund, 260

Callot, Jacques, 30, 43–46, 53–55, 231
canonicity, 222
Carlyle, Thomas, 210, 270
Carnegy, Patrick, 225, 249
Carr, Jonathan, 229, 232, 235, 245
Catholicism, 17, 157, 161, 164, 217
childhood, 32–33, 40–41, 229
children, 34, 48, 54, 67, 71, 74, 95, 97, 108, 110–11, 115, 118–19, 121–22, 124, 189–93, 264

Christianity, 3, 37, 90–92, 109–12, 114, 120, 122, 127, 163–64, 168, 176, 190, 193–94, 201, 206, 264, 266
Christlich-deutsche Tischgesellschaft (Christian-German Dining Club), 67
cognition, 214–15, 221
Cohen, Joshua, 271
commonality, 153, 177, 210, 213, 221
cosmopolitanism in German culture, 3, 19, 32, 58–59, 130–31, 144, 147, 160–63, 175, 178, 211, 254
countertypes, 68, 81
creativity, 49, 193, 207, 209, 212
crisis, 21, 36, 57, 87, 126, 128, 218–19, 227
Critchley, Simon, 246
cultural memory, 10, 80–82, 146, 238
culture, 1, 6–9, 11–12, 17–25, 31–34, 57–62, 72, 80–82, 86–87, 90, 92, 124–31, 137, 143–51, 154, 157–60, 163, 169, 173, 177–83, 194–96, 210–11, 213, 218–22, 224, 238, 260; and anti-Semitism, 12; as apolitical, 24; Austrian, 189, 254; and crisis, 129; decline of, 89; Dutch, 141, 148; fin-de-siècle, 17, 21, 86, 179, 195, 208; German, 6–8, 15, 17–21, 23–24, 33, 126, 128, 130–31, 136–37, 143–46, 149, 151, 154, 159–60, 163, 173, 177, 180–81, 211–13, 218–21, 254; German-Austrian, 4, 11, 17; German-Jewish, 4, 18, 25, 34, 92, 127, 136, 158, 173, 220, 255, 272; high, 7–8, 22, 80; as homogenizing, 24; and identity, 222; Jewish, 127, 147, 159, 181, 196; low, 7–8, 22, 80; and mobility, 82; and nationalism, 19, 58, 78–79, 129, 157; oriental, 34, 189, 196; and otherness, 20–21, 82, 124, 129, 131, 147, 178–79, 181; and politics, 11; popular, 21, 126
Cusack, Andrew, 235

Dante, 232

Danuser, Hermann, 263, 267–69
Dargie, E. Mary, 264–65
Darwin, Charles, 103–4, 113
Davison, Peter, 250
death, 33, 37–38, 42–47, 50, 65, 71, 76–77, 92, 95, 98–100, 105, 117, 119, 121–22, 124, 152, 167, 172, 183, 187–95, 198–201, 203, 205–9, 245, 264–66, 269; on the battlefield, 76–77; Fechner on, 269; Freud on, 264; of God (Nietzsche), 83, 105; humor and, 46, 117, 119, 121; Jean Paul on, 37–38, 42–46; and *Des Knaben Wunderhorn*, 65, 71, 76–77; love and, 43, 46–47, 99, 152; Rückert and, 187, 189–93, 264; as symbol, 33
Debussy, Claude, 139, 185, 213
Decsey, Ernst, 130, 249
Degeneration, 90–91
Dehmel, Ida, 67, 78, 235
Dehmel, Richard, 249
Diepenbrock, Alphons, 53, 138–43, 150–51, 232, 250–51
Diepenbrock, Alphons, works by: *Im großen Schweigen* (*In Great Silence*), 139–41; *Incidental Music for Goethe's 'Faust,'* 139; *Die Nacht* (*The Night*), 139; "Schemeringen" ("Twilights"), 139–40, 251; *Te deum*, 138; *Veni Creator Spiritus*, 139
Dijkstra, Bram, 266
Dilthey, Wilhelm, 232
Dingelstedt, Franz, 156
diversity, 4, 21, 23, 25, 55–56, 97, 177, 179, 209–10, 212, 216, 219–22, 227, 272
Doré, Gustav, 68
Duchamp, Marcel, 22
Düntzer, Heinrich, 254
Dürer, Albrecht, 144

Eckermann, Johann Peter, 162–64, 257, 270
Eckermann, Johann Peter, works by: *Gespräche mit Goethe* (*Conversations with Goethe*), 162–64, 257, 270

Eco, Umberto, 232, 270
Eggebrecht, Hans Heinrich, 73, 94, 236, 264
Eichendorff, Joseph von, 135
Ekirch, A. Roger, 252
emotions, 2–3, 21, 23, 35–37, 40–43, 46–50, 52, 85, 99–100, 108–9, 113–15, 137, 152, 156, 172, 176, 186–87, 191–92, 208, 210–11, 213–16, 221, 242, 270; and commonality, 100, 210–11, 213; diverging, 43, 47, 50, 52, 85, 108–9, 115, 152, 187, 191, 215–16; and individual development, 35, 42, 46; music and, 2–3, 23, 43, 48, 100, 215–16, 221; Nussbaum on, 100, 215; Spinoza on, 172; and value, 99–100, 114, 215, 221
Enlightenment, 17, 58, 60, 97, 136, 144, 172, 218, 226, 230
ethnomusicology, 23, 56

Fechner, Gustav Theodor, 208, 269
Feder, Stuart, 247, 263, 265, 269
femininity, 38, 70, 82, 169, 196
Finke, Michael C., 230
Fischer, Bernd, 233
Fischer, Jens Malte, 89, 138, 234, 248, 260, 269
Fischer-Dieskau, Dietrich, 225
Floros, Constantin, 223–24, 231–32, 239, 243, 245, 258
Fohrmann, Jürgen, 229–31
Förster-Nietzsche, Elisabeth, 247
Förster-Nietzsche, Elisabeth, works by: *Das Leben Friedrich Nietzsche's*, 247–48
Franco-Prussian war, 78
Frank, Manfred, 239–40
Franke, Ursula, 229
Frankfurt School, 6–7
Franklin, Peter, 240, 243–44
Franz Joseph, emperor, 17
French Revolution, 24, 32, 79
Freud, Sigmund, 11–12, 18–19, 24, 36, 42, 65, 85, 88, 109, 116, 120, 123–24, 161, 179, 190, 199, 208, 228, 230, 247, 264, 272

Freud, Sigmund, works by: "Der Dichter und das Phantasieren" ("The Creative Writer and Day-Dreaming"), 123, 247; *Traumdeutung* (*The Interpretation of Dreams*), 123, 247
Freund Hein (the grim reaper), 117, 245
Furness, Raymond, 238, 243–44

Gay, Peter, 272
Geiger, Ludwig, 174
gender, 81, 169
Gerlach, Reinhard, 264
Gesamtkunstwerk (total work of art), 15
Gilman, Sander L., 127, 226, 248, 256, 261, 266–67, 272–73
Giskes, Johan, 271
Goethe, Johann Wolfgang von, 18–19, 33–34, 36, 38, 44–46, 48–51, 64, 71, 75, 88, 90–93, 128–29, 131, 139, 144, 154–77, 181–84, 186, 193–94, 196–98, 206, 209–11, 221, 228–29, 232, 236, 240, 243, 254–59, 262–64, 266, 269–70; and Beethoven, 161, 169; on Bildung, 51, 159; and cosmopolitanism, 19, 155, 159; and Heine, 255; and Jean Paul, 33–34, 45–46, 48, 50–51, 93, 229; and Jews, 158–59, 173, 255; and Kant, 259; and Langbehn, 144; and Lipiner, 170–73, 257; on love, 44, 167–69; on music, 163, 174, 257; as a national symbol, 154–57, 160; and nature, 164–66, 269; and the Orient, 33, 174–76, 181–83, 186, 194, 196, 209, 261; and pantheism, 92; on religion, 164, 167, 169, 258; and Rückert, 183–84, 210, 262; contra Schiller, 154–55, 158, 160–61, 254, 256; and Friedrich Schlegel, 181–82; and Schopenhauer, 194, 261; and Spinoza, 172–73, 177, 258–59, 266; on symbols, 90–91; and Vienna, 160; and Wagner, 129, 131, 139, 156, 158–59, 240; on

wandering, 64; on world literature, 210–11, 221, 270; and Zelter, 174, 257
Goethe, Johann Wolfgang von, works by: "Der Chinese in Rom," 229; *Dichtung und Wahrheit* (*Poetry and Truth*), 232; *Egmont*, 161; "Erlkönig" ("King of Elves"), 71; *Faust*, 34, 128, 131, 139, 154–57, 159–64, 166–73, 175–77, 206, 221, 254–55, 257–59, 264; *Die Leiden des jungen Werther* (*The Sorrows of Young Werther*), 36, 44–51, 93, 240; *Maximen und Reflexionen*, 240, 259; *Noten und Abhandlungen zu besserem Verständnis des West-östlichen Divans* (*Notes and Treatises to Further the Understanding of the West-Eastern Divan*), 181–82, 229, 261; *West-östlicher Divan*, 33–34, 174–76, 181–84, 193–94, 196, 198, 209–10, 229, 259, 261–63; *Wilhelm Meisters Lehrjahre* (*Wilhelm Meister's Apprenticeship*), 38, 51, 64, 228; *Wilhelm Meisters Wanderjahre* (*Wilhelm Meister's Journeyman Years*), 64
Goethe monument, 160
goetheln, 159, 256
Goetschel, Willi, 240, 259
Gomperz, Theodor, 136–37, 250
Gomperz, Theodor, works by: "Über die Grenzen der jüdischen intellectuellen Begabung" ("On the Limits of Jewish Intellectual Aptitude"), 136–37, 250
Görner, Rüdiger, 248
Griffin, Roger, 234, 272
Grimm, Herman, 156
Grimm, Jacob, and Wilhelm Grimm, 80, 234–35
Grimme, Hubert, 263

Hafiz, 174–75, 181, 184, 193
Hahn, Barbara, 255
Haitink, Bernard, 269
Hamburger, Paul, 71, 236–37
Hammer-Purgstall, Joseph von, 174

Hanslick, Eduard, 73
Haslinger, Josef, 228
Haydn, Joseph, 117
Hefling, Steven E., 240, 246, 263–64, 267–69
Hein, Peter Ulrich, 252
Heine, Heinrich, 64, 92, 136, 157–58, 254–55
Herder, Johann Gottfried, 56–62, 82, 147, 178, 180–81, 210, 233, 260–61
Herder, Johann Gottfried, works by: *Briefe zu Beförderung der Humanität* (*Letters for the Advancement of Humanity*), 233; *Ideen zur Philosophie der Geschichte der Menschheit* (*Ideas for the Philosophy of History of Humanity*), 233, 260–61; *Volkslieder* (*Folk songs*), 233
Hermand, Jost, 229, 231
Herz, Henriette, 158
Hess, Jonathan M., 272
heterogeneity, 6, 9, 23–24, 34, 52, 64, 82, 131, 172, 181, 221–22, 230
heterophony, 185, 187, 189, 198, 203–5, 209, 213, 219–20, 222, 262, 269
Hillebrand, Bruno, 238–39, 244, 247
Hilmes, Oliver, 271–72
Hindemith, Paul, 213
Hinduism, 90
Hobsbawm, Eric, 78–80, 223, 237–38
Hoffmann, E. T. A., 44, 46, 135, 231–32
Hoffmann, E. T. A., works by: *Fantasiestücke in Callots Manier* (*Fantasy Pieces in Callot's Manner*), 44; *Nachtstücke* (*Night Pieces*), 135
Hofmannsthal, Hugo von, 229
Holbein, Hans, 117, 245
Hölderlin, Friedrich, 139, 141, 243
Hölderlin, Friedrich, works by: "Die Nacht" ("The Night"), 139, 141; "Der Rhein" ("The Rhine"), 243
Holocaust (Shoah), 3–4, 23, 216, 271
Holtzmann, Robert, 228
Homer, 61
Horace, 181

Humboldt, Wilhelm von, 164, 257
humor, 32–33, 46, 50, 52, 54, 71–72, 82, 94, 101–3, 106, 109, 111, 114–19, 121–22, 125, 129, 222, 246

Indo-Germanic tradition, 180–81
Israel, Jonathan, 259

Jacobs, Jürgen, 232
Jean Paul, 18–19, 29–52, 56, 64, 71, 93, 107, 116, 120–22, 128–29, 162, 165, 167, 183, 225, 229–32, 236, 239–40, 243–44, 246, 248, 250–51, 260; on Bildung, 31, 35, 39–40, 47, 128, 232; and Callot, 44; and emotion, 40; and Goethe, 33–34, 44–46, 48, 50–51, 93, 229; and Hoffmann, 44, 231; and humor, 32–33, 52, 116, 122, 129, 246; on irony, 121; on Jews, 34; on love, 38–39, 41–43, 165; on memory, 39–40; and Mozart, 45–46, 51; on nature, 37–41; and politics, 32; on religion, 37, 39; and Rückert, 183; and Bruno Walter, 30–31, 231
Jean Paul, works by: *Hesperus*, 32; *Selbsterlebensbeschreibung*, 229–30; *Siebenkäs*, 42, 231; *Titan*, 29–55, 93, 128, 165, 221, 230–32; *Vorschule der Ästhetik* (*School for Aesthetics*), 246
Jelavich, Barbara, 226
jester's cap (Schellenkappe), 116, 122, 124, 245
Jewish artists, 220
Jewish audiences, 145
Jewish composers, 7, 151, 219
Jewish cosmopolitanism, 3, 147, 254
Jewish culture, 19, 34, 92, 97, 127, 147, 159, 173, 180–81, 196
Jewish emancipation, 226
Jewish identity, 12, 19
Jewish intellectuals, 18, 136–37, 260
Jewish music, 11–12, 20, 23, 25, 128, 179, 195, 216, 228, 248

Jewish musicians, 216
Jewish neighborhood (Amsterdam), 142
"Jewish question," 10–20, 136, 226
Jewish responses to Wagner, 226
Jewish self-hatred, 225
Jewish speech. *See* mauscheln
Jewishness, 3–4, 6–7, 10–12, 14–15, 17, 19–21, 23, 25, 34, 68, 92, 146, 151, 158, 163, 173, 178–79, 216, 218, 220, 228, 242, 272
Joyce, James, 214
Judaism, 19, 91–92, 97, 127, 137, 146, 266, 272

Kafka, Franz, 18
Kaiser, Gerhard, 242
Kalbeck, Max, 121
Kant, Immanuel, 75, 246, 259
Kapner, Gerhardt, 256
Karbusicky, Vladimír, 242
Karpath, Ludwig, 34, 228
Kerr, Alfred, 32
Kienzle, Ulrike, 244
Kittler, Friedrich A., 228
Klimt, Gustav, 11, 22, 124, 161–62, 176, 180, 195, 198, 200, 256–57, 266
Klimt, Gustav, works by: *Beethoven-Frieze*, 161–62, 176, 200, 256; *Judith I / II* (*Salome*), 195, 198; *Nuda Veritas*, 257
Klopstock, Friedrich Gottlieb, 18, 97–100, 128, 242
Klopstock, Friedrich Gottlieb, works by: "Die Auferstehung" ("The Resurrection"), 97–99, 242; *Der Messias* (*The Messiah*), 98
Knapp, Raymond, 245
Koepnick, Lutz, 263
Kokoschka, Oskar, 22, 124, 180, 247, 265
Kokoschka, Oskar, works by: *Die träumenden Knaben* (*The Dreaming Boys*), 124, 180, 247, 265
Kontje, Todd, 228, 230, 232, 261
Korngold, Erich Wolfgang, 222
Koselleck, Reinhart, 233

Krause, Markus, 232
Kravitt, Edward F., 264–65
Křenek, Ernst, 12, 21, 131, 222, 225–27, 249, 271
Kreutzer, Hans Joachim, 254, 257
Krisper, Anton, 13
Kropfinger, Klaus, 223
Krzyzanowski, Rudolf, 13
Kuper, Adam, 238

La Grange, Henry-Louis de, 227, 235–36, 245, 253, 263, 265, 267–69
Langbehn, Julius, 143–47, 149–52
Langbehn, Julius, works by: *Rembrandt als Erzieher* (*Rembrandt as Educator*), 143–47, 149–52
Le Rider, Jacques, 227
Lehár, Franz, 151, 253
Lehár, Franz, works by: *Die lustige Witwe* (*The Merry Widow*), 151, 253
Leibniz, Gottfried, 171–72
Lepenies, Wolf, 24, 228, 237
Leppert, Richard, 224
Leseverein der deutschen Studenten (Reading Society of German Students), 87, 101
Lessing, Gotthold Ephraim, 92, 160, 230
Lessing, Gotthold Ephraim, works by: *Nathan der Weise*, 230
Levin, David J., 225, 249
Levin (Varnhagen), Rahel, 158
Li Tai Po (Li Bai), 199–200, 268
Lipiner, Clementine, 258
Lipiner, Siegfried, 15–16, 83–84, 86–94, 97–101, 105, 125–26, 142–43, 159, 170–73, 177, 226, 231, 239–41, 243, 251, 257–59; on aesthetics, 88–89, 91–92; and Goethe, 159, 170–73, 177, 257–59; and mauscheln, 159, 256; and Mickiewicz, 93, 240–41; on nature, 231; and Nietzsche, 83–84, 86–89, 125–26, 143, 239–40; on pantheism, 88, 91–92, 100, 105; on religion, 87–92, 97, 99, 101; and Rembrandt, 142–43; and Schopenhauer, 86, 88, 170; and Spinoza, 171–73, 177; on tragedy, 89, 91, 98; and Wagner, 15–16, 86, 88–92, 94, 97, 126
Lipiner, Siegfried, works by: *Adam. Ein Vorspiel. Hyppolytos. Tragödie*, 251; *Homunkulus: Eine Studie über Faust und die Philosophie Goethes* (*Homunculus: A Study on Faust and Goethe's Philosophy*), 170–73; *Prometheus entfesselt* (*Prometheus Unbound*), 86; *Todtenfeier / Dziady*, introduction, 93, 240–41 (see also Mickiewicz); *Über die Elemente einer Erneuerung religiöser Ideen in der Gegenwart* (*On the Elements of a Renewal of Religious Ideas in the Present*), 87–92, 94, 97–101, 105, 126, 240, 243
Lippitt, John, 244
Liszt, Franz, 155
Loeper, Gustav von, 156–57, 255
Löhr, Friedrich, 101–2, 107, 112–13, 234, 242, 244
love, 31, 35–39, 41–44, 46–51, 63, 65–66, 68–72, 74–75, 77–78, 95, 99–100, 110–12, 114–15, 118, 124, 141, 152, 165–69, 174–75, 186–88, 201–4, 228, 263, 268; and compassion, 38, 111–12; and death, 43, 46–47, 99, 152; and friendship, 201, 203; of God, 103; Goethe on, 165–69, 258; Jean Paul on, 31, 35–39, 41–44, 46–47; in *Des Knaben Wunderhorn*, 63, 65–72, 74–75, 78; and laughter, 115, 118; as a metaphor, 112; of nature, 37; as passion, 68–70; romantic, 38, 71; Rückert on, 187–88, 263; in *Veni Creator Spiritus*, 175; in *Werther*, 44, 48
Lovejoy, Arthur O., 242–43
Lueger, Karl, 17
Luhmann, Niklas, 236

Magee, Bryan, 265
Magon, Leopold, 262

Mahler, Alma, 33, 48, 95, 125, 135, 140, 159, 164, 168–70, 172, 180, 188, 192, 197, 212, 217, 227, 229, 232, 235, 241, 243, 247, 249, 251, 256, 258, 260, 267, 271
Mahler, Anna, 96
Mahler, Gustav, works by: *Blumine*, 41, 43, 49–50, 53–55; *Kindertotenlieder* (*Songs on the Death of Children*), 20, 148, 179, 182–83, 185, 189–94, 198–99, 209, 213, 263–64; *Das klagende Lied* (*Song of Lament*), 16, 52, 80; *Das Lied von der Erde* (*Song of the Earth*), 7, 11, 20, 22, 147–48, 176–77, 179, 185, 187–89, 194, 197–211, 213, 216–17, 227, 239, 264, 267–69; *Lieder eines fahrenden Gesellen* (*Songs of a Wayfarer*), 62–68, 80–82, 128, 183, 186, 195, 200, 206–7, 213, 216–17, 271; *Rückert songs*, 20, 177, 179, 182–90, 192–94, 198, 202, 209, 213, 262–65; *Symphony No. 1*, 17, 22, 29–55, 62, 65, 92–94, 101, 107, 117–18, 121, 128, 148, 207, 213, 215, 221, 227, 231–32, 271; *Symphony No. 2*, 29–30, 84, 87–100, 111, 118, 121–22, 124–25, 128, 166, 209, 213, 215, 217–18, 241, 266, 270–71; *Symphony No. 3*, 52, 83–87, 100–15, 118, 122, 125–26, 128, 139–40, 187, 209, 213, 215, 243, 246, 264; *Symphony No. 4*, 72, 83–85, 102, 109, 111, 114–25, 128, 131, 148, 152, 187, 209, 213, 223, 245–46, 271; *Symphony No. 5*, 135, 148, 183, 185, 189, 193, 217, 227; *Symphony No. 6*, 22, 135, 137, 148, 183, 185; *Symphony No. 7*, 20, 53, 74, 135–53, 183, 194–95, 213, 220, 250–51, 253, 265–66; *Symphony No. 8*, 8, 19–20, 100, 111, 128, 131, 139, 147–48, 154–77, 209–10, 213, 215, 217–18, 221, 257–58, 264, 268; *Symphony No. 9*, 7, 147–48, 217; *Symphony No. 10*, 147–48; *Todtenfeier* (*Celebration of the Dead*), 93, 240–41; "Vergessene Liebe" ("Forgotten Love"), 207; *Wunderhorn songs*, 20, 22, 56–82, 94–95, 101, 108–9, 111, 115, 119, 128, 136, 147–48, 183, 185, 188, 195, 213, 220, 235–37, 241–42, 246

Maier, Charles, 225, 227, 249
Mandelkow, Karl Robert, 254–55
Marchand, Suzanne L., 260–61, 265
marginality, 32, 63–64, 67, 79, 136, 145, 148, 178, 213, 218
Markx, Francien, 232
Marschalk, Max, 29, 43, 50, 92–94
masculinity, 62, 68, 72, 78, 81–82, 156, 169, 238
masochism, 36–37, 65, 121, 165, 220–21, 230, 272–73
Maurus, Hrabanus, 174
mauscheln, 11, 14, 159, 196, 226
Mauthausen, 24
Mayer, Mathias, 174, 259
McBride, Patrizia, 21, 273
McCarthy, John A., 114, 243–44
McGrath, William, 84, 101, 114, 226–27, 239, 242, 244, 254
melancholy, 51, 150, 190, 251
memory, 30, 39–40, 51, 58, 66, 69, 74, 76–77, 79–82, 93, 146, 182, 231, 272
Mendelssohn, Dorothea (Veit-Schlegel), 158
Mendelssohn, Moses, 92, 136, 158, 230
Mendelssohn-Bartholdy, Felix, 14, 155, 174
Mendes-Flohr, Paul, 260
Mengelberg, Willem, 13, 49, 117, 138–42, 223, 232, 245, 250–51, 271
Meng Haoran (Mong Kao Yen), 204
Menzel, Wolfgang, 155, 254
Menzel, Wolfgang, works by: *Die deutsche Literatur*, 155, 254
Meyerbeer, Giacomo, 163
Meyer-Kalkus, Reinhard, 270
Meysenbug, Malwina von, 89, 100, 240

Meysenbug, Malwina von, works by: *Memoiren einer Idealistin* (*Memoirs of an Idealist*), 89, 100, 240
Micheels, Pauline, 251, 260
Mickiewicz, Adam, 86, 93, 240
Mildenburg, Anna von, 13, 102, 105, 225, 244
Mitchell, Donald, 62–63, 119, 175, 185, 187, 190, 199, 201, 203–4, 226, 232, 238, 242, 245, 247, 264, 268–69
modernism, 21, 24, 40, 76, 87, 128, 130, 136, 142, 212–13, 216, 218–21, 227, 233, 256, 272; and aesthetic autonomy, 213; and the avant-garde, 212; and crisis, 21, 76, 128, 227, 272; European, 256; and Jewishness, 220, 272; nostalgic, 21, 212, 224; reactionary, 213; in Vienna, 218–19
modernity, 4, 19–21, 35–36, 60, 82, 84, 97, 116, 128–30, 136, 138, 143, 147, 155, 157, 159, 162, 164, 166, 172–73, 212–13, 218, 271; and ambiguity, 128; and the anti-modern, 60, 129; and crisis, 143; and criticism, 129–30, 218; and Jewishness, 145–47, 218; and materialism, 155; and normativity, 4, 166; and a post-metaphysical world view, 36, 84, 164, 213, 218; and religion, 97; and science, 157; and society, 82; and Spinoza, 171–73; and tradition, 130
Mosse, George L., 81, 159, 234–35, 238, 250, 255
Mottle, Felix, 13
Mozart, Wolfgang Amadeus, 45–46, 51, 117, 135, 163, 225, 231, 249, 256
Mozart, Wolfgang Amadeus, works by: *Don Giovanni*, 45–46, 51, 163, 231; *Zauberflöte* (*Magic Flute*), 163, 256
Multatuli (Eduard Douwes Dekker), 179, 260
musicology, 1–2, 5–6, 8, 10–12, 20, 73, 94, 97, 115, 117, 151, 185, 219, 264, 266, 268

Musil, Robert, 141–42, 251

Nachtmusik, 135, 152
Nadler, Steven, 252
Napoleon, 156, 182
narrative, 3, 16–17, 25, 31–32, 34, 36, 46, 51–52, 57, 60, 64, 68, 72, 77, 81, 90, 93, 101, 118–19, 121, 128, 152, 162, 186, 189, 204–6, 219–20, 245
Nathorp, Paul, 251
nationalism, 4, 14, 18–19, 32, 56–60, 62, 67, 74, 78–79, 81–82, 86, 101, 127–30, 136–37, 154–57, 159–62, 173, 177, 182, 184, 211–13, 220, 227, 233, 238, 248, 254, 270–71
nature, 31–32, 37–41, 46–47, 54, 64–66, 72–73, 84–85, 88–89, 91–92, 94, 96–100, 102–7, 113–14, 124–25, 128, 140, 149, 152–53, 165–66, 174, 190–92, 194, 200–201, 203–4, 206–8, 231, 234, 239, 242–43, 264, 268–69
nazism, 8, 11, 113
new mythology, the idea of a, 84, 89, 239
Nietzsche, Friedrich, 18–19, 33, 61–62, 73, 82–131, 136, 139–41, 143–44, 150–51, 154, 157–59, 171, 176–77, 182–83, 202, 208–9, 213, 218–19, 234, 238–40, 242–44, 247–49, 251–52, 255–56, 264, 268–69, 271; and the affirmation of life, 109–11, 113; and anti-Semitism, 127, 158, 248–49; and atheism, 83; and children, 110–11, 115; on compassion, 111–12; and cosmopolitanism, 19, 130, 159; and the death of God, 83, 105; and Diepenbrock, 139–41, 151; and Dionysian art, 61, 84–86, 104, 234; on eternal recurrence, 99, 208, 242; and fin-de-siècle Vienna, 83–84, 86–87, 126, 218, 247; on German culture, 33, 61–62, 87, 128–29, 144, 159, 177, 209; and Goethe, 157–59; on humor, 106, 109, 114–15, 118, 125; and Jean

Nietzsche, Friedrich—*(cont'd)* Paul, 33; and *Des Knaben Wunderhorn*, 61; and Langbehn, 143–44, 150, 252; and Lipiner, 83–84, 86–89, 125–26, 143, 239–40; on love, 112, 115, 118; on music, 85–86, 129–30; and nationalism, 86, 127, 130, 154, 158–59; on nature, 73, 99, 102, 105–6, 114, 125, 208, 239, 269; and nihilism, 125; and orientalism, 182, 202, 239; and pessimism, 85, 114; in popular culture, 126, 213; and religion, 86–87, 89, 94, 99, 108, 110, 112, 114, 122, 125, 127, 130; and the renaturalization of mankind, 114; and Romanticism, 84, 129, 139, 248; and Schopenhauer, 85–86; and skepticism, 92, 106, 122, 125–26, 141; and tragedy, 85, 89, 91, 98, 100, 114; and the Übermensch, 112–13, 244; and Wagner, 61–62, 86–88, 111–12, 125–30, 150, 154, 157–58, 176, 239, 247–49; and Western metaphysics, 83–84, 87, 99, 107, 109, 128–29, 139, 176, 208, 213; and the world as aesthetic phenomenon, 84, 89, 122, 125, 129, 239

Nietzsche, Friedrich, works by: *Also sprach Zarathustra* (*Thus Spoke Zarathustra*), 85, 101–2, 107–15, 126, 140, 182, 187, 202, 208, 239, 242–44; *Ecce homo*, 242, 244, 249; *Der Fall Wagner* (*The Case of Wagner*), 128–29, 158, 255; *Die fröhliche Wissenschaft* (*The Gay Science*), 83, 100, 105–7, 109, 111; *Die Geburt der Tragödie aus dem Geiste der Musik* (*The Birth of Tragedy out of the Spirit of Music*), 61–62, 84–86, 89, 91, 102, 104, 106, 108, 113, 118, 129, 144, 151; *Menschliches, Allzumenschliches* (*Human, All Too Human*), 86, 140, 248, 251; *Morgenröthe* (*Daybreak*), 139, 251; *Nietzsche contra Wagner*, 126–27; "Zur Kritik Wagners" ("On a Critique of Wagner"), 157–58

nihilism, 33, 125, 244

Nikkels, Eveline, 238–39, 247, 268

nostalgia, 21, 94, 212

Novalis (Friedrich von Hardenberg), 51, 56, 135, 138, 141

Novalis, works by: *Hymnen an die Nacht* (*Hymns to the Night*), 135, 138, 141

Nowak, Adolf, 94, 123, 241, 246–47

Nussbaum, Martha, 96–97, 100, 215–16, 242

open narratives, 16–17, 31, 52–53, 64, 78, 214, 216, 232, 270

opera, 13–16, 20, 45–46, 79, 87, 90, 151, 163, 194–97

orientalism, 11, 33–34, 96, 174, 176, 178–90, 193–204, 206, 208–11, 239, 260–63, 267–68; Adorno and, 11, 179, 204; and Brentano, 96; German, 180–81, 196, 261; and German literature, 178; Goethe and, 33, 174–76, 181–83, 186, 194, 196, 209, 261; Jean Paul and, 33–34; Jewish interest in, 179, 260; Klimt and, 180; Kokoschka and, 180; and music, 185, 209, 268; Nietzsche and, 182, 202, 239; Rückert and, 182–85, 190; Edward Said on, 178–79, 260, 267; Friedrich Schlegel and, 180–82, 194, 260; Schopenhauer and, 194, 199, 206, 208; Richard Strauss and, 180, 194–97, 209

Origen, 258

Osmond-Smith, David, 270

otherness (alterity), 20–21, 60, 82, 136, 148, 169, 173, 177–79, 181, 210, 213, 221

Paddison, Max, 224

Padua, Anthony of, 72

Painter, Karen, 142, 219–20, 223, 225, 227, 249–50, 265–66, 272

pantheism, 88, 91–92, 99–100, 105, 269

Partsch, Susanna, 266
Pechefsky, Rebecca, 231, 267, 272
pentatonic scale, 185, 189
Pernerstorfer, Engelbert, 86, 254
Pernerstorfer Kreis (Pernerstorfer Circle), 18, 79, 86, 191, 125–26, 154, 254
Pfitzner, Hans, 255
Pietism, 97
Pizer, John, 270
Polaschegg, Andrea, 261–63, 267
Ponte, Lorenzo da, 46, 51, 163
popular music, 7, 228
Potter, Pamela M., 273
pregnancy, 71
Prochaska, David, 260
programs, 5–6, 12, 14–16, 29–31, 39–44, 46–47, 50, 52–54, 61–62, 66–68, 83, 92–94, 98, 101–8, 111, 115–16, 119, 124, 131, 135, 141, 147, 149–50, 152, 163, 169–70, 188, 201, 214, 223–24, 231, 233, 236, 240–42, 243, 245–46; and anti-programmatic statements, 5–6, 30, 52–53, 115, 135, 147, 214; Berio on musical, 214; cultural, 12, 163; and *Das Lied von der Erde*, 201; Nietzsche and musical, 61; and *Symphony No. 1*, 40–55, 107; and *Symphony No. 2*, 92–94, 98, 241; and *Symphony No. 3*, 83, 101–8, 111, 243; and *Symphony No. 4*, 115–16, 119; and *Symphony No. 7*, 135, 141, 149, 152; Wagner and musical, 12, 14, 16; Walter on musical, 5–6, 30–31, 40, 52, 231
Pulzer, Peter, 252

race, 11–12, 14, 81, 113, 136, 147, 158, 194–95, 225
Rathaus, Karol, 222
Rattle, Simon, 24
Ravel, Maurice, 185, 213
reading, 1, 5, 9, 15, 19–20, 24, 31, 33, 42, 46, 49, 51, 53, 57–58, 73, 87, 94–96, 99, 103, 108, 120, 129, 135–36, 154, 162, 168–70, 176–78, 201, 213, 218–23, 271; culture, 9, 15, 20, 24, 31, 51, 62, 129, 148–49, 154, 176, 213, 218–22; Mahler's (anti-)programs, 42, 49, 52, 103, 169; Mahler's summertime, 162; music, 8, 31, 46, 53, 87, 94, 96–97, 101, 177, 201, 213; nature, 99, 105–6; paintings, 153; Romanticism, 135–36
Reeser, Eduard, 232, 250–53
Reginster, Bernard, 244
Reik, Theodor, 265
Reilly, Edward R., 241
Reitter, Paul, 225
religion, 31, 37, 39, 59, 69, 84, 87–97, 99, 101, 105, 114, 121–22, 125, 127–29, 137, 170, 176, 182, 194, 196, 240–41, 258, 266; art and, 84, 87, 89–90, 129, 170, 176, 240, 258; in decline, 90–91, 101; Goethe on, 164, 167, 169, 258; as institution, 97; Jean Paul on, 37, 39; Lipiner on, 87–92, 97, 99, 101; Nietzsche on, 86–87, 89, 94, 99, 108, 110, 112, 114, 122, 125, 127, 130; revelatory, 95, 97, 241
Rembrandt, 138, 141–47, 149–50, 152–53, 213, 252–53
Rembrandt, works by: *Nachtwacht (Night Watch)*, 141–42
Revers, Peter, 66, 235–36, 253
Richter, Johann Paul Friedrich. *See* Jean Paul
Richter, Thomas, 259
Rietschel, Ernst, 256
Robertson, Ritchie, 226
Rölleke, Heinz, 237
Roller, Alfred, 8, 13, 19, 130, 161, 256
Romanticism, 33, 39, 58, 67, 79, 82, 84, 86, 129, 135–36, 143, 148, 183, 248–49
Rose, Paul Lawrence, 225
Rott, Hans, 13
Rousseau, Jean-Jacques, 32, 37, 39, 64
Rückert, Friedrich, 18, 177, 182–94, 198, 202, 209–10, 213, 261–65, 270

Rückert, Friedrich, works by: *Haus- und Jahreslieder*, 192, 262–63; *Kindertodtenlieder*, 189, 192, 263–65; *Liebesfrühling* (*Spring of Love*), 187, 192, 263, 265; *Östliche Rosen* (*Eastern Roses*), 184, 262
Russell, Peter, 262, 264
Ryding, Erik, 231, 267, 272

Said, Edward W., 178–79, 260, 266–67
Salaquarda, Jörg, 239, 249
Sammons, Jeffrey L., 254, 256
Samuel, Emanuel, 34
Schäfer, Thomas, 270
Schama, Simon, 142, 252
Scheffer, Frank, 269
Schein, Ida, 170–73, 257, 259
Schein, Ida, works by: *Die Gedanken- und Ideenwelt Siegfried Lipiners* (*Siegfried Lipiner's World of Thoughts and Ideas*), 170–73, 257, 259
Scheit, Gerhard, 223, 227, 249, 271
Schiedermair, Ludwig, 5, 116–17, 224, 245
Schiller, Friedrich, 24, 33–34, 51, 75, 90, 144, 154–55, 158–62, 178, 228, 240, 254–57
Schiller, Friedrich, works by: "Ode an die Freude" ("Ode to Joy"), 24, 161, 228; "Thekla," 158; *Votivtafeln*, 257
Schiller monument, 160
Schimmel, Annemarie, 262–63, 265, 270
Schlegel, August Wilhelm, 56
Schlegel, Friedrich, 56, 90, 180–82, 184, 194, 196, 198, 209, 260–61
Schlegel, Friedrich, works by: *Über die Sprache und Weisheit der Indier* (*On the Language and Wisdom of the Indians*), 180, 184, 209, 261
Schmidt, James, 228
Schnitzler, Arthur, 11–12, 18, 194–95
Schnurrjude (Jewish peddler), 34, 230
Schoenberg, Arnold, 7–8, 148, 213, 219–20, 272
Schönberg, Jutta, 230
Schöne, Albrecht, 257–58
Schopenhauer, Arthur, 85–86, 170–71, 182–83, 193–94, 199, 201, 206, 209, 243–44, 261, 265–66, 269; and Goethe, 261; and metaphysics, 170; on music, 61, 85; on nature, 243; and Nietzsche, 85; and orientalism, 182–83, 193–94, 199, 206; on religion, 193, 243, 265; and Wagner, 266; on the will, 85–86, 170, 194
Schopenhauer, Arthur, works by: *Aphorismen zur Lebensweisheit* (*Aphorisms on the Wisdom of Life*), 182, 193–94, 199, 261, 265
Schorske, Carl E., 11–12, 224–26
Schreker, Franz, 220, 222
Schubert, Franz, 66, 71, 135, 186
Schumann, Robert, 135, 155
Schuschnigg, Kurt, 217, 220, 271
Schwerte, Hans (Hans Schneider), 254–55
See, Klaus von, 237–38
Seidl, Arthur, 242
Semitic race, theory of, 181, 266
sex, 63, 69, 158–59, 168–69, 195–96, 198, 202–4
Seyhan, Azade, 238
Sezession (Secession), 13, 161–62
Shakespeare, William, 144
Singer, Peter, 246
Solvik, Morten, 224, 273
Sorgner, Stefan Lorenz, 239
Spazier, Richard Otto, 230
Specht, Richard, 253
Spengler, Oswald, 143
Spielmann, Heinz, 247
Spielmann, Julius, 15
Spieß, August, 254
Spinoza, Baruch / Benedict / Bento de, 92, 137, 146–47, 171–73, 176–77, 250, 252, 258–59, 266
Sprengel, Peter, 229
Stark-Voit, Renate, 233, 236, 241–42
Steinberg, Michael P., 218, 257, 272
Steiner, Josef, 68, 236
Stern, Fritz, 252
Strauss, Richard, 115, 126, 148, 180, 194–98, 201–4, 209, 212, 214, 219–20, 253, 266–67

Strauss, Richard, works by: *Also sprach Zarathustra* (*Thus Spoke Zarathustra*), 126; *Betrachtungen und Erinnerungen* (*Reflections and Memories*), 261, 266; *Ein Heldenleben* (*A Hero's Life*), 115; *Der Rosenkavalier*, 214; *Salome*, 180, 194–98, 201–4, 209, 220, 266–67
Stravinsky, Igor, 7–8, 10, 213–14, 219, 272
Sue, Eugène, 68
Sutcliffe, Adam, 259
Svoboda, Wilhelm, 223, 227, 249, 271
symbol, 87–88, 90–100, 110–11, 121, 155–56, 169, 186, 237, 258

Tchang Tsi, 268
text, 2, 5–6, 10, 16, 18, 20–25, 29, 31, 41, 48, 52–53, 61–62, 64–65, 81, 115, 121, 128, 131, 139, 154, 156–57, 161–62, 168–69, 174, 178, 185, 190, 200, 202, 209, 213–16, 218, 220–22; Adorno on, 10; closed, 52; Mahler's choice of, 67, 102, 107, 161, 168; and memory, 10; and music, 5–6, 10, 16, 20, 25, 31, 41, 48, 52–53, 61–62, 64, 115, 121, 174, 190, 213–16, 221; national, 154, 156–57, 169; open, 52, 78, 232, 270
Third Reich, 11–12, 58, 143, 216, 271
Tieck, Ludwig, 51, 56
tradition, 1, 3–4, 6, 8, 10–11, 15, 18, 20–25, 31, 33, 40, 50–52, 57–58, 61, 64, 68, 76, 78–82, 91, 97, 109, 116, 124–25, 128, 130–31, 135, 137, 139, 141, 144–48, 153–54, 158–59, 162–64, 166, 168, 173, 175–77, 180–81, 198, 210, 212, 216–18, 221–22, 228, 232, 238, 245–46, 252, 258, 264; against, 78–82, 109, 120, 128, 166; German cultural, 10–11, 15, 20–21, 24, 51, 68, 139, 146–48, 159, 218; inventing, 4, 78–80, 238; Jewish cultural, 19, 97, 146–47, 180, 216, 228; loss of, 21; margins of, 131, 222; and nationalism, 8, 154, 159, 162, 169
Türnau, Dietrich, 259
twenty-first century, 2, 217

Ueberkultur, 151–52
Ueding, Gert, 229–30
Ullmann, Viktor, 222
United States, 3, 131

Vaget, Hans Rudolf, 225
Valéry, Paul, 214
Varnhagen, Rahel. *See* Levin, Rahel
vegetarianism, 90, 120
Veni Creator Spiritus (anonymous medieval hymn), 139, 173, 175–76, 259
Venturelli, Aldo, 240
Vergo, Peter, 247, 256, 260
Vill, Susanne, 232
violence, 65, 77, 82, 124, 165
visual arts, 1, 6, 20, 47, 161, 170, 179, 245
Volk, 56–61, 63, 66–68, 74, 76–81, 128, 195, 213, 234
völkische Bewegung, 60, 79, 234
Voltaire (François-Marie Arouet), 193
Vordermayer, Martina, 235

Wackenroder, Wilhelm Heinrich, 56
Wagner, Cosima, 89, 225, 240
Wagner, Manfred, 260
Wagner, Nike, 239, 243
Wagner, Richard, 9–19, 32, 60–62, 73–74, 79, 82, 86–92, 94, 97, 99, 111–12, 120, 125–31, 135, 138–39, 149–52, 154–63, 176, 197, 212–13, 219, 224–26, 233–34, 237, 239–40, 243–44, 246–49, 253, 255–57, 260, 264, 266; and Adorno, 9–10; and anti-Semitism, 12, 14–15, 17–19, 74, 127–28, 163, 219, 225–26, 248–49, 253; and Beethoven, 161, 255–57; on Brahmanism and Buddhism, 90; and Christianity, 91–92, 99, 120, 127; on compassion, 111, 244; and

Wagner, Richard—*(cont'd)*
  German cultural history, 16–17, 79, 128, 130, 151, 163, 219; and Goethe, 129, 156, 159–60, 255; on Judaism, 90–92; and Langbehn, 149–50; and Lipiner, 88–91, 94; and nationalism, 62, 82, 86, 128, 130, 162; on a new mythology, 89; and Nietzsche, 61–62, 86–88, 111–12, 125–30, 150, 154, 157–58, 176, 239, 247–49; and politics, 10, 13–14; and reactionary modernism, 213; and his reception in Vienna, 13–14, 79; and religion, 89–91, 97, 99, 127, 130; and Romanticism, 129; and Schiller, 159, 240, 255; and Richard Strauss, 266; on vegetarianism, 120; on the "Volk," 60–61, 79
Wagner, Richard, works by: "Autobiographische Skizze (bis 1842)" ("Autobiographical Sketch (until 1842)"), 249; "Beethoven," 158, 255–57; "Bericht über die Aufführung der neunten Symphonie von Beethoven im Jahre 1846 in Dresden" ("Report on the Performance of Beethoven's Ninth Symphony in the Year 1846 in Dresden"), 161, 256; *Faust Overture*, 160; "Das Judentum in der Musik" ("Jewishness in Music"), 17, 127, 224, 248; "Das Kunstwerk der Zukunft" ("The Art-Work of the Future"), 60–61, 225; *Die Meistersinger von Nürnberg*, 73–74, 76, 151, 170, 253; *Parsifal*, 13–15, 111, 129–30, 219, 243–44; "Publikum und Popularität" ("Public and Popularity"), 247–48; "Religion und Kunst" ("Religion and Art"), 17, 89–92, 99, 120, 129, 240; *Ring des Nibelungen*, 14, 127, 156, 253; *Siegfried*, 14–15, 20, 74, 156, 159; *Tannhäuser*, 139; *Tristan und Isolde*, 13, 86, 130, 225, 249, 264; "Was ist Deutsch?" ("What is German?"), 234
Wallenstein, Duke of, 178

Walter, Bruno, 3, 5–6, 23, 30–31, 37, 40, 43–44, 48, 50, 52, 103, 116–18, 125–26, 135, 148, 198–99, 212, 217–18, 223–25, 228, 231–32, 237, 245, 247, 249–50, 252, 261, 267, 271–72
wandering, 34, 59, 63–64, 66, 68, 81, 103, 235–36, 268
Wang Wei, 204
Weber, Carl Maria von, 48
Weber, Marion von, 48–50, 62, 232
Webern, Anton, 148, 150
Wedekind, Frank, 196
Wedekind, Frank, works by: *Frühlings Erwachen* (*Spring's Awakening*), 196
Weiner, Marc A., 224–26, 233, 253, 257
Weininger, Otto, 250
Weininger, Otto, works by: *Geschlecht und Charakter: Eine prinzipielle Untersuchung* (*Sex and Character: An Investigation of Fundamental Principles*), 250
Weissberg, Liliane, 238
Wellesz, Egon, 222
Wenk, Arthur, 202, 268
Wieland, Christoph Martin, 51
Wieland, Christoph Martin, works by: *Geschichte des Agathon* (*History of Agathon*), 51
Wiener Akademischer Wagner Verein (Vienna Academic Wagner Society), 13–14
Wilde, Oscar, 195–96
Williamson, John G., 251
Winckelmann, Johann Joachim, 144
Wolf, Hugo, 13–14, 150, 212
Wolf, Karl, 13
world literature, 210–11, 221, 270
Wotruba, Fritz, 217
Wuthenow, Ralph-Rainer, 230

Zelter, Carl Friedrich, 174, 257, 259
Zemlinsky, Alexander, 150, 220, 222
Zimmermann, Robert, 259
Zoroastrianism, 107, 182
Zwart, Frits, 250–51
Zychowicz, James L., 245–46, 253, 267

Praise for the hardcover edition:

Thought provoking. . . . Should be a part of all serious academic and public classical music collections.
                    AMERICAN JEWISH LIBRARIES REVIEWS

Although the Mahler literature is extensive and growing, one can find nothing quite like this volume. Highly recommended.
                                        CHOICE

Riveting. . . . [A] compelling book, an example of interdisciplinary scholarship at its finest. It is a major contribution to our understanding of this pivotal epoch in Western civilization and represents an invaluable resource for any future research into the period as a whole.
                    Andrew Barker, MODERN LANGUAGE REVIEW

Carl Niekerk's *Reading Mahler* is a notable addition to the composer's bibliography because it counters conventional images of Mahler as a "nostalgic modernist" or a "neoromanticist". . . . Niekerk investigates Mahler in a rewarding and challenging way. His study also provides readers with a solid grounding in texts and sources that are not always considered in the field of Mahler studies.
                    MUSICA JUDAICA ONLINE REVIEWS

www.ingramcontent.com/pod-product-compliance
Lightning Source LLC
Chambersburg PA
CBHW051600230426
43668CB00013B/1922